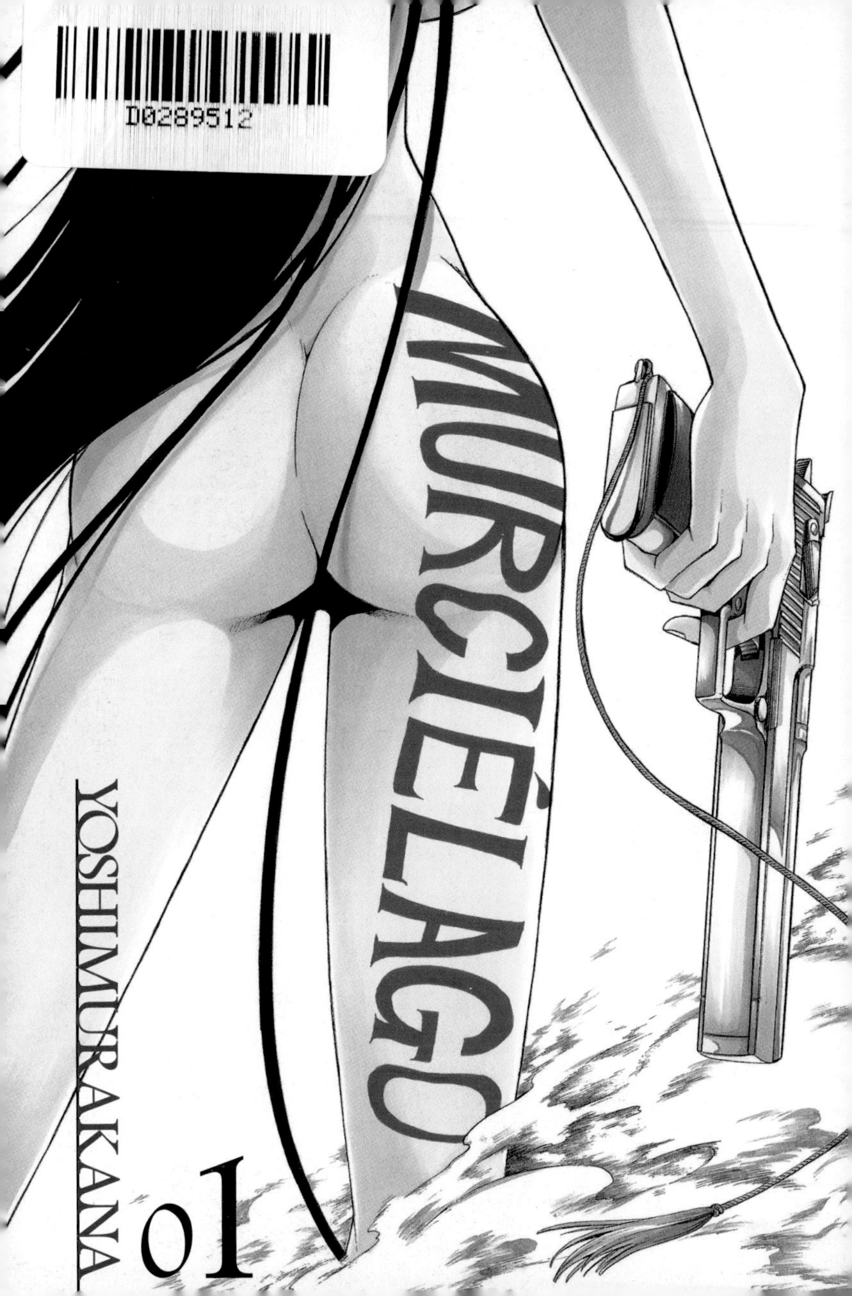
MURCIÉLAGO
YOSHIMURAKANA
01

MURCIÉLAGO 01

CONTENTS

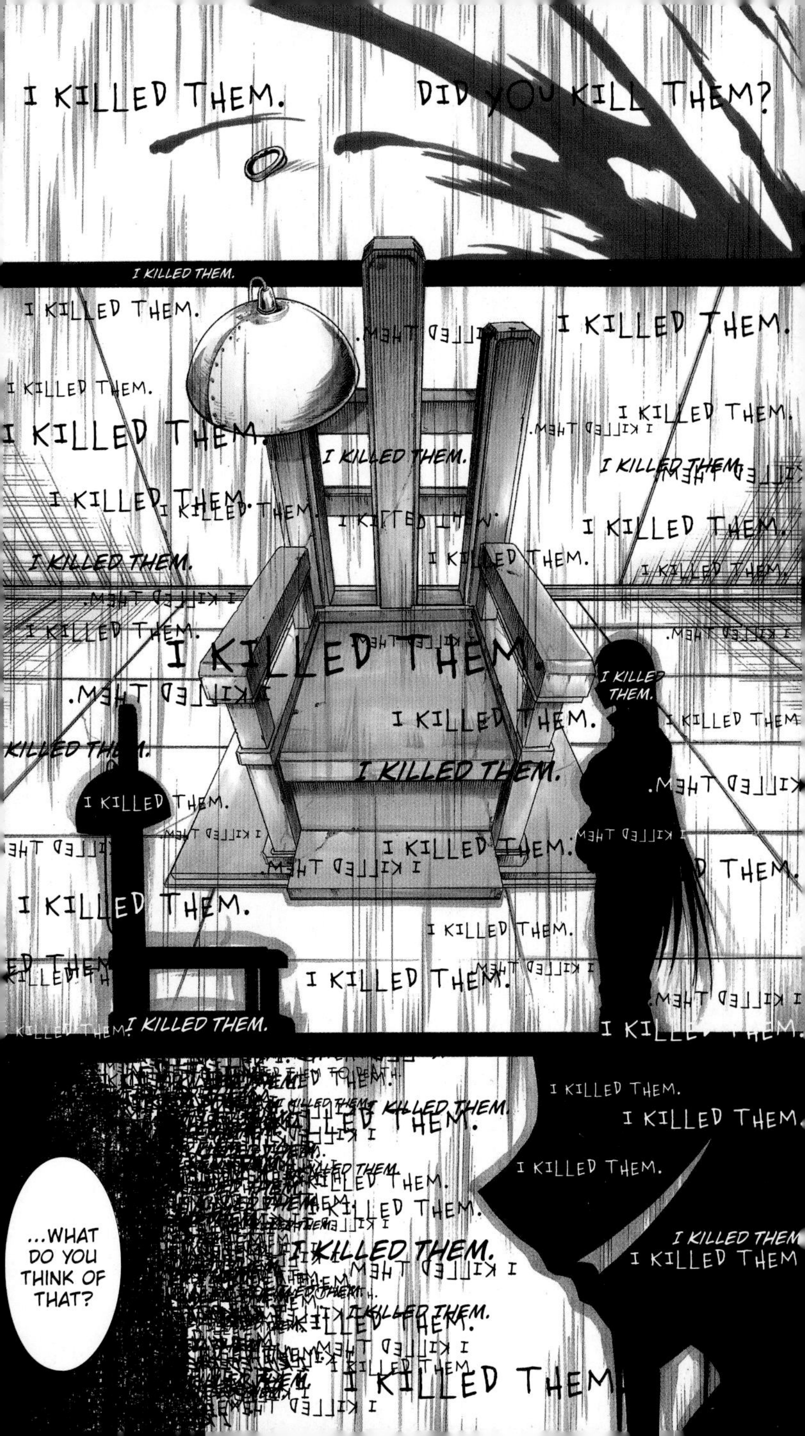
DID YOU KILL THEM?
I KILLED THEM.
I KILLED THEM.
I KILLED THEM.
I KILLED THEM.
I KILLED THEM.
I KILLED THEM.
I KILLED THEM.
I KILLED THEM.
I KILLED THEM.
I KILLED THEM.
I KILLED THEM.
I KILLED THEM.
I KILLED THEM.
I KILLED THEM.
I KILLED THEM
I KILLED THEM
I KILLED THEM.
...WHAT DO YOU THINK OF THAT?

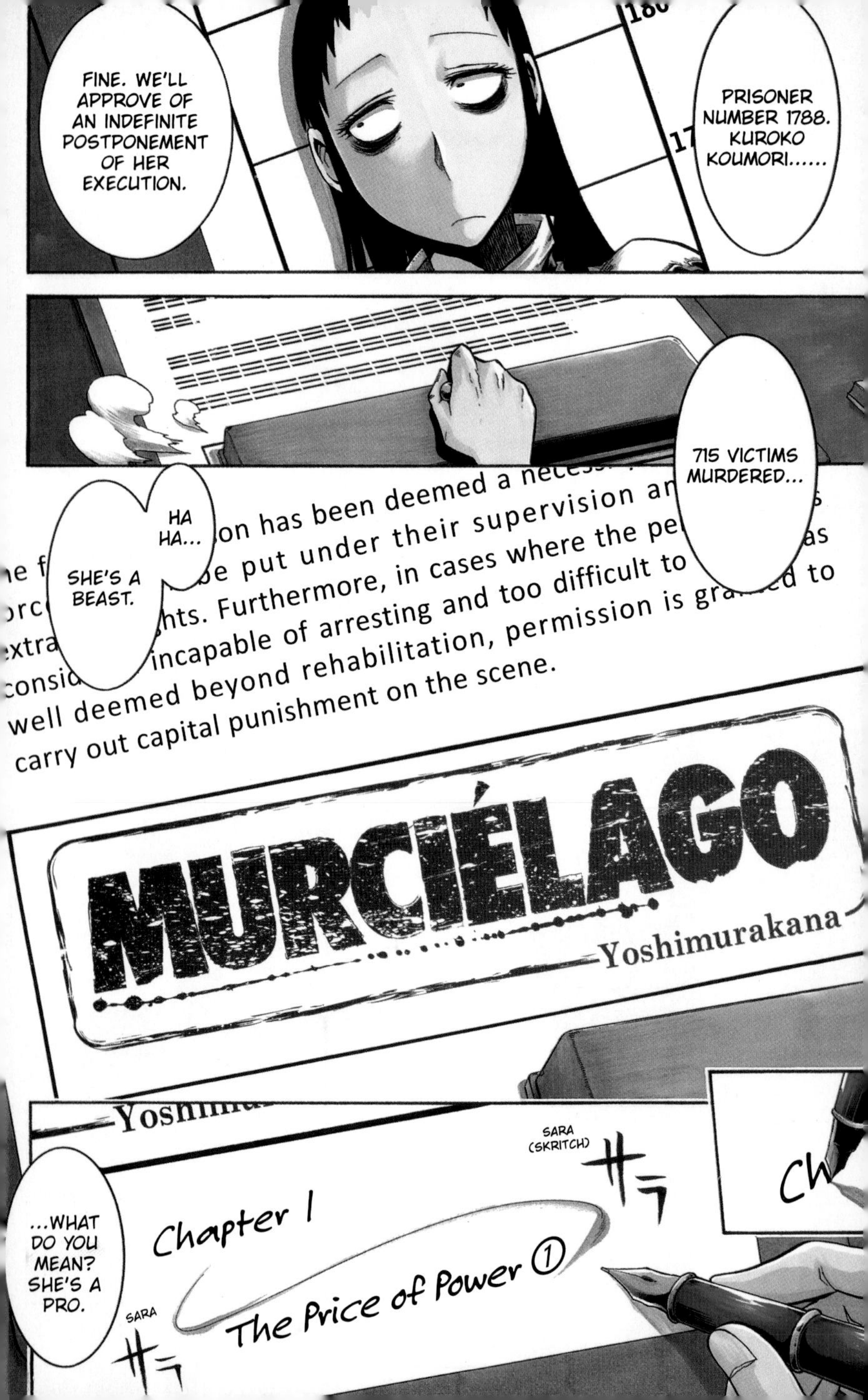

PRISONER NUMBER 1788. KUROKO KOUMORI......
FINE. WE'LL APPROVE OF AN INDEFINITE POSTPONEMENT OF HER EXECUTION.
715 VICTIMS MURDERED...
HA HA... SHE'S A BEAST.
on has been deemed a nece
be put under their supervision an
in cases where the pe
hts. Furthermore, in cases where the pe as
incapable of arresting and too difficult to
permission is gra ed to
well deemed beyond rehabilitation, permission is gra
carry out capital punishment on the scene.
MURCIÉLAGO
Yoshimurakana
SARA (SKRITCH)
Ch
Chapter 1
The Price of Power ①
...WHAT DO YOU MEAN? SHE'S A PRO.
SARA

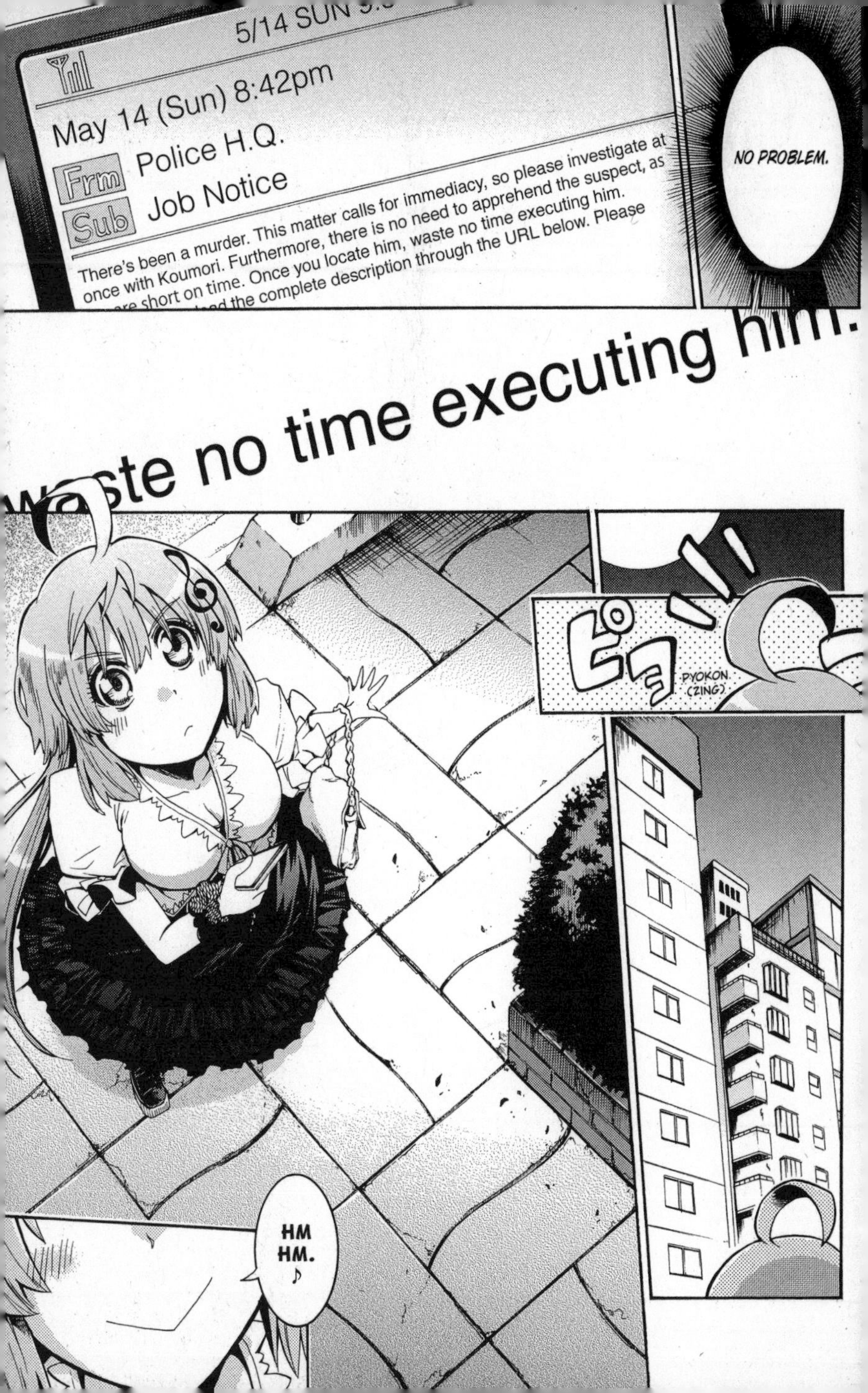
NO PROBLEM.
5/14 SUN
May 14 (Sun) 8:42pm
Frm Police H.Q.
Sub Job Notice
There's been a murder. This matter calls for immediacy, so please investigate at once with Koumori. Furthermore, there is no need to apprehend the suspect, as we are short on time. Once you locate him, waste no time executing him. Please ... the complete description through the URL below. Please
waste no time executing him.
ピョ
PYOKON (ZING)
HM HM. ♪

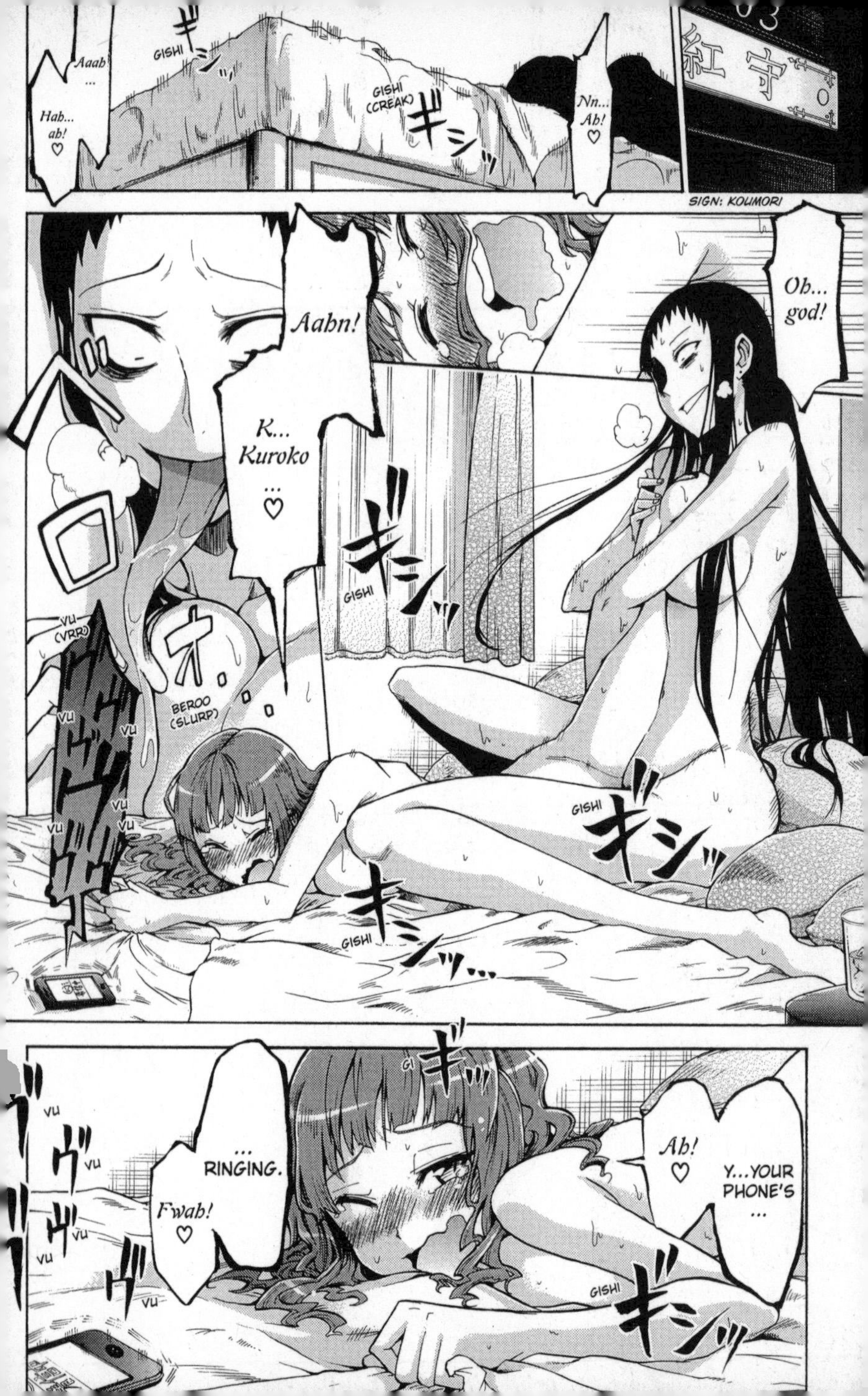
紅守
SIGN: KOUMORI
Nn... Ah! ♡
GISHI (CREAK)
GISHI
Aaah ...
Hah... ah! ♡
Oh... god!
GISHI
GISHI
Aahn!
K... Kuroko ... ♡
BEROO (SLURP)
VU (VRR)
VU VU VU VU VU
GISHI
Ah! ♡
Y...YOUR PHONE'S ...
GISHI
GI
... RINGING.
Fwah! ♡
VU VU VU VU

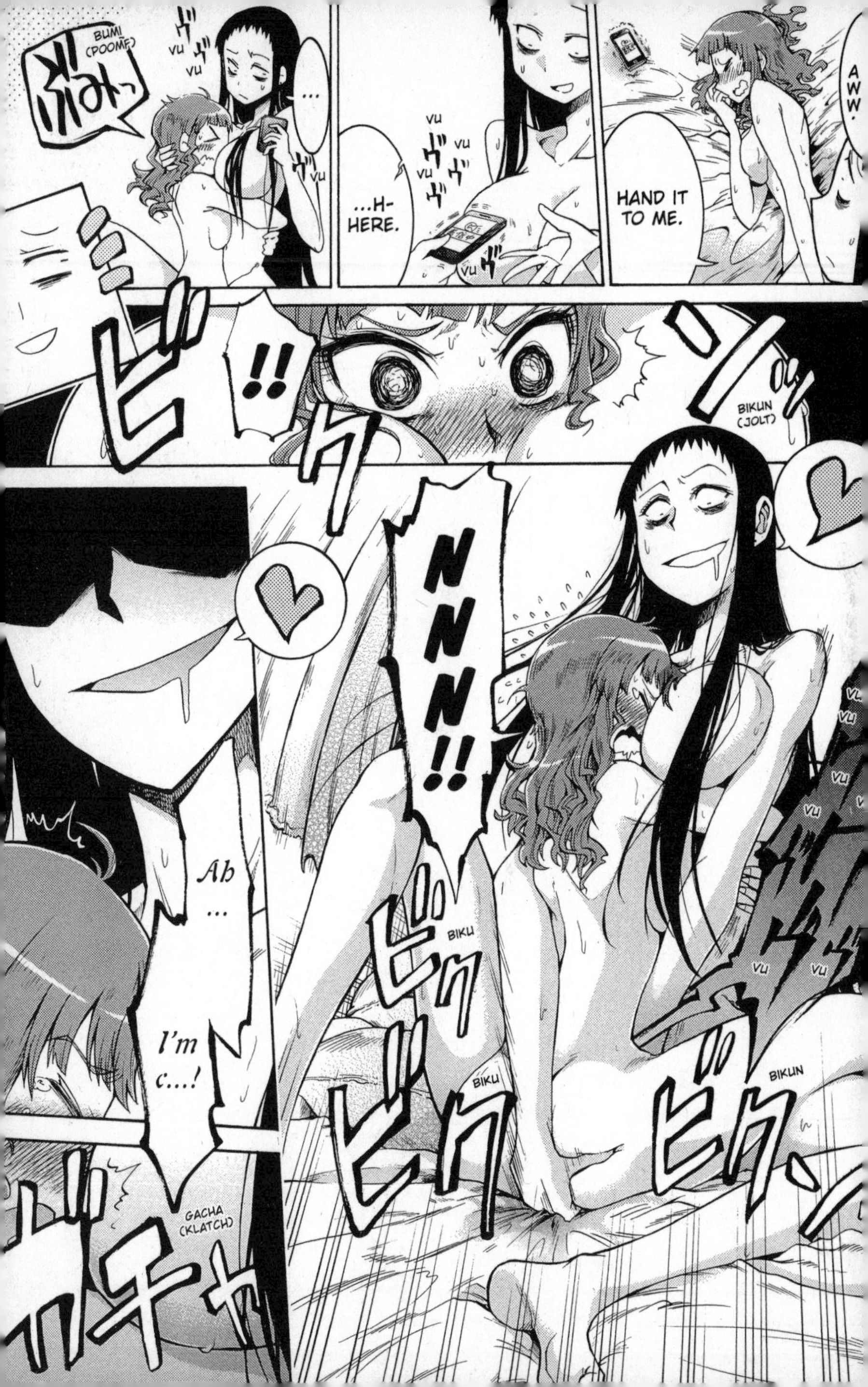

AWW.
HAND IT TO ME.
VU VU VU VU VU
...H- HERE.
VU
...
VU VU
VU
BUMI (POOMF)
BIKUN (JOLT)
!!
NNNN!!
VU VU VU VU VU VU
BIKUN
BIKU
BIKU
Ah ... I'm c...!
GACHA (KLATCH)

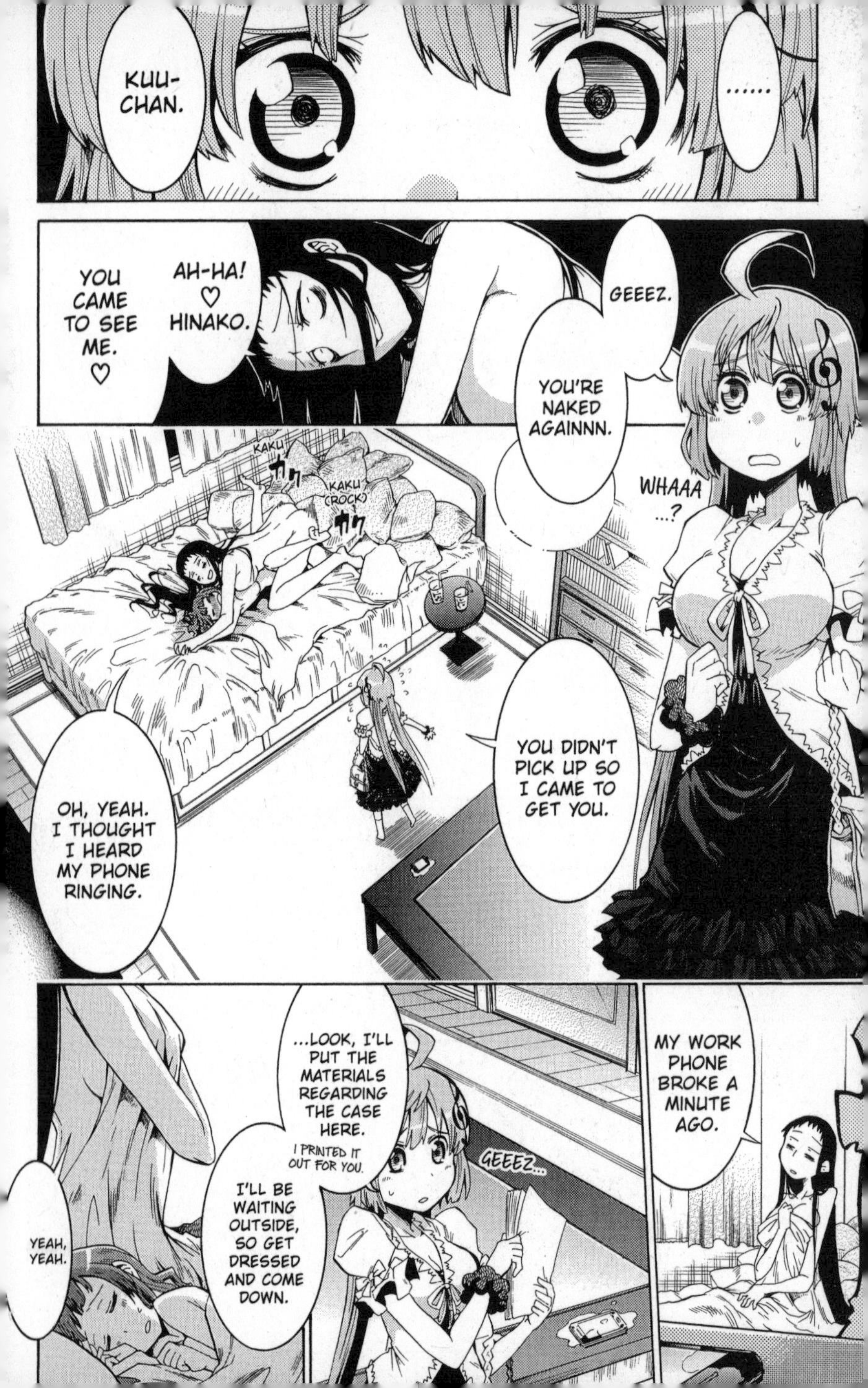
......
KUU-CHAN.
GEEEZ.
YOU'RE NAKED AGAINNN.
WHAAA ...?
AH-HA! ♡ HINAKO.
YOU CAME TO SEE ME. ♡
KAKU
KAKU (ROCK)
YOU DIDN'T PICK UP SO I CAME TO GET YOU.
OH, YEAH. I THOUGHT I HEARD MY PHONE RINGING.
MY WORK PHONE BROKE A MINUTE AGO.
...LOOK, I'LL PUT THE MATERIALS REGARDING THE CASE HERE.
I PRINTED IT OUT FOR YOU.
GEEEZ...
I'LL BE WAITING OUTSIDE, SO GET DRESSED AND COME DOWN.
YEAH, YEAH.

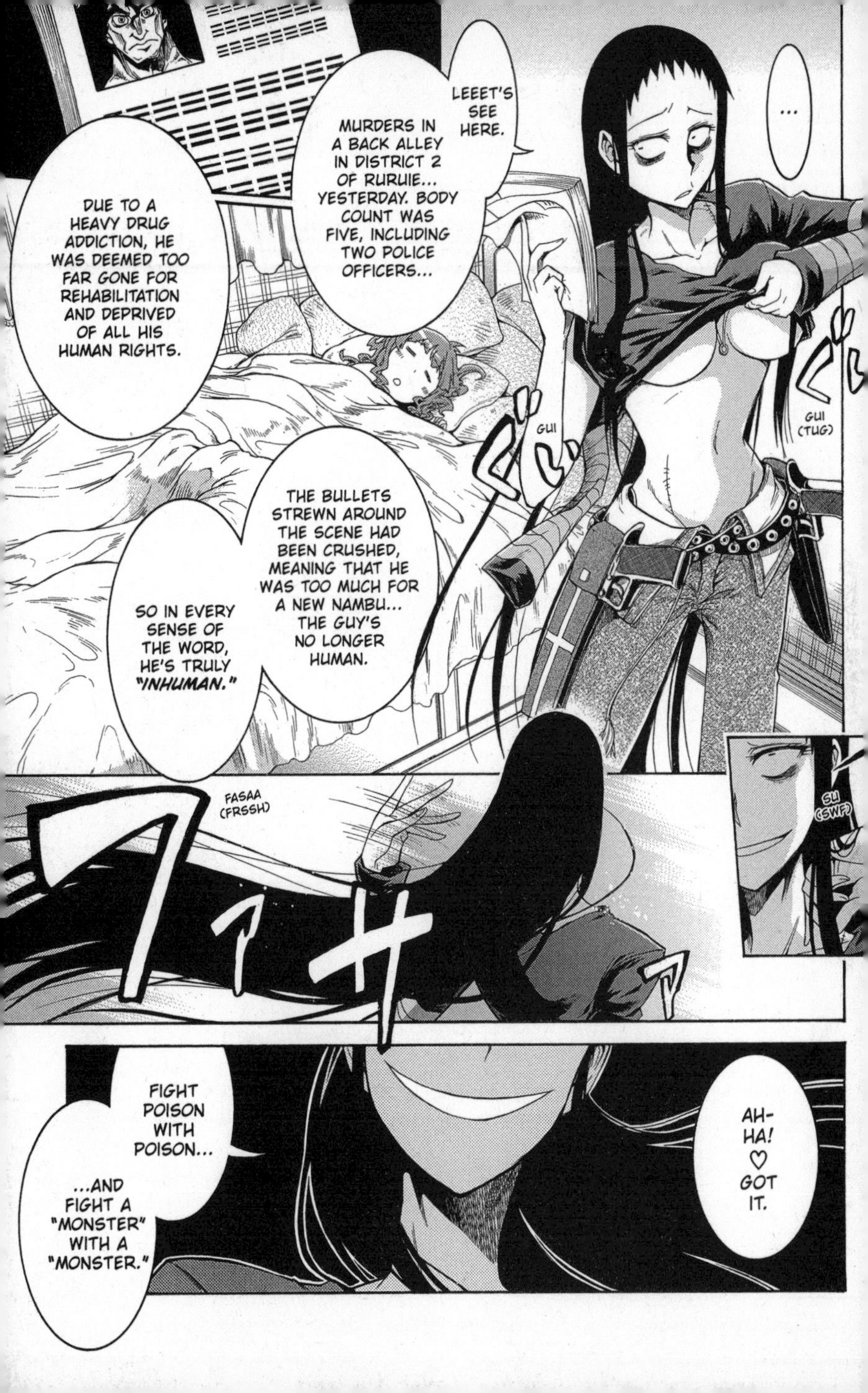
...
LEEET'S SEE HERE.
MURDERS IN A BACK ALLEY IN DISTRICT 2 OF RURUIE... YESTERDAY. BODY COUNT WAS FIVE, INCLUDING TWO POLICE OFFICERS...
DUE TO A HEAVY DRUG ADDICTION, HE WAS DEEMED TOO FAR GONE FOR REHABILITATION AND DEPRIVED OF ALL HIS HUMAN RIGHTS.
GUI (TUG)
GUI
THE BULLETS STREWN AROUND THE SCENE HAD BEEN CRUSHED, MEANING THAT HE WAS TOO MUCH FOR A NEW NAMBU... THE GUY'S NO LONGER HUMAN.
SO IN EVERY SENSE OF THE WORD, HE'S TRULY *"INHUMAN."*
SU (SWF)
FASAA (FRSSH)
AH-HA! ♡ GOT IT.
FIGHT POISON WITH POISON...
...AND FIGHT A "MONSTER" WITH A "MONSTER."

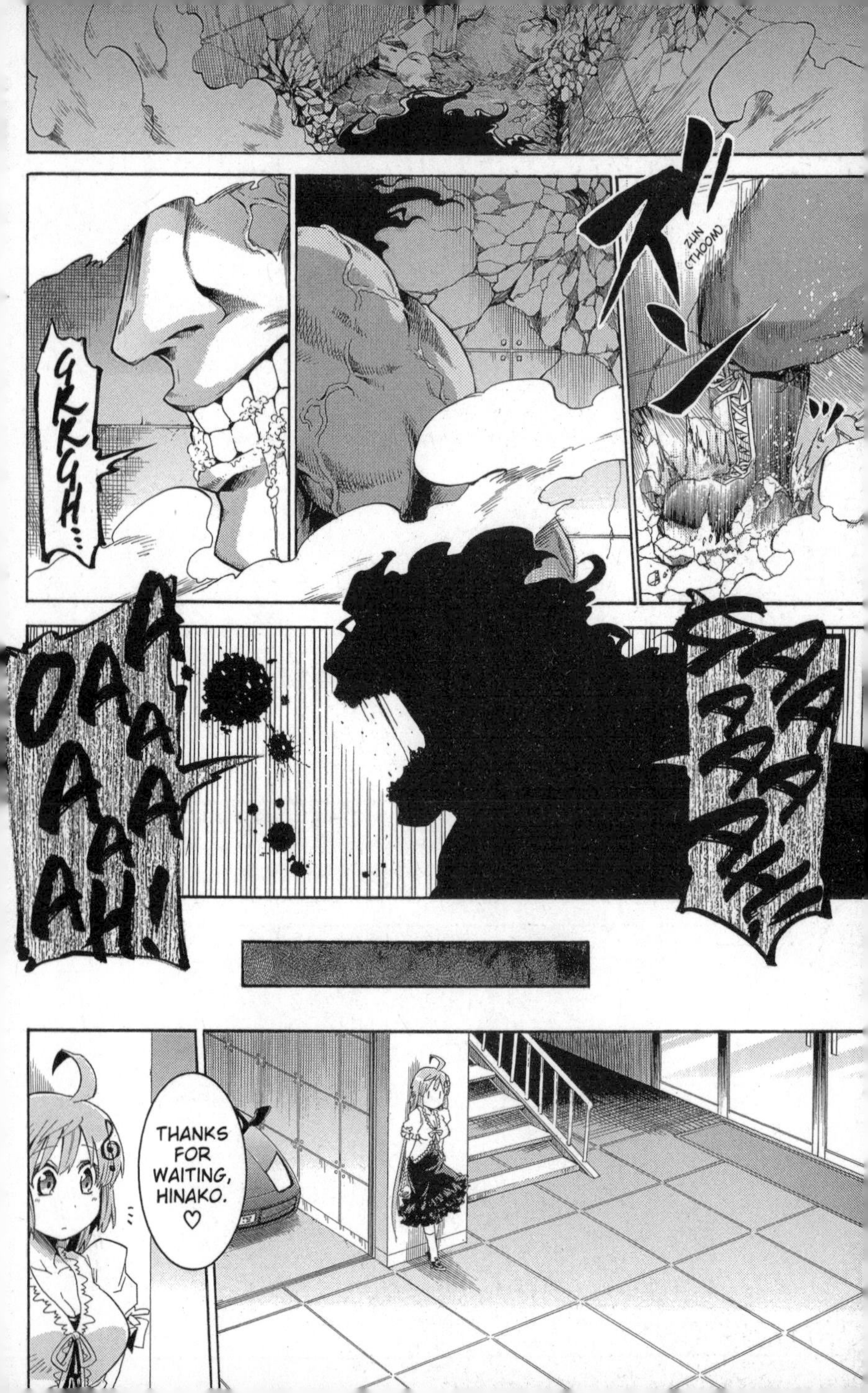
ZUN (THOOM)
GRRGH...
GAAAAAAAH!
OAAAAAAAAH!
THANKS FOR WAITING, HINAKO. ♡

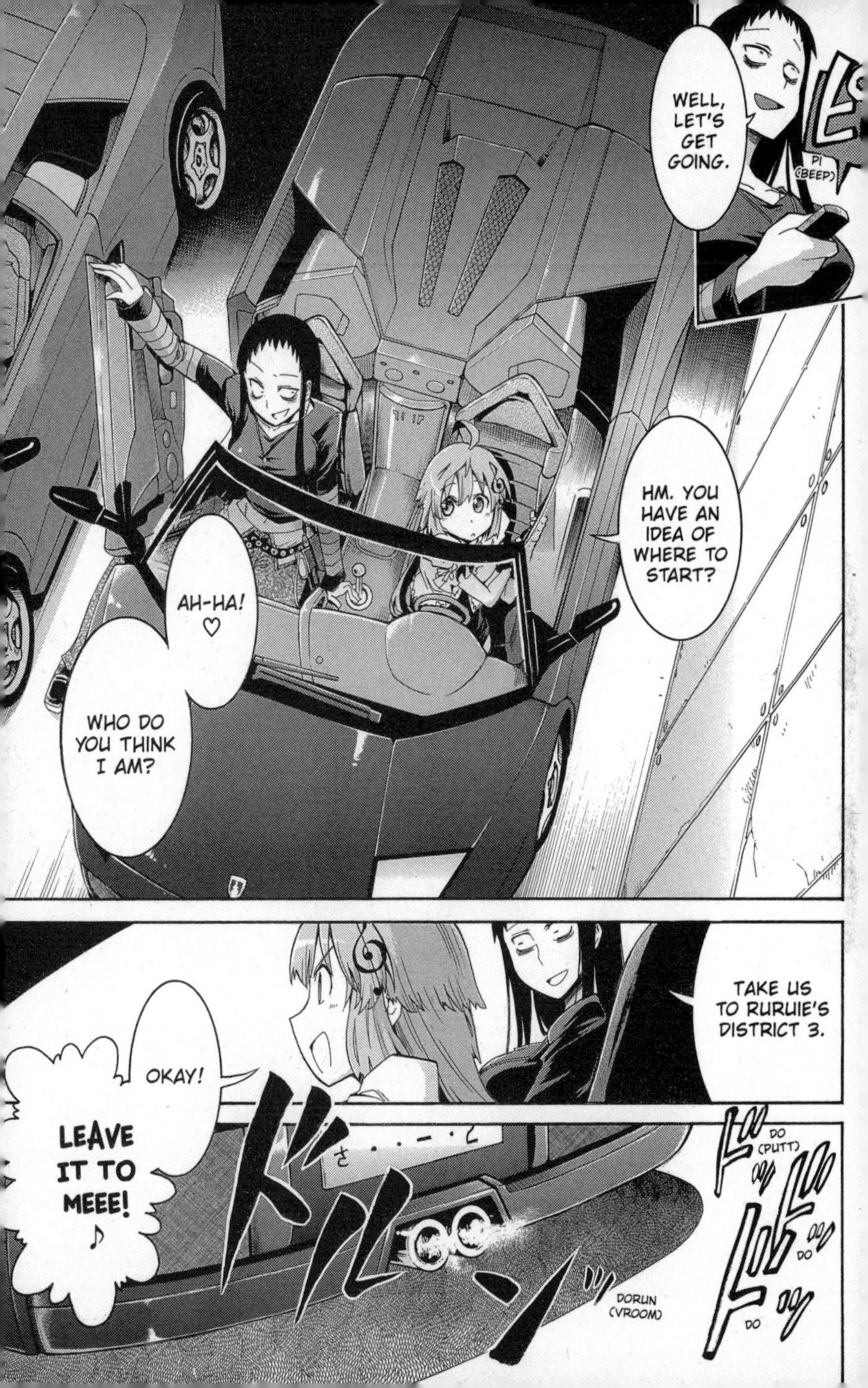
WELL, LET'S GET GOING.
PI (BEEP)
HM. YOU HAVE AN IDEA OF WHERE TO START?
AH-HA! ♡
WHO DO YOU THINK I AM?
TAKE US TO RURUIE'S DISTRICT 3.
OKAY!
LEAVE IT TO MEEE! ♪
DO (PUTT)
DO
DO
DORUN (VROOM)

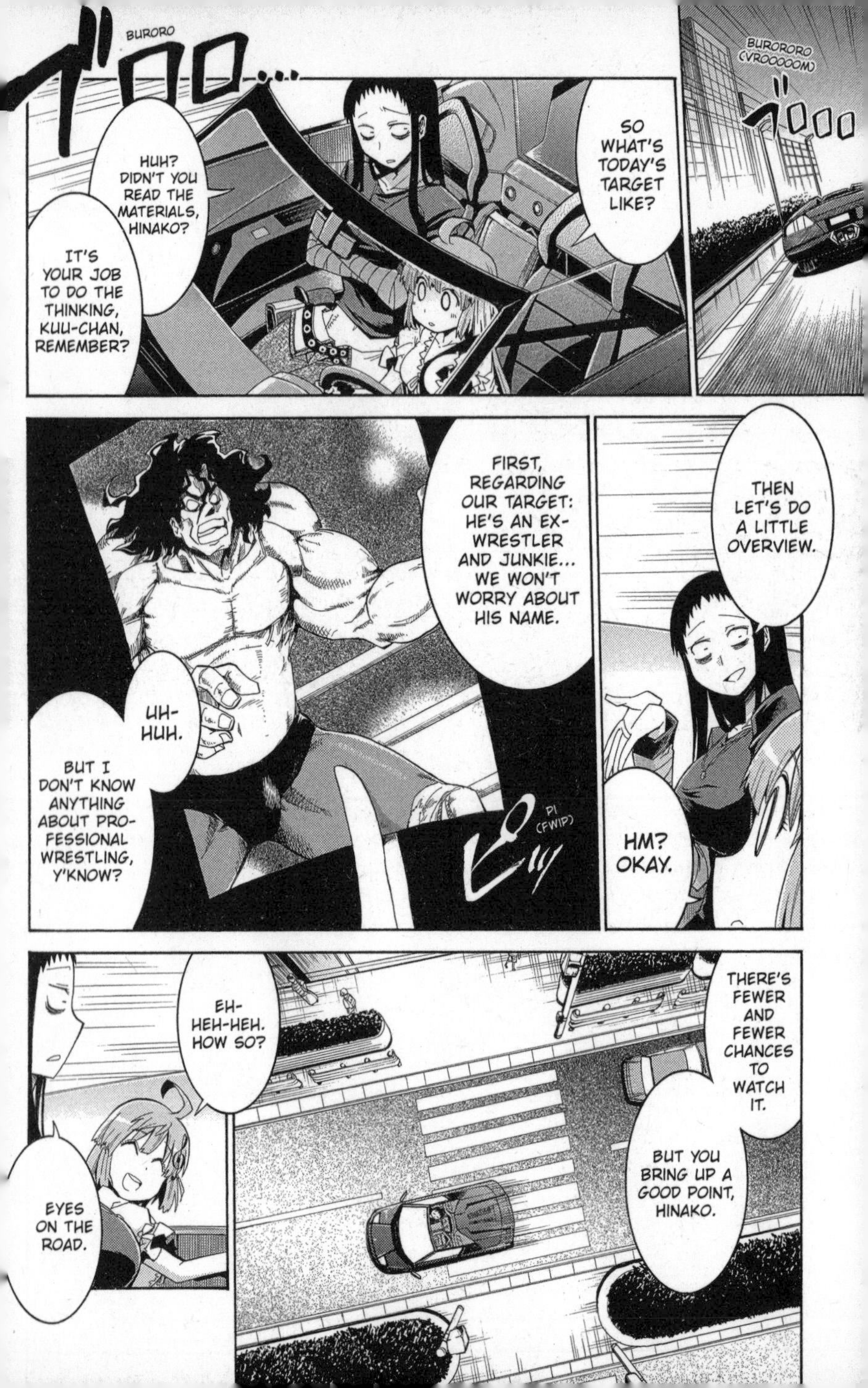
BURORORO (VROOOOOM)
BURORO
SO WHAT'S TODAY'S TARGET LIKE?
HUH? DIDN'T YOU READ THE MATERIALS, HINAKO?
IT'S YOUR JOB TO DO THE THINKING, KUU-CHAN, REMEMBER?
THEN LET'S DO A LITTLE OVERVIEW.
HM? OKAY.
FIRST, REGARDING OUR TARGET: HE'S AN EX-WRESTLER AND JUNKIE... WE WON'T WORRY ABOUT HIS NAME.
PI (FWIP)
UH-HUH.
BUT I DON'T KNOW ANYTHING ABOUT PRO-FESSIONAL WRESTLING, Y'KNOW?
THERE'S FEWER AND FEWER CHANCES TO WATCH IT.
EH-HEH-HEH. HOW SO?
BUT YOU BRING UP A GOOD POINT, HINAKO.
EYES ON THE ROAD.

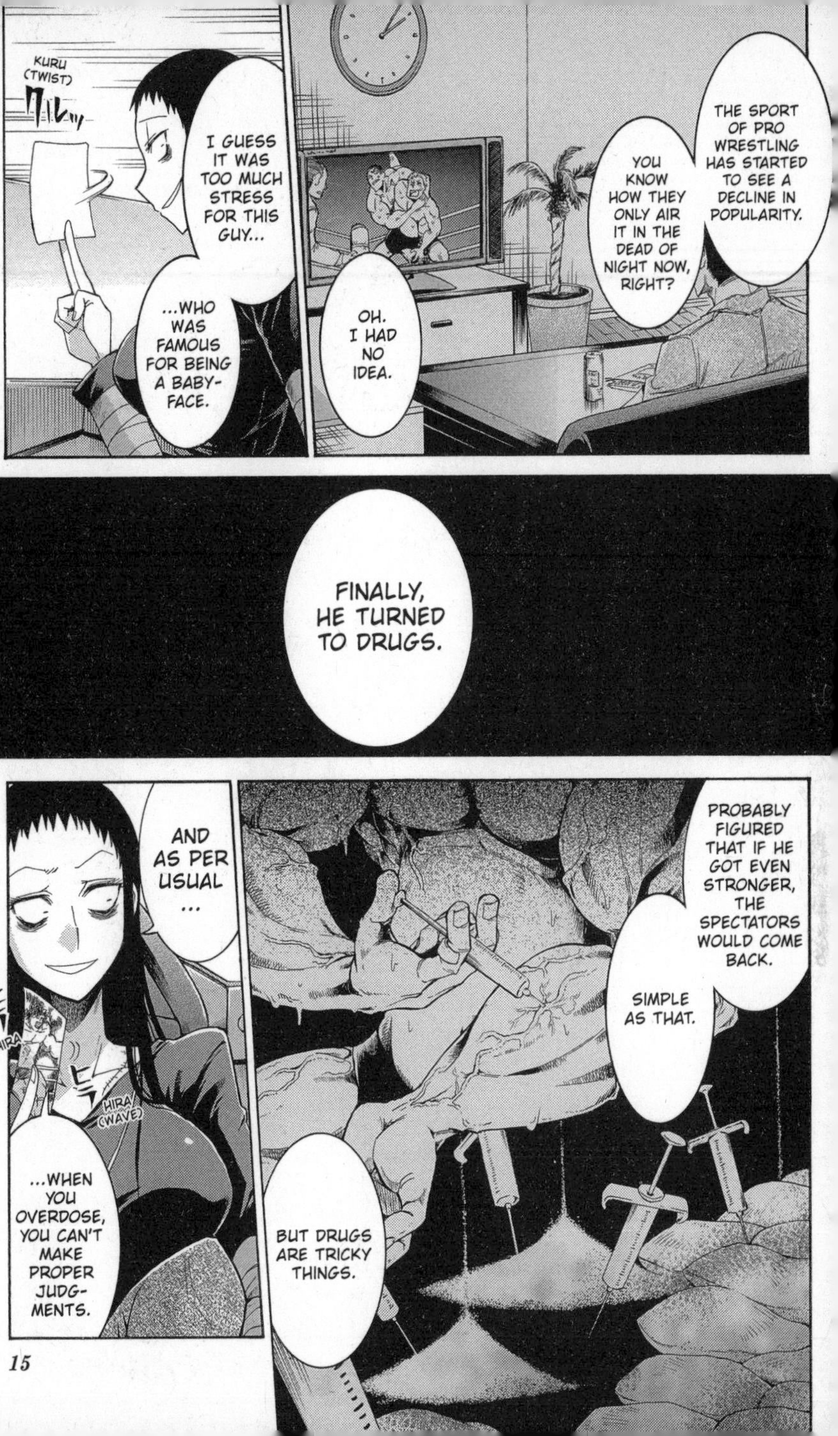
THE SPORT OF PRO WRESTLING HAS STARTED TO SEE A DECLINE IN POPULARITY.
YOU KNOW HOW THEY ONLY AIR IT IN THE DEAD OF NIGHT NOW, RIGHT?
OH. I HAD NO IDEA.
KURU (TWIST)
I GUESS IT WAS TOO MUCH STRESS FOR THIS GUY...
...WHO WAS FAMOUS FOR BEING A BABY-FACE.
FINALLY, HE TURNED TO DRUGS.
PROBABLY FIGURED THAT IF HE GOT EVEN STRONGER, THE SPECTATORS WOULD COME BACK.
SIMPLE AS THAT.
BUT DRUGS ARE TRICKY THINGS.
AND AS PER USUAL ...
HIRA
HIRA (WAVE)
...WHEN YOU OVERDOSE, YOU CAN'T MAKE PROPER JUDG-MENTS.

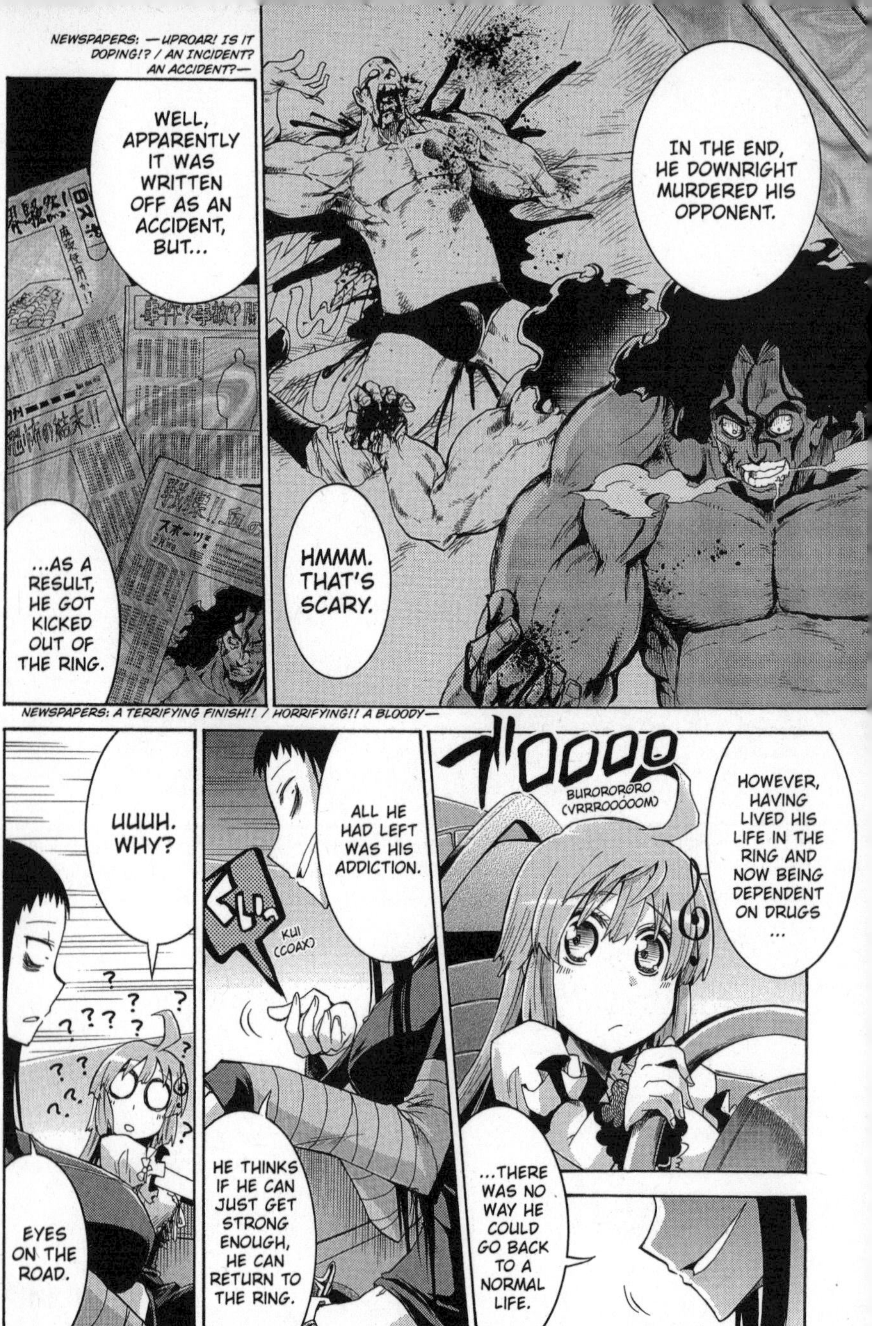
NEWSPAPERS: —UPROAR! IS IT DOPING!? / AN INCIDENT? AN ACCIDENT?—
IN THE END, HE DOWNRIGHT MURDERED HIS OPPONENT.
HMMM. THAT'S SCARY.
WELL, APPARENTLY IT WAS WRITTEN OFF AS AN ACCIDENT, BUT...
...AS A RESULT, HE GOT KICKED OUT OF THE RING.
NEWSPAPERS: A TERRIFYING FINISH!! / HORRIFYING!! A BLOODY—
BURORORORO (VRRROOOOOM)
HOWEVER, HAVING LIVED HIS LIFE IN THE RING AND NOW BEING DEPENDENT ON DRUGS ...
...THERE WAS NO WAY HE COULD GO BACK TO A NORMAL LIFE.
ALL HE HAD LEFT WAS HIS ADDICTION.
KUI (COAX)
HE THINKS IF HE CAN JUST GET STRONG ENOUGH, HE CAN RETURN TO THE RING.
UUUH. WHY?
EYES ON THE ROAD.

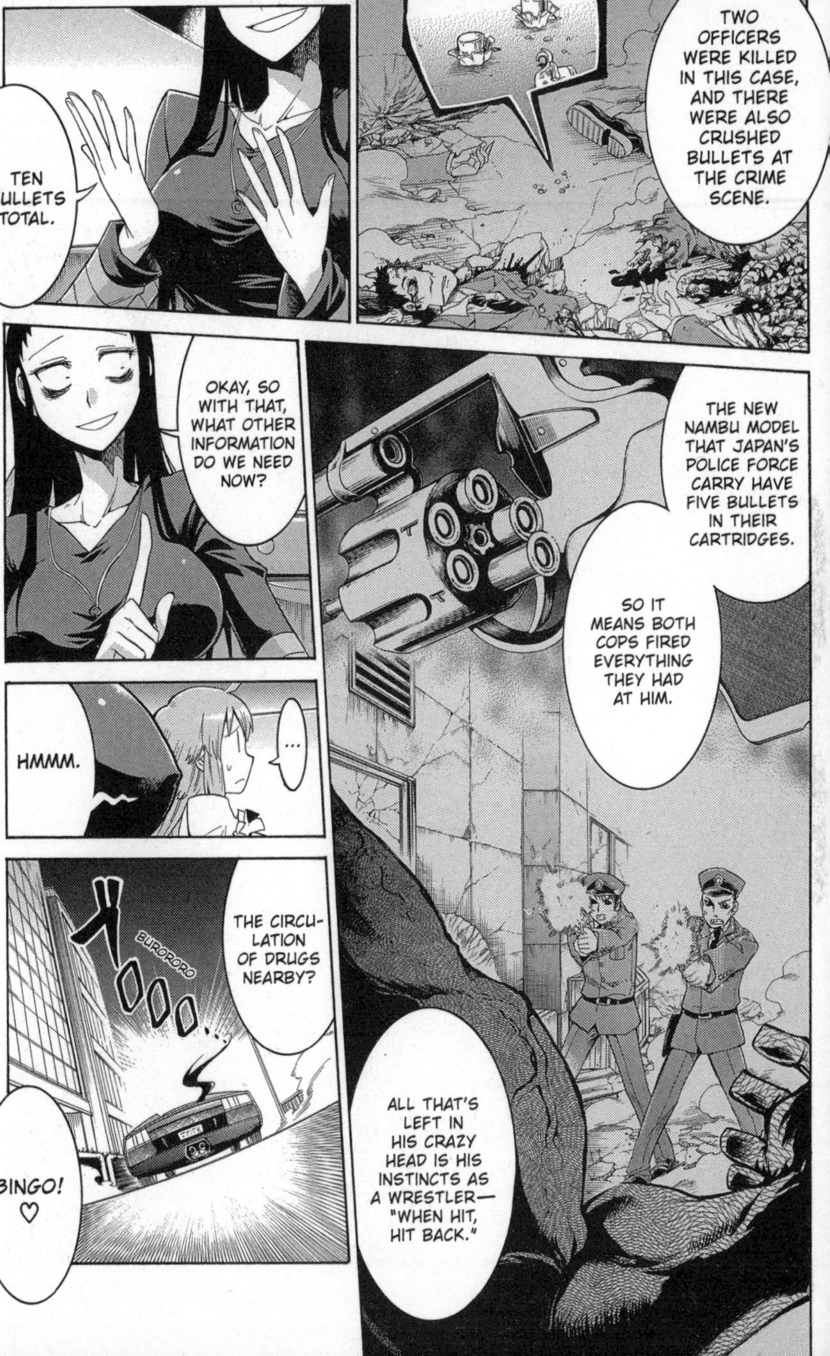
TWO OFFICERS WERE KILLED IN THIS CASE, AND THERE WERE ALSO CRUSHED BULLETS AT THE CRIME SCENE.
TEN BULLETS TOTAL.
THE NEW NAMBU MODEL THAT JAPAN'S POLICE FORCE CARRY HAVE FIVE BULLETS IN THEIR CARTRIDGES.
SO IT MEANS BOTH COPS FIRED EVERYTHING THEY HAD AT HIM.
ALL THAT'S LEFT IN HIS CRAZY HEAD IS HIS INSTINCTS AS A WRESTLER— "WHEN HIT, HIT BACK."
OKAY, SO WITH THAT, WHAT OTHER INFORMATION DO WE NEED NOW?
...
HMMM.
THE CIRCU-LATION OF DRUGS NEARBY?
BURORORO
BINGO! ♡

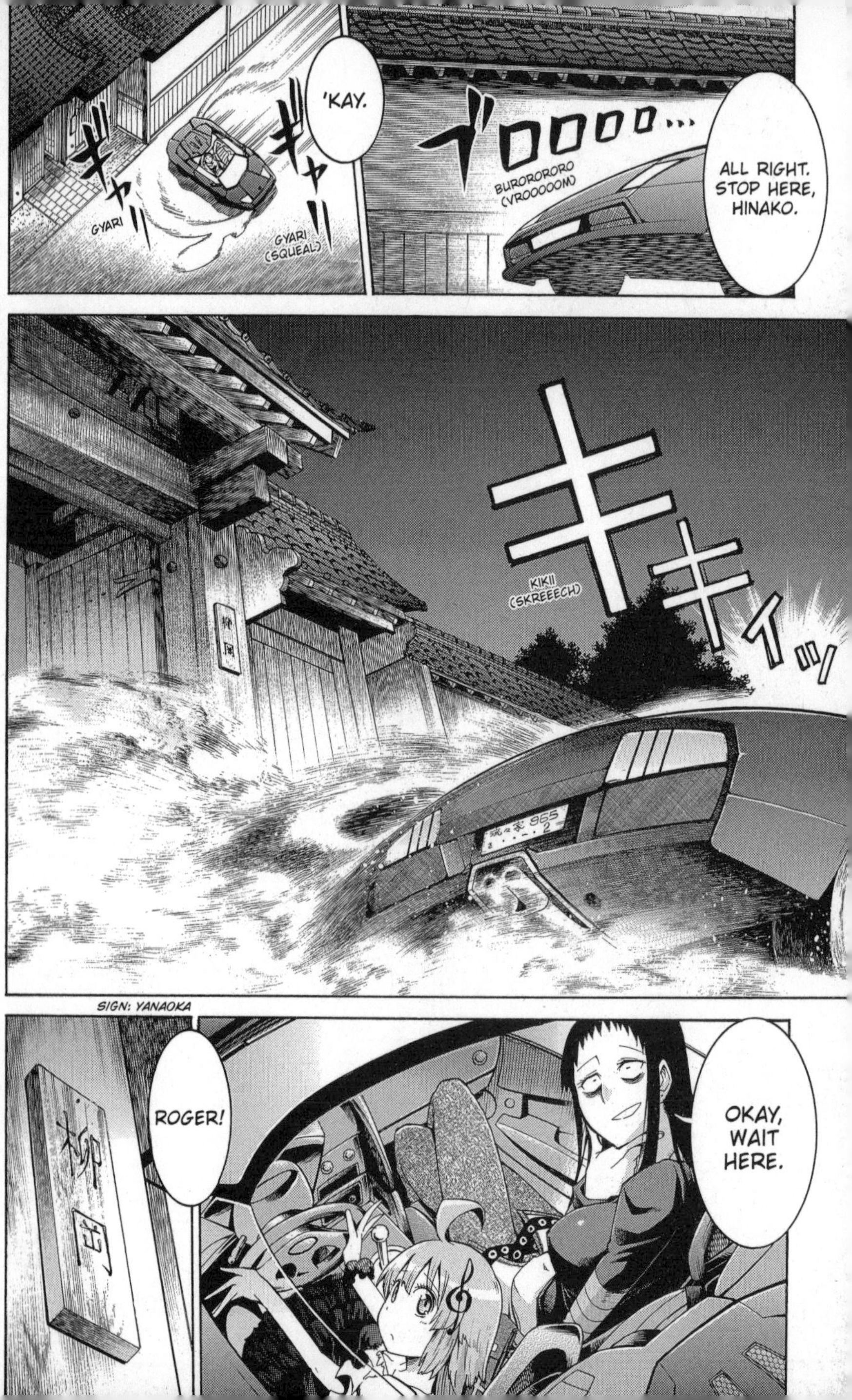
ALL RIGHT. STOP HERE, HINAKO.
BURORORO (VROOOOOM)
'KAY.
GYARI (SQUEAL)
GYARI
KIKII (SKREEECH)
SIGN: YANAOKA
OKAY, WAIT HERE.
ROGER!

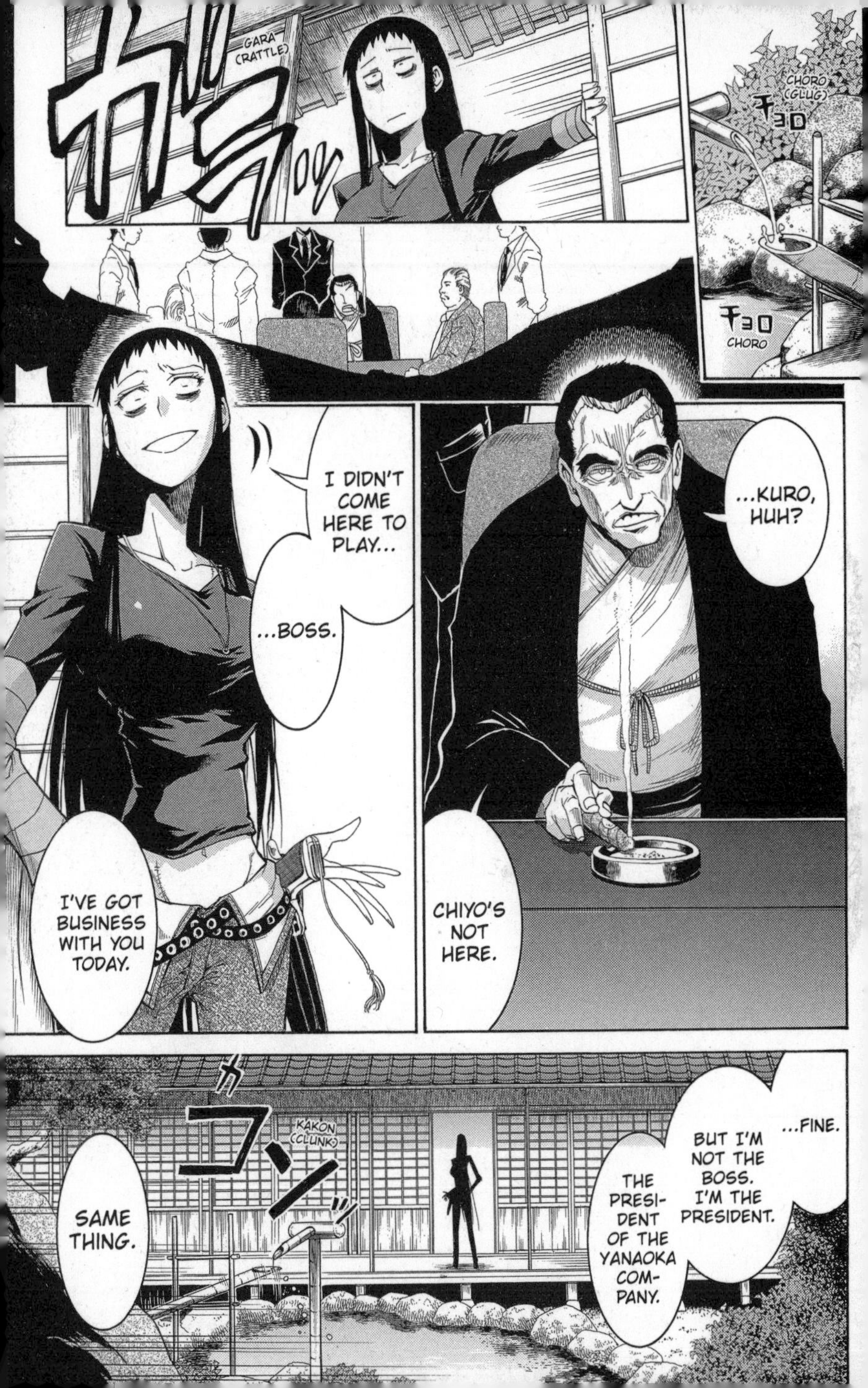
CHORO (GLUG)
チョロ
チョロ
CHORO
カラッ
GARA (RATTLE)
...KURO, HUH?
CHIYO'S NOT HERE.
I DIDN'T COME HERE TO PLAY...
...BOSS.
I'VE GOT BUSINESS WITH YOU TODAY.
...FINE.
BUT I'M NOT THE BOSS. I'M THE PRESIDENT.
THE PRESI-DENT OF THE YANAOKA COM-PANY.
KAKON (CLUNK)
SAME THING.

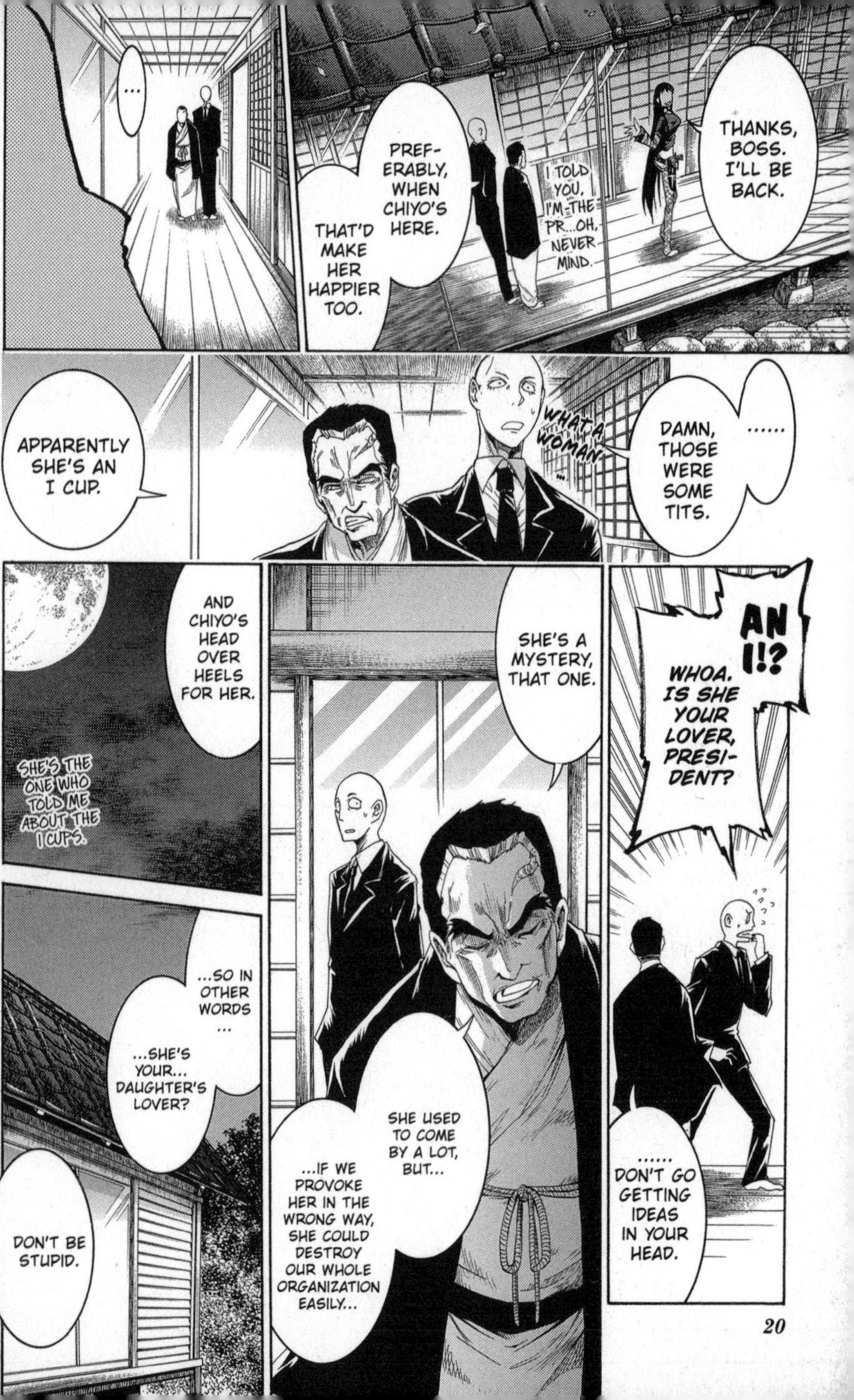
THANKS, BOSS. I'LL BE BACK.
I TOLD YOU, I'M THE PR...OH, NEVER MIND.
PREF-ERABLY, WHEN CHIYO'S HERE.
THAT'D MAKE HER HAPPIER TOO.
...
......
DAMN, THOSE WERE SOME TITS.
WHAT A WOMAN...
APPARENTLY SHE'S AN I CUP.
AN I!?
WHOA. IS SHE YOUR LOVER, PRESIDENT?
...... DON'T GO GETTING IDEAS IN YOUR HEAD.
SHE'S A MYSTERY, THAT ONE.
SHE USED TO COME BY A LOT, BUT...
...IF WE PROVOKE HER IN THE WRONG WAY, SHE COULD DESTROY OUR WHOLE ORGANIZATION EASILY...
AND CHIYO'S HEAD OVER HEELS FOR HER.
SHE'S THE ONE WHO TOLD ME ABOUT THE I CUPS.
...SO IN OTHER WORDS...
...SHE'S YOUR... DAUGHTER'S LOVER?
DON'T BE STUPID.

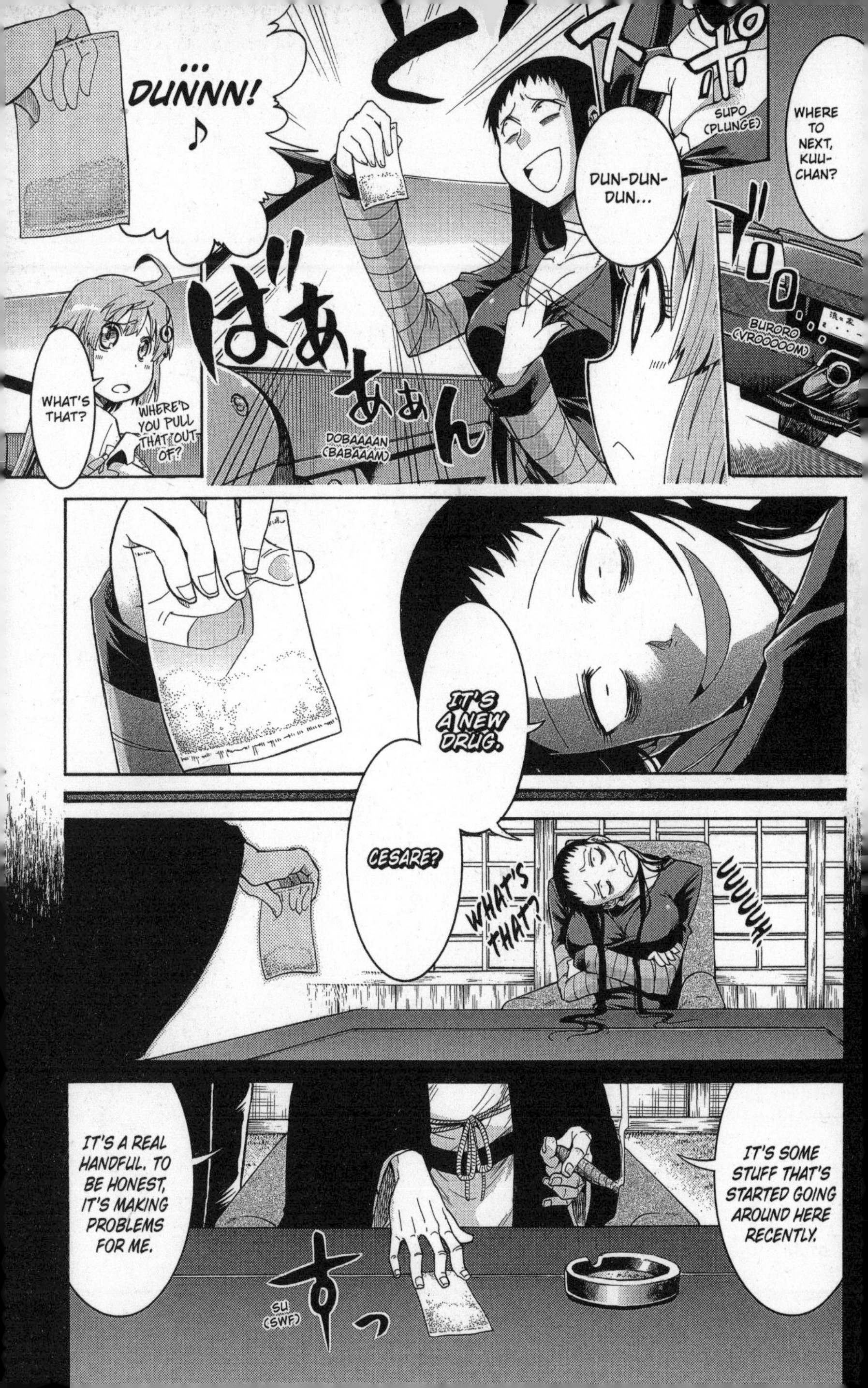
WHERE TO NEXT, KUU-CHAN?
SUPO (PLUNGE)
BURORO (VROOOOOM)
DUN-DUN-DUN...
...DUNNN! ♪
DOBAAAAN (BABAAAM)
WHAT'S THAT?
WHERE'D YOU PULL THAT OUT OF?
IT'S A NEW DRUG.
CESARE?
UUUUH.
WHAT'S THAT?
IT'S SOME STUFF THAT'S STARTED GOING AROUND HERE RECENTLY.
IT'S A REAL HANDFUL. TO BE HONEST, IT'S MAKING PROBLEMS FOR ME.
SU (SWF)

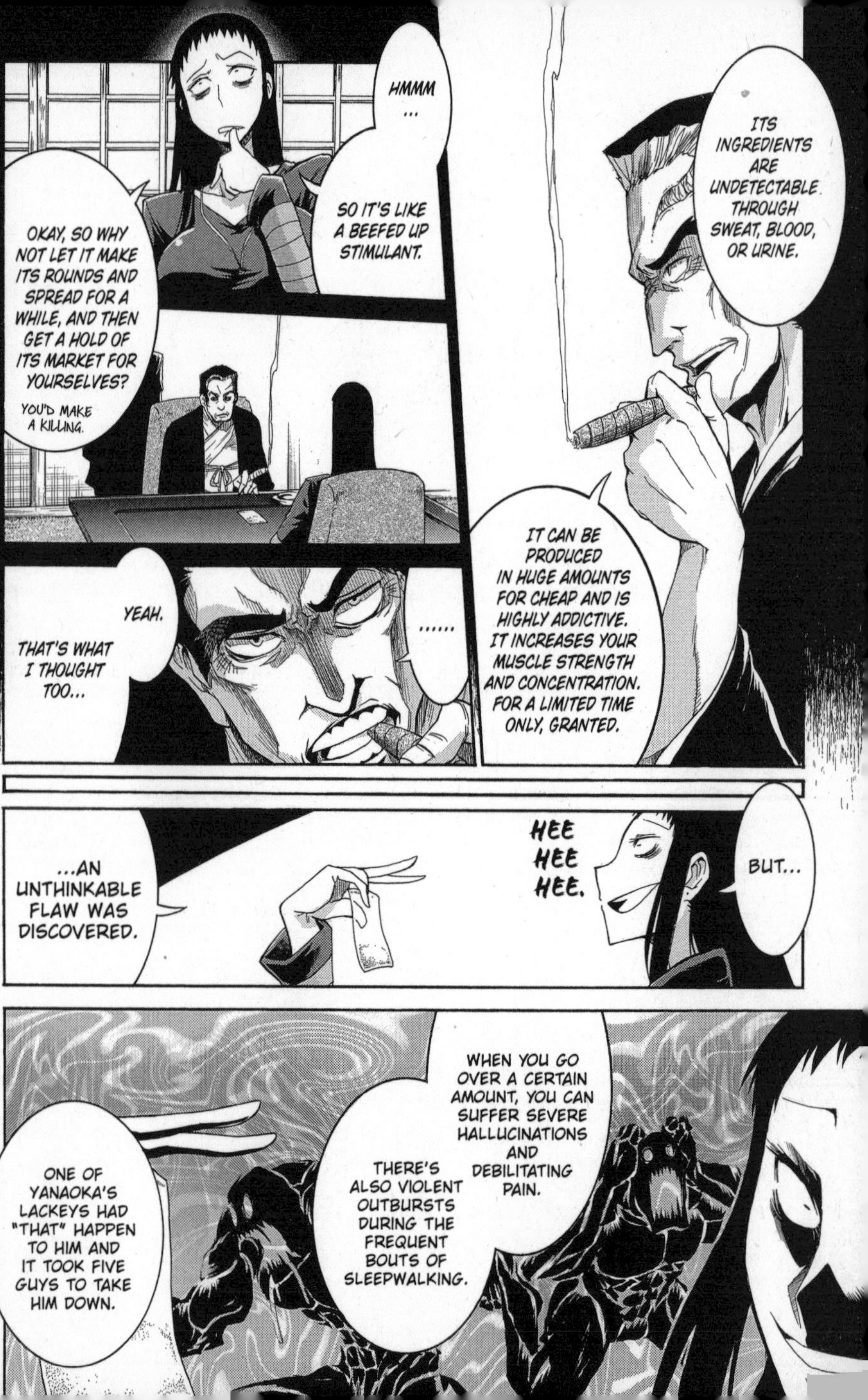
ITS INGREDIENTS ARE UNDETECTABLE THROUGH SWEAT, BLOOD, OR URINE.
IT CAN BE PRODUCED IN HUGE AMOUNTS FOR CHEAP AND IS HIGHLY ADDICTIVE. IT INCREASES YOUR MUSCLE STRENGTH AND CONCENTRATION. FOR A LIMITED TIME ONLY, GRANTED.
HMMM...
SO IT'S LIKE A BEEFED UP STIMULANT.
OKAY, SO WHY NOT LET IT MAKE ITS ROUNDS AND SPREAD FOR A WHILE, AND THEN GET A HOLD OF ITS MARKET FOR YOURSELVES?
YOU'D MAKE A KILLING.
......
YEAH.
THAT'S WHAT I THOUGHT TOO...
BUT...
HEE HEE HEE.
...AN UNTHINKABLE FLAW WAS DISCOVERED.
WHEN YOU GO OVER A CERTAIN AMOUNT, YOU CAN SUFFER SEVERE HALLUCINATIONS AND DEBILITATING PAIN.
THERE'S ALSO VIOLENT OUTBURSTS DURING THE FREQUENT BOUTS OF SLEEPWALKING.
ONE OF YANAOKA'S LACKEYS HAD "THAT" HAPPEN TO HIM AND IT TOOK FIVE GUYS TO TAKE HIM DOWN.

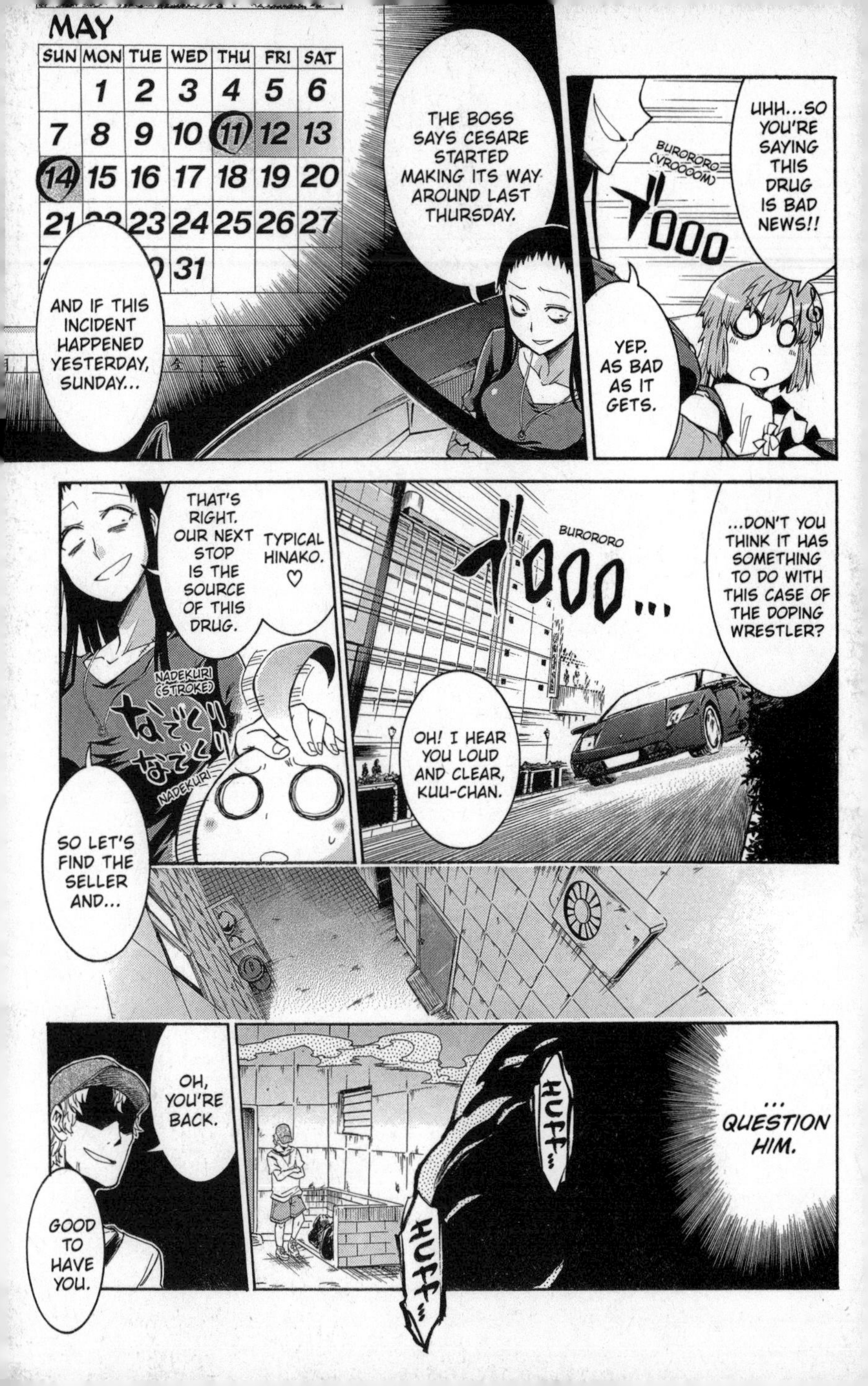
UHH...SO YOU'RE SAYING THIS DRUG IS BAD NEWS!!
BURORORO (VROOOOM)
YEP. AS BAD AS IT GETS.
MAY
SUN MON TUE WED THU FRI SAT
THE BOSS SAYS CESARE STARTED MAKING ITS WAY AROUND LAST THURSDAY.
AND IF THIS INCIDENT HAPPENED YESTERDAY, SUNDAY...
...DON'T YOU THINK IT HAS SOMETHING TO DO WITH THIS CASE OF THE DOPING WRESTLER?
BURORORO
OH! I HEAR YOU LOUD AND CLEAR, KUU-CHAN.
THAT'S RIGHT. OUR NEXT STOP IS THE SOURCE OF THIS DRUG.
TYPICAL HINAKO. ♡
NADEKURI (STROKE)
なでくり なでくり
NADEKURI
SO LET'S FIND THE SELLER AND...
... QUESTION HIM.
HUFF..
HUFF..
OH, YOU'RE BACK.
GOOD TO HAVE YOU.

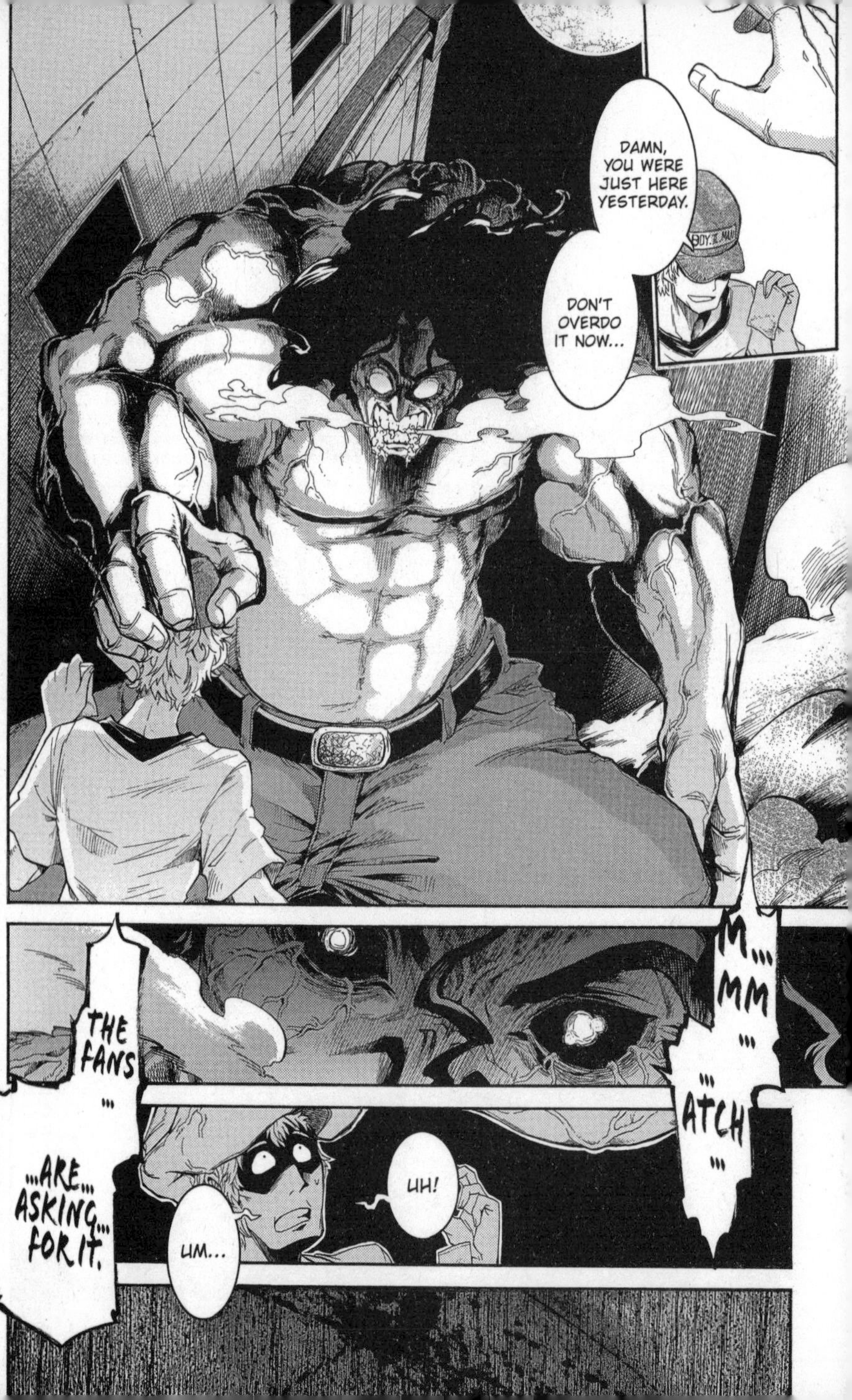
DAMN, YOU WERE JUST HERE YESTERDAY.
DON'T OVERDO IT NOW...
M... MM... ...ATCH...
THE FANS...
...ARE... ASKING... FOR IT.
UH!
UM...

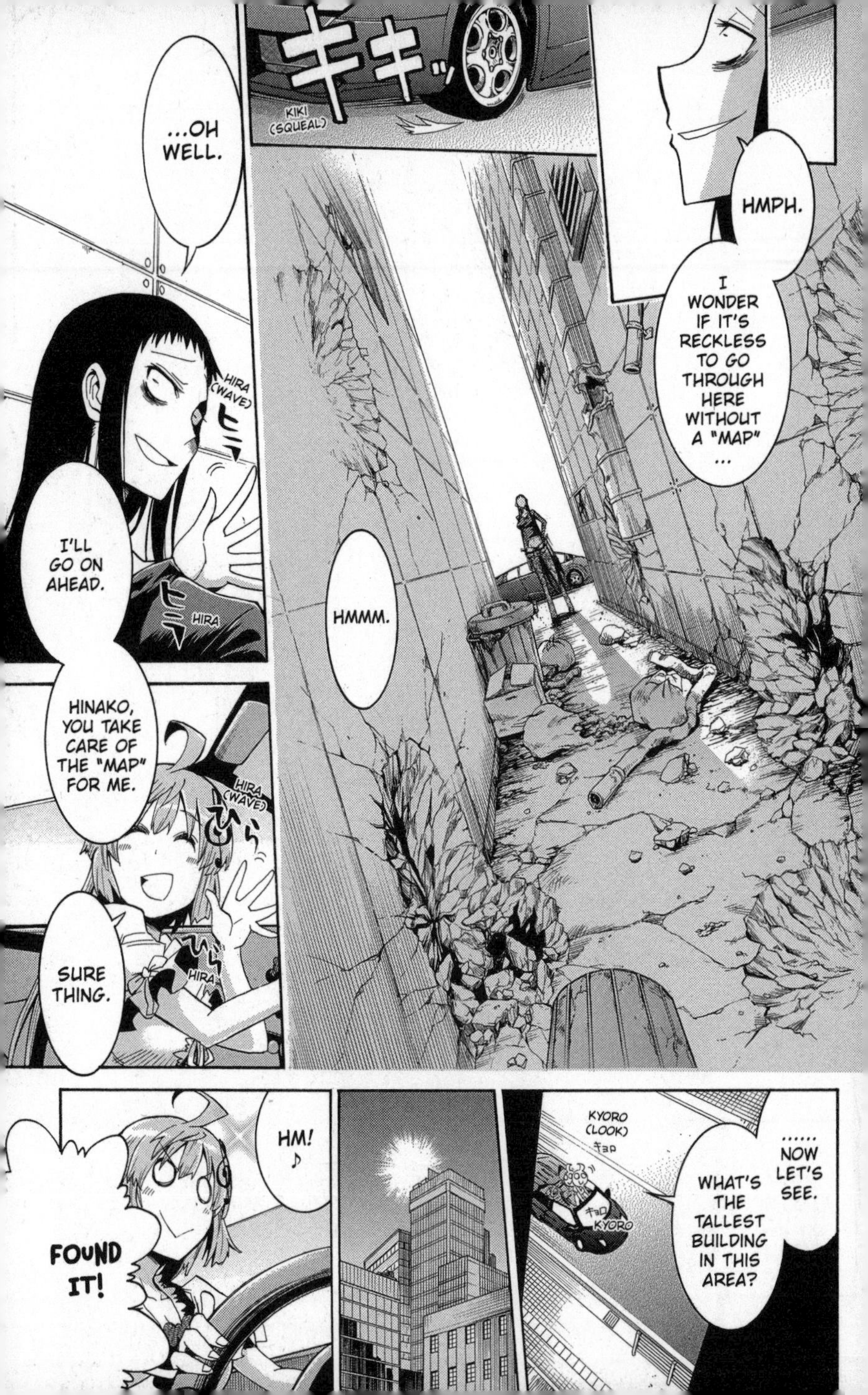
HMPH.
キキッ
KIKI (SQUEAL)
I WONDER IF IT'S RECKLESS TO GO THROUGH HERE WITHOUT A "MAP"...
HMMM.
...OH WELL.
HIRA (WAVE)
I'LL GO ON AHEAD.
HIRA
HINAKO, YOU TAKE CARE OF THE "MAP" FOR ME.
HIRA (WAVE)
ひら
SURE THING.
HIRA
...... NOW LET'S SEE.
WHAT'S THE TALLEST BUILDING IN THIS AREA?
KYORO (LOOK)
キョロ
KYORO
HM! ♪
FOUND IT!

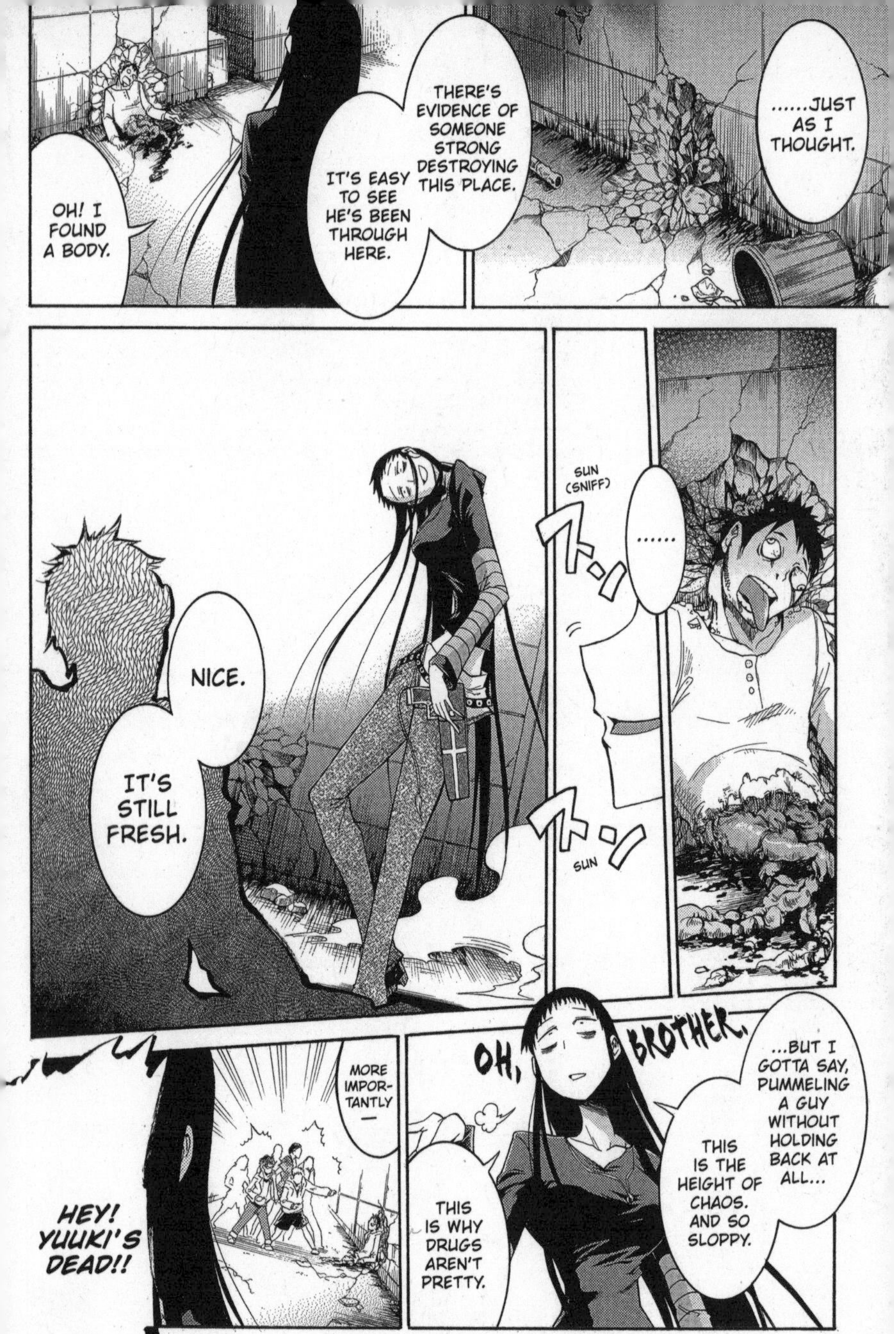
......JUST AS I THOUGHT.
THERE'S EVIDENCE OF SOMEONE STRONG DESTROYING THIS PLACE.
IT'S EASY TO SEE HE'S BEEN THROUGH HERE.
OH! I FOUND A BODY.
SUN (SNIFF)
......
SUN
NICE.
IT'S STILL FRESH.
OH, BROTHER.
...BUT I GOTTA SAY, PUMMELING A GUY WITHOUT HOLDING BACK AT ALL...
THIS IS THE HEIGHT OF CHAOS. AND SO SLOPPY.
THIS IS WHY DRUGS AREN'T PRETTY.
MORE IMPORTANTLY—
HEY! YUUKI'S DEAD!!

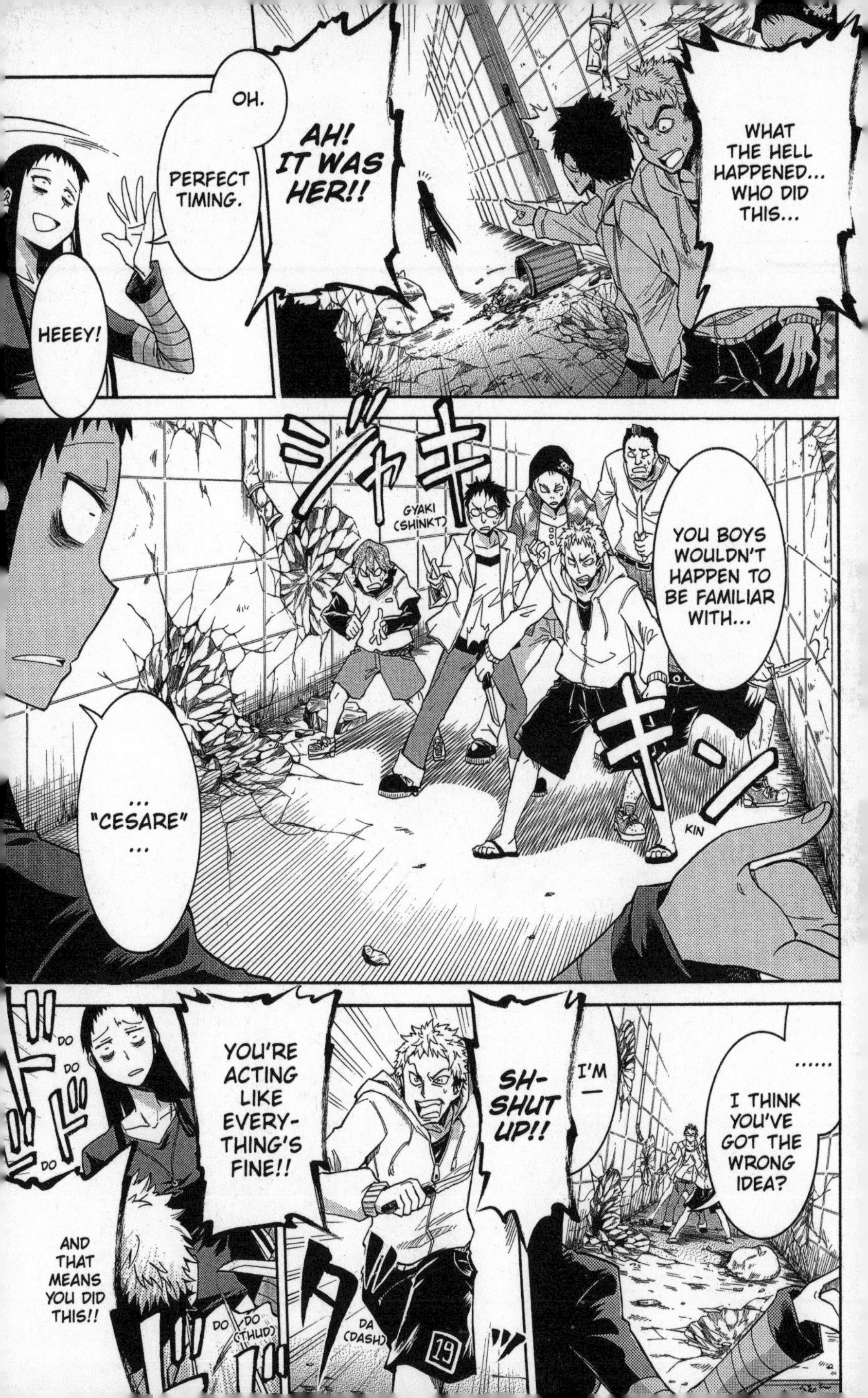
WHAT THE HELL HAPPENED... WHO DID THIS...
AH! IT WAS HER!!
OH.
PERFECT TIMING.
HEEEY!
GYAKI (SHINKT)
YOU BOYS WOULDN'T HAPPEN TO BE FAMILIAR WITH...
KIN
... "CESARE" ...
......
I THINK YOU'VE GOT THE WRONG IDEA?
I'M —
SH-SHUT UP!!
YOU'RE ACTING LIKE EVERY-THING'S FINE!!
DA (DASH)
DO DO (THUD)
AND THAT MEANS YOU DID THIS!!
DO
DO
DO

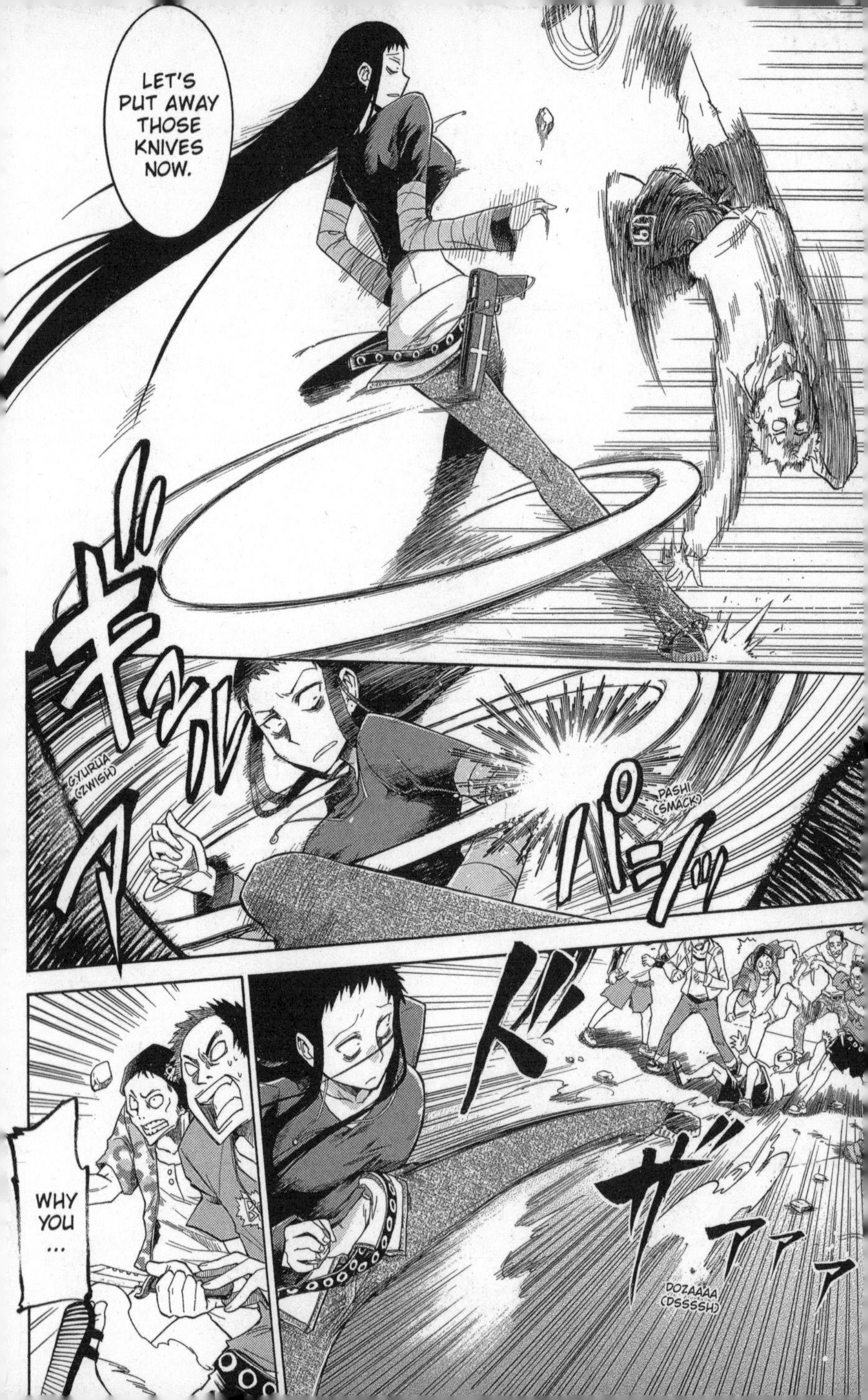
LET'S PUT AWAY THOSE KNIVES NOW.
PASHI (SMACK)
GYURUA (ZWISH)
DOZAAAA (DSSSSH)
WHY YOU ...

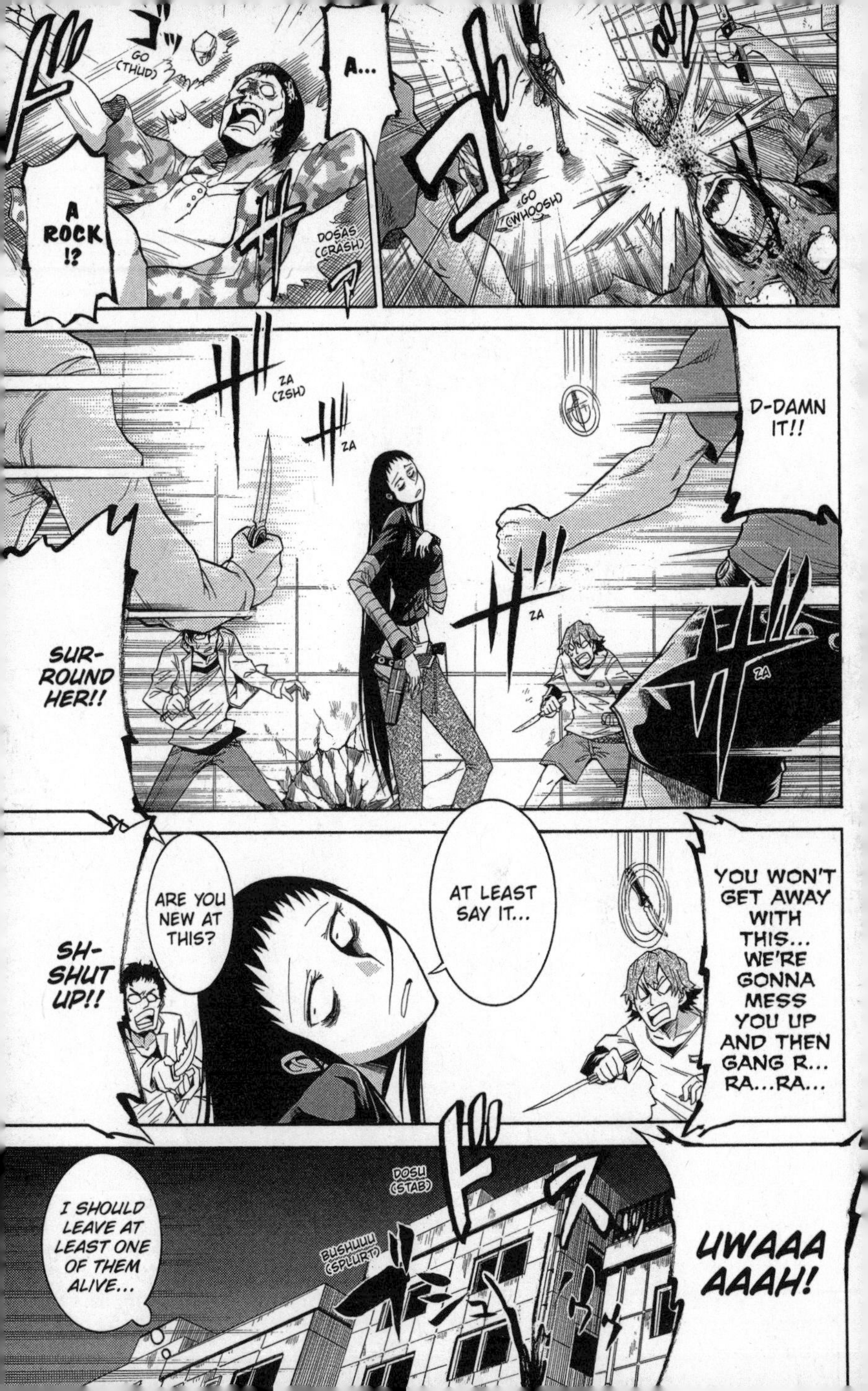
GO (WHOOSH)
DOSAS (CRASH)
A...
GO (THUD)
A ROCK !?
D-DAMN IT!!
ZA
ZA
ZA (ZSH)
ZA
SUR-ROUND HER!!
YOU WON'T GET AWAY WITH THIS... WE'RE GONNA MESS YOU UP AND THEN GANG R... RA...RA...
AT LEAST SAY IT...
ARE YOU NEW AT THIS?
SH-SHUT UP!!
UWAAA AAAH!
DOSU (STAB)
BUSHUUU (SPLURT)
I SHOULD LEAVE AT LEAST ONE OF THEM ALIVE...

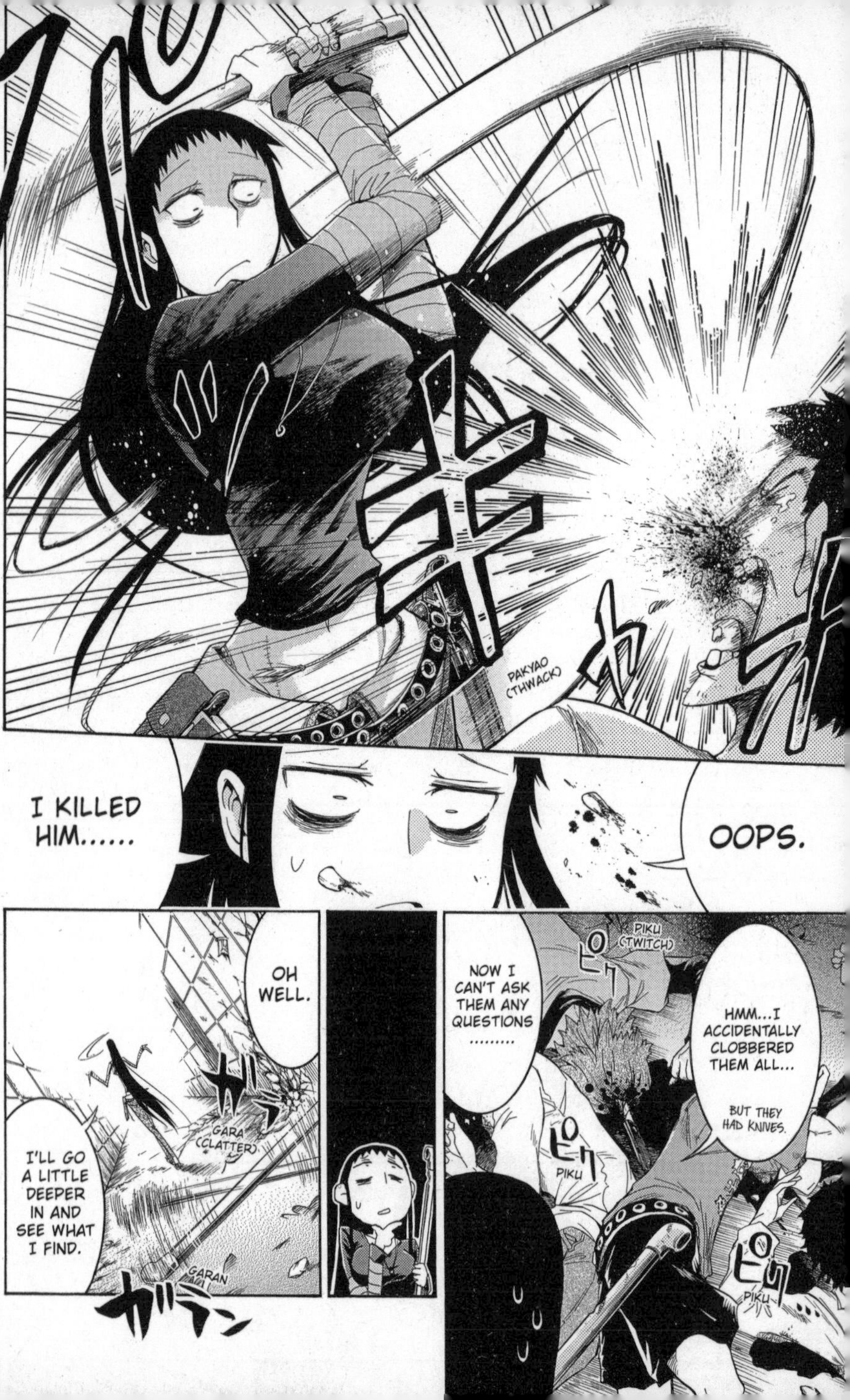
PAKYAO (THWACK)
OOPS.
I KILLED HIM......
PIKU (TWITCH)
HMM...I ACCIDENTALLY CLOBBERED THEM ALL...
NOW I CAN'T ASK THEM ANY QUESTIONS ....
BUT THEY HAD KNIVES.
PIKU
PIKU
OH WELL.
GARA (CLATTER)
I'LL GO A LITTLE DEEPER IN AND SEE WHAT I FIND.
GARAN

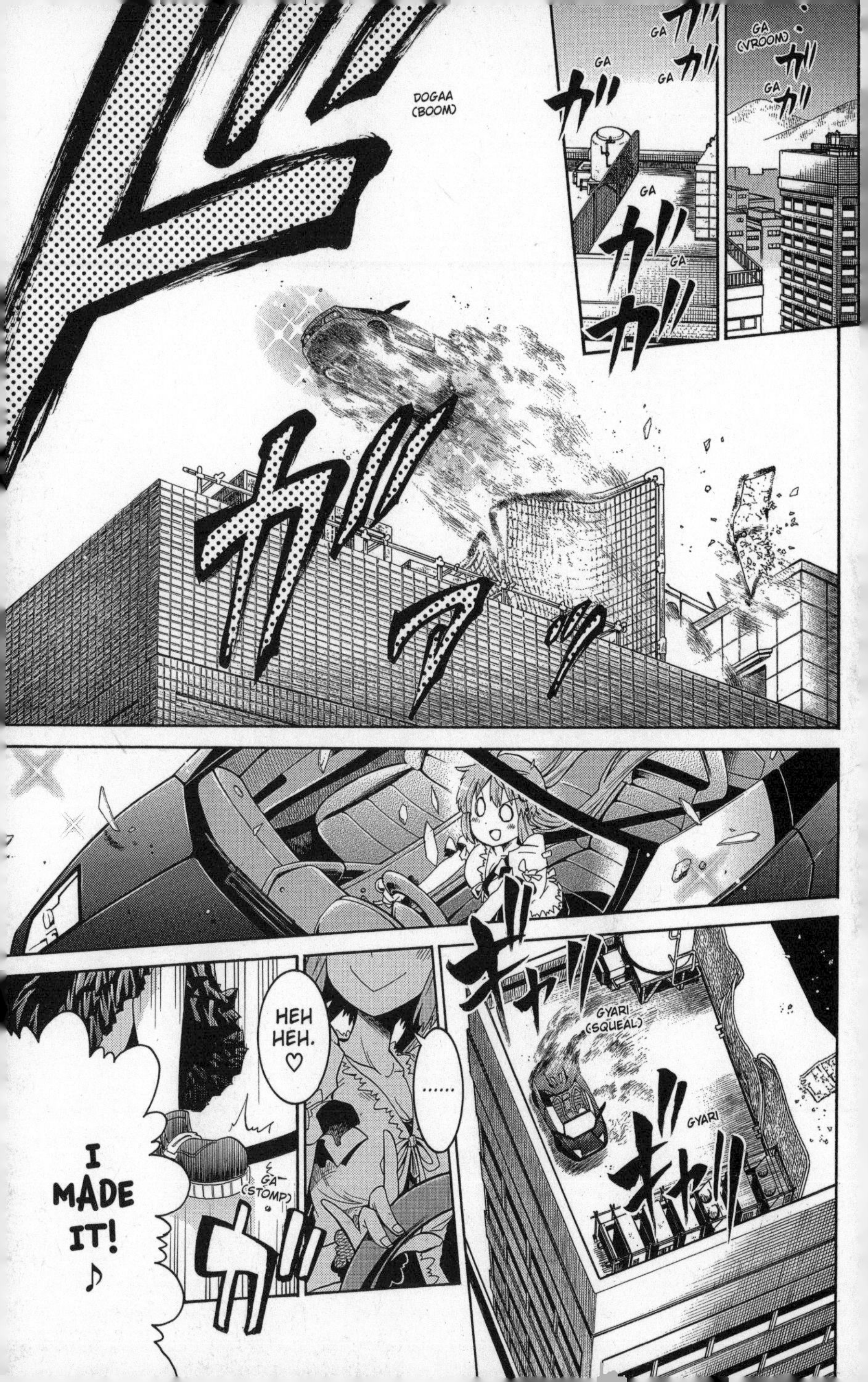

GA (VROOM)
GA
GA
GA
GA
GA
GA
DOGAA (BOOM)
GYARI (SQUEAL)
GYARI
HEH HEH. ♡
......
GA (STOMP)
I MADE IT! ♪

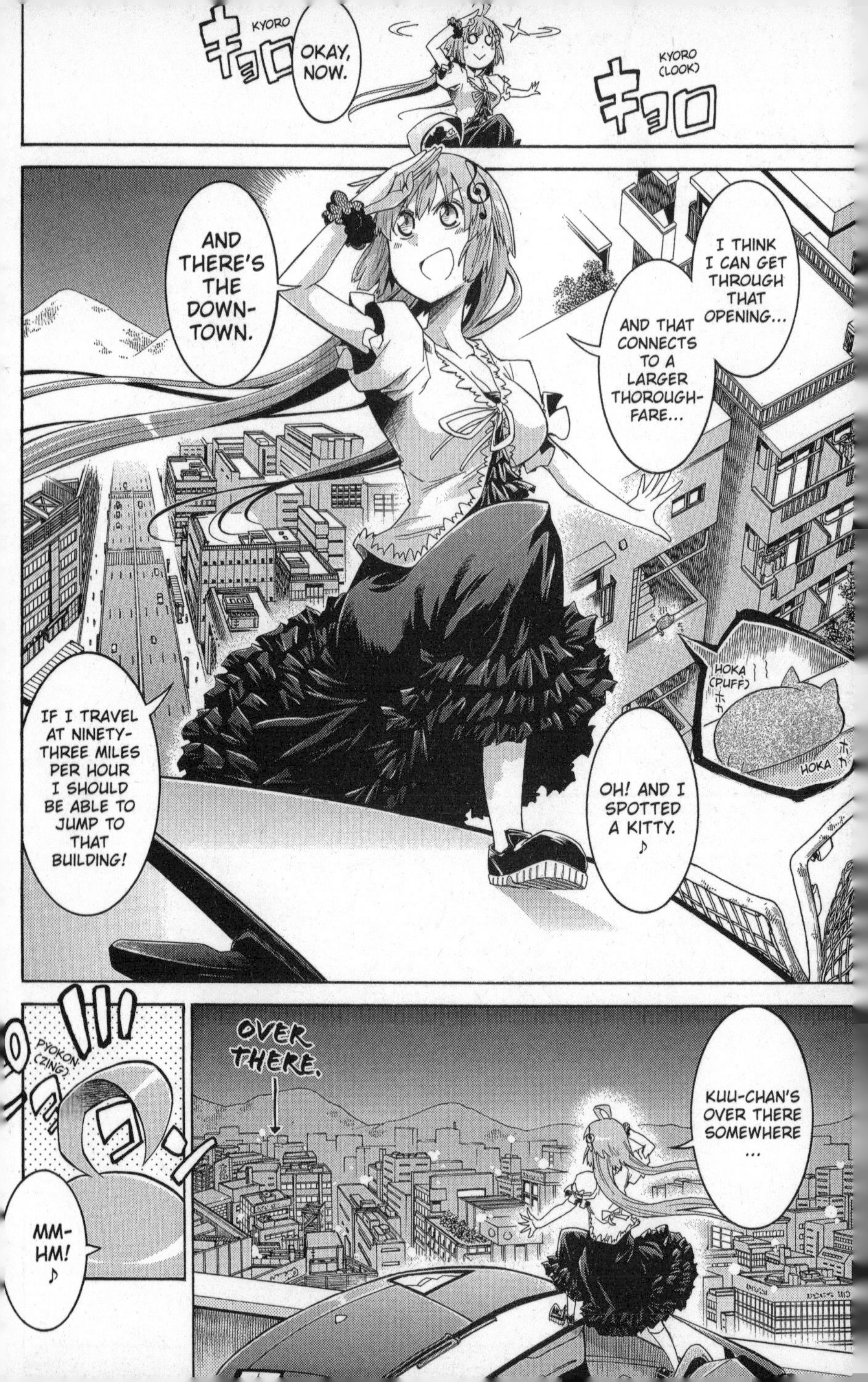
KYORO (LOOK)
キョロ
OKAY, NOW.
KYORO
キョロ
I THINK I CAN GET THROUGH THAT OPENING...
AND THAT CONNECTS TO A LARGER THOROUGH-FARE...
AND THERE'S THE DOWN-TOWN.
HOKA (PUFF)
HOKA
OH! AND I SPOTTED A KITTY. ♪
IF I TRAVEL AT NINETY-THREE MILES PER HOUR I SHOULD BE ABLE TO JUMP TO THAT BUILDING!
KUU-CHAN'S OVER THERE SOMEWHERE ...
OVER THERE.
PYOKON (ZING)
MM-HM! ♪

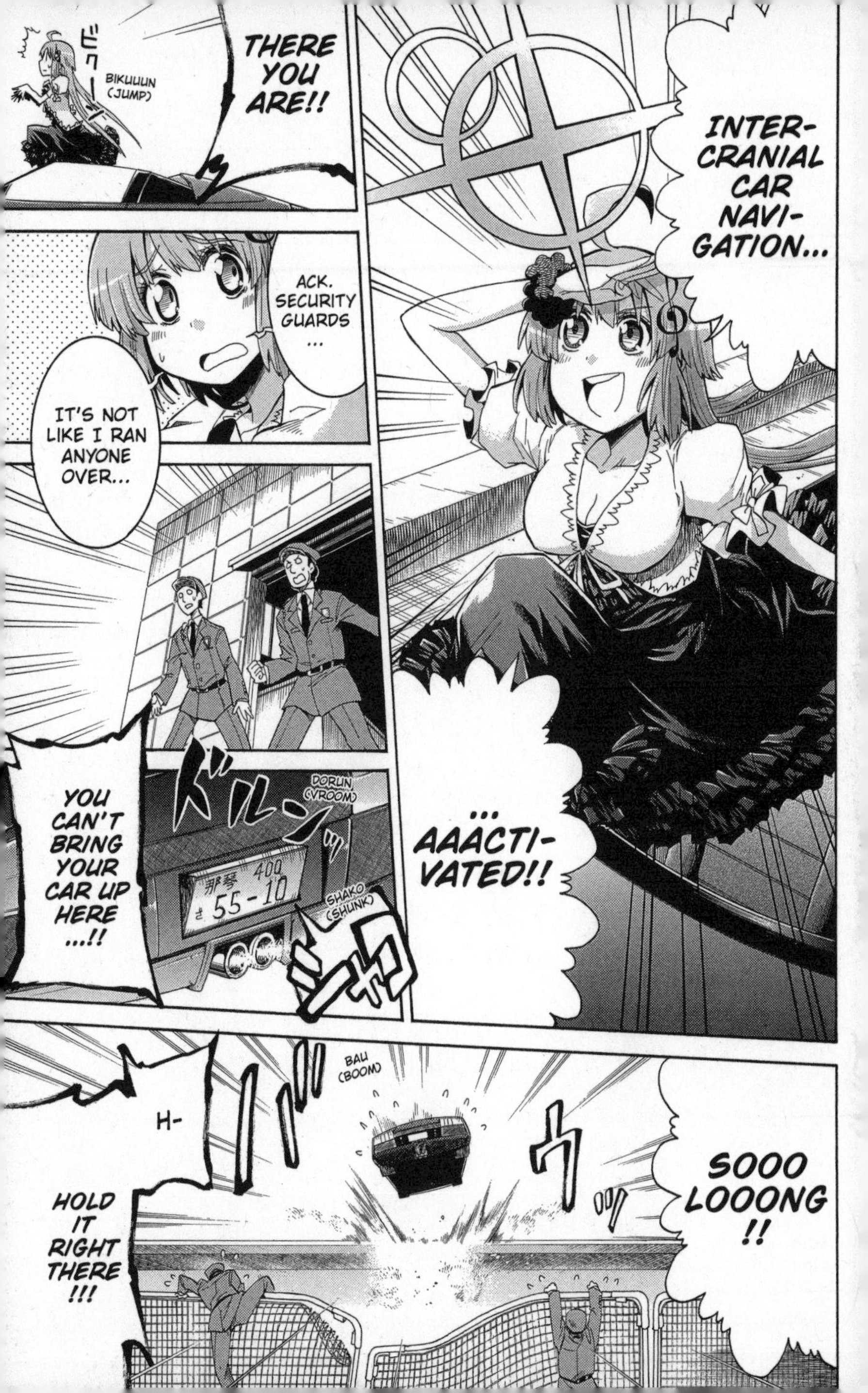
INTER-CRANIAL CAR NAVI-GATION...
...AAÄCTI-VATED!!
THERE YOU ARE!!
ビクー
BIKUUUN (JUMP)
ACK. SECURITY GUARDS...
IT'S NOT LIKE I RAN ANYONE OVER...
ドルンッ
DORUN (VROOM)
那琴 400 さ 55-10
SHAKO (SHUNK)
シャコ
YOU CAN'T BRING YOUR CAR UP HERE ...!!
SOOO LOOONG!!
バウッ
BAU (BOOM)
H-
HOLD IT RIGHT THERE!!!

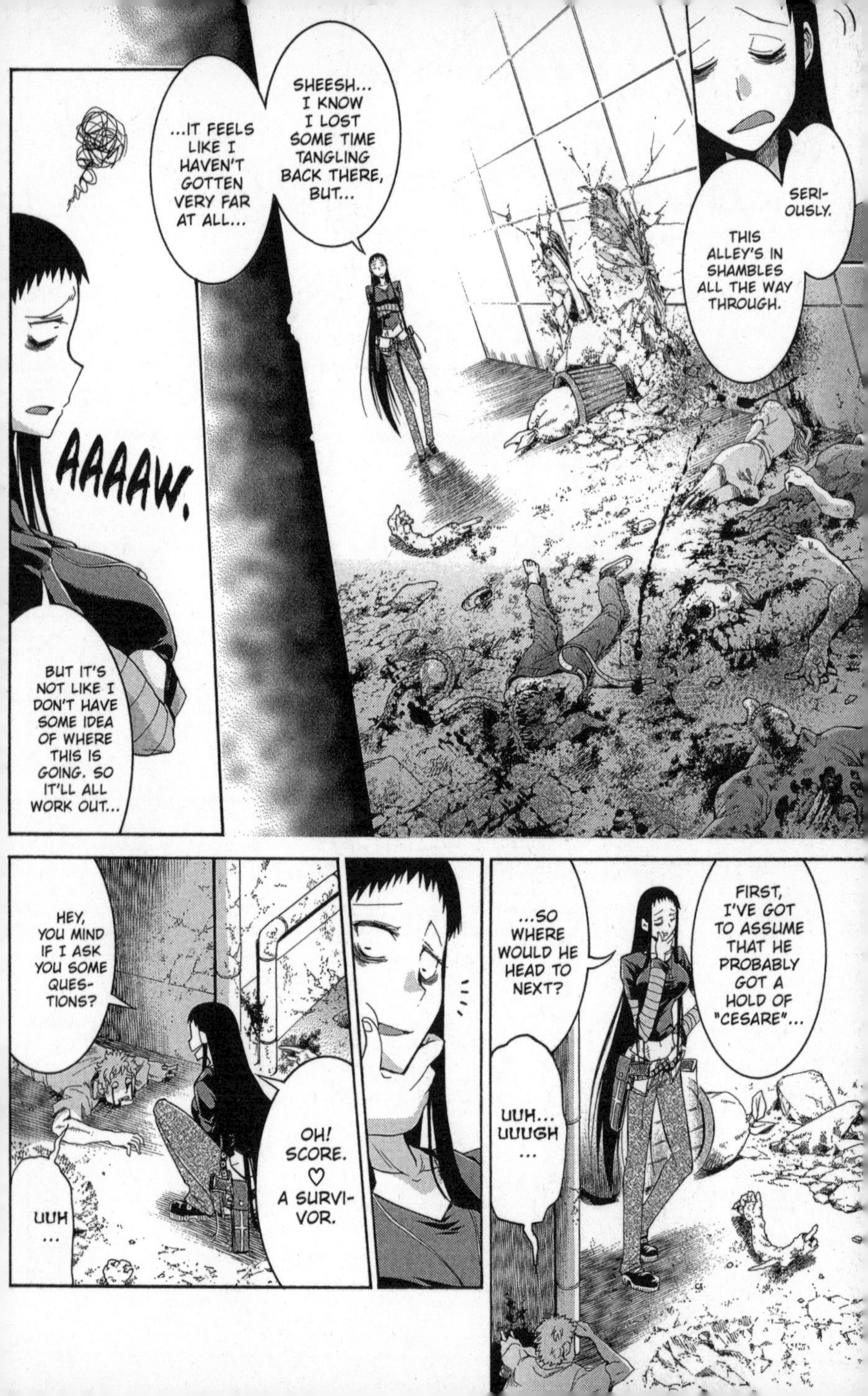
SERIOUSLY.
THIS ALLEY'S IN SHAMBLES ALL THE WAY THROUGH.
SHEESH... I KNOW I LOST SOME TIME TANGLING BACK THERE, BUT...
...IT FEELS LIKE I HAVEN'T GOTTEN VERY FAR AT ALL...
AAAAW.
BUT IT'S NOT LIKE I DON'T HAVE SOME IDEA OF WHERE THIS IS GOING. SO IT'LL ALL WORK OUT...
FIRST, I'VE GOT TO ASSUME THAT HE PROBABLY GOT A HOLD OF "CESARE"...
...SO WHERE WOULD HE HEAD TO NEXT?
UUH... UUUGH ...
OH! SCORE. ♡ A SURVIVOR.
HEY, YOU MIND IF I ASK YOU SOME QUESTIONS?
UUH ...

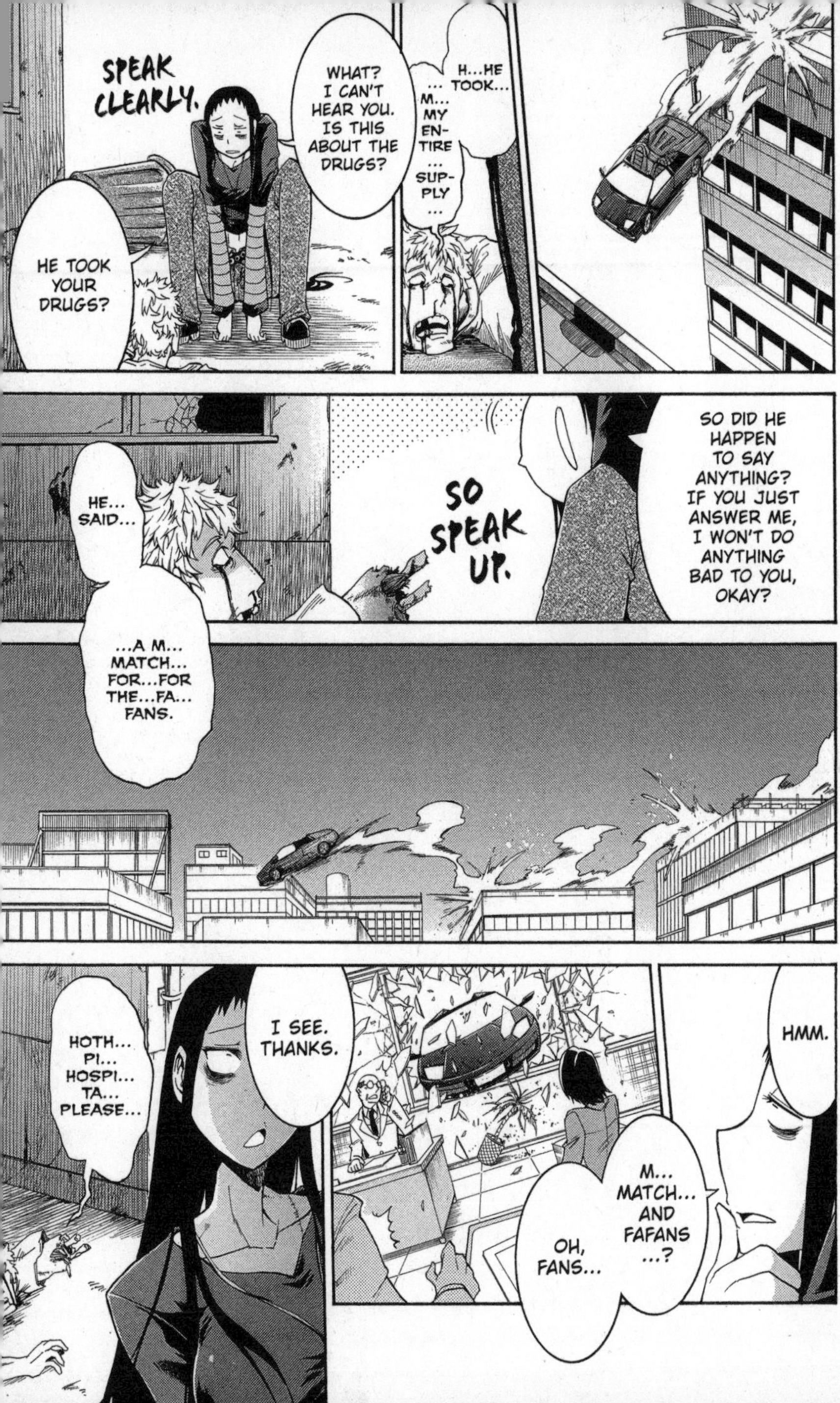
H...HE TOOK... ...M... MY EN-TIRE ... SUP-PLY ...
WHAT? I CAN'T HEAR YOU. IS THIS ABOUT THE DRUGS?
SPEAK CLEARLY.
HE TOOK YOUR DRUGS?
SO DID HE HAPPEN TO SAY ANYTHING? IF YOU JUST ANSWER ME, I WON'T DO ANYTHING BAD TO YOU, OKAY?
SO SPEAK UP.
HE... SAID...
...A M... MATCH... FOR...FOR THE...FA... FANS.
HMM.
M... MATCH... AND FAFANS ...?
OH, FANS...
I SEE. THANKS.
HOTH... PI... HOSPI... TA... PLEASE...

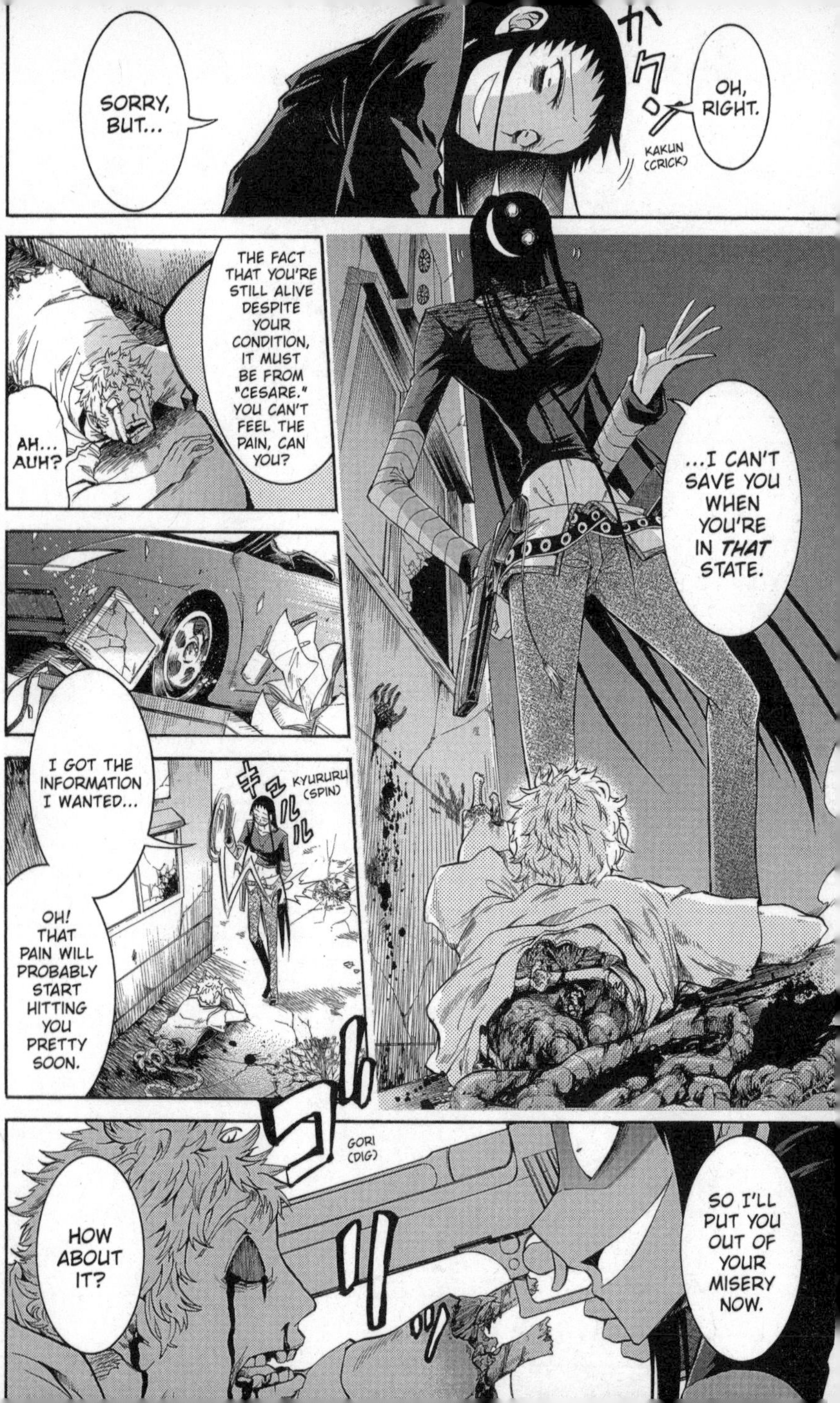
OH, RIGHT.
KAKUN (CRICK)
SORRY, BUT...
...I CAN'T SAVE YOU WHEN YOU'RE IN *THAT* STATE.
THE FACT THAT YOU'RE STILL ALIVE DESPITE YOUR CONDITION, IT MUST BE FROM "CESARE." YOU CAN'T FEEL THE PAIN, CAN YOU?
AH... AUH?
I GOT THE INFORMATION I WANTED...
KYURURU (SPIN)
OH! THAT PAIN WILL PROBABLY START HITTING YOU PRETTY SOON.
SO I'LL PUT YOU OUT OF YOUR MISERY NOW.
GORI (DIG)
HOW ABOUT IT?

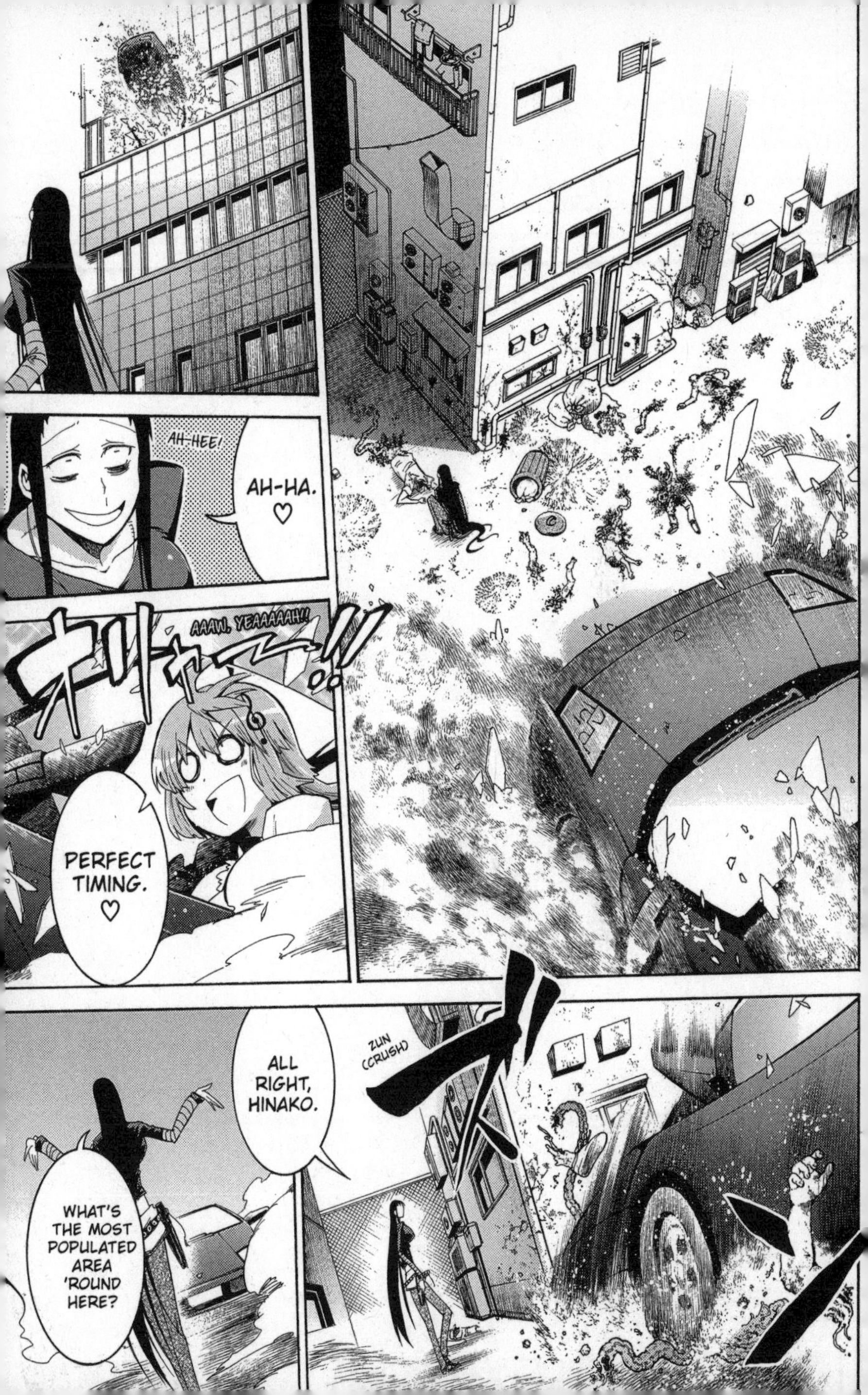

AH-HEE!
AH-HA. ♡
AAAW, YEAAAAAH!!
PERFECT TIMING. ♡
ZUN (CRUSH)
ALL RIGHT, HINAKO.
WHAT'S THE MOST POPULATED AREA 'ROUND HERE?

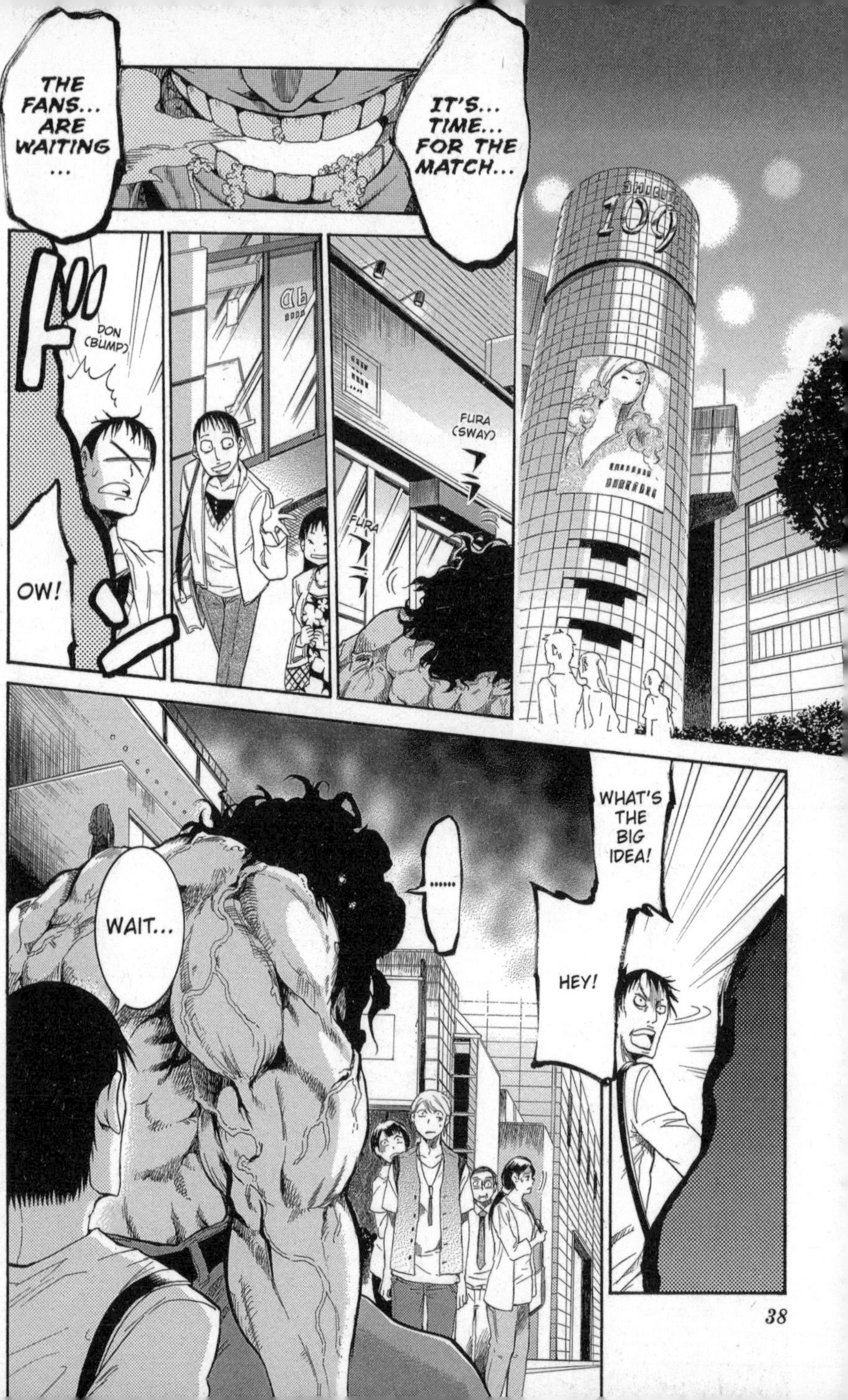
109
IT'S... TIME... FOR THE MATCH...
THE FANS... ARE WAITING ...
FURA (SWAY)
FURA
DON (BUMP)
OW!
HEY!
WHAT'S THE BIG IDEA!
......
WAIT...

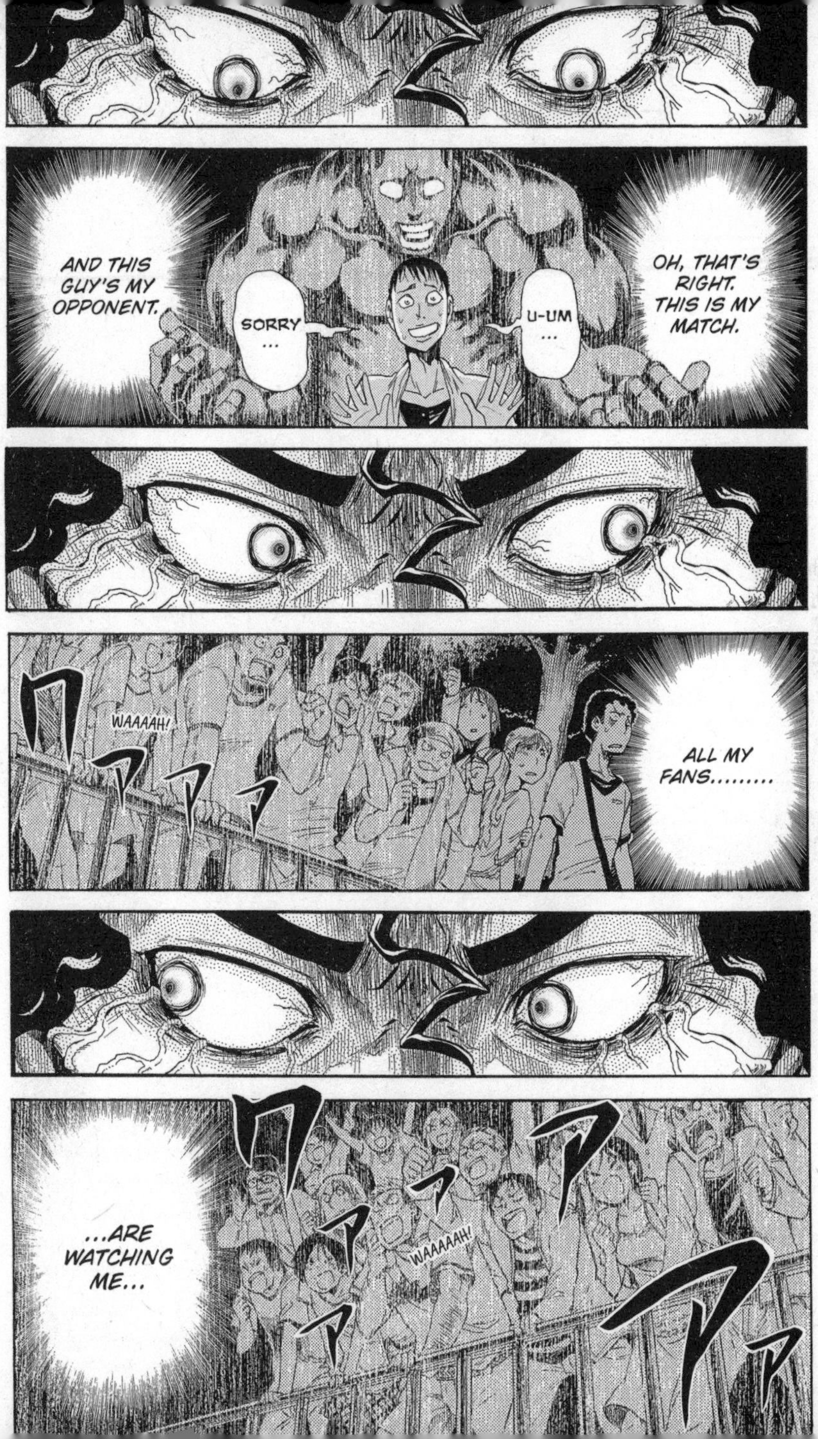
OH, THAT'S RIGHT. THIS IS MY MATCH.
U-UM ...
SORRY ...
AND THIS GUY'S MY OPPONENT.
ALL MY FANS.........
WAAAAH!
...ARE WATCHING ME...
WAAAAAH!

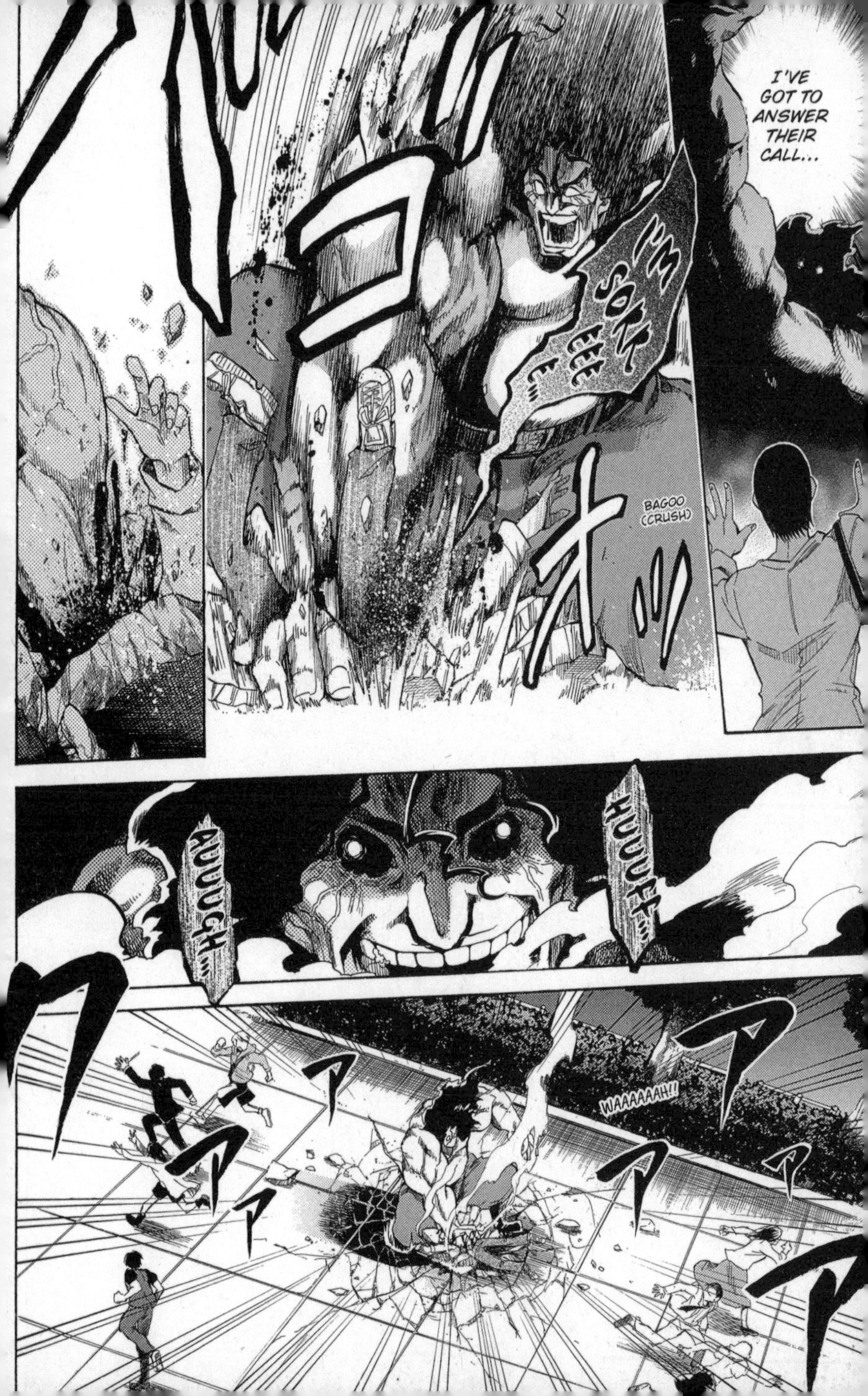
I'VE GOT TO ANSWER THEIR CALL...
I'M SORREEEE...
BAGOO (CRUSH)
HUUUFF...
AUUUGH...
WAAAAAAH!!

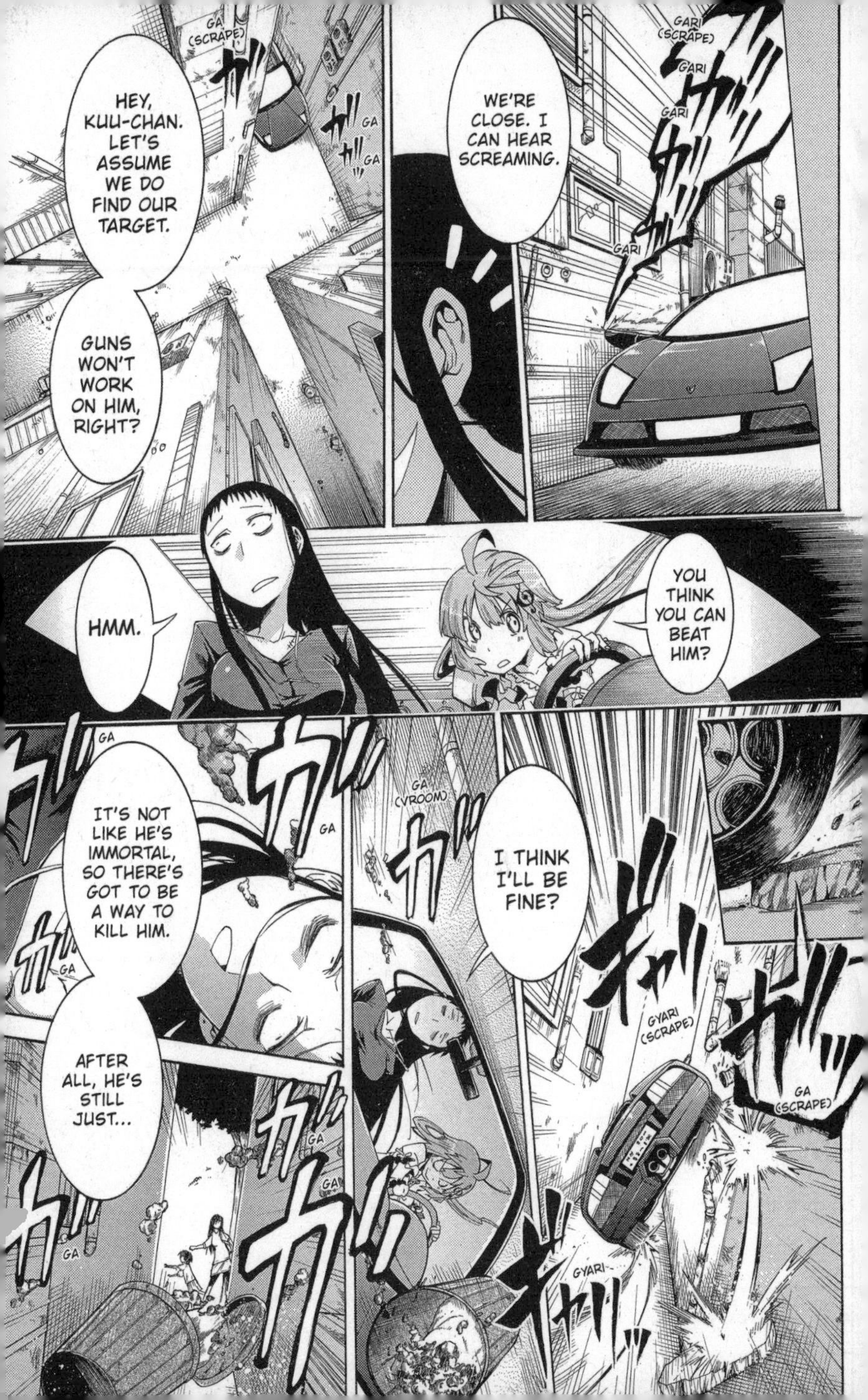
GARI (SCRAPE)
GARI
GARI
GARI
WE'RE CLOSE. I CAN HEAR SCREAMING.
GA (SCRAPE)
GA
GA
HEY, KUU-CHAN. LET'S ASSUME WE DO FIND OUR TARGET.
GUNS WON'T WORK ON HIM, RIGHT?
YOU THINK YOU CAN BEAT HIM?
HMM.
GYARI (SCRAPE)
GA (SCRAPE)
GYARI
GA (VROOM)
I THINK I'LL BE FINE?
GA
GA
IT'S NOT LIKE HE'S IMMORTAL, SO THERE'S GOT TO BE A WAY TO KILL HIM.
GA
AFTER ALL, HE'S STILL JUST...
GA
GA
GA

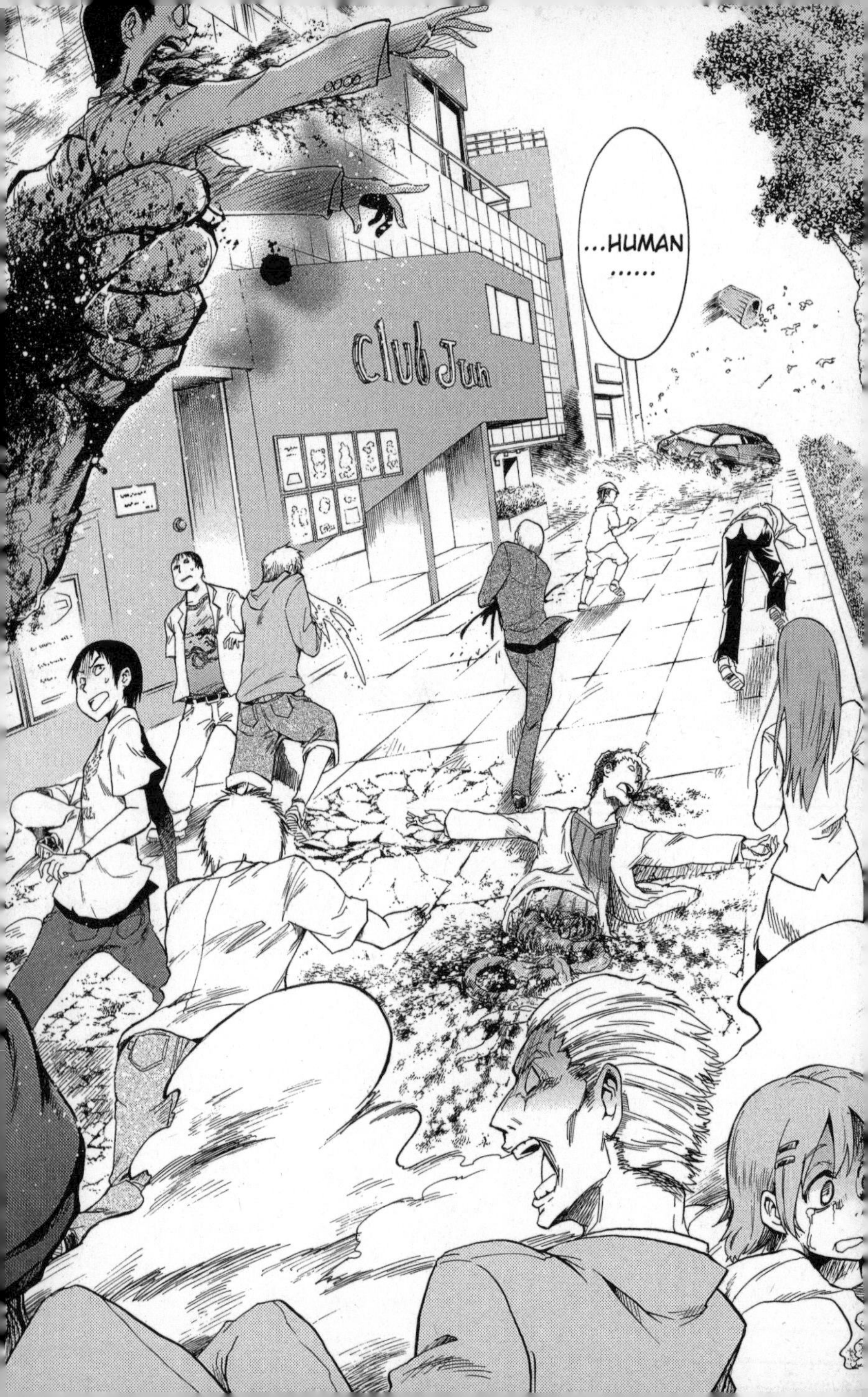
...HUMAN
......
Club Jun

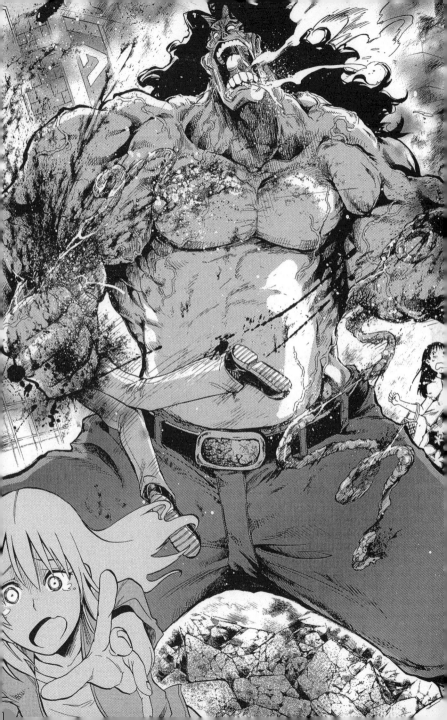

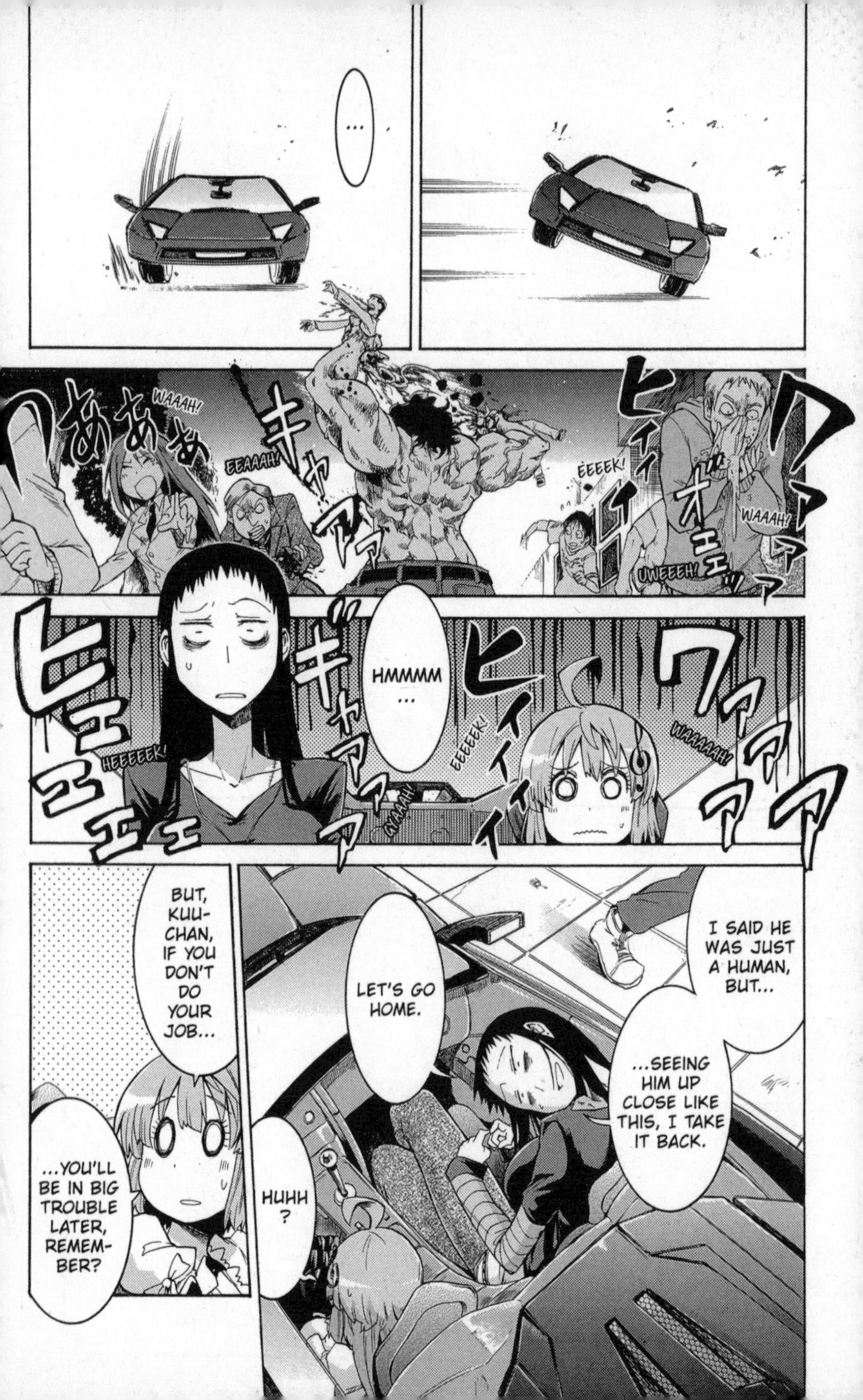
!!
...
ワァァァ
WAAAH!
オェェッ
UWEEEH!
ヒィイイ
EEEEK!
キャアア
EEAAAH!
あああ
WAAAH!
ワァァァァァ
WAAAAAH!
ヒィイイイ
EEEEEK!
HMMMM...
ギャアアア
GYAAAH!
ヒェエエエ
HEEEEEK!
I SAID HE WAS JUST A HUMAN, BUT...
...SEEING HIM UP CLOSE LIKE THIS, I TAKE IT BACK.
LET'S GO HOME.
HUHH?
BUT, KUU-CHAN, IF YOU DON'T DO YOUR JOB...
...YOU'LL BE IN BIG TROUBLE LATER, REMEMBER?

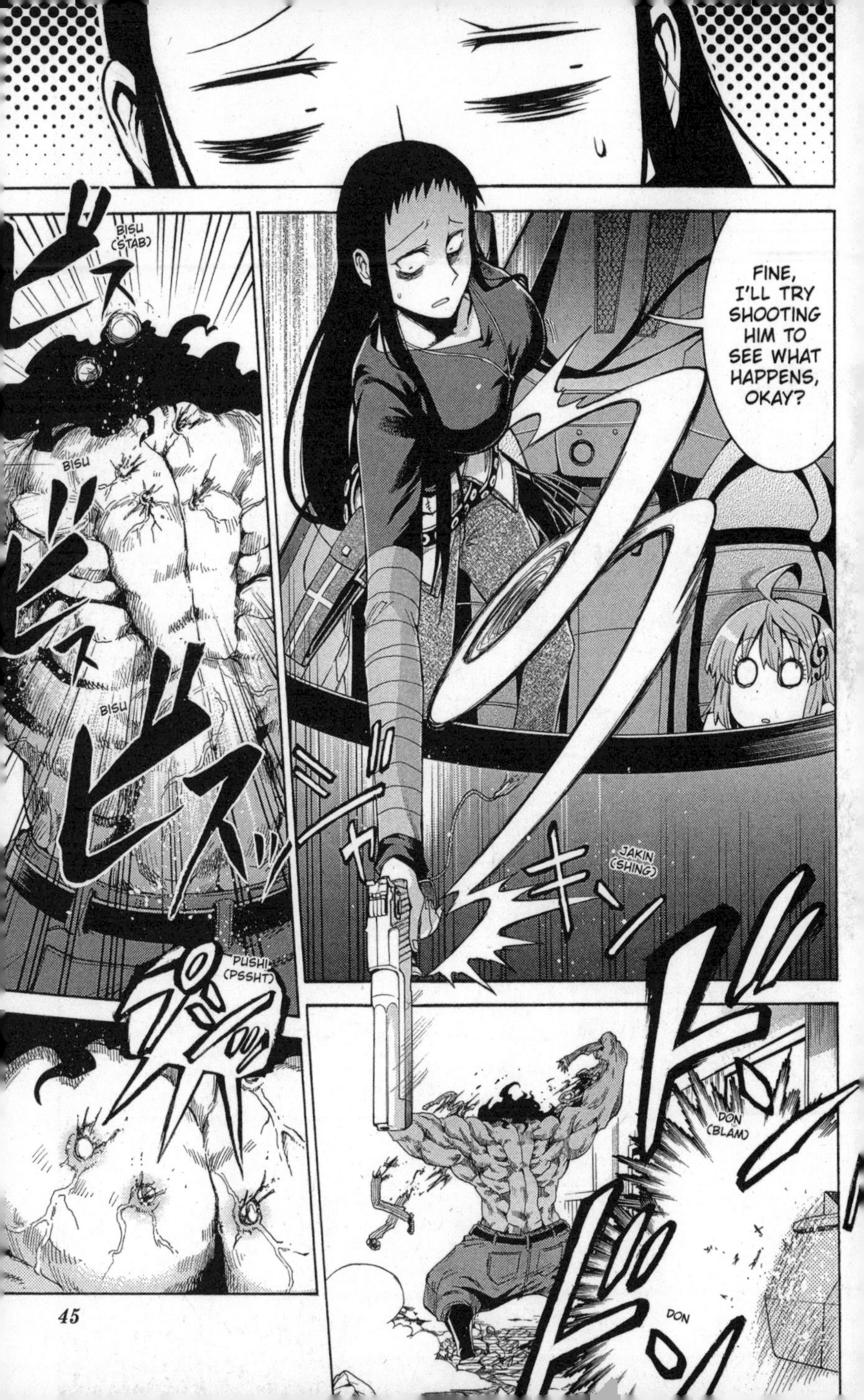
FINE, I'LL TRY SHOOTING HIM TO SEE WHAT HAPPENS, OKAY?
JAKIN (SHING)
BISU (STAB)
BISU
BISU
DON (BLAM)
DON
PUSHI (PSSHT)

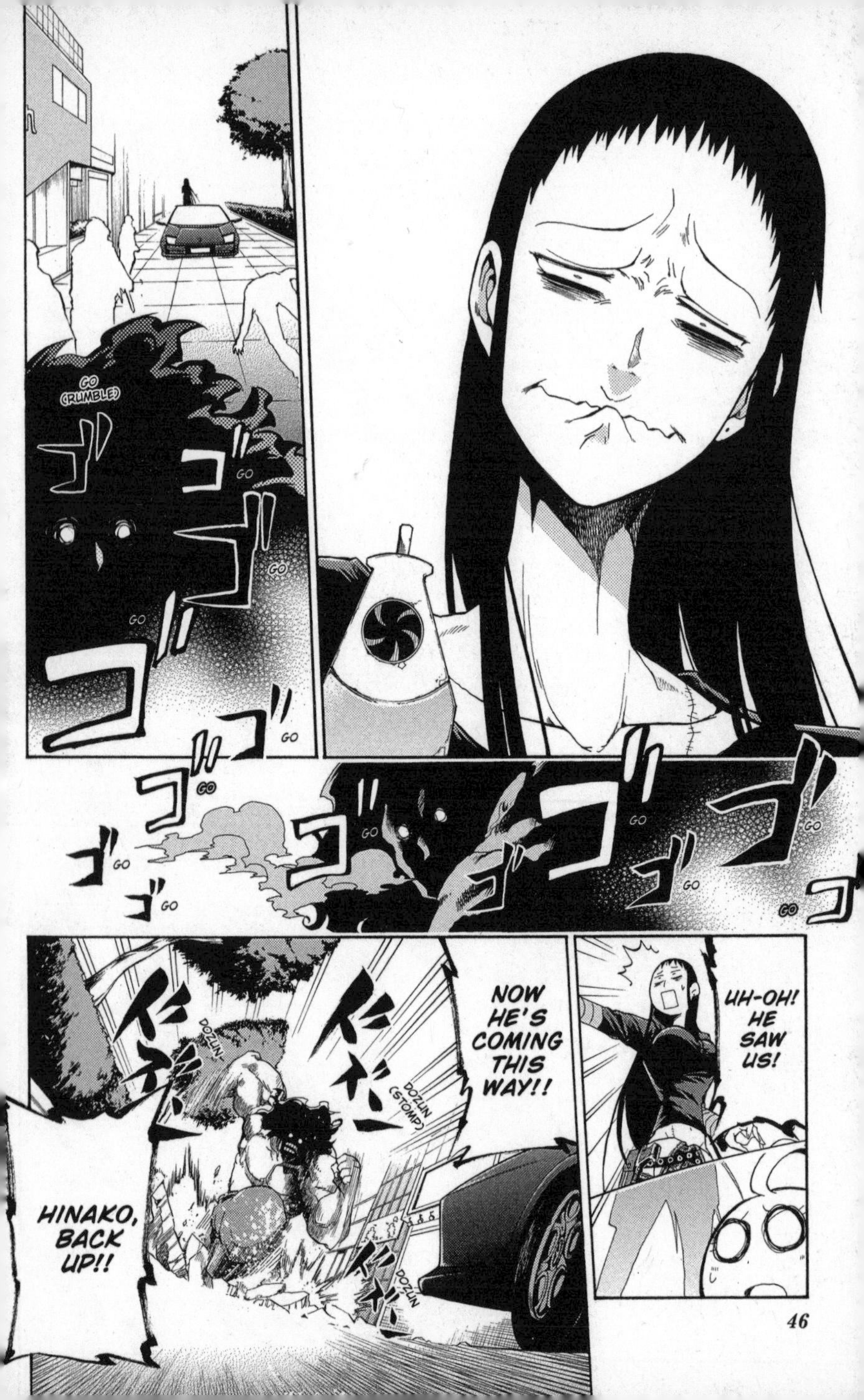
GO (RUMBLE)
GO
GO
GO
GO
GO
GO
GO
GO
GO
GO
GO
GO
UH-OH! HE SAW US!
NOW HE'S COMING THIS WAY!!
DOZUN (STOMP)
DOZUN-
DOZUN
HINAKO, BACK UP!!

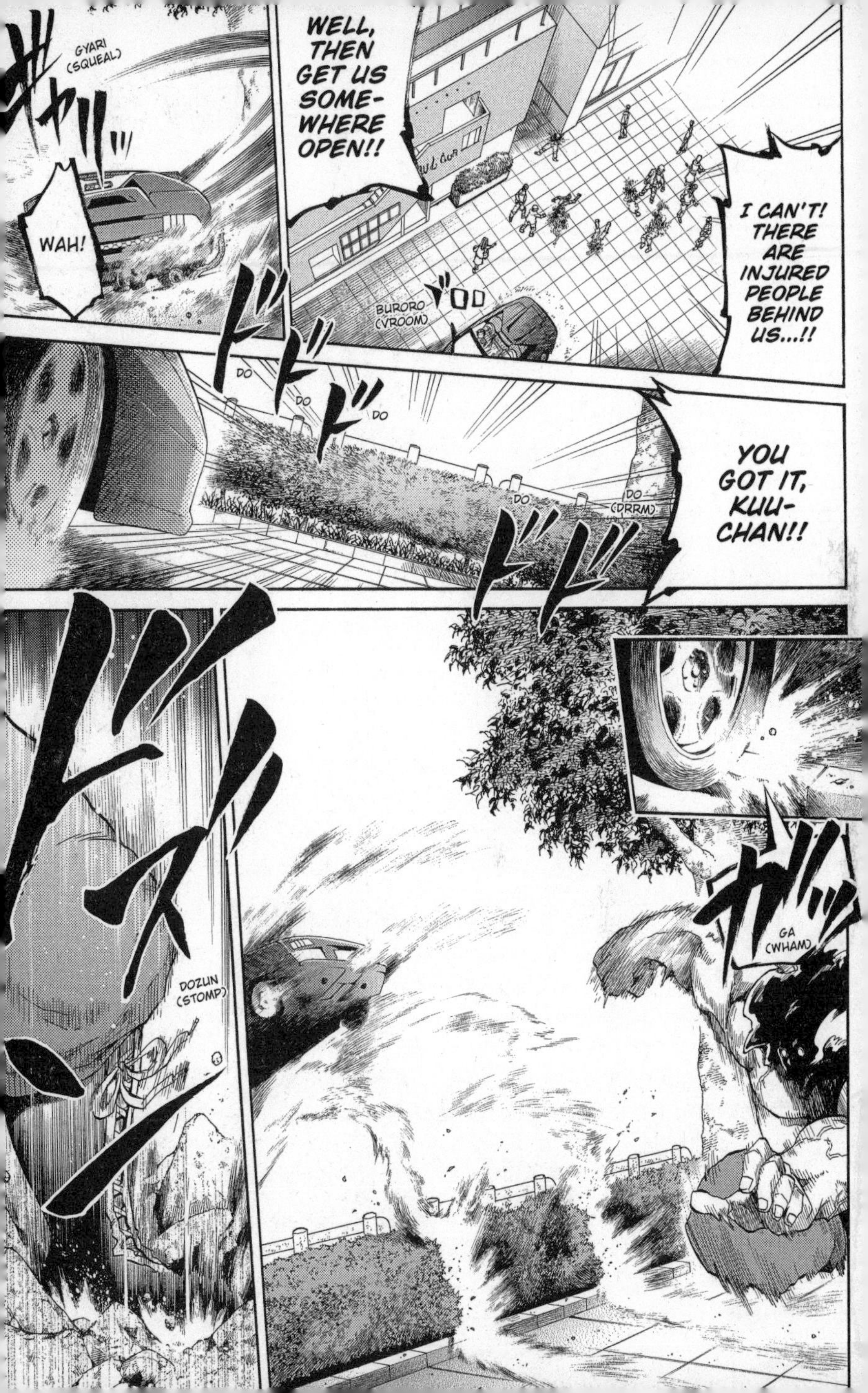
WELL, THEN GET US SOMEWHERE OPEN!!
I CAN'T! THERE ARE INJURED PEOPLE BEHIND US...!!
BURORO (VROOM)
GYARI (SQUEAL)
WAH!
YOU GOT IT, KUU-CHAN!!
DO DO (DRRM)
DO DO DO
GA (WHAM)
DOZUN (STOMP)

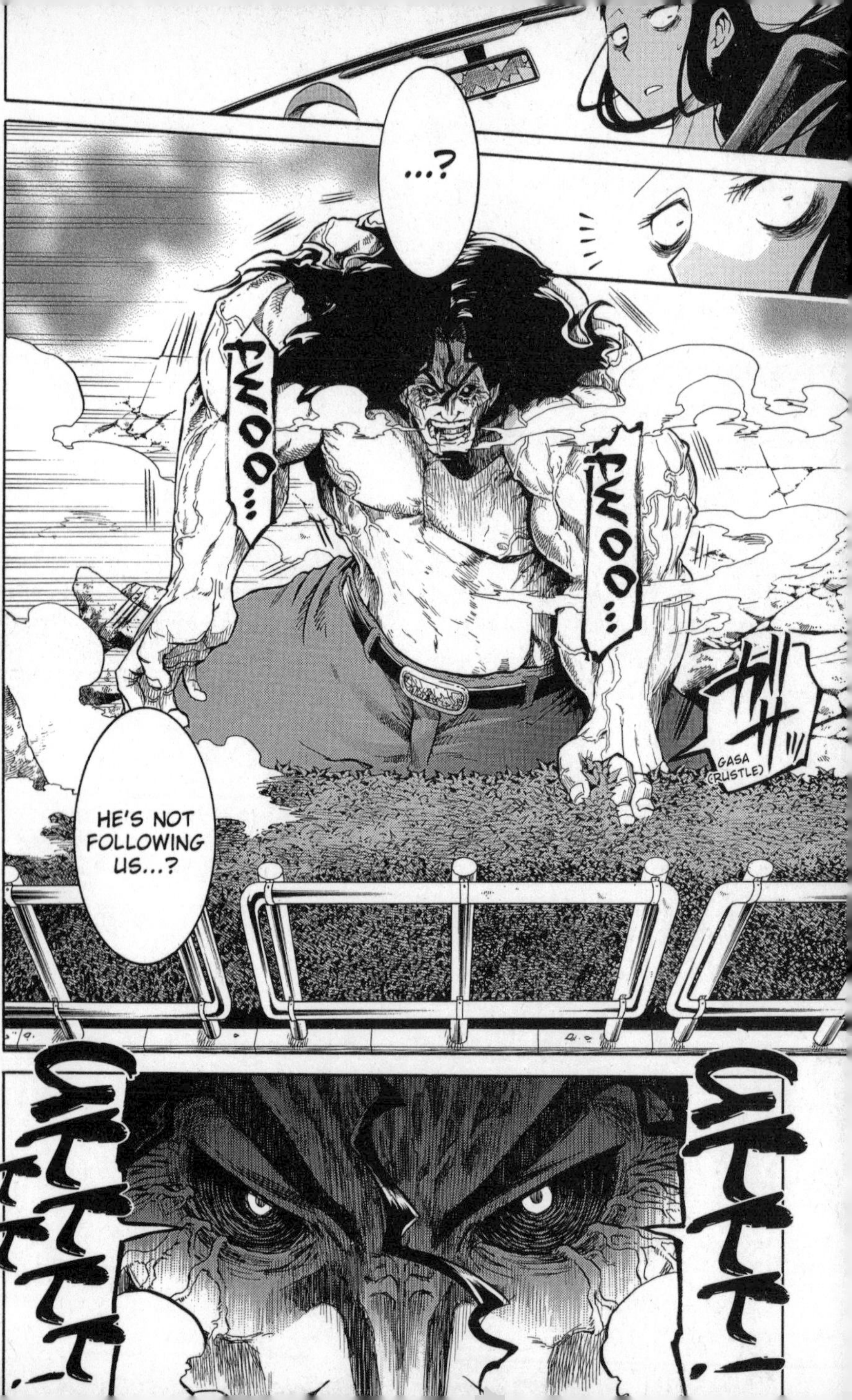
...?
FWOO...
GASA (RUSTLE)
FWOO...
HE'S NOT FOLLOWING US...?

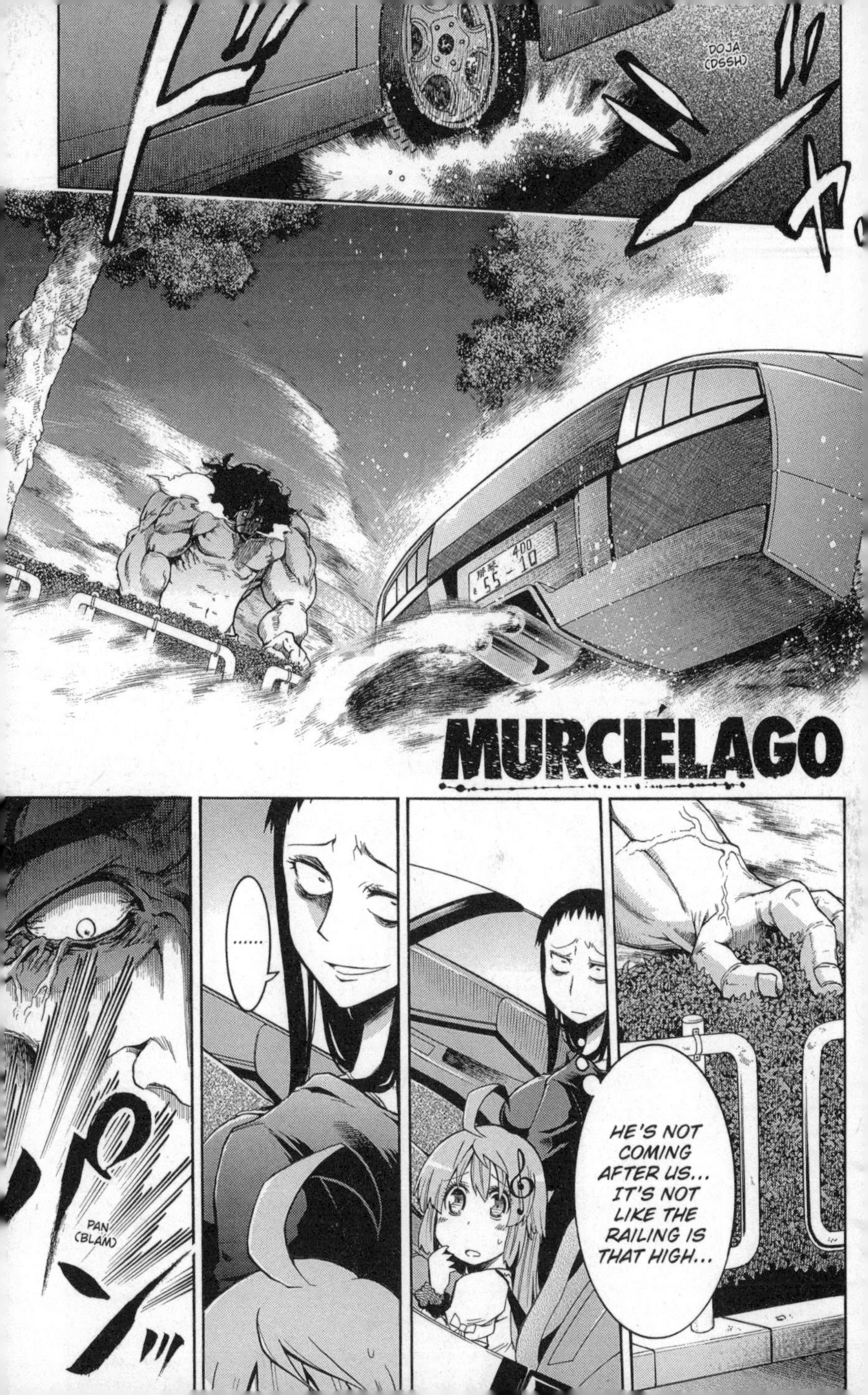
DOJA
(DSSH)
MURCIÉLAGO
HE'S NOT COMING AFTER US... IT'S NOT LIKE THE RAILING IS THAT HIGH...
......
PAN
(BLAM)

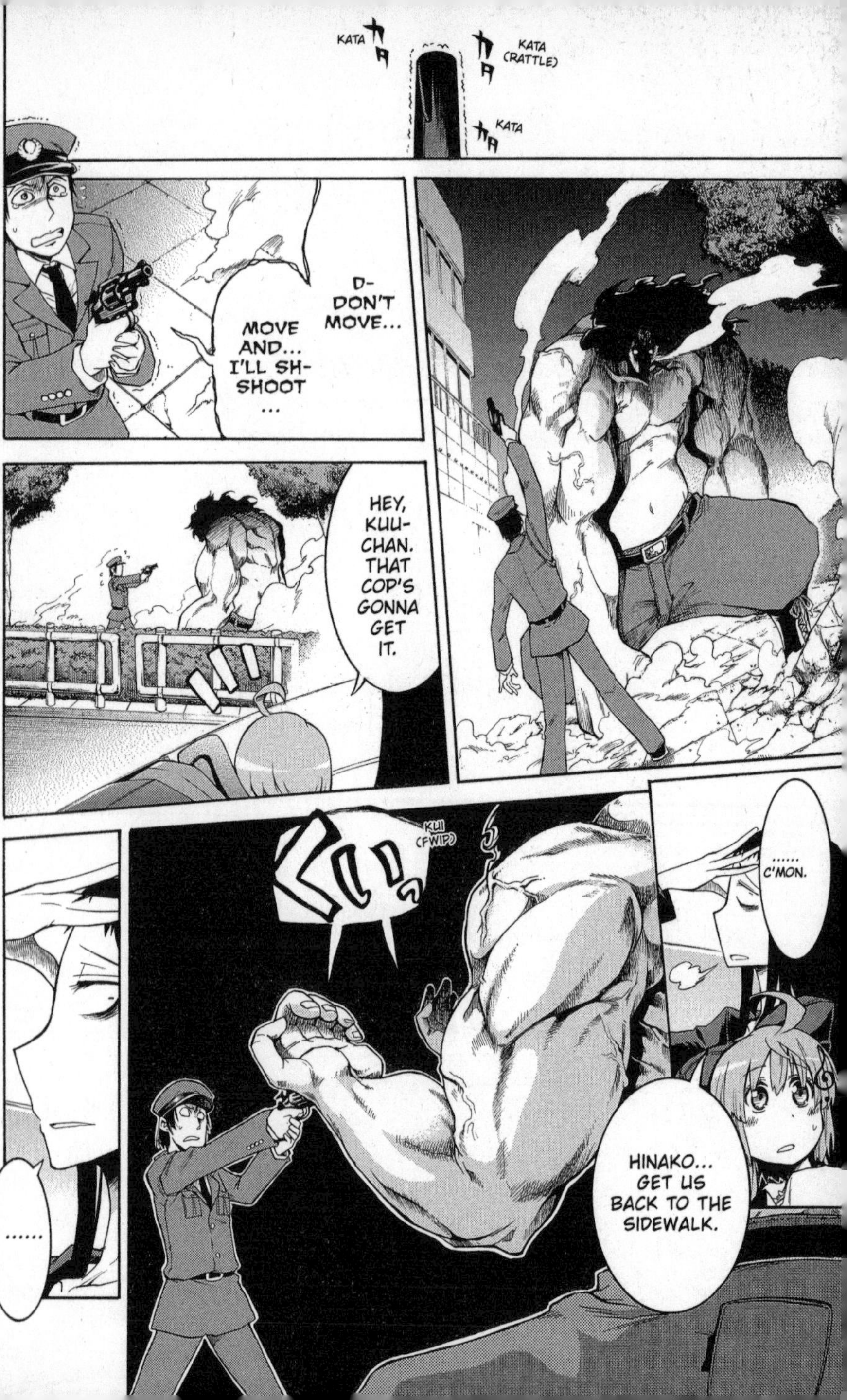

KATA (RATTLE)
KATA
KATA
D-DON'T MOVE...
MOVE AND... I'LL SH-SHOOT ...
HEY, KUU-CHAN. THAT COP'S GONNA GET IT.
...... C'MON.
HINAKO... GET US BACK TO THE SIDEWALK.
KUI (FWIP)
......

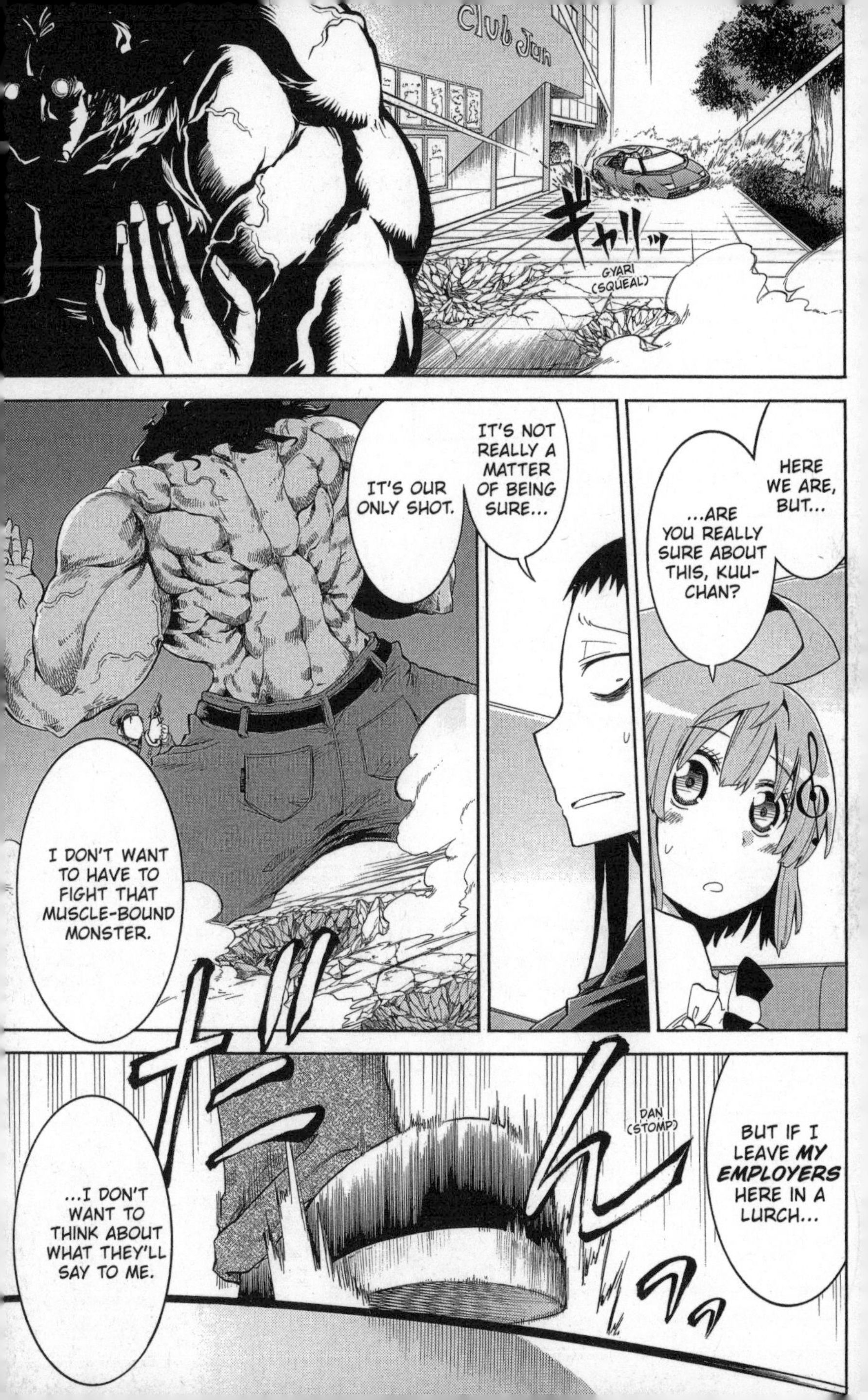
Club Jun
GYARI (SQUEAL)
HERE WE ARE, BUT...
...ARE YOU REALLY SURE ABOUT THIS, KUU-CHAN?
IT'S NOT REALLY A MATTER OF BEING SURE...
IT'S OUR ONLY SHOT.
I DON'T WANT TO HAVE TO FIGHT THAT MUSCLE-BOUND MONSTER.
BUT IF I LEAVE *MY EMPLOYERS* HERE IN A LURCH...
DAN (STOMP)
...I DON'T WANT TO THINK ABOUT WHAT THEY'LL SAY TO ME.

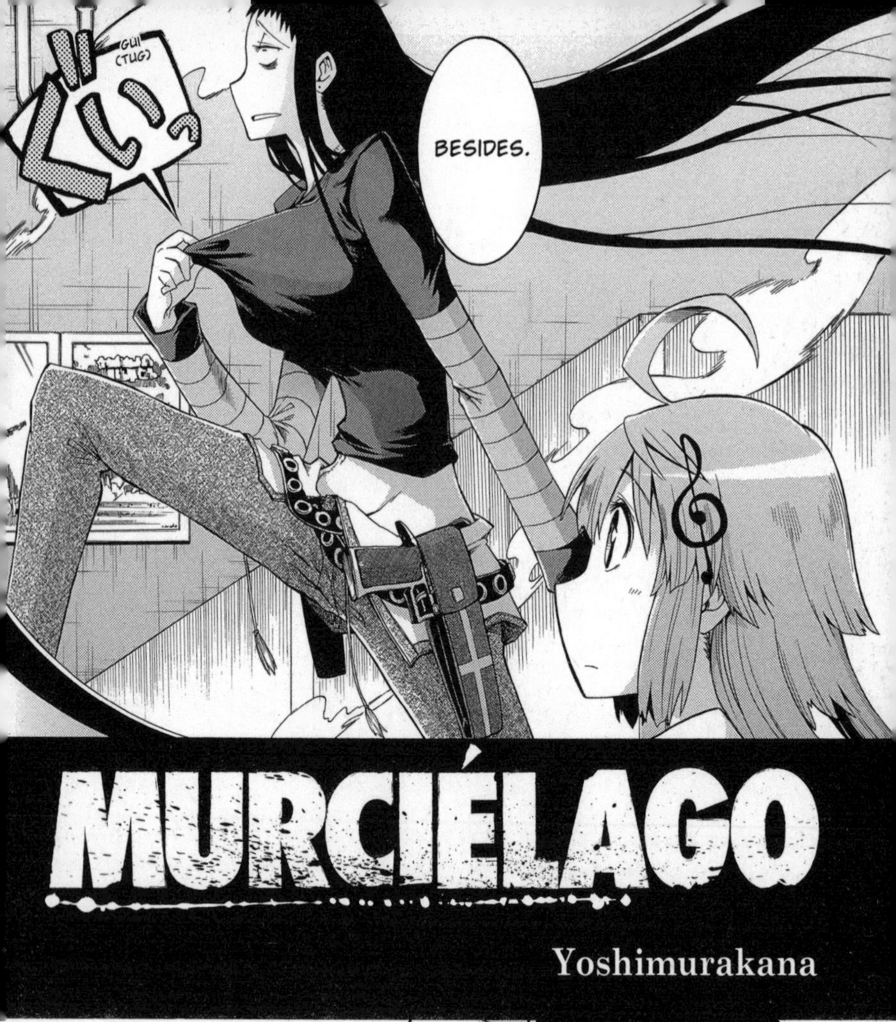
BESIDES.
GUI (TUG)

MURCIÉLAGO

Yoshimurakana

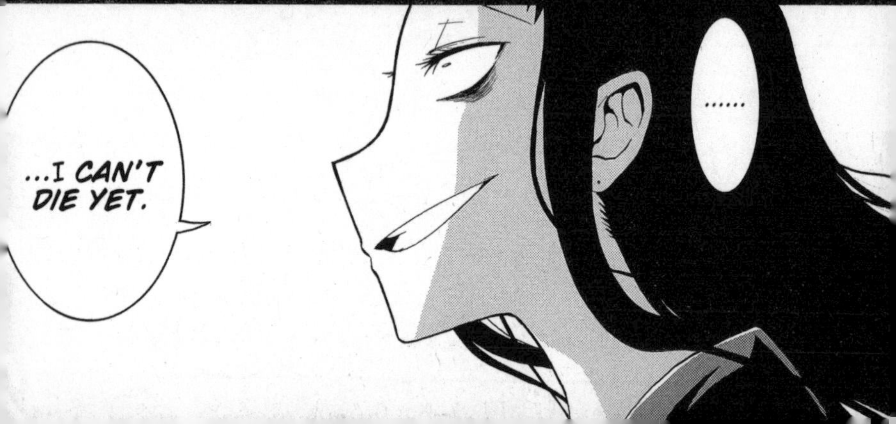
......
...I CAN'T DIE YET.

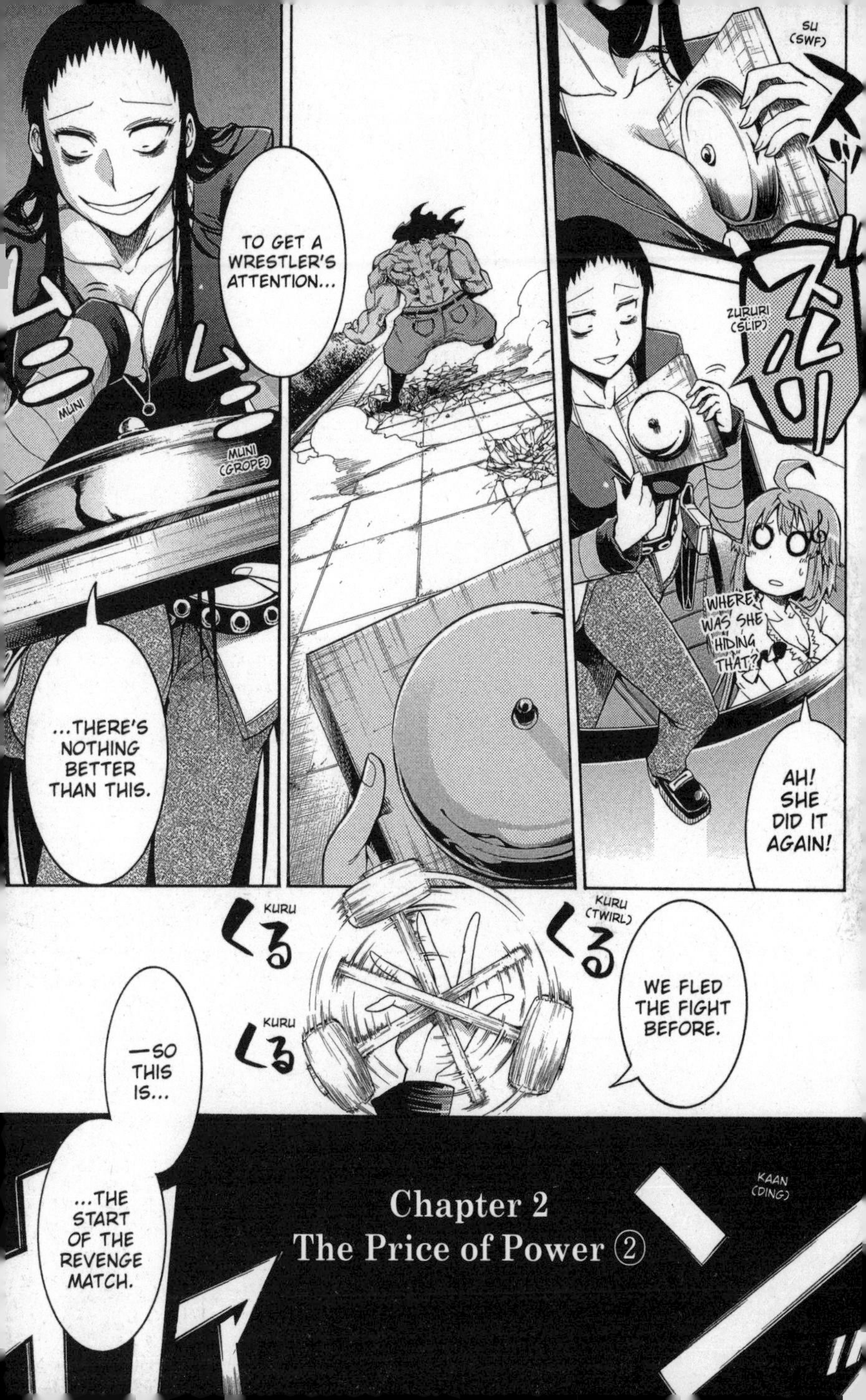
SU (SWF)
ZURURI (SLIP)
WHERE WAS SHE HIDING THAT?
AH! SHE DID IT AGAIN!
TO GET A WRESTLER'S ATTENTION...
MUNI
MUNI (GROPE)
...THERE'S NOTHING BETTER THAN THIS.
KURU (TWIRL)
WE FLED THE FIGHT BEFORE.
KURU
KURU
—SO THIS IS...
KAAN (DING)
...THE START OF THE REVENGE MATCH.

Chapter 2
The Price of Power ②

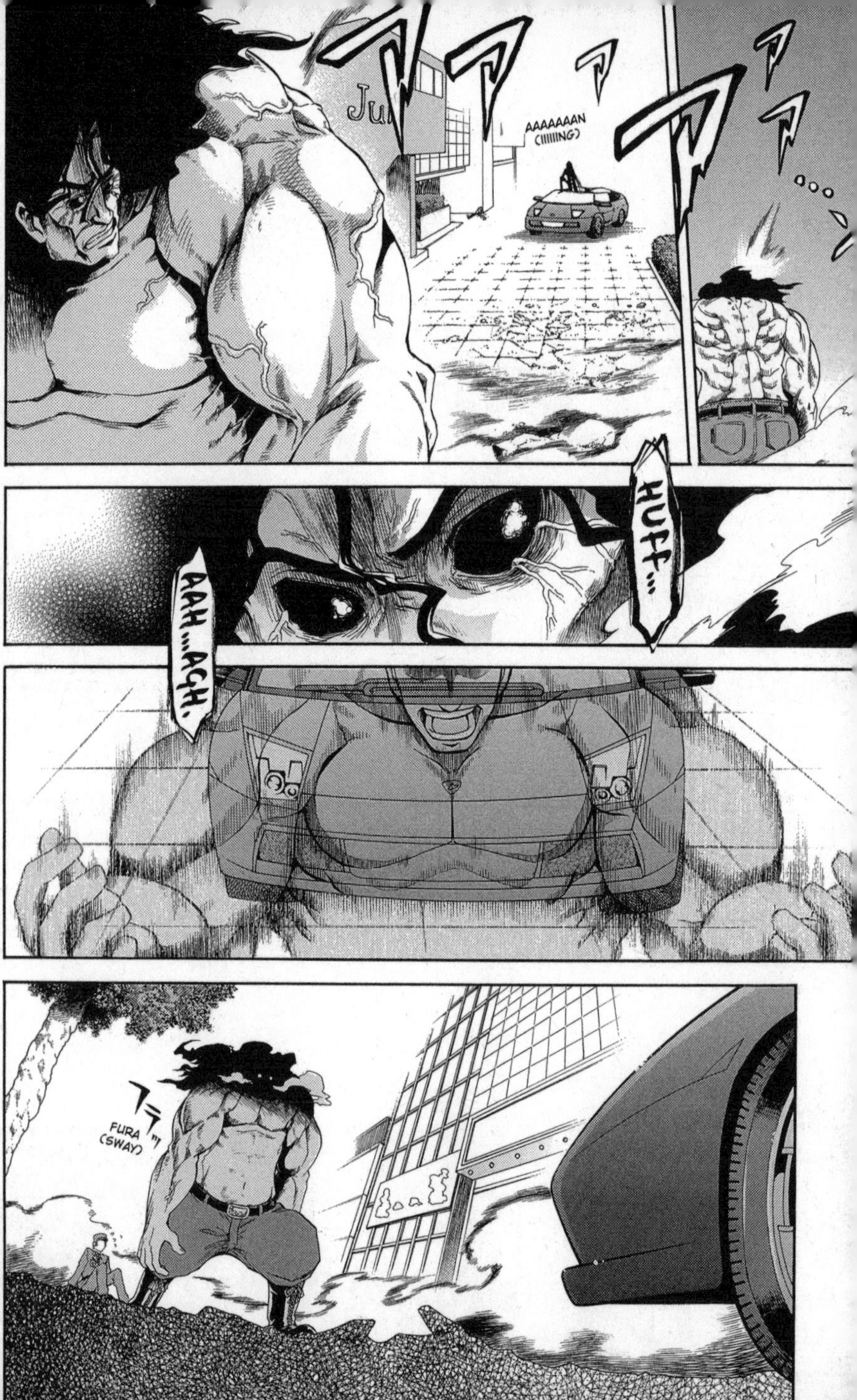
AAAAAAAN (IIIIING)
HUFF...
AAH...AGH.
FURA (SWAY)

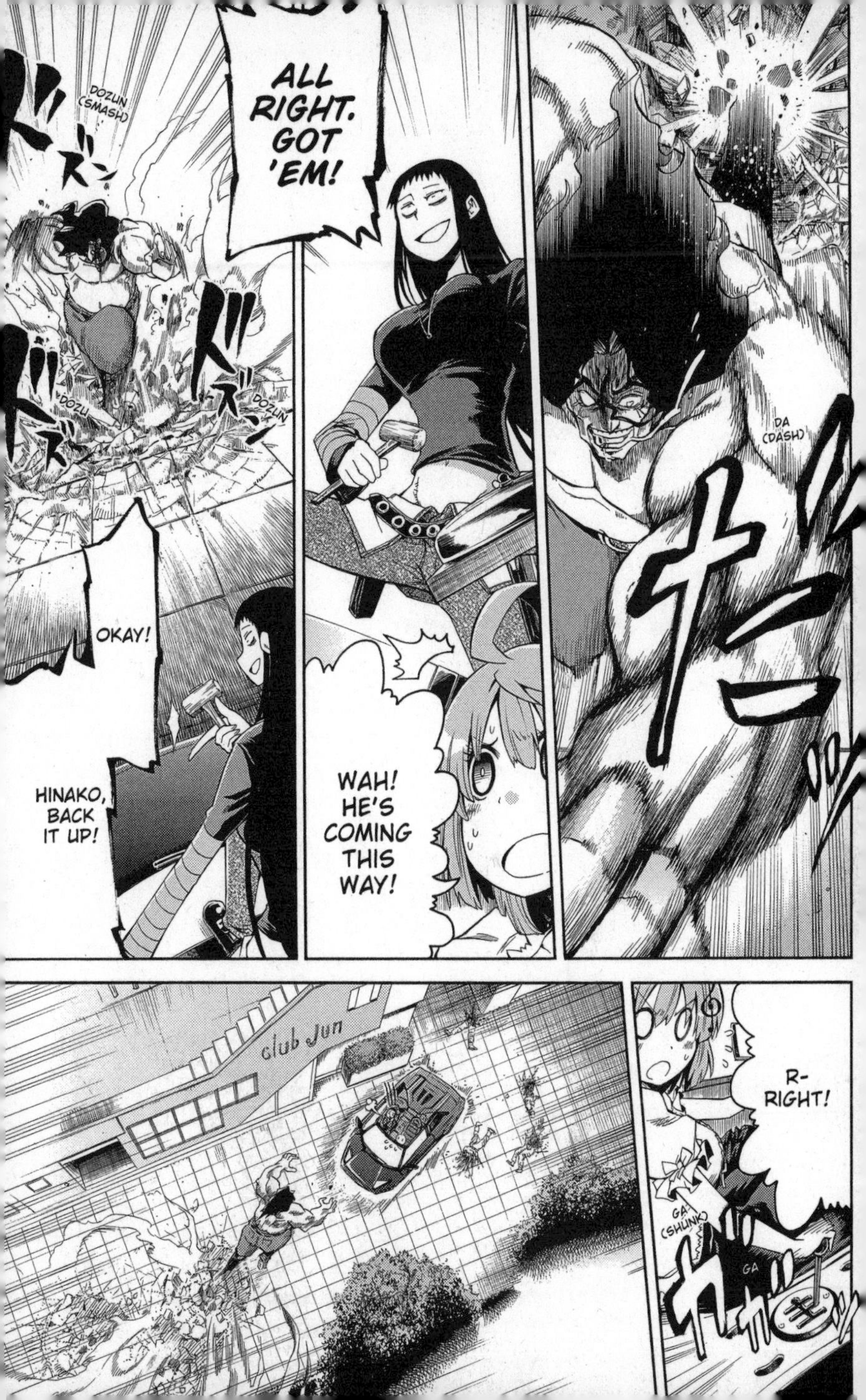
DA (DASH)
ALL RIGHT. GOT 'EM!
WAH! HE'S COMING THIS WAY!
DOZUN (SMASH)
DOZUN
DOZU
OKAY!
HINAKO, BACK IT UP!
R-RIGHT!
GA (SHUNK)
GA
club Jun

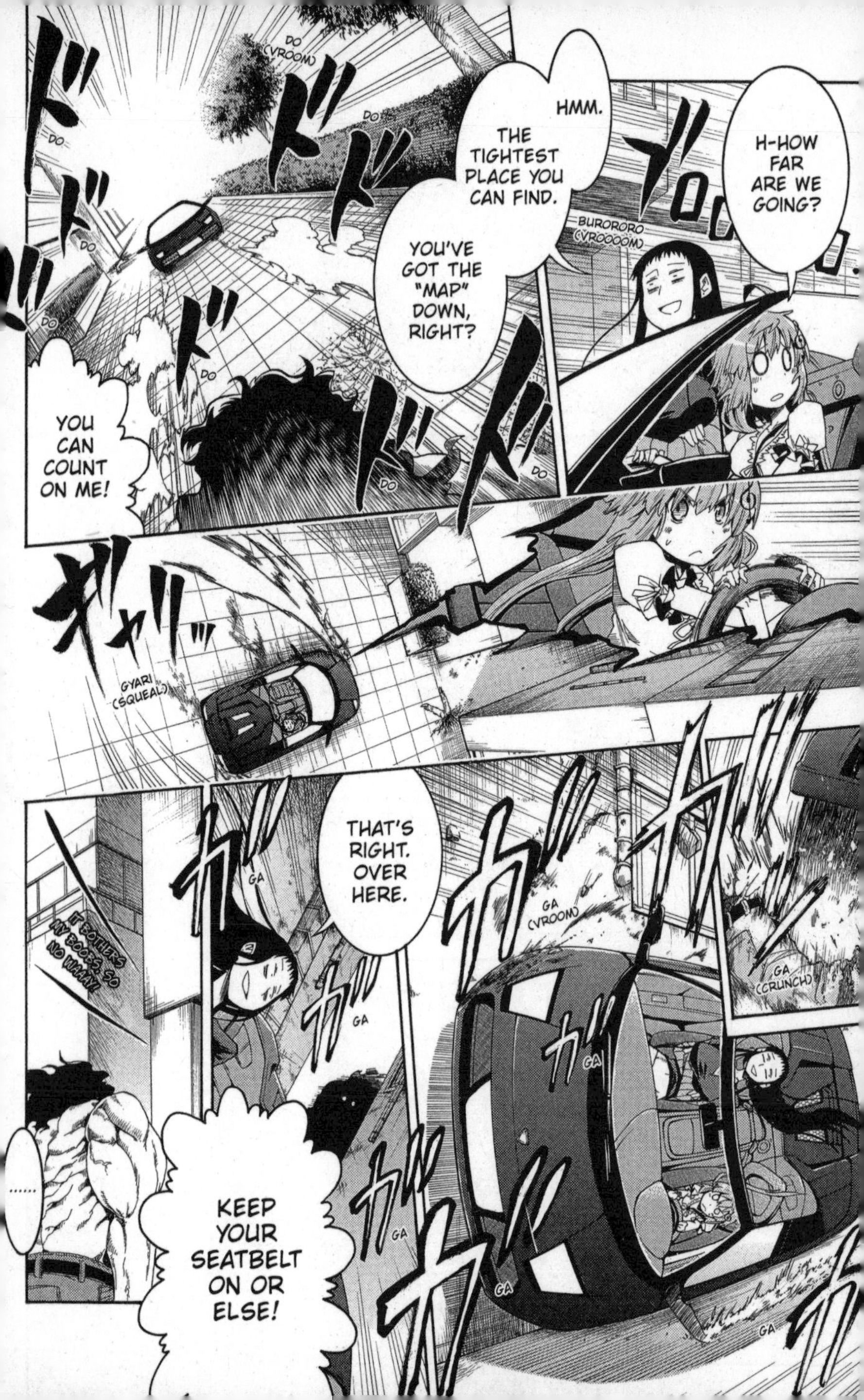
H-HOW FAR ARE WE GOING?
BUROROROO (VROOOOM)
HMM. THE TIGHTEST PLACE YOU CAN FIND.
YOU'VE GOT THE "MAP" DOWN, RIGHT?
DO (VROOM)
DO
DO
DO
DO
DO
DO
YOU CAN COUNT ON ME!
GYARI (SQUEAL)
GA (CRUNCH)
GA (VROOM)
THAT'S RIGHT. OVER HERE.
GA
GA
IT BOTHERS MY BOOBS, SO NO WAAAY!
GA
GA
GA
GA
KEEP YOUR SEATBELT ON OR ELSE!
......

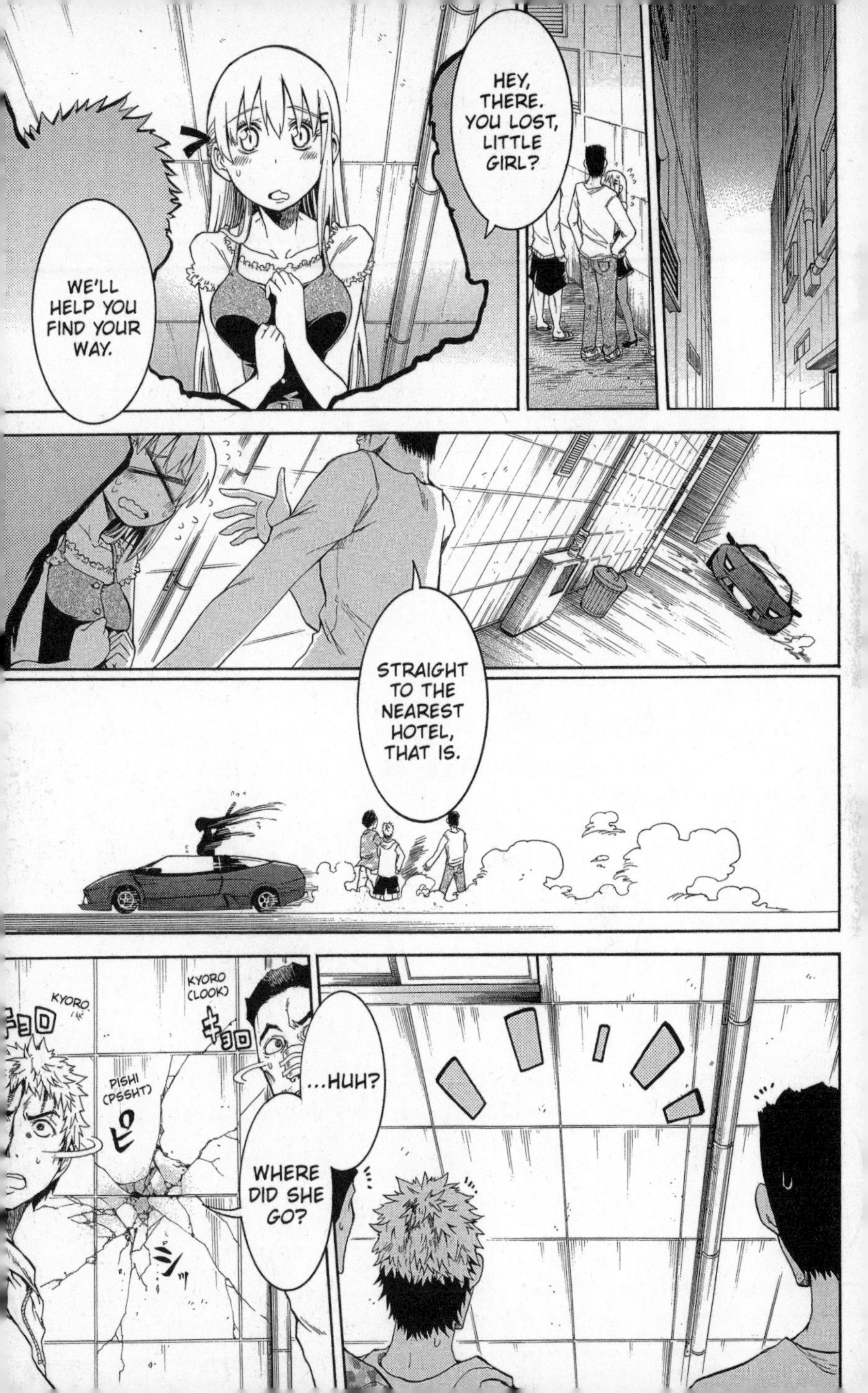
HEY, THERE. YOU LOST, LITTLE GIRL?
WE'LL HELP YOU FIND YOUR WAY.
STRAIGHT TO THE NEAREST HOTEL, THAT IS.
...HUH?
WHERE DID SHE GO?
KYORO (LOOK)
KYORO
PISHI (PSSHT)

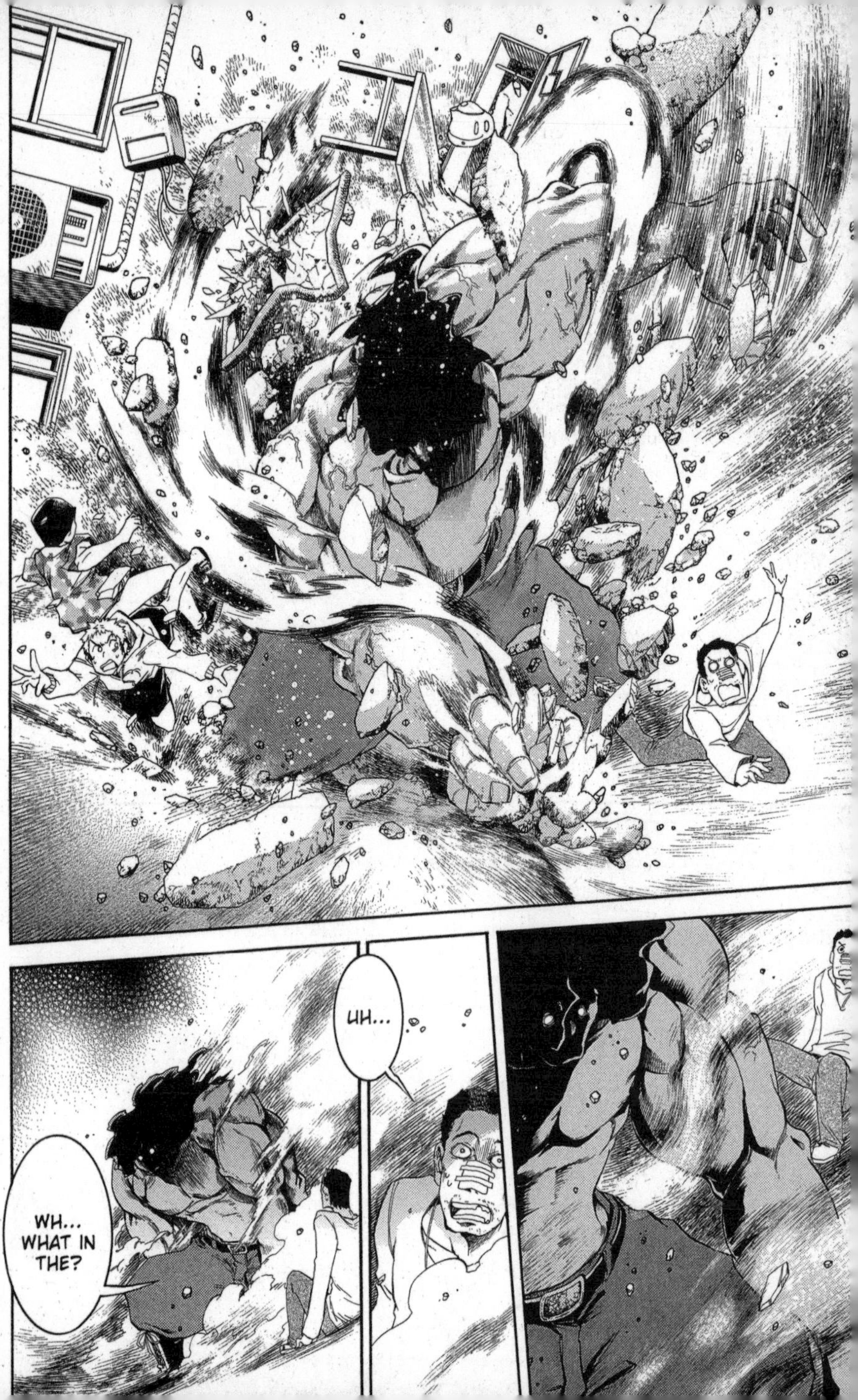
UH...
WH... WHAT IN THE?

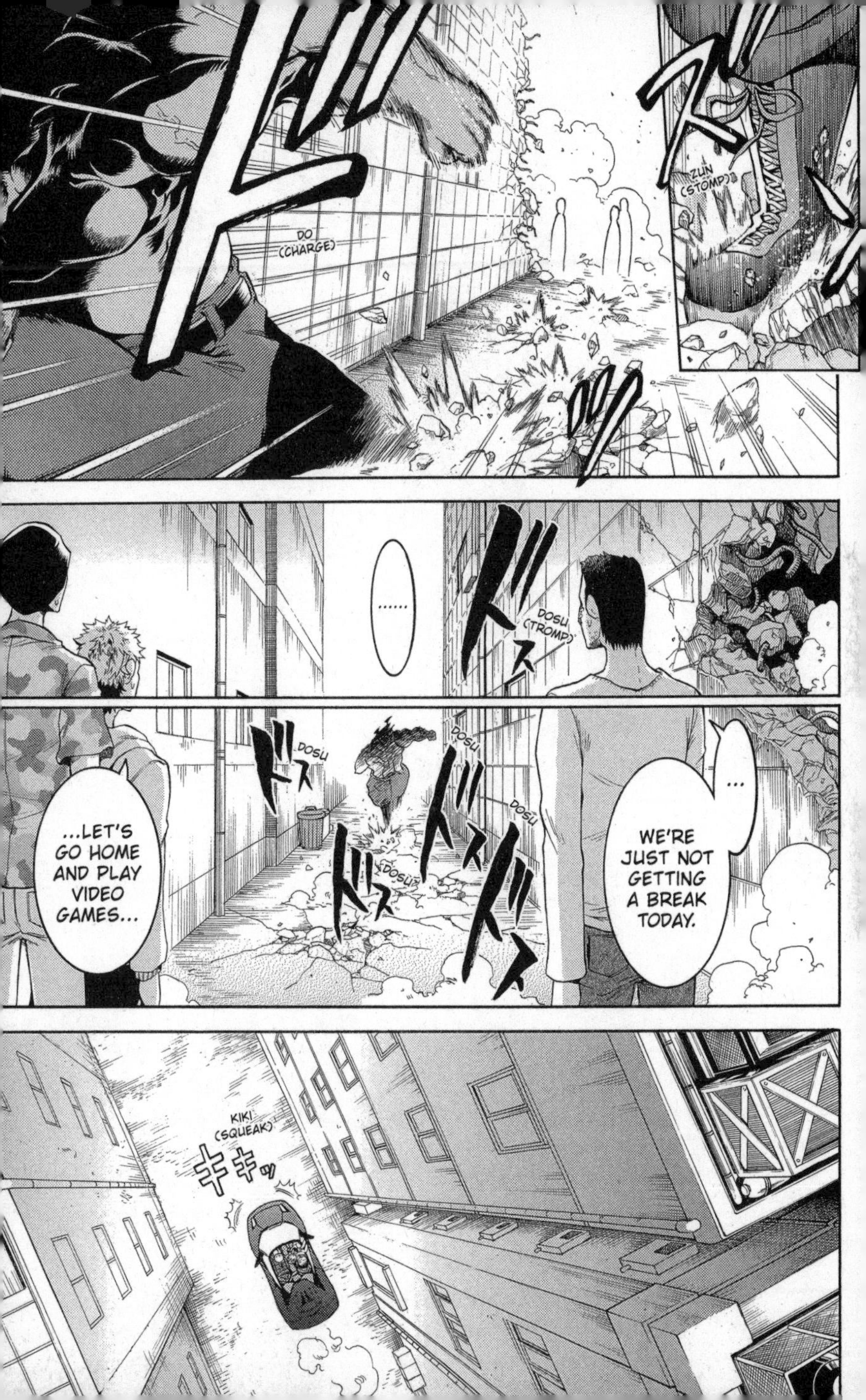
ZUN (STOMP)
DO (CHARGE)
DOSU (TROMP)
......
...
WE'RE JUST NOT GETTING A BREAK TODAY.
DOSU
DOSU
DOSU
DOSU
...LET'S GO HOME AND PLAY VIDEO GAMES...
KIKI (SQUEAK)

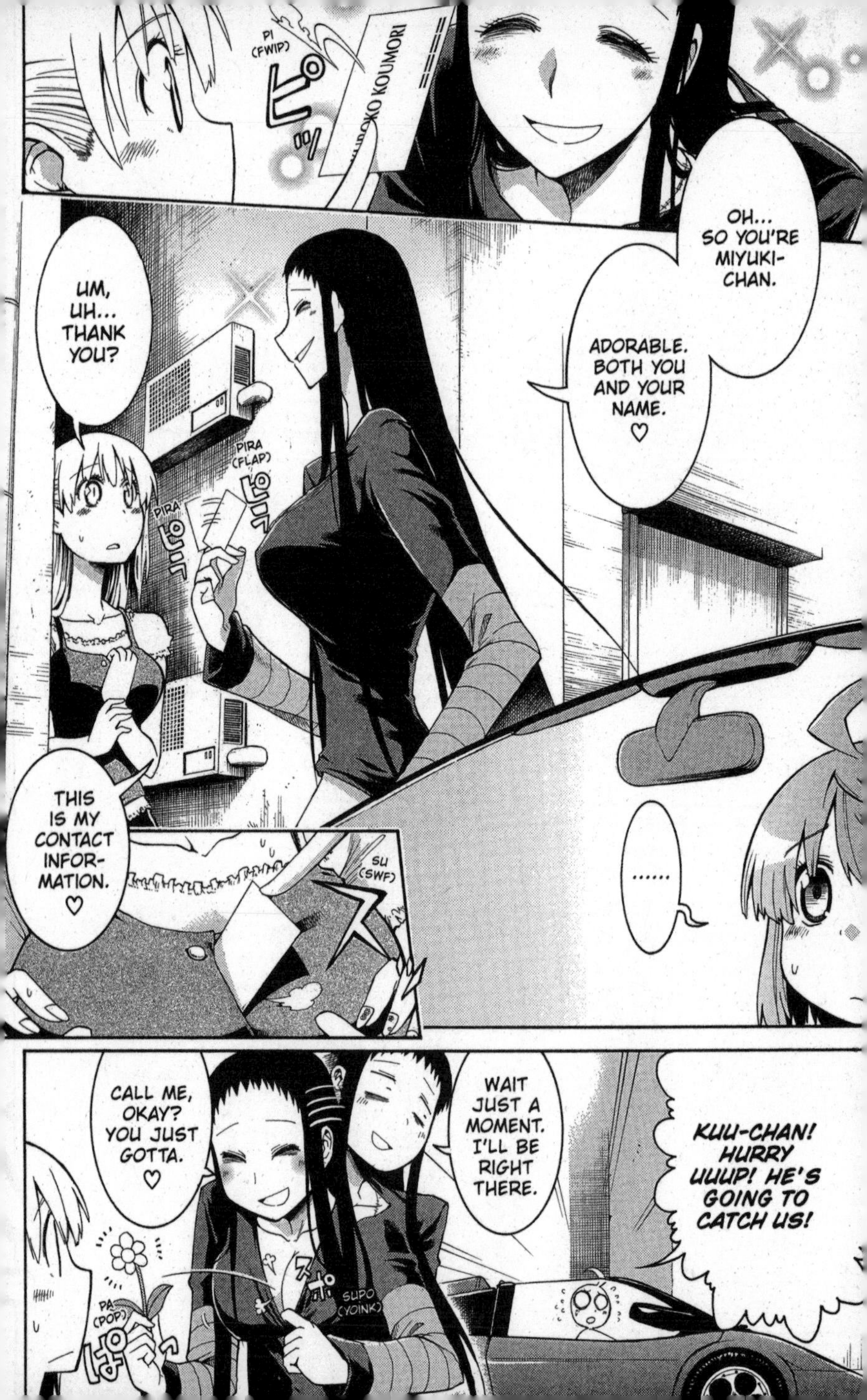
PI (FWIP)
KOUMORI
OH... SO YOU'RE MIYUKI-CHAN.
ADORABLE. BOTH YOU AND YOUR NAME. ♡
......
UM, UH... THANK YOU?
PIRA (FLAP)
PIRA
THIS IS MY CONTACT INFORMATION. ♡
SU (SWF)
KUU-CHAN! HURRY UUUP! HE'S GOING TO CATCH US!
WAIT JUST A MOMENT. I'LL BE RIGHT THERE.
CALL ME, OKAY? YOU JUST GOTTA. ♡
SUPO (YOINK)
PA (POP)

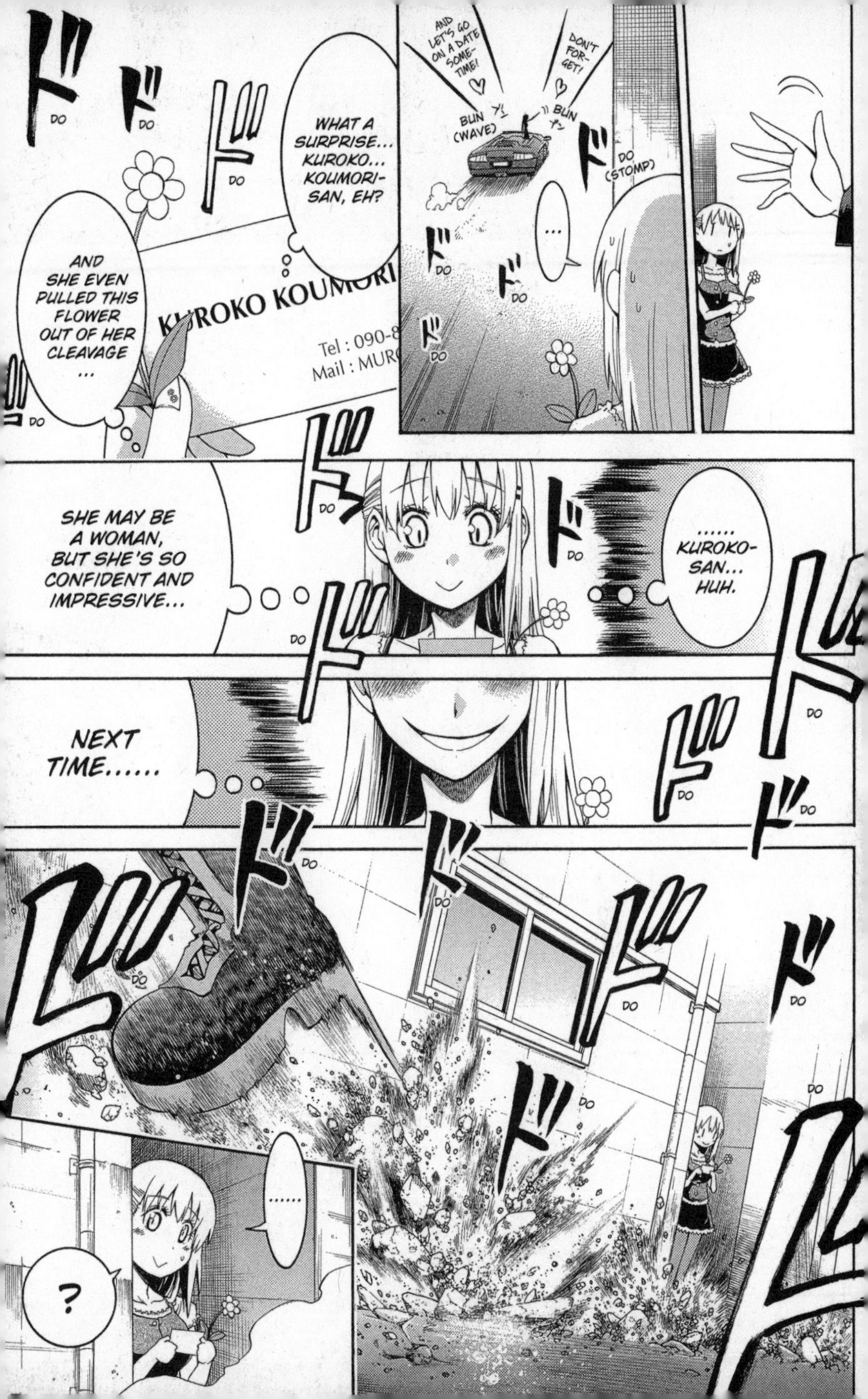
DON'T FORGET!
AND LET'S GO ON A DATE SOMETIME!
BUN
BUN (WAVE)
DO (STOMP)
...
DO
DO
DO
WHAT A SURPRISE... KUROKO... KOUMORI-SAN, EH?
KUROKO KOUMORI
Tel : 090-8
Mail : MURO
AND SHE EVEN PULLED THIS FLOWER OUT OF HER CLEAVAGE...
DO
DO
DO
DO
......KUROKO-SAN... HUH.
DO
SHE MAY BE A WOMAN, BUT SHE'S SO CONFIDENT AND IMPRESSIVE...
DO
DO
DO
DO
DO
NEXT TIME......
DO
DO
DO
DO
DO
DO
DO
......
?

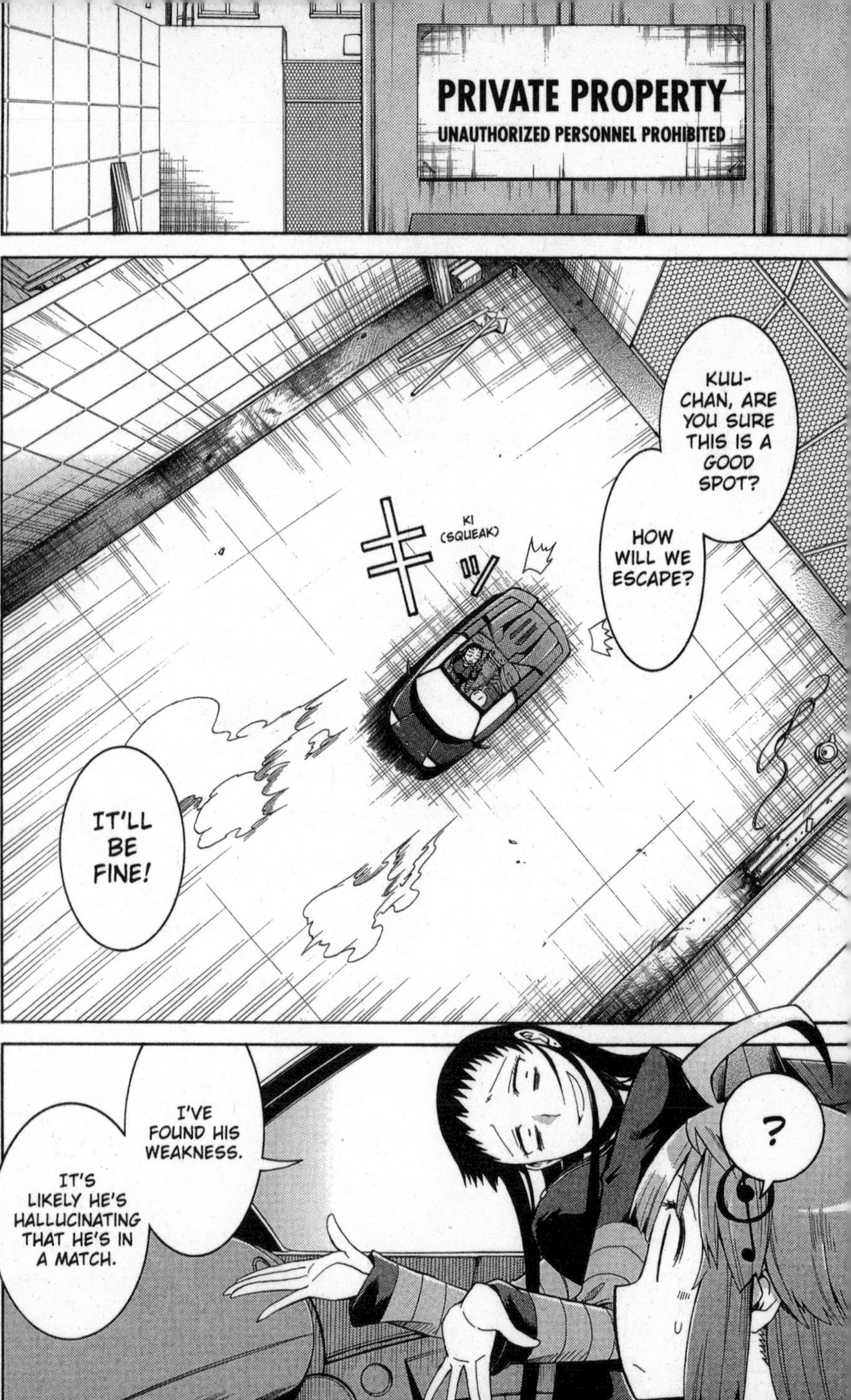
PRIVATE PROPERTY
UNAUTHORIZED PERSONNEL PROHIBITED
KUU-CHAN, ARE YOU SURE THIS IS A GOOD SPOT?
HOW WILL WE ESCAPE?
KI (SQUEAK)
IT'LL BE FINE!
?
I'VE FOUND HIS WEAKNESS.
IT'S LIKELY HE'S HALLUCINATING THAT HE'S IN A MATCH.

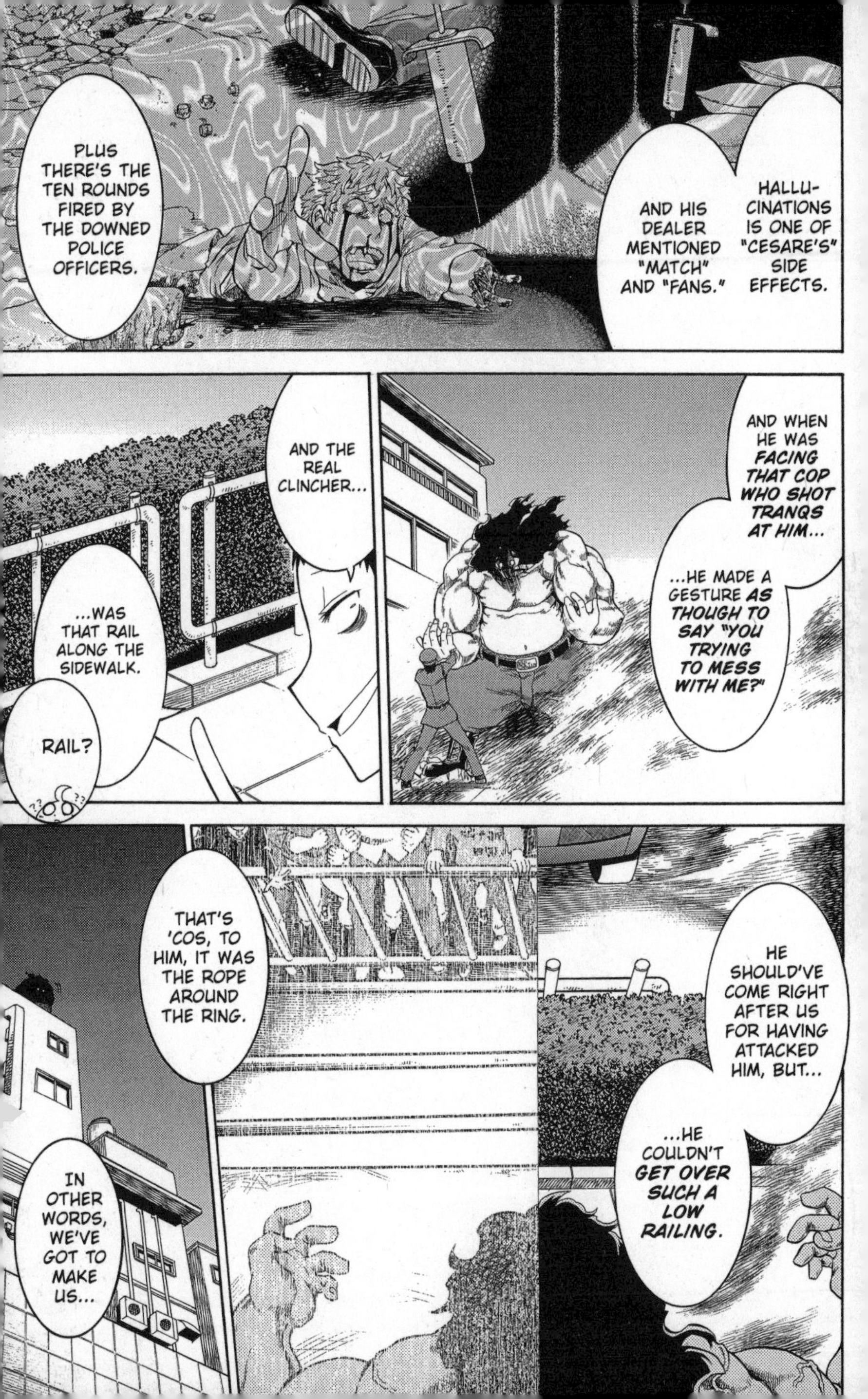
HALLUCINATIONS IS ONE OF "CESARE'S" SIDE EFFECTS.
AND HIS DEALER MENTIONED "MATCH" AND "FANS."
PLUS THERE'S THE TEN ROUNDS FIRED BY THE DOWNED POLICE OFFICERS.
AND WHEN HE WAS FACING THAT COP WHO SHOT TRANQS AT HIM...
...HE MADE A GESTURE AS THOUGH TO SAY "YOU TRYING TO MESS WITH ME?"
AND THE REAL CLINCHER...
...WAS THAT RAIL ALONG THE SIDEWALK.
RAIL?
HE SHOULD'VE COME RIGHT AFTER US FOR HAVING ATTACKED HIM, BUT...
...HE COULDN'T GET OVER SUCH A LOW RAILING.
THAT'S 'COS, TO HIM, IT WAS THE ROPE AROUND THE RING.
IN OTHER WORDS, WE'VE GOT TO MAKE US...

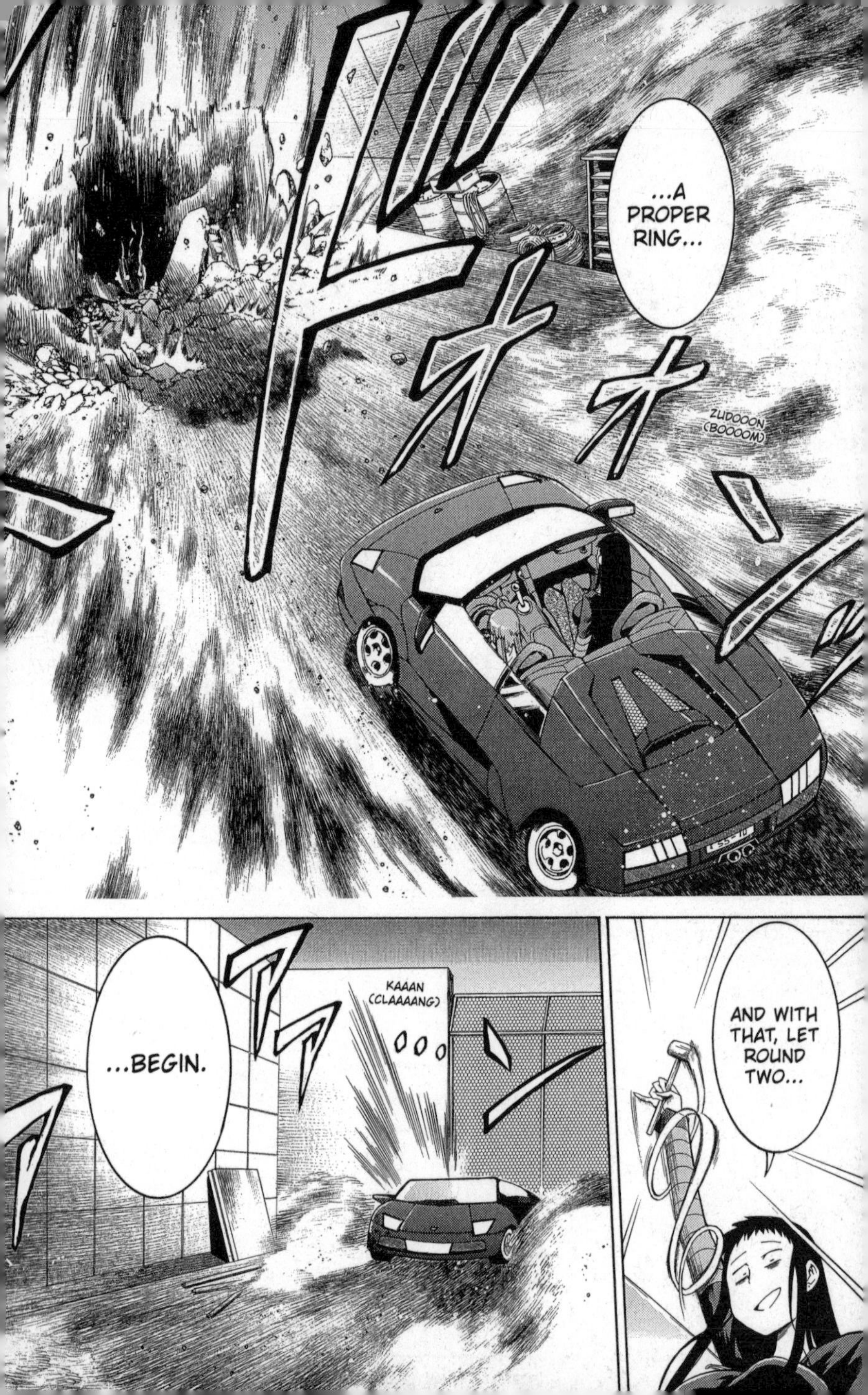
...A PROPER RING...
ZUDOOON (BOOOOM)
AND WITH THAT, LET ROUND TWO...
KAAAN (CLAAAANG)
...BEGIN.

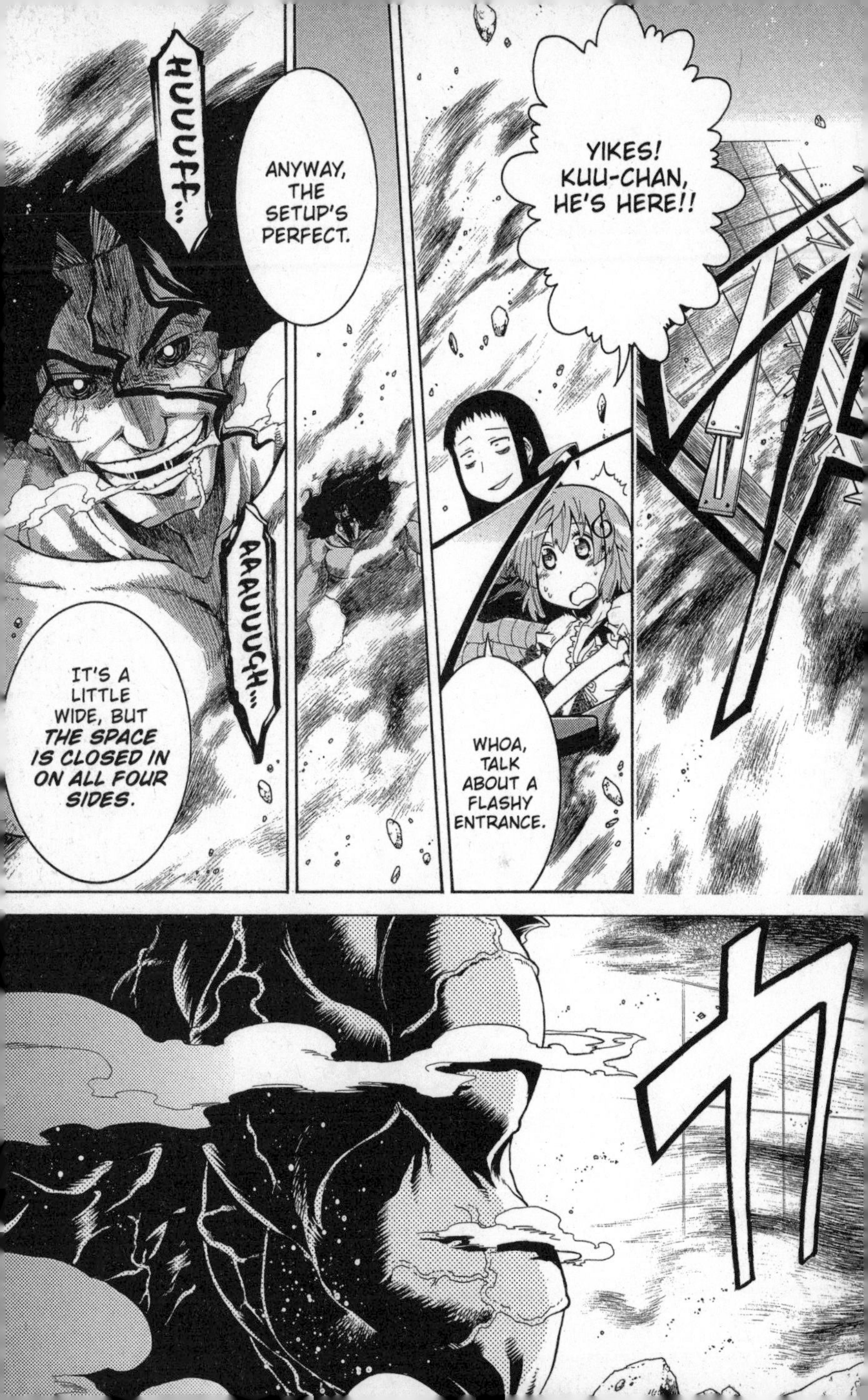
YIKES! KUU-CHAN, HE'S HERE!!
WHOA, TALK ABOUT A FLASHY ENTRANCE.
ANYWAY, THE SETUP'S PERFECT.
HUUUFF...
AAAUUUGH...
IT'S A LITTLE WIDE, BUT *THE SPACE IS CLOSED IN ON ALL FOUR SIDES.*

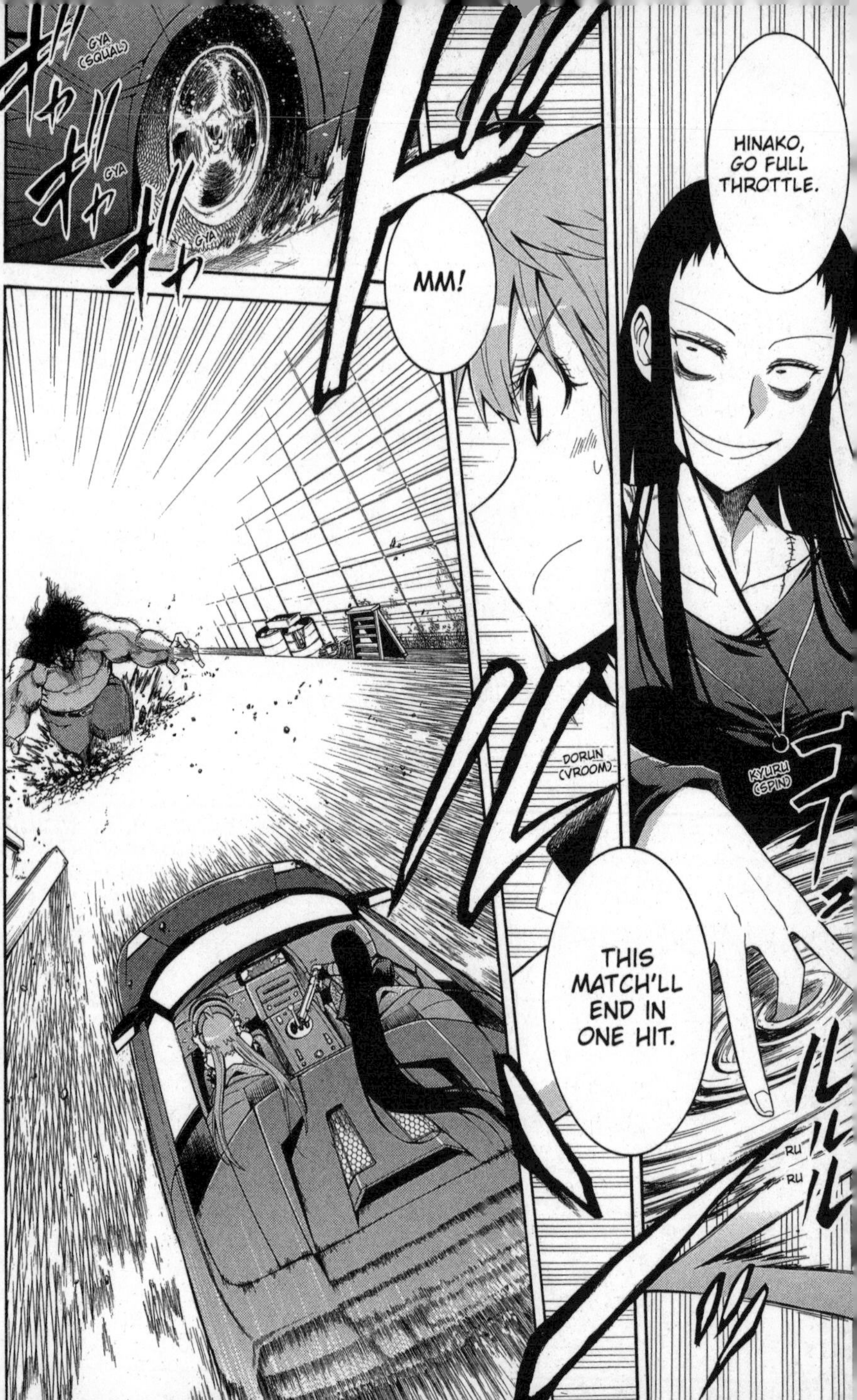
HINAKO, GO FULL THROTTLE.
MM!
KYURU (SPIN)
THIS MATCH'LL END IN ONE HIT.
RU
RU
GYA (SQUAL)
GYA
GYA
DORUN (VROOM)

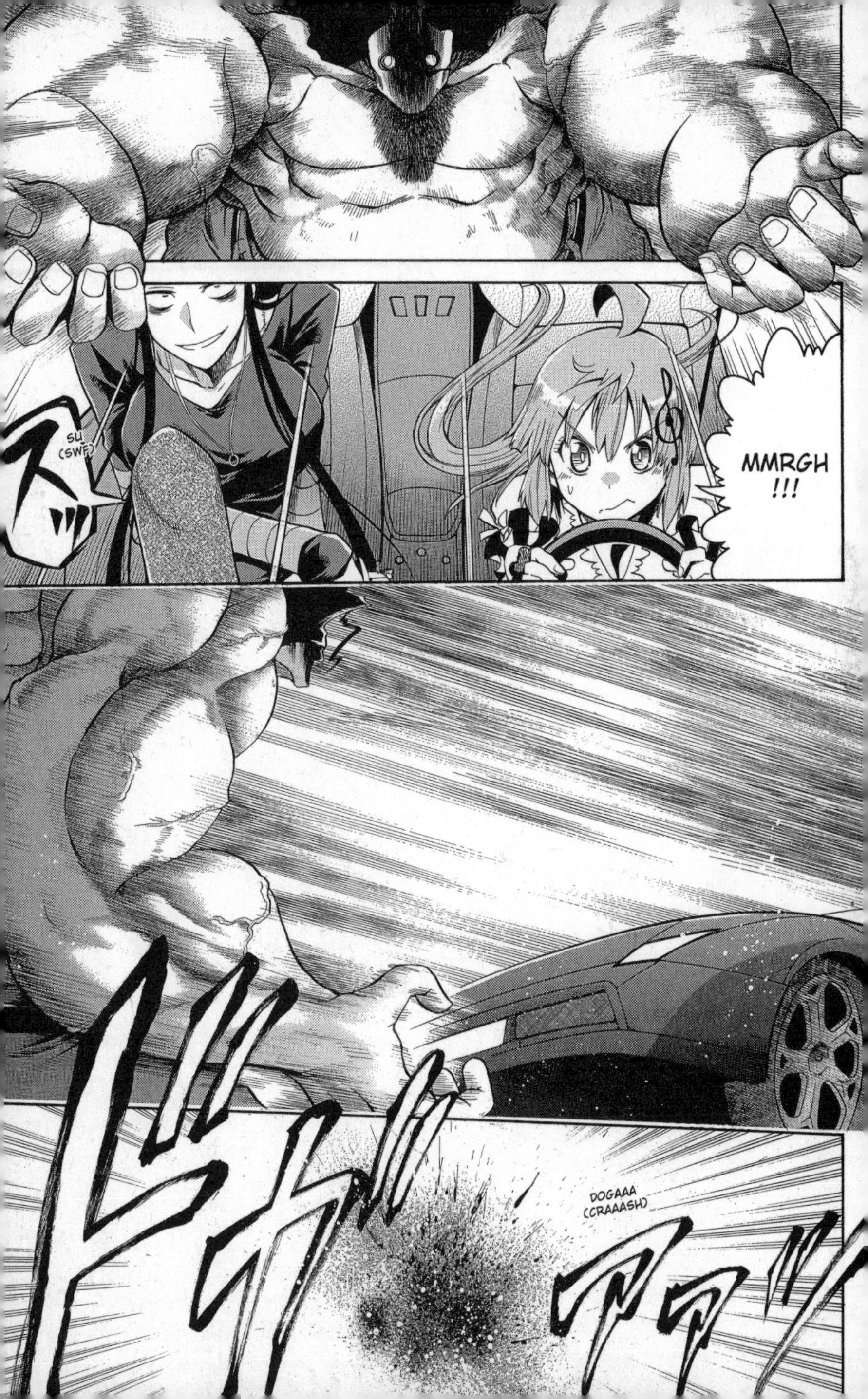
MMRGH
!!!
ス
SU
(SWF)
ドガァ
DOGAAA
(CRAAASH)

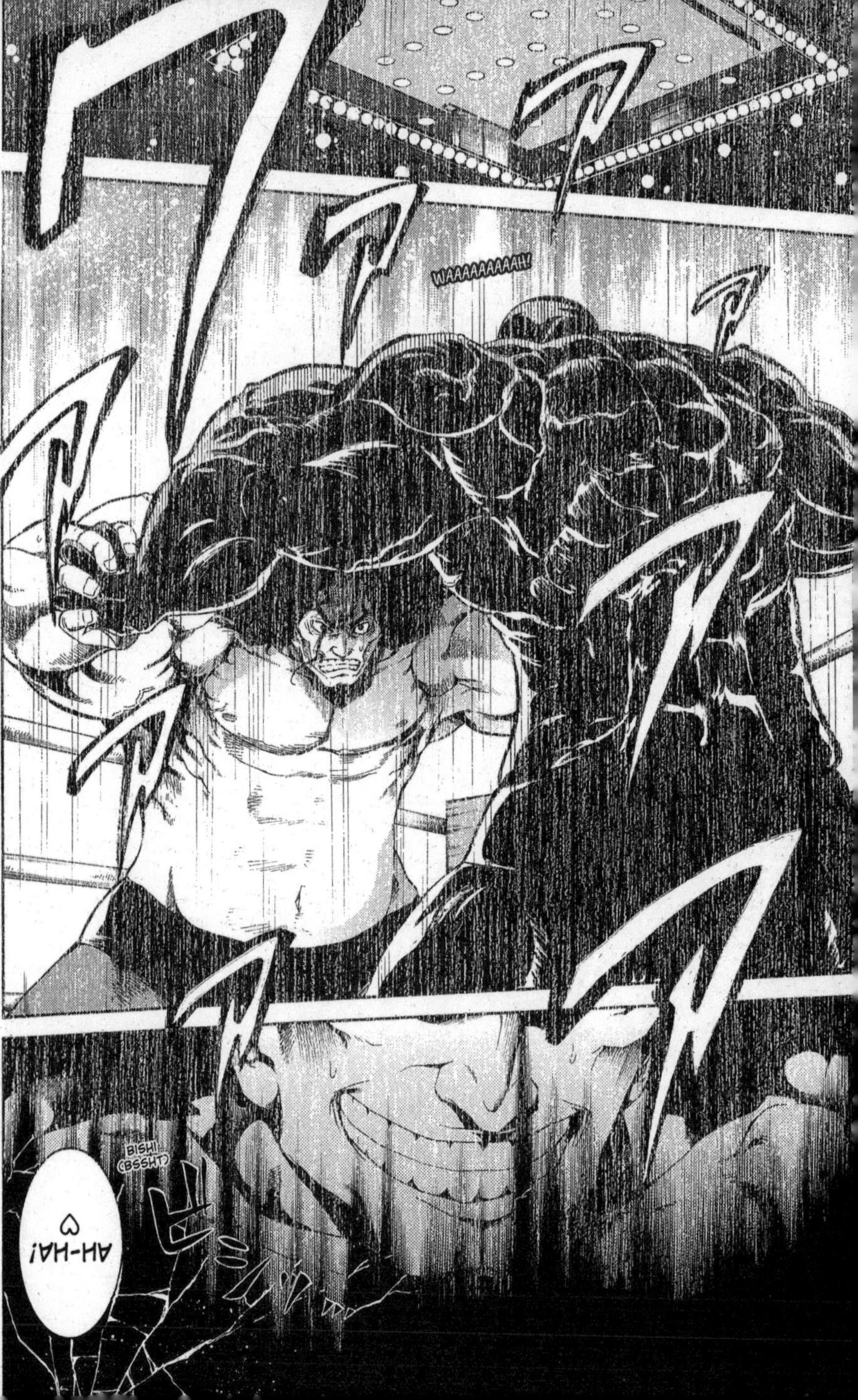
WAAAAAAAAAH!
BISHI (BSSHT)
AH-HA! ♡

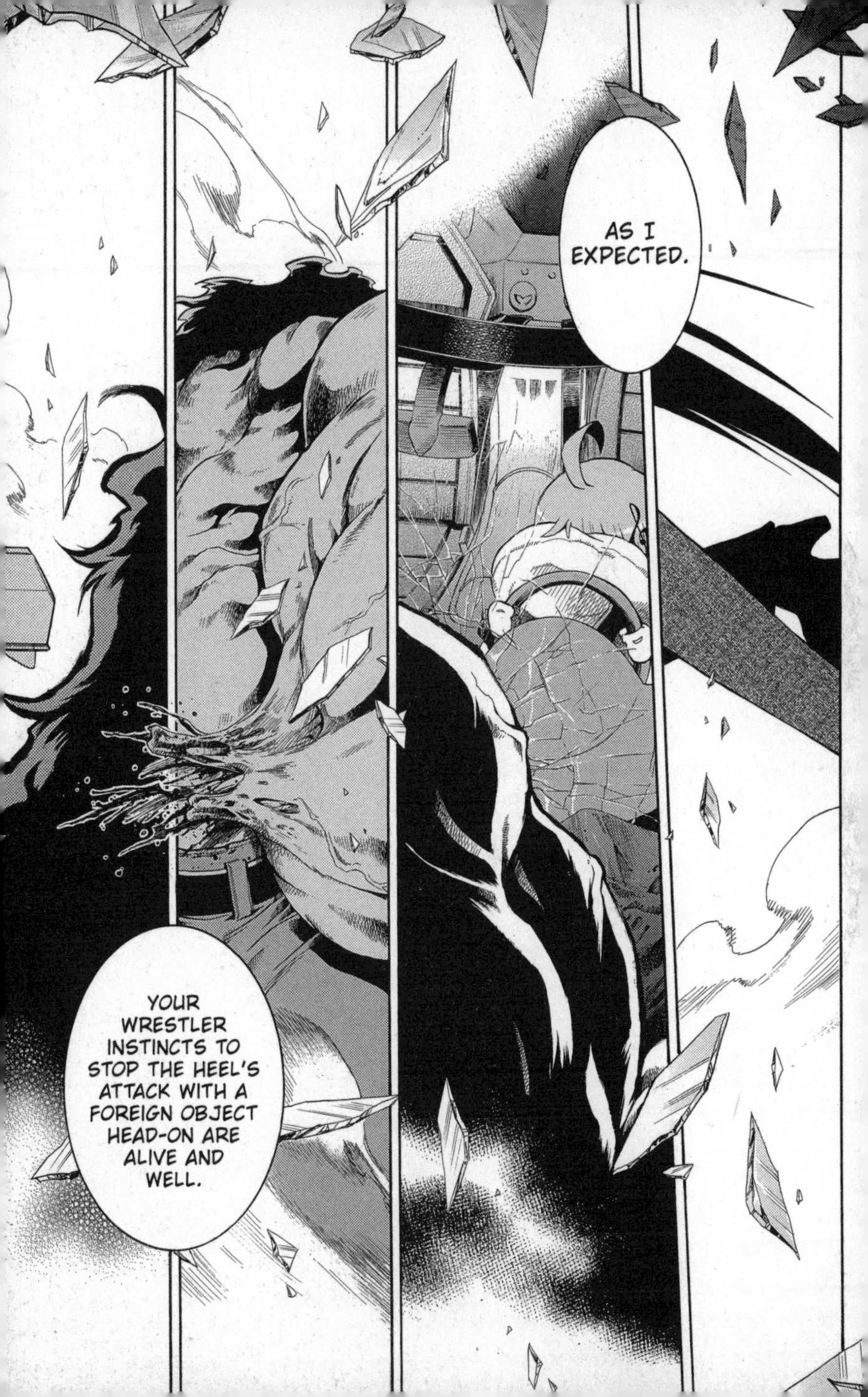
AS I EXPECTED.
YOUR WRESTLER INSTINCTS TO STOP THE HEEL'S ATTACK WITH A FOREIGN OBJECT HEAD-ON ARE ALIVE AND WELL.

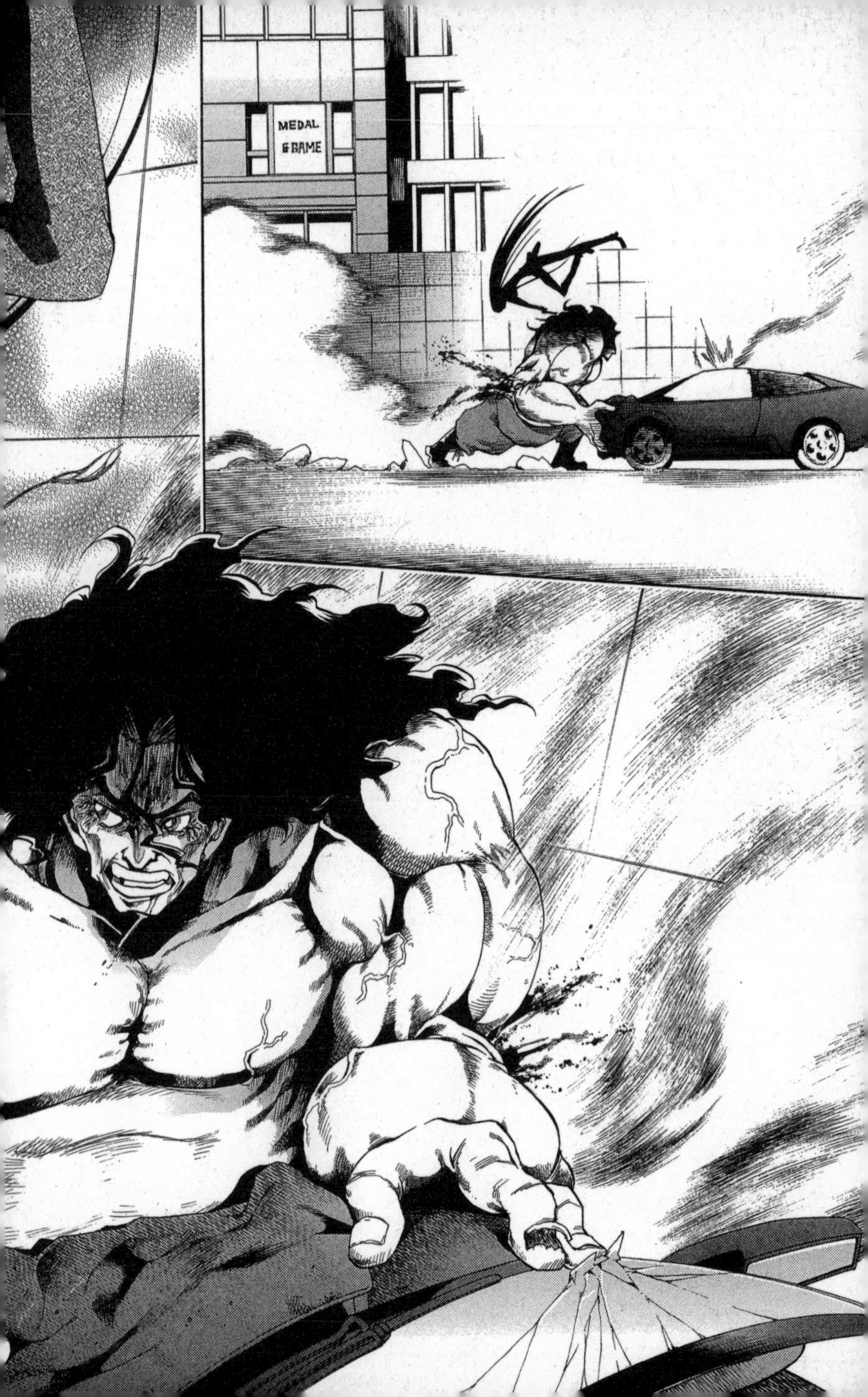
MEDAL
& GAME

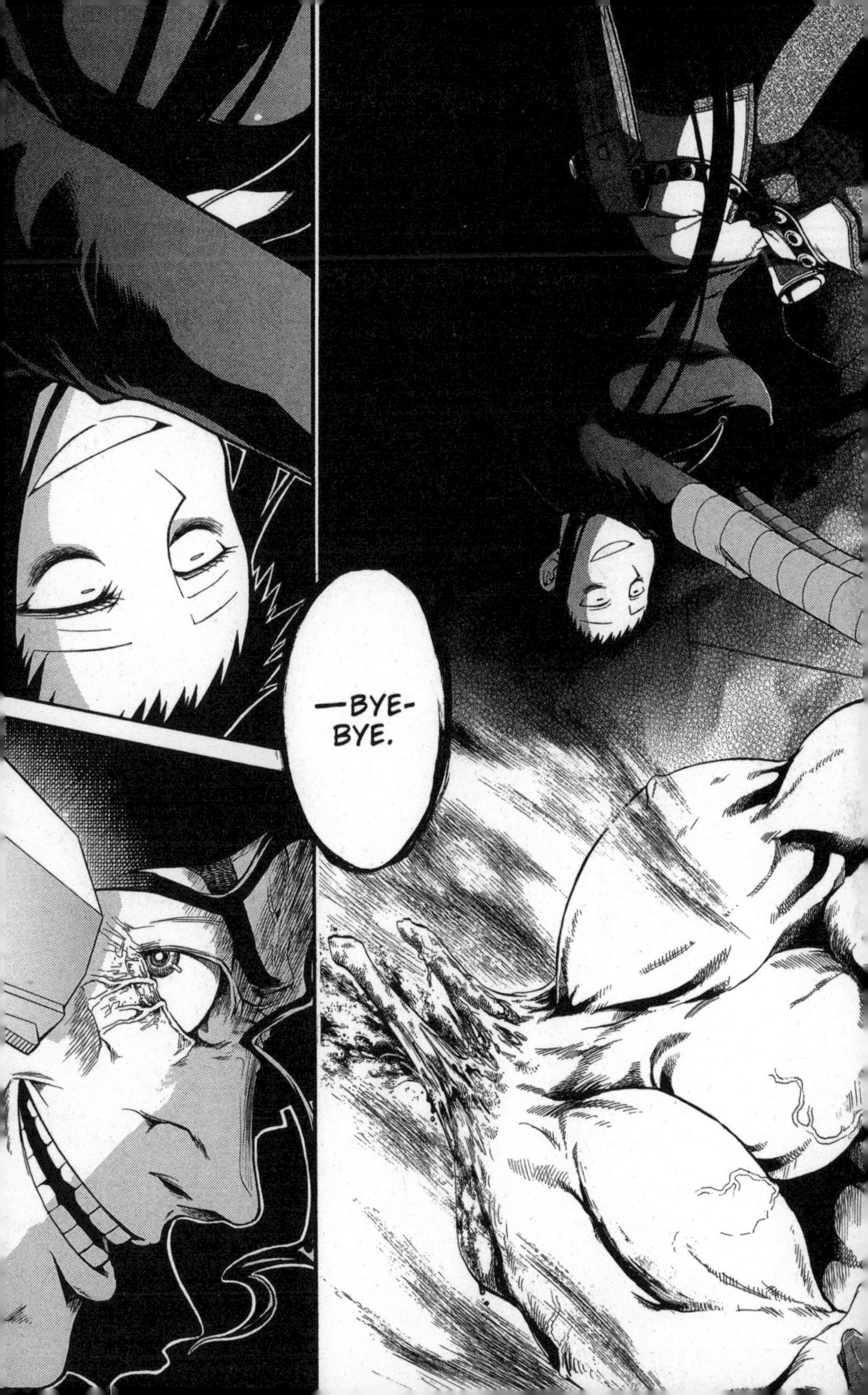
—BYE-BYE.

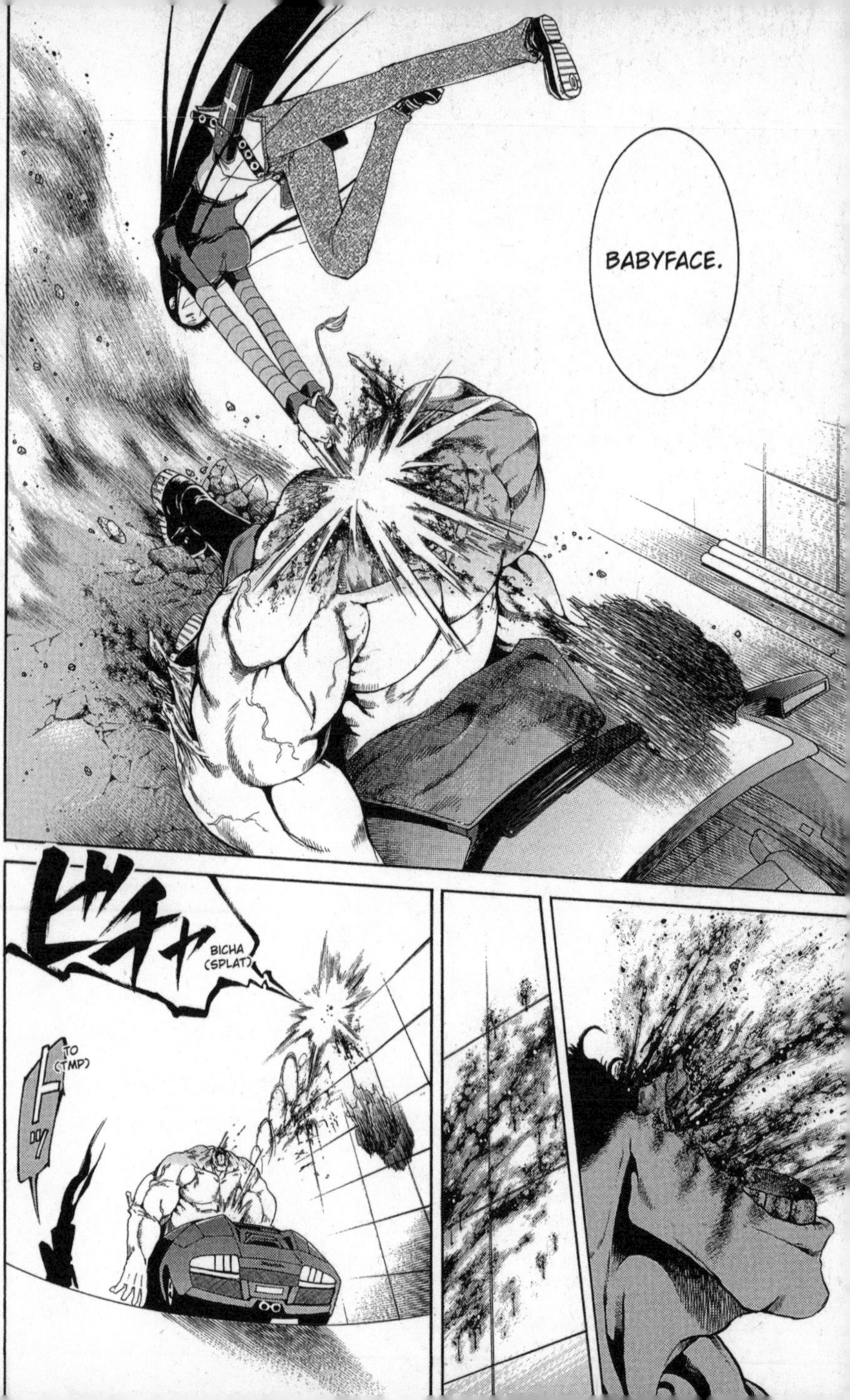
BABYFACE.
ビチャ
BICHA (SPLAT)
トッ
TO (TMP)

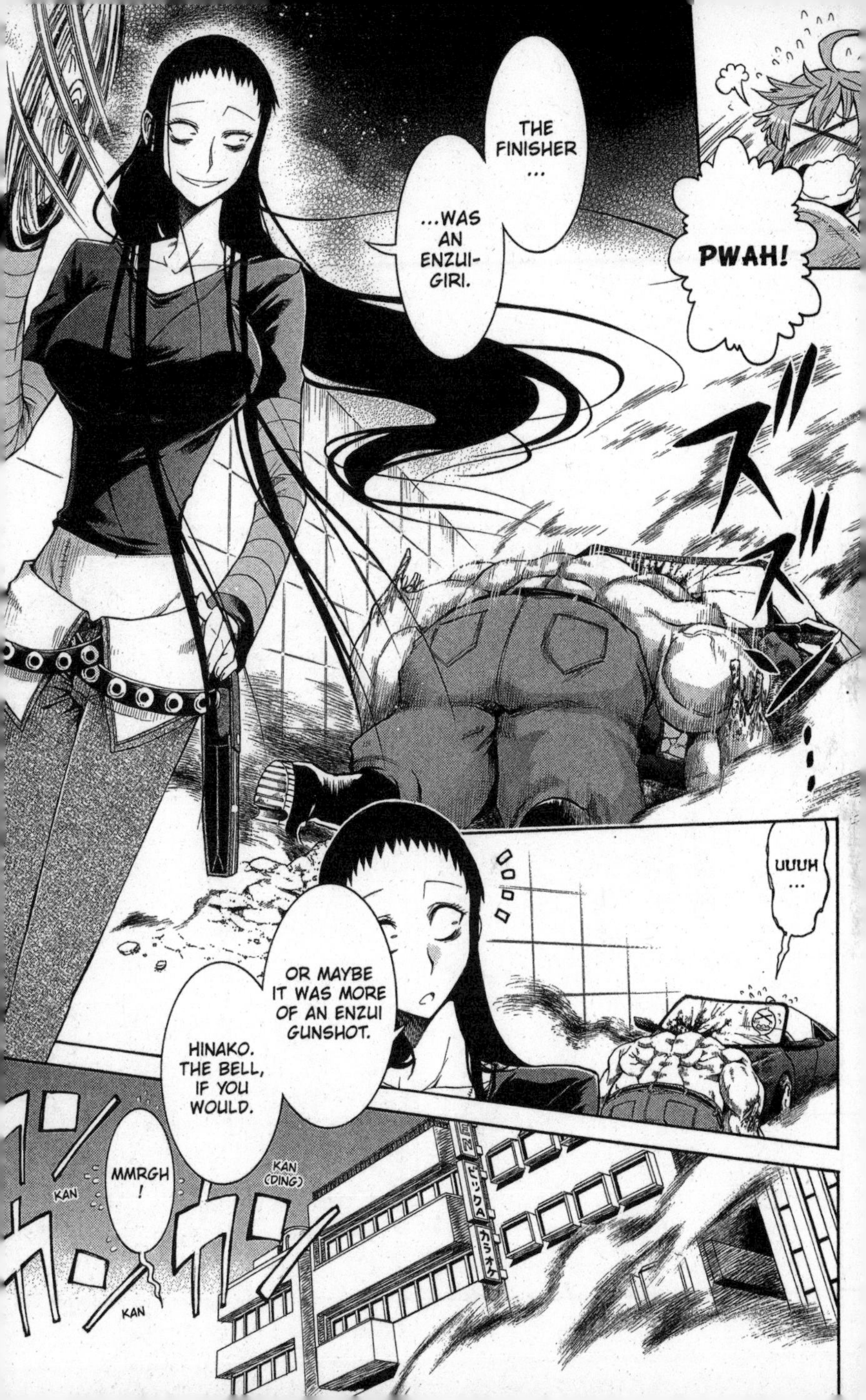

PWAH!
THE FINISHER ...
...WAS AN ENZUI-GIRI.
ズズ
UUUH ...
OR MAYBE IT WAS MORE OF AN ENZUI GUNSHOT.
HINAKO. THE BELL, IF YOU WOULD.
KAN (DING)
MMRGH!
KAN
KAN
ビックA
カラオケ

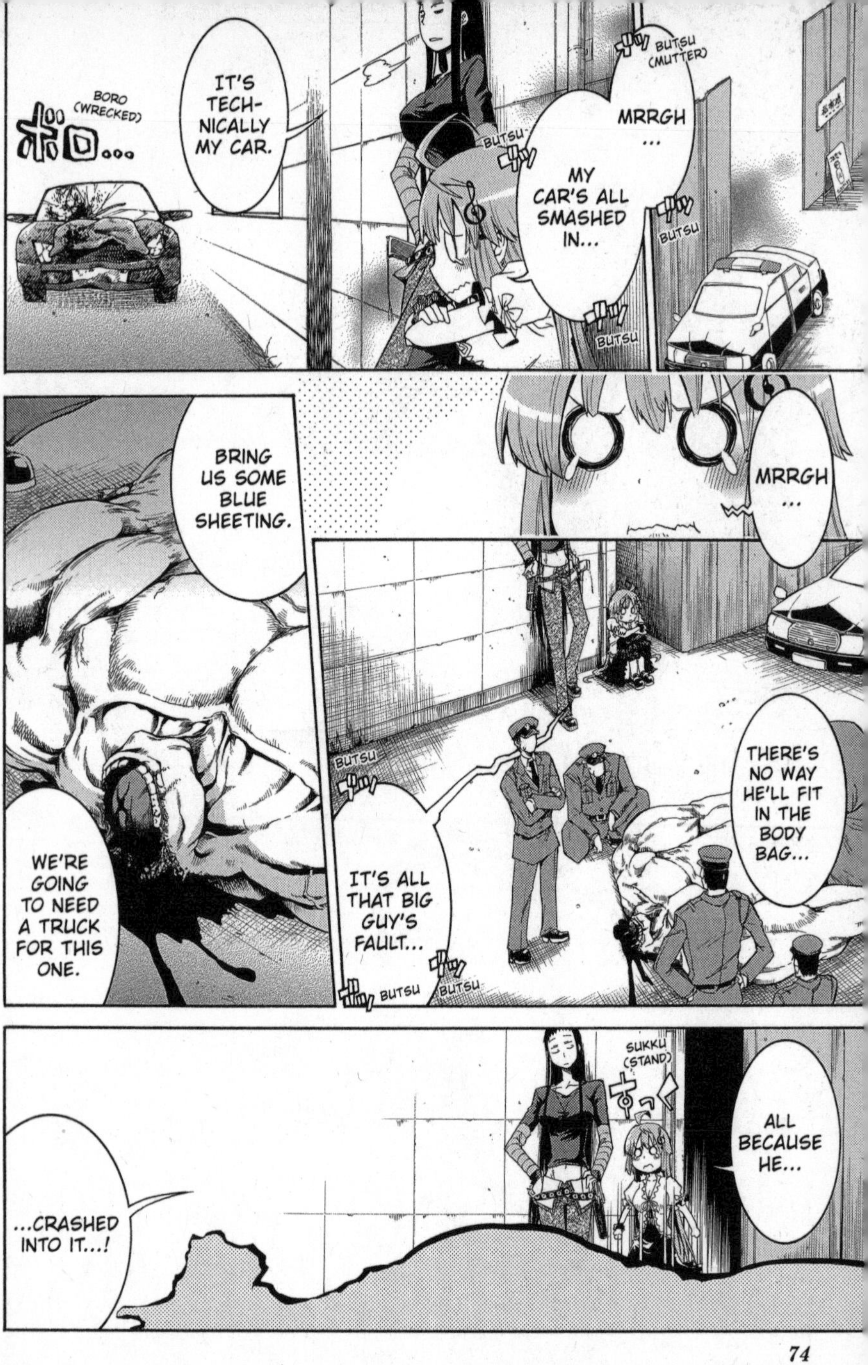
BUTSU (MUTTER)
MRRGH... MY CAR'S ALL SMASHED IN...
BUTSU
BUTSU
BUTSU
IT'S TECHNICALLY MY CAR.
BORO (WRECKED)
MRRGH...
THERE'S NO WAY HE'LL FIT IN THE BODY BAG...
BUTSU
IT'S ALL THAT BIG GUY'S FAULT...
BUTSU
BUTSU
BRING US SOME BLUE SHEETING.
WE'RE GOING TO NEED A TRUCK FOR THIS ONE.
SUKKU (STAND)
ALL BECAUSE HE...
...CRASHED INTO IT...!

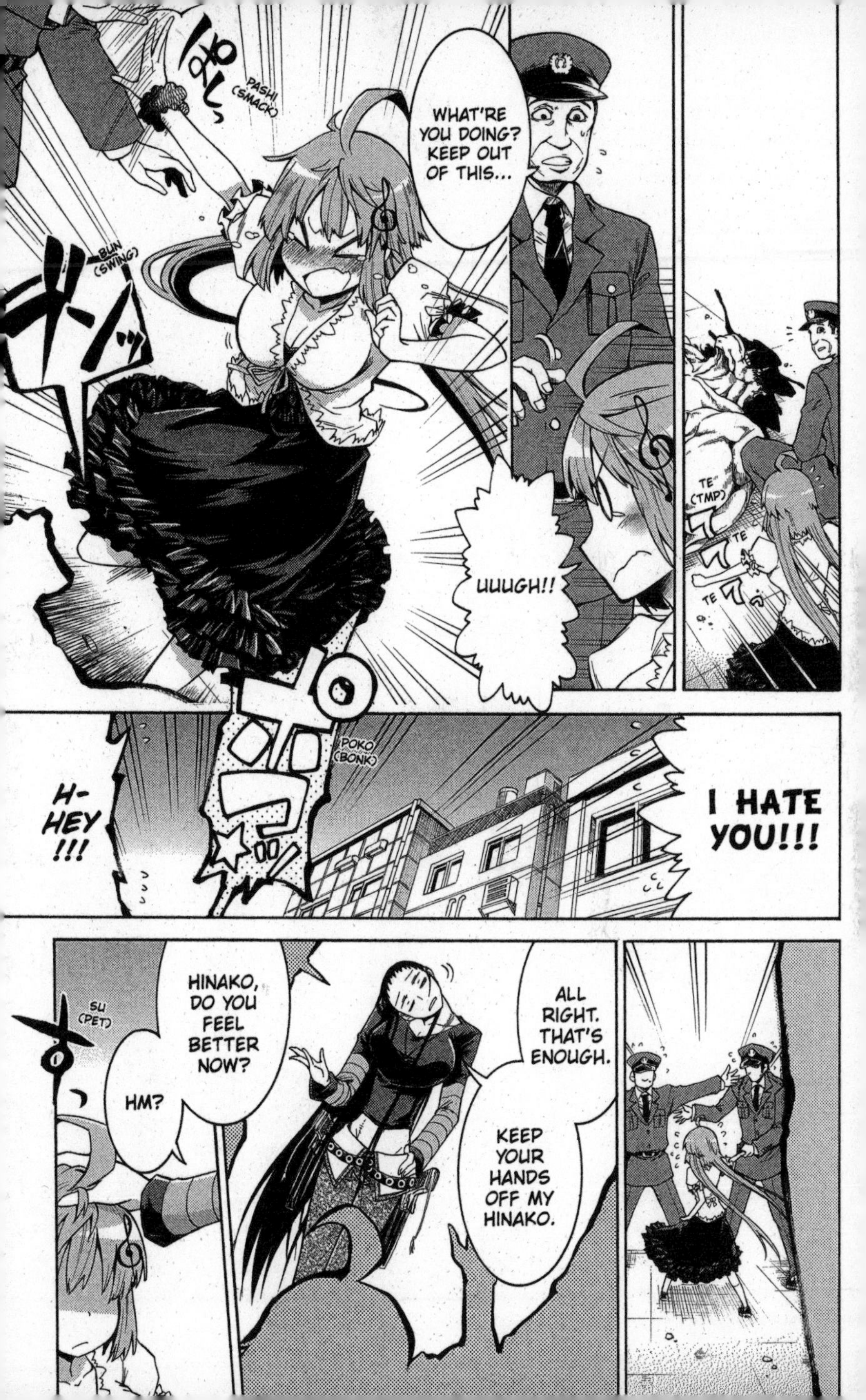
TE" (TMP)
TE
TE
WHAT'RE YOU DOING? KEEP OUT OF THIS...
UUUGH!!
PASHI (SMACK)
BUN (SWING)
I HATE YOU!!!
POKO (BONK)
H-HEY!!!
ALL RIGHT. THAT'S ENOUGH.
KEEP YOUR HANDS OFF MY HINAKO.
HINAKO, DO YOU FEEL BETTER NOW?
HM?
SU (PET)

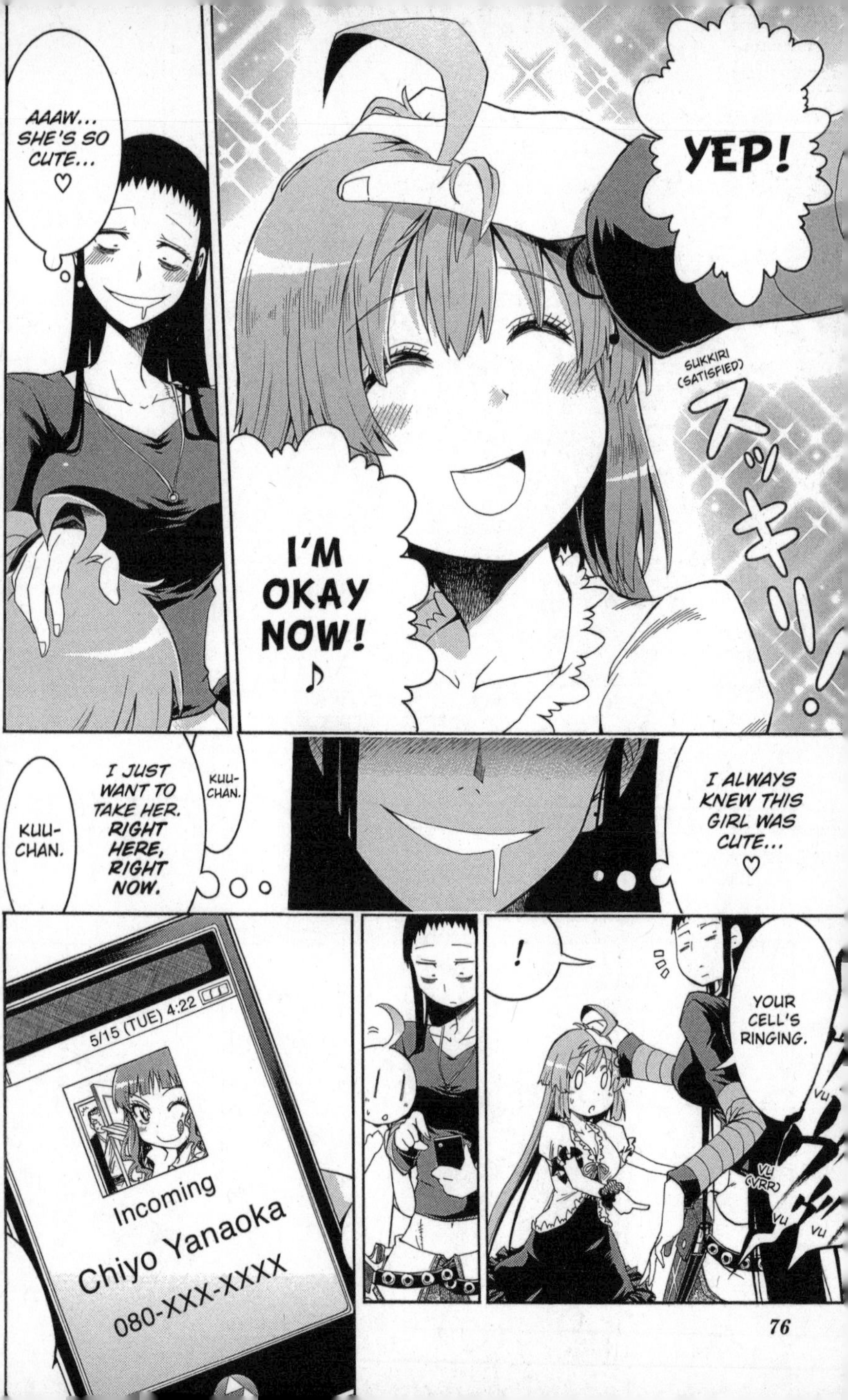
YEP!
SUKKIRI (SATISFIED)
I'M OKAY NOW! ♪
AAAW... SHE'S SO CUTE... ♡
I ALWAYS KNEW THIS GIRL WAS CUTE... ♡
KUU-CHAN.
I JUST WANT TO TAKE HER. RIGHT HERE, RIGHT NOW.
KUU-CHAN.
YOUR CELL'S RINGING.
!
VU
VU (VRR)
VU
VU
5/15 (TUE) 4:22
Incoming
Chiyo Yanaoka
080-XXX-XXXX

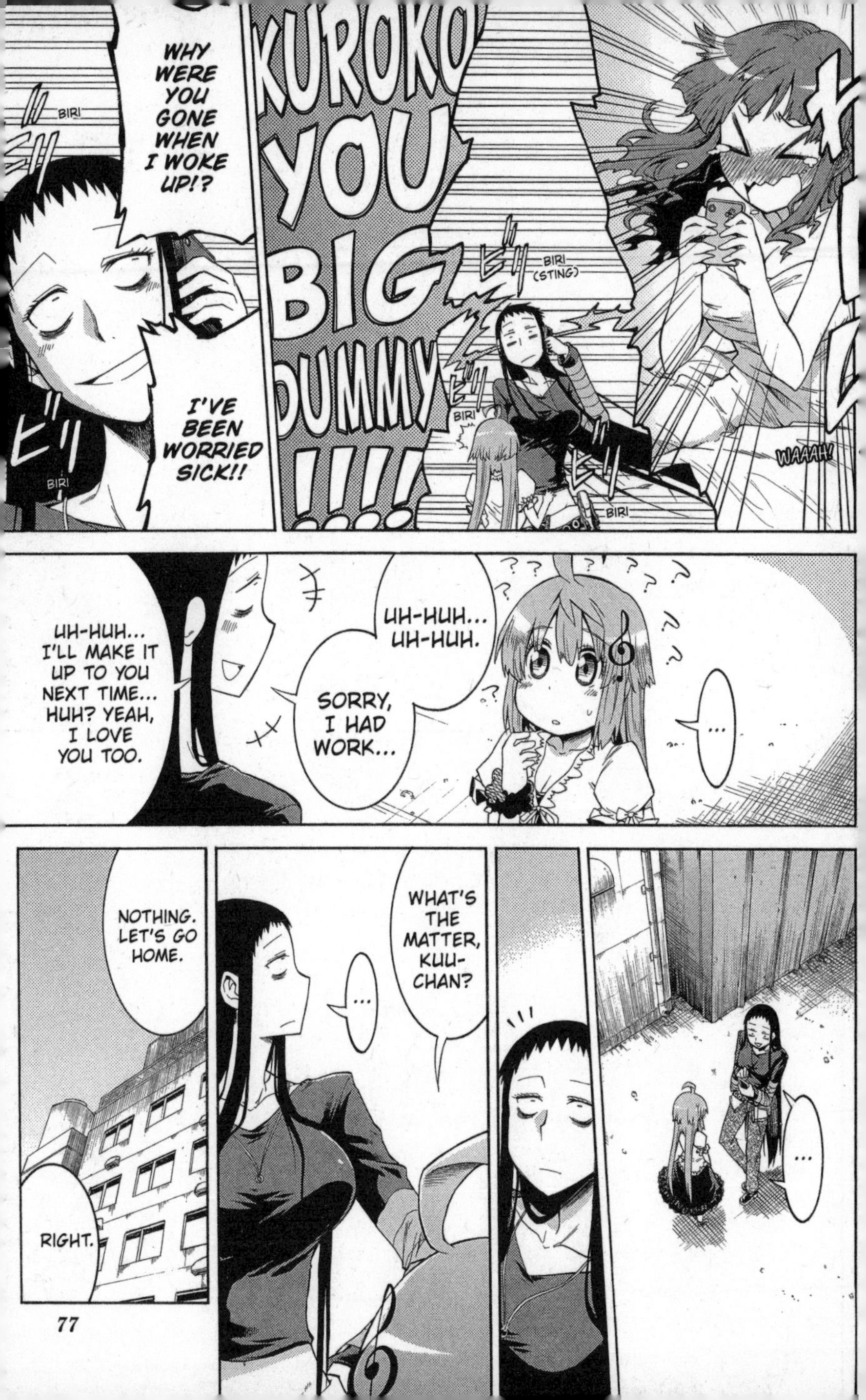
WAAAH!
KUROKO YOU BIG DUMMY!!!!
BIRI (STING)
BIRI
BIRI
BIRI
WHY WERE YOU GONE WHEN I WOKE UP!?
I'VE BEEN WORRIED SICK!!
BIRI
...
UH-HUH... UH-HUH.
SORRY, I HAD WORK...
UH-HUH... I'LL MAKE IT UP TO YOU NEXT TIME... HUH? YEAH, I LOVE YOU TOO.
...
WHAT'S THE MATTER, KUU-CHAN?
...
NOTHING. LET'S GO HOME.
RIGHT.

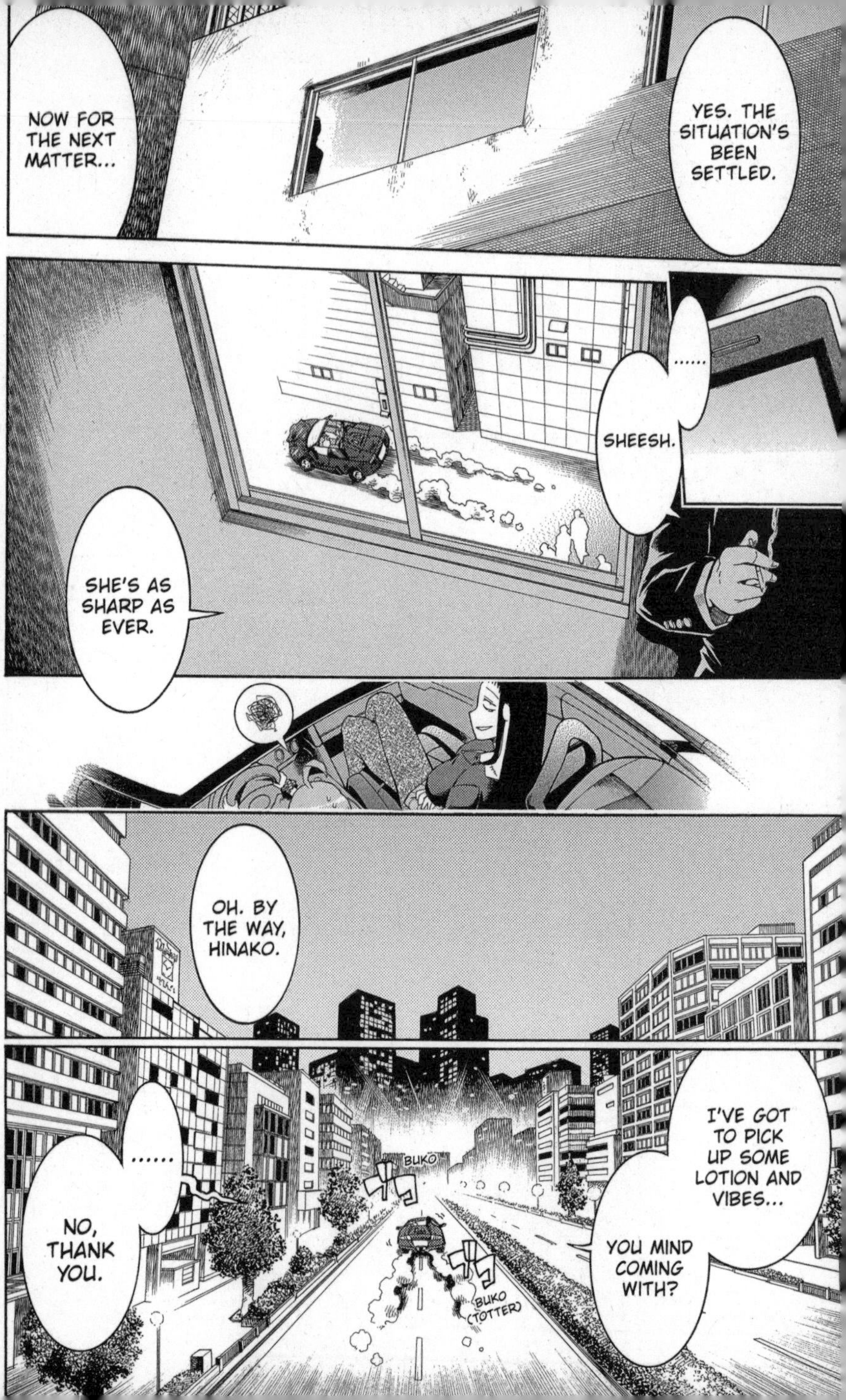
YES. THE SITUATION'S BEEN SETTLED.
NOW FOR THE NEXT MATTER...
......
SHEESH.
SHE'S AS SHARP AS EVER.
OH. BY THE WAY, HINAKO.
I'VE GOT TO PICK UP SOME LOTION AND VIBES...
YOU MIND COMING WITH?
BUKO
BUKO (TOTTER)
......
NO, THANK YOU.

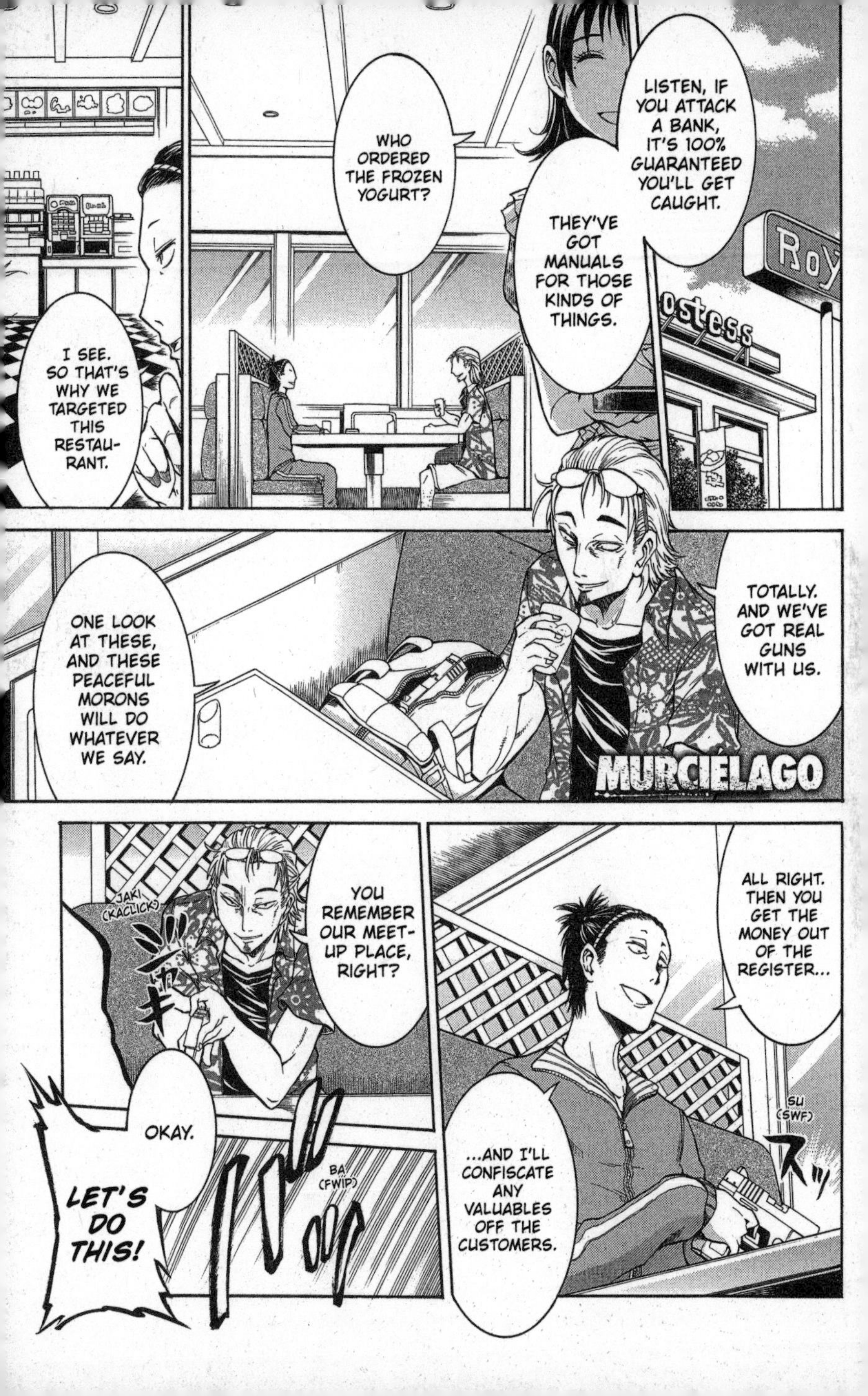
LISTEN, IF YOU ATTACK A BANK, IT'S 100% GUARANTEED YOU'LL GET CAUGHT.
THEY'VE GOT MANUALS FOR THOSE KINDS OF THINGS.
Roy
ostess
WHO ORDERED THE FROZEN YOGURT?
I SEE. SO THAT'S WHY WE TARGETED THIS RESTAURANT.
TOTALLY. AND WE'VE GOT REAL GUNS WITH US.
ONE LOOK AT THESE, AND THESE PEACEFUL MORONS WILL DO WHATEVER WE SAY.
MURCIELAGO
ALL RIGHT. THEN YOU GET THE MONEY OUT OF THE REGISTER...
...AND I'LL CONFISCATE ANY VALUABLES OFF THE CUSTOMERS.
SU (SWF)
YOU REMEMBER OUR MEET-UP PLACE, RIGHT?
JAKI (KACLICK)
OKAY.
BA (FWIP)
LET'S DO THIS!

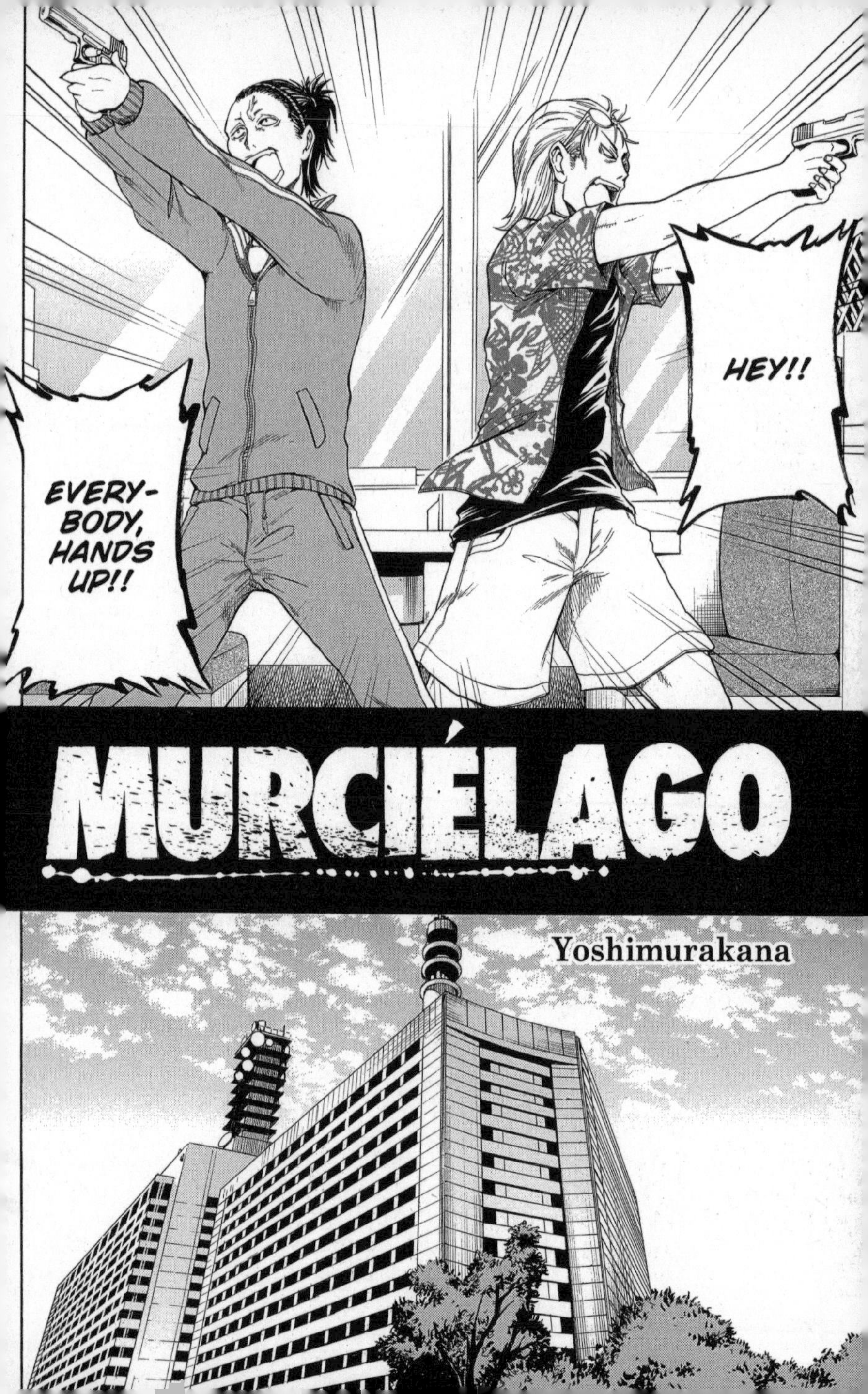
HEY!!
EVERY-BODY, HANDS UP!!
MURCIÉLAGO
Yoshimurakana

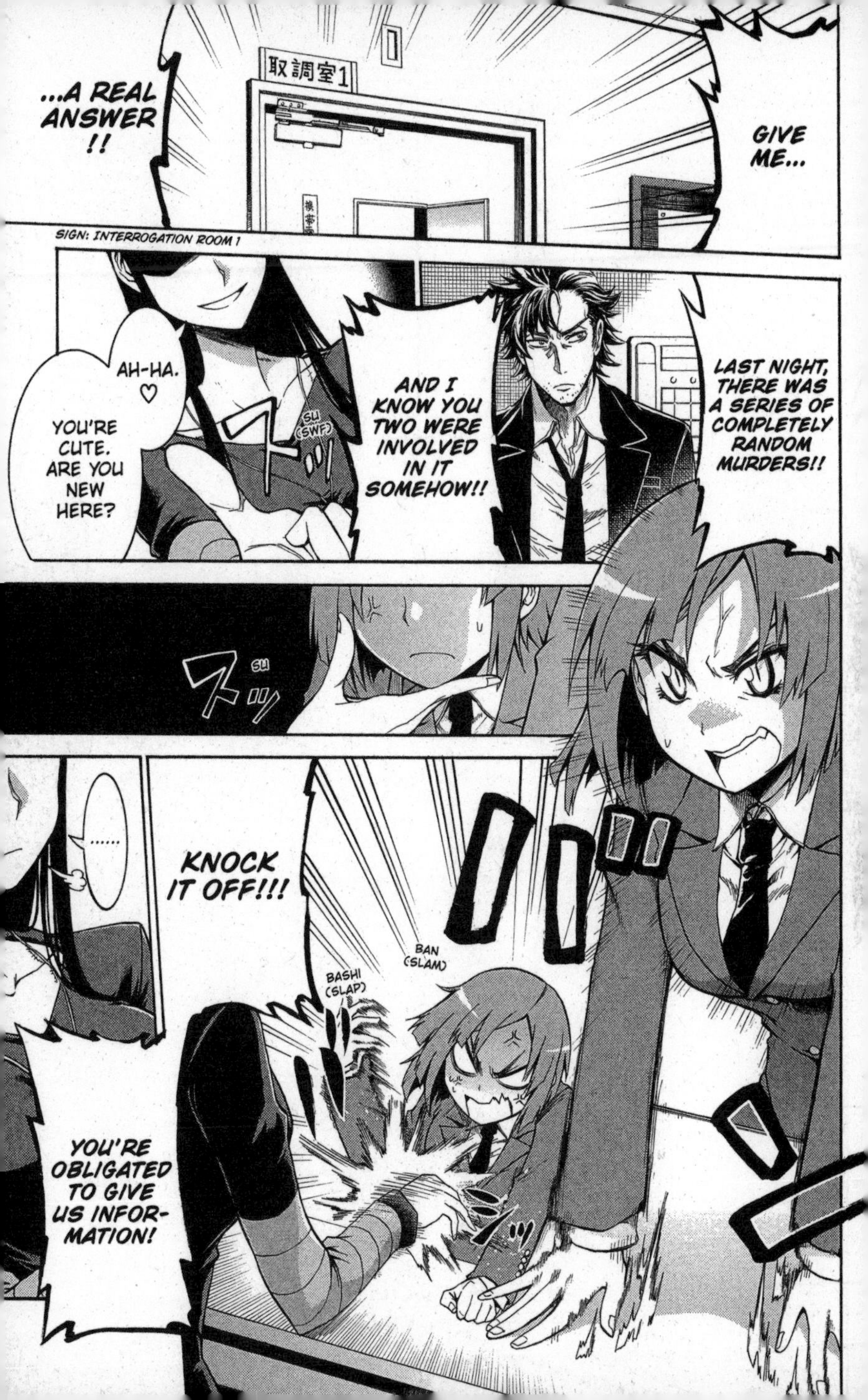
GIVE ME...
取調室1
...A REAL ANSWER!!
SIGN: INTERROGATION ROOM 1
LAST NIGHT, THERE WAS A SERIES OF COMPLETELY RANDOM MURDERS!!
AND I KNOW YOU TWO WERE INVOLVED IN IT SOMEHOW!!
SU (SWF)
AH-HA. ♡
YOU'RE CUTE. ARE YOU NEW HERE?
SU
KNOCK IT OFF!!!
BAN (SLAM)
BASHI (SLAP)
YOU'RE OBLIGATED TO GIVE US INFORMATION!
......

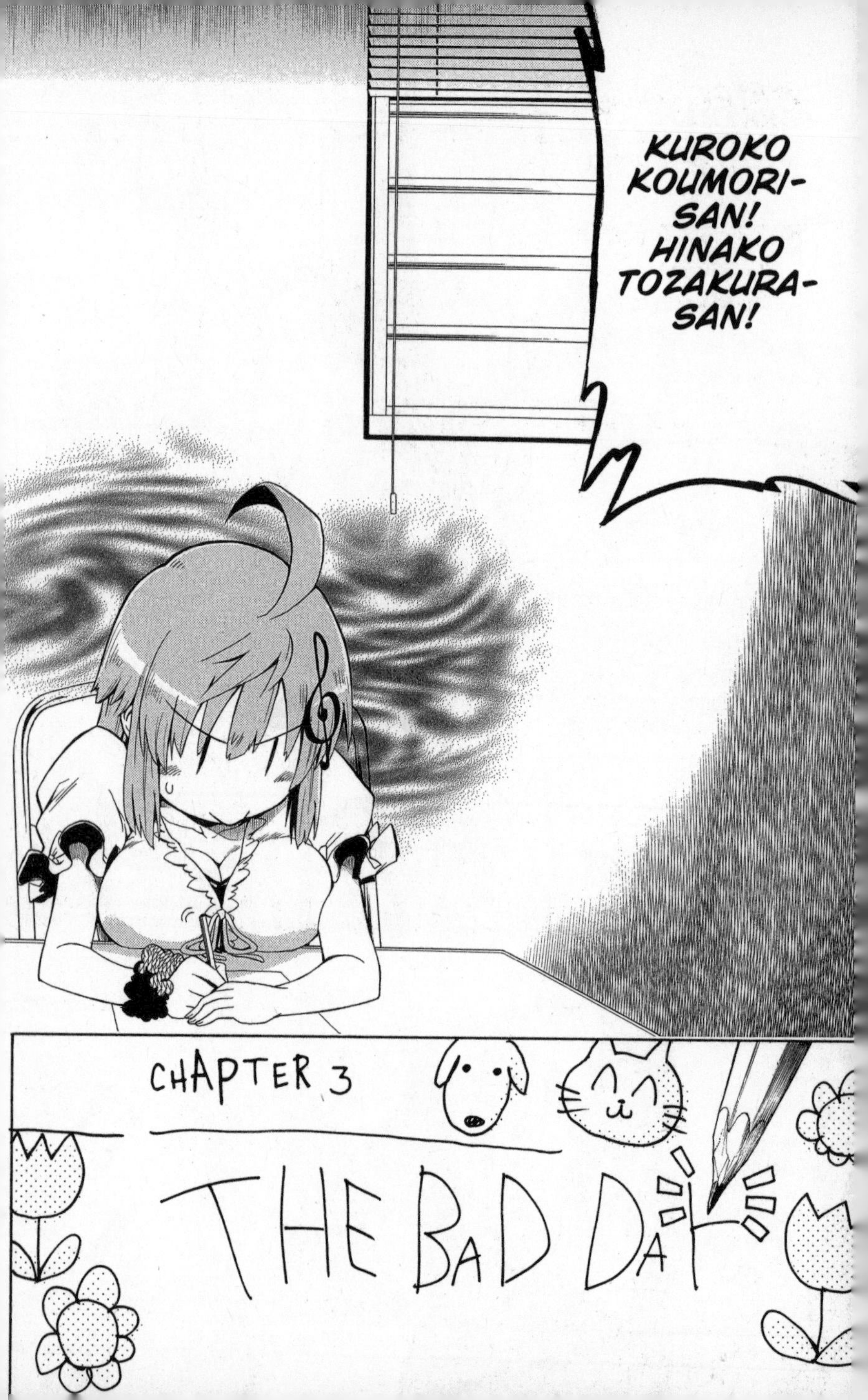
KUROKO KOUMORI-SAN! HINAKO TOZAKURA-SAN!
CHAPTER 3
THE BAD DAY

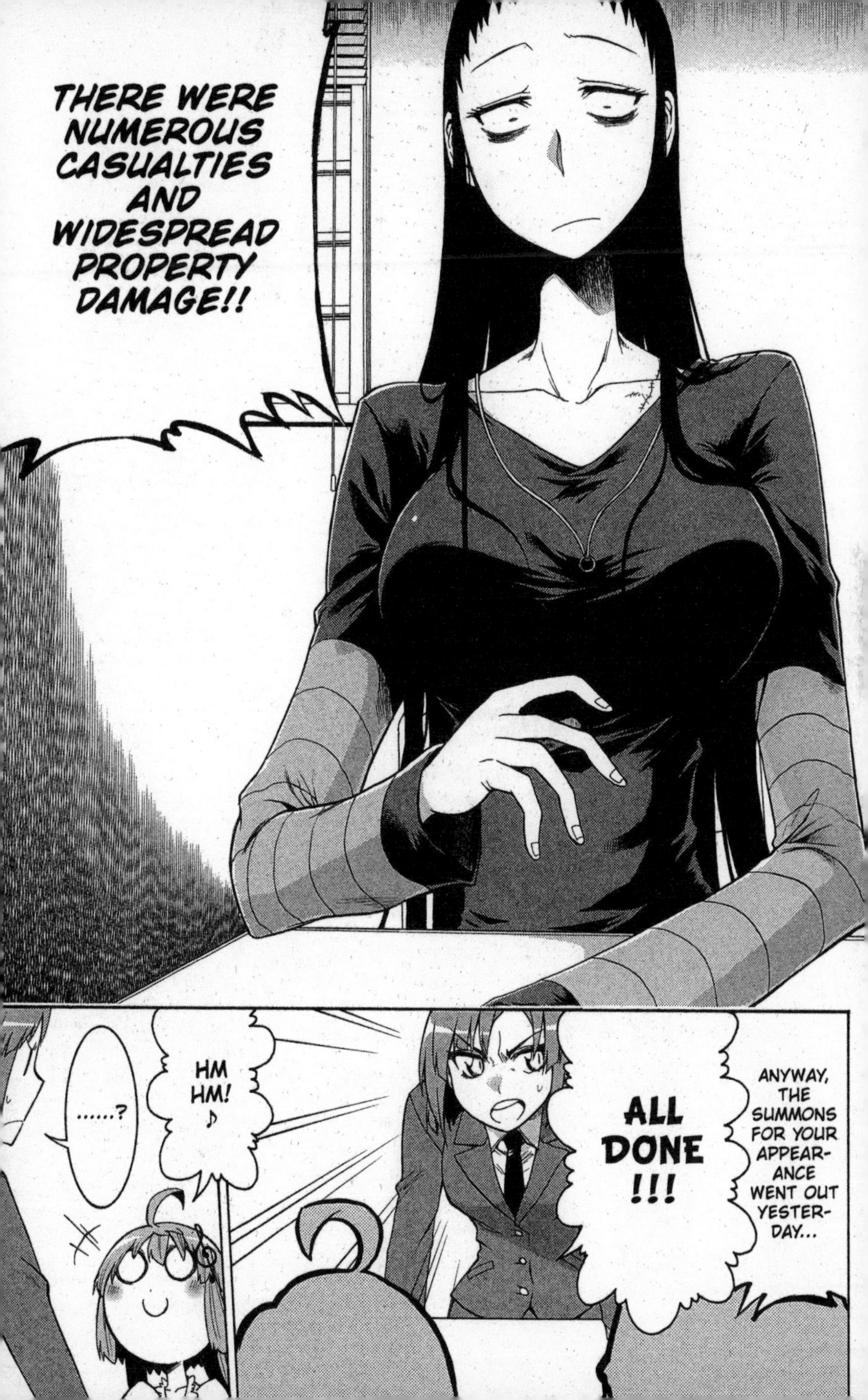
THERE WERE NUMEROUS CASUALTIES AND WIDESPREAD PROPERTY DAMAGE!!
ANYWAY, THE SUMMONS FOR YOUR APPEAR-ANCE WENT OUT YESTER-DAY...
ALL DONE !!!
HM HM! ♪
......?

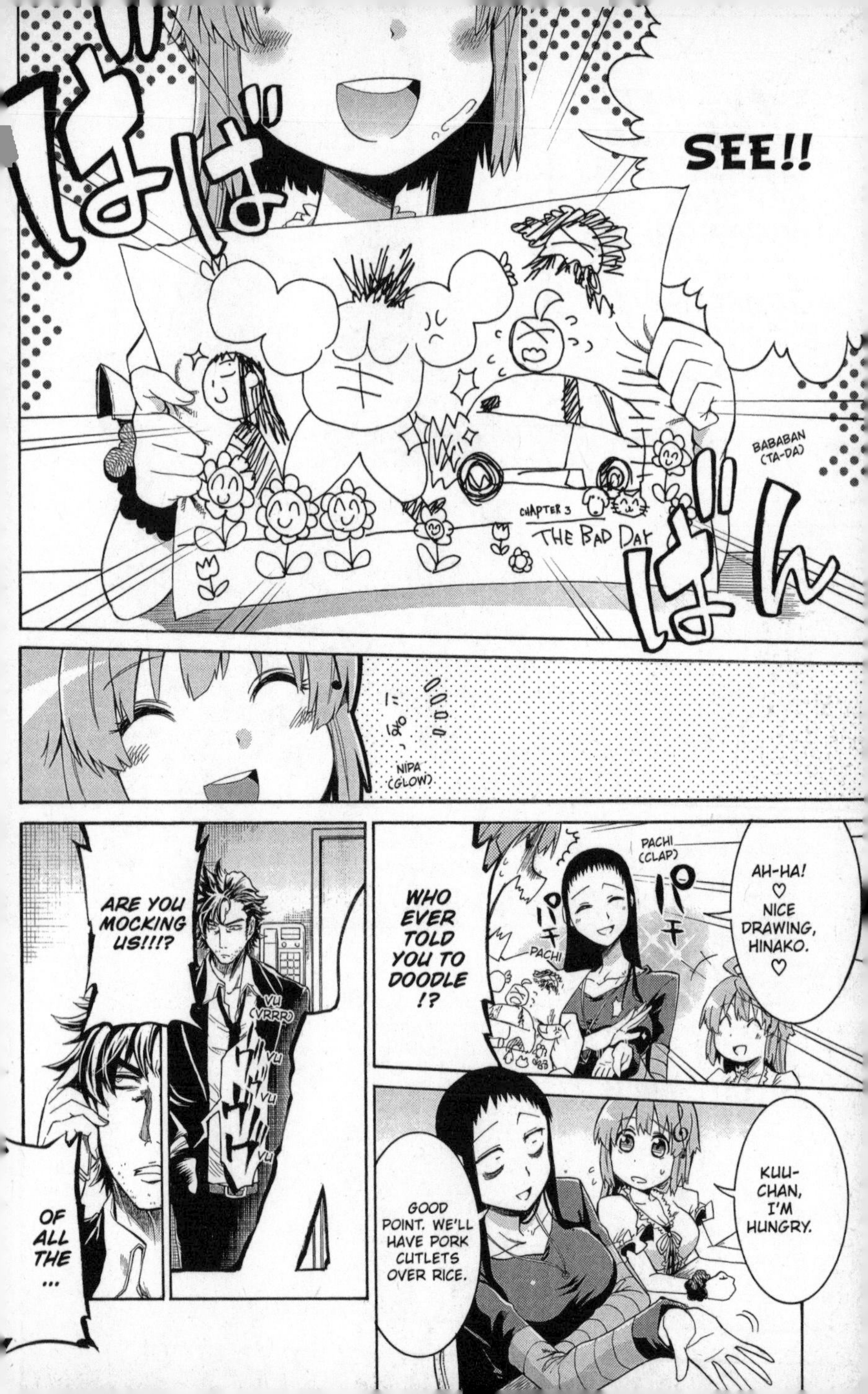
SEE!!
CHAPTER 3
THE BAD DAY
BABABAN (TA-DA)
ばん
NIPA (GLOW)
AH-HA! ♡ NICE DRAWING, HINAKO. ♡
PACHI (CLAP)
PACHI
WHO EVER TOLD YOU TO DOODLE!?
KUU-CHAN, I'M HUNGRY.
GOOD POINT. WE'LL HAVE PORK CUTLETS OVER RICE.
ARE YOU MOCKING US!!!?
VU (VRRR)
VU
VU
VU
OF ALL THE ...

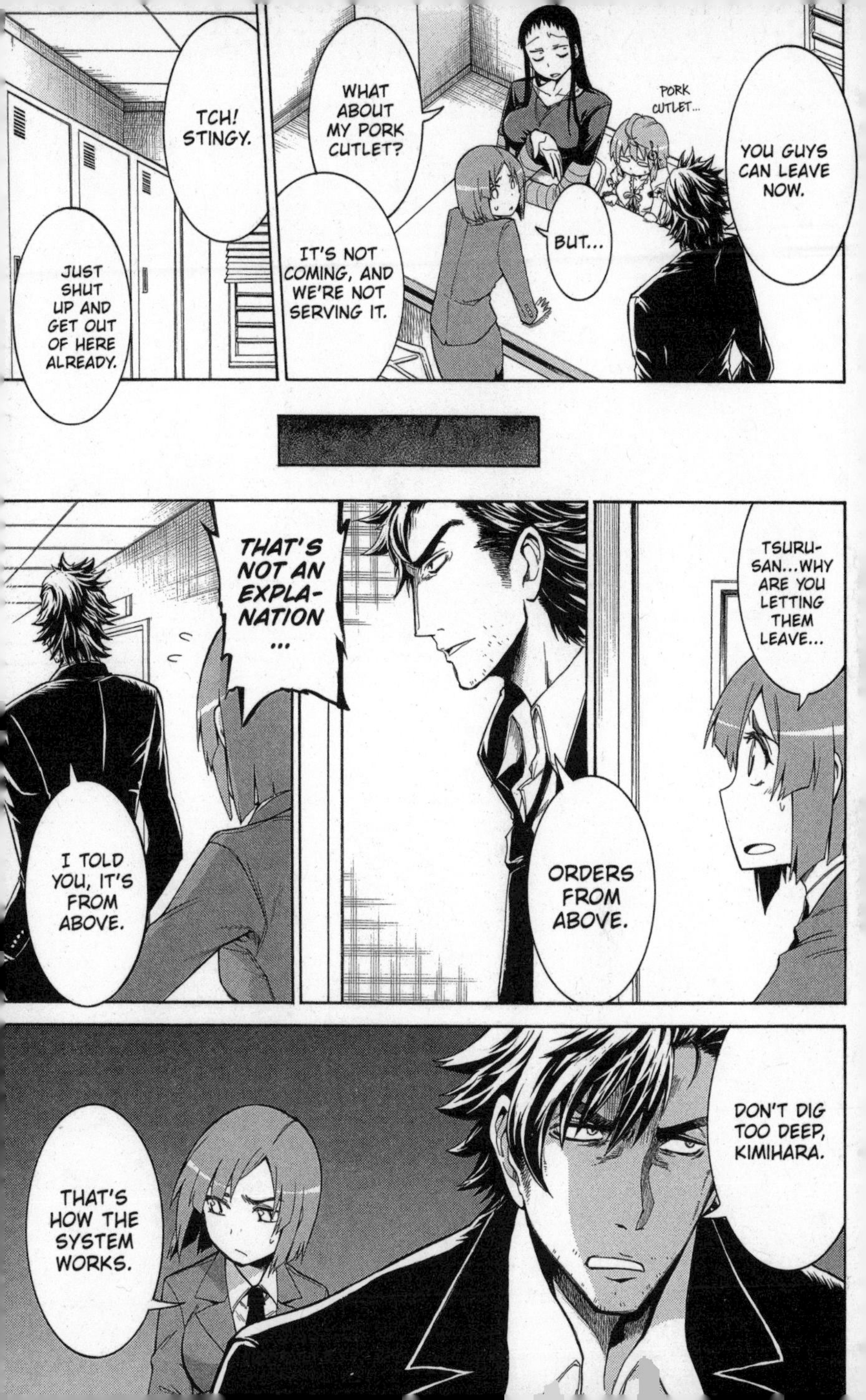
YOU GUYS CAN LEAVE NOW.
PORK CUTLET...
WHAT ABOUT MY PORK CUTLET?
BUT...
IT'S NOT COMING, AND WE'RE NOT SERVING IT.
TCH! STINGY.
JUST SHUT UP AND GET OUT OF HERE ALREADY.
TSURU-SAN...WHY ARE YOU LETTING THEM LEAVE...
ORDERS FROM ABOVE.
THAT'S NOT AN EXPLANATION...
I TOLD YOU, IT'S FROM ABOVE.
DON'T DIG TOO DEEP, KIMIHARA.
THAT'S HOW THE SYSTEM WORKS.

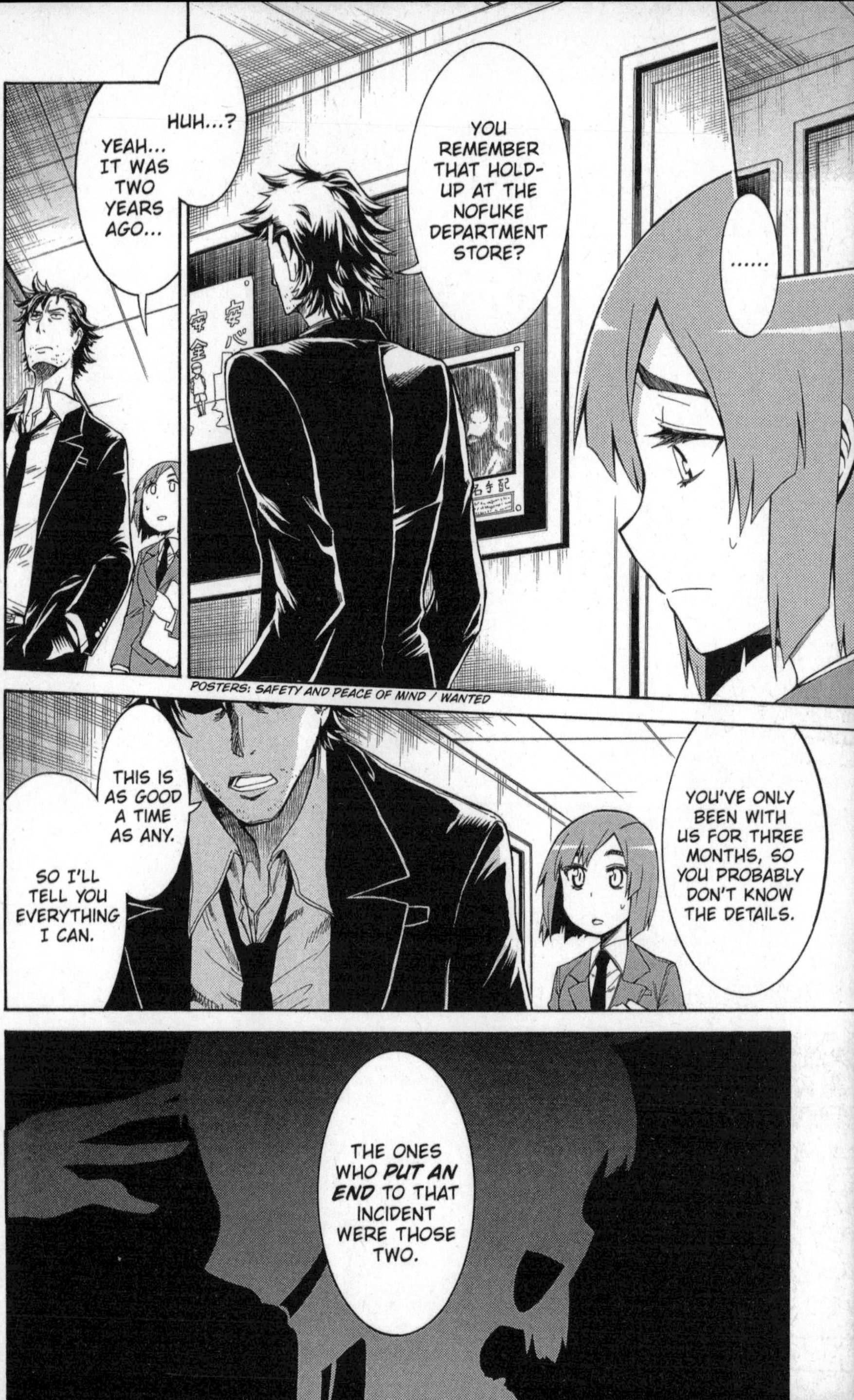
......
YOU REMEMBER THAT HOLD-UP AT THE NOFUKE DEPARTMENT STORE?
HUH...? YEAH... IT WAS TWO YEARS AGO...
POSTERS: SAFETY AND PEACE OF MIND / WANTED
YOU'VE ONLY BEEN WITH US FOR THREE MONTHS, SO YOU PROBABLY DON'T KNOW THE DETAILS.
THIS IS AS GOOD A TIME AS ANY.
SO I'LL TELL YOU EVERYTHING I CAN.
THE ONES WHO ***PUT AN END*** TO THAT INCIDENT WERE THOSE TWO.

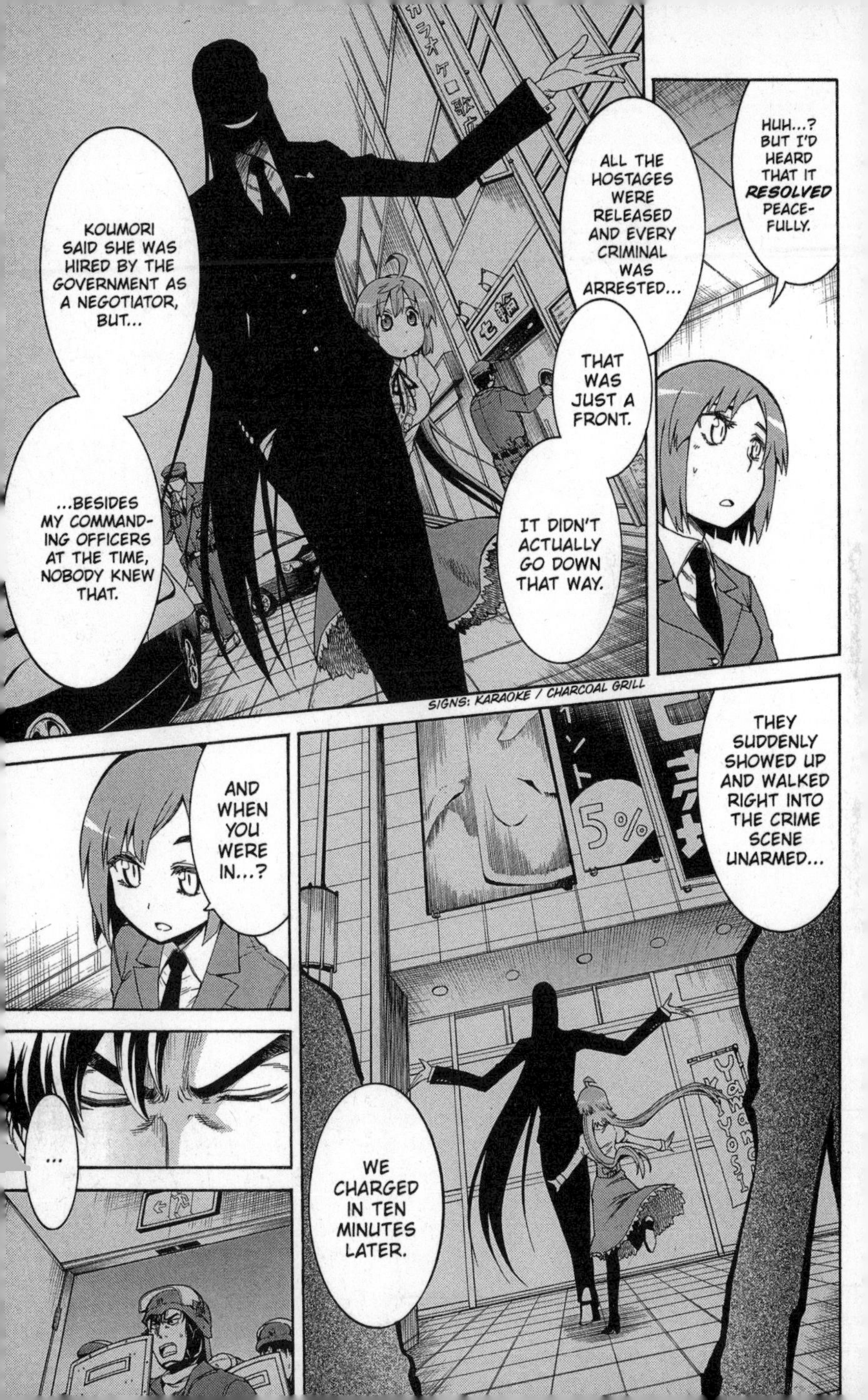
HUH...? BUT I'D HEARD THAT IT **RESOLVED** PEACE-FULLY.
ALL THE HOSTAGES WERE RELEASED AND EVERY CRIMINAL WAS ARRESTED...
THAT WAS JUST A FRONT.
IT DIDN'T ACTUALLY GO DOWN THAT WAY.
KOUMORI SAID SHE WAS HIRED BY THE GOVERNMENT AS A NEGOTIATOR, BUT...
...BESIDES MY COMMAND-ING OFFICERS AT THE TIME, NOBODY KNEW THAT.
SIGNS: KARAOKE / CHARCOAL GRILL
THEY SUDDENLY SHOWED UP AND WALKED RIGHT INTO THE CRIME SCENE UNARMED...
WE CHARGED IN TEN MINUTES LATER.
AND WHEN YOU WERE IN...?
...

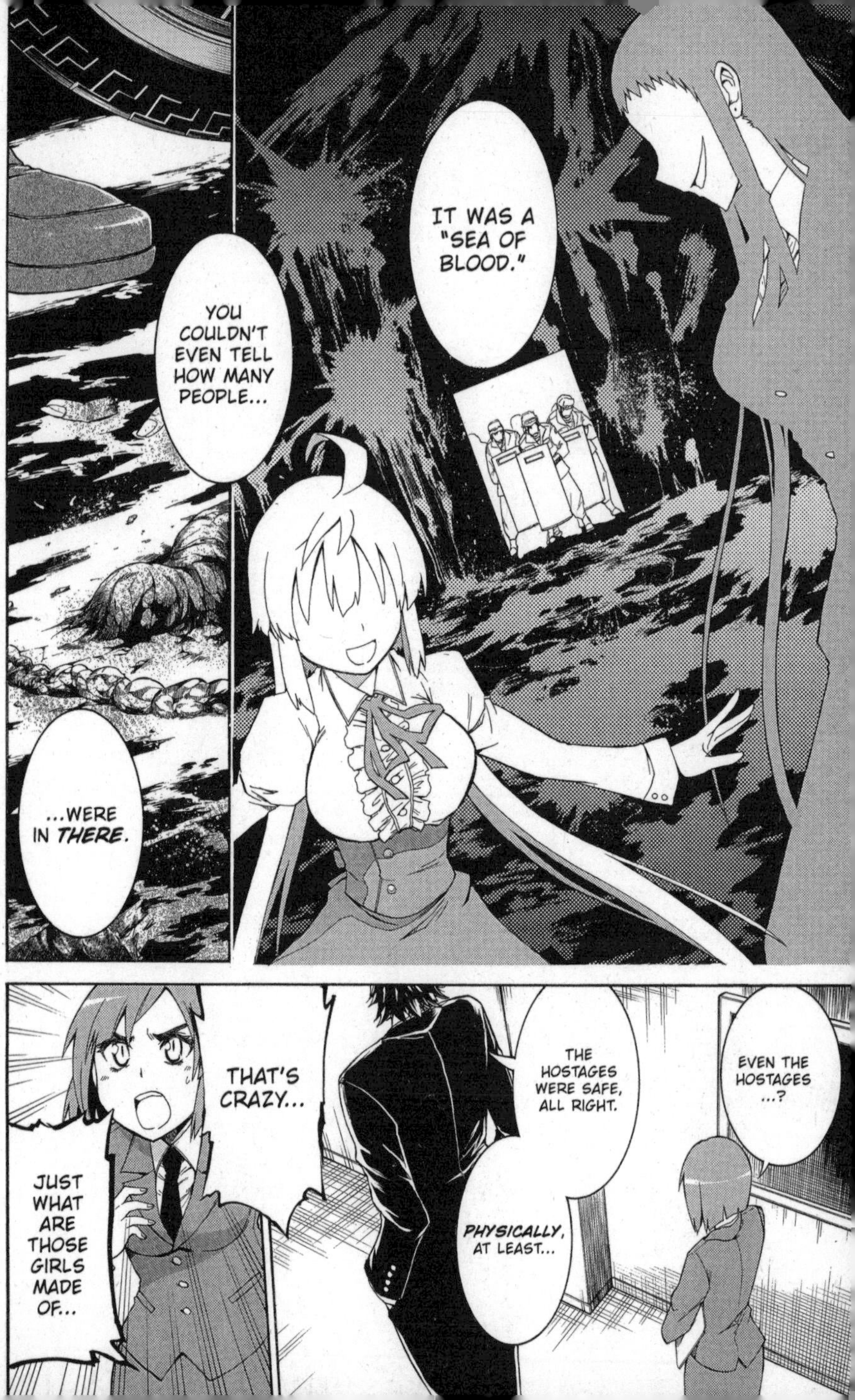
IT WAS A "SEA OF BLOOD."
YOU COULDN'T EVEN TELL HOW MANY PEOPLE...
...WERE IN *THERE*.
EVEN THE HOSTAGES ...?
THE HOSTAGES WERE SAFE, ALL RIGHT.
PHYSICALLY, AT LEAST...
THAT'S CRAZY...
JUST WHAT ARE THOSE GIRLS MADE OF...

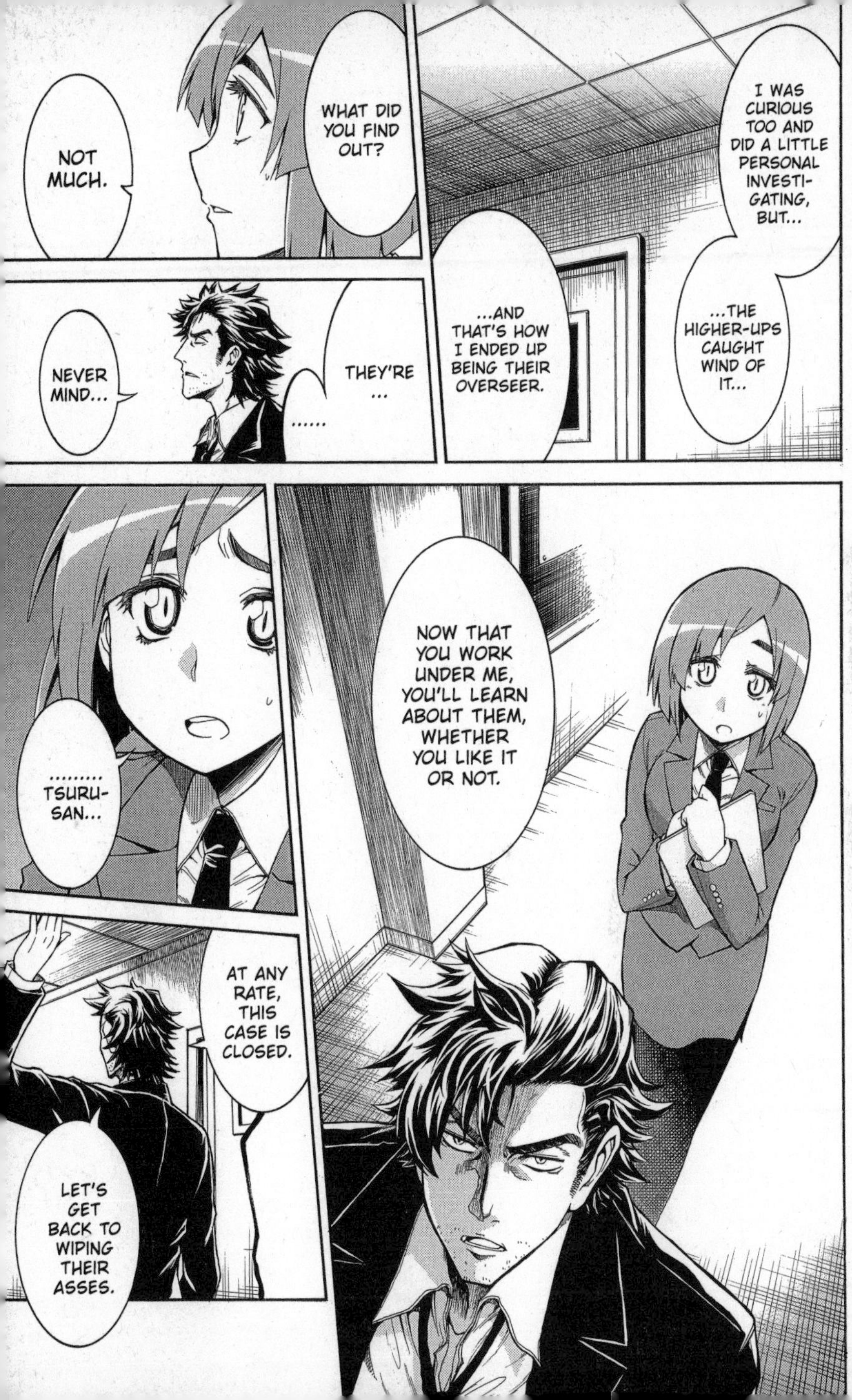
I WAS CURIOUS TOO AND DID A LITTLE PERSONAL INVESTIGATING, BUT...
...THE HIGHER-UPS CAUGHT WIND OF IT...
...AND THAT'S HOW I ENDED UP BEING THEIR OVERSEER.
WHAT DID YOU FIND OUT?
NOT MUCH.
THEY'RE ...
......
NEVER MIND...
NOW THAT YOU WORK UNDER ME, YOU'LL LEARN ABOUT THEM, WHETHER YOU LIKE IT OR NOT.
.... TSURU-SAN...
AT ANY RATE, THIS CASE IS CLOSED.
LET'S GET BACK TO WIPING THEIR ASSES.

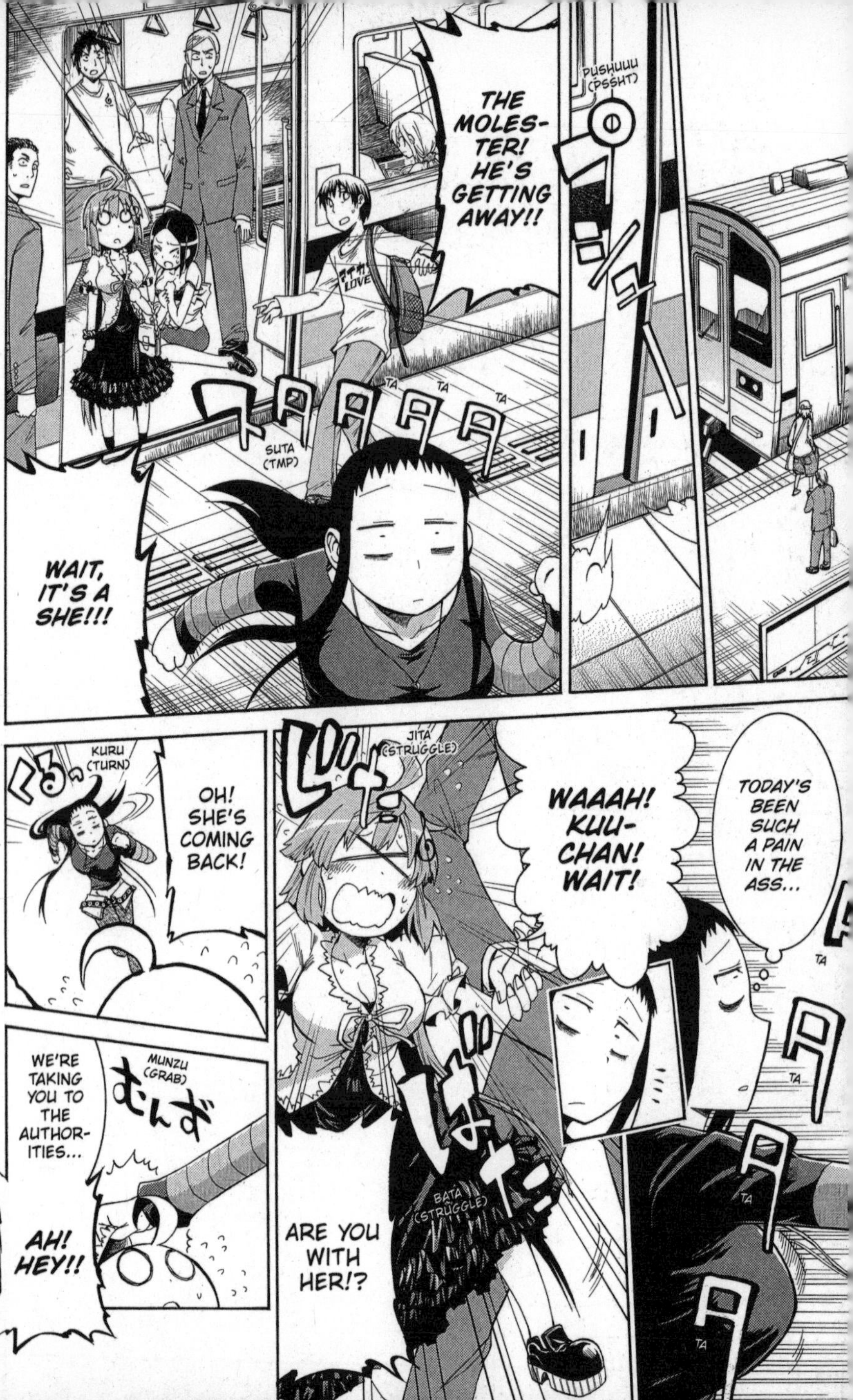
PUSHUUU (PSSHT)
THE MOLES-TER! HE'S GETTING AWAY!!
TA TA TA
SUTA (TMP)
WAIT, IT'S A SHE!!!
TODAY'S BEEN SUCH A PAIN IN THE ASS...
TA TA TA TA
JITA (STRUGGLE)
WAAAH! KUU-CHAN! WAIT!
BATA (STRUGGLE)
ARE YOU WITH HER!?
KURU (TURN)
OH! SHE'S COMING BACK!
MUNZU (GRAB)
WE'RE TAKING YOU TO THE AUTHOR-ITIES...
AH! HEY!!

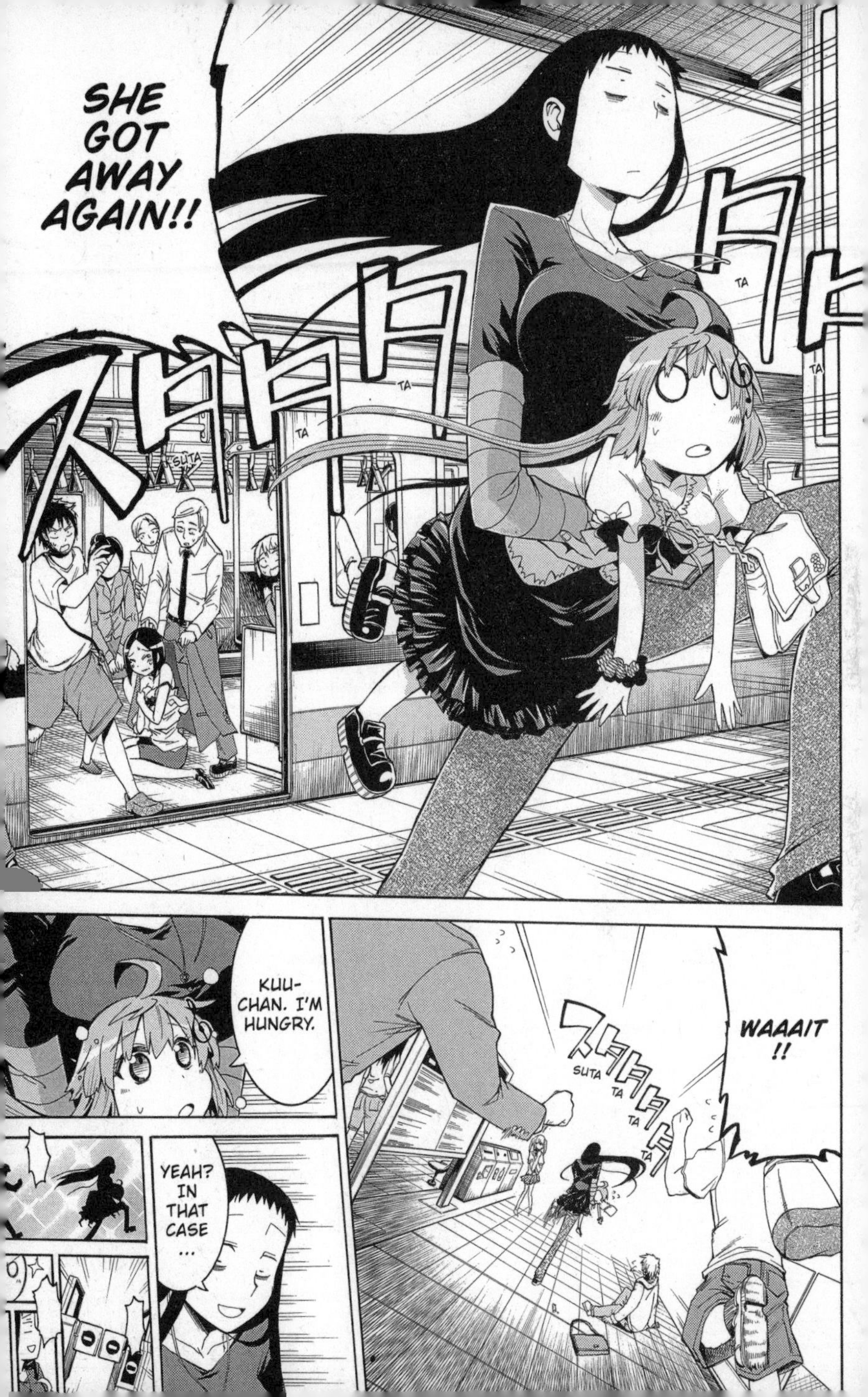
TA
TA
TA
TA
SUTA
SHE GOT AWAY AGAIN!!
WAAAIT !!
SUTA
TA
TA
TA
KUU-CHAN. I'M HUNGRY.
YEAH? IN THAT CASE ...

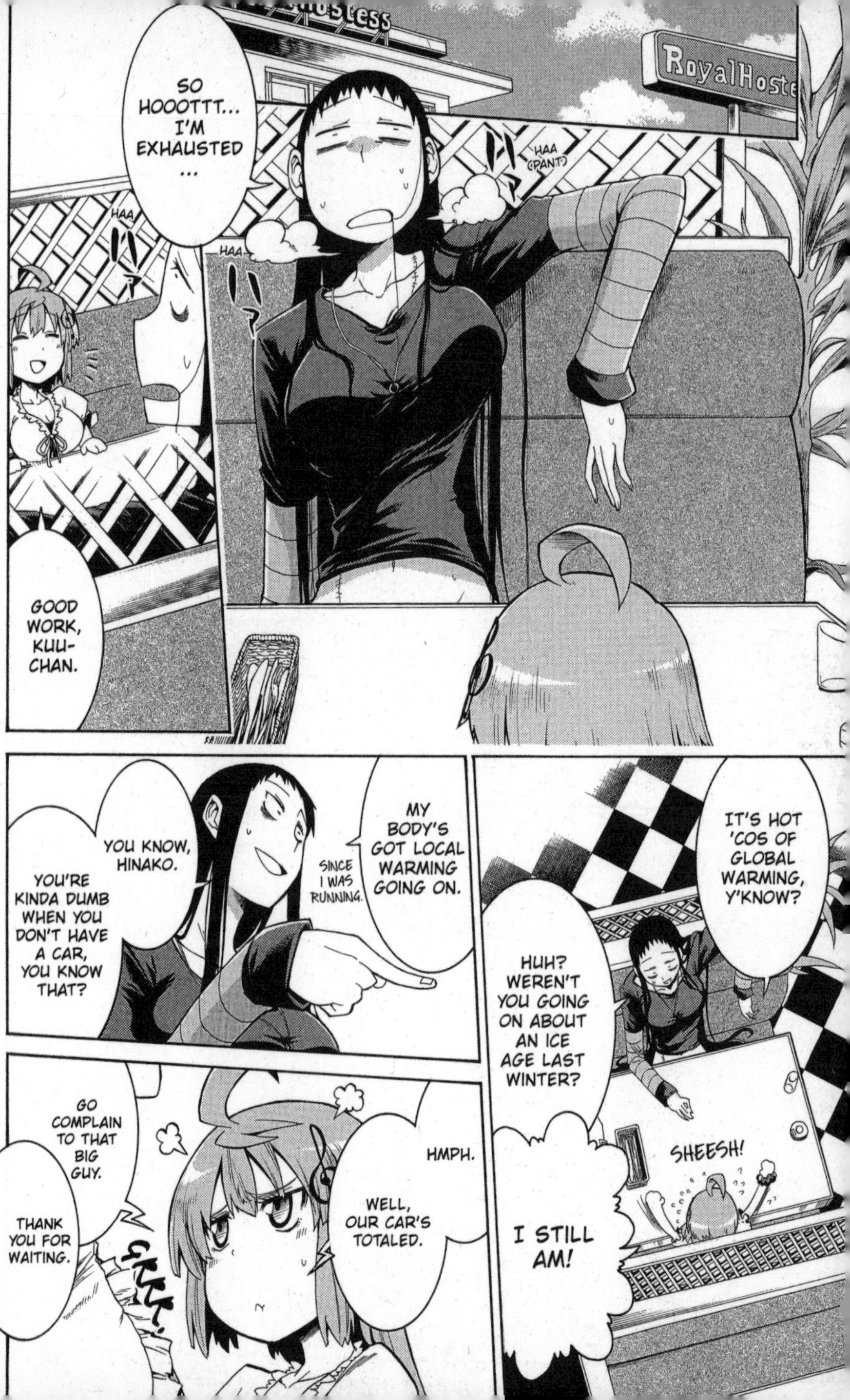
RoyalHoste
HAA (PANT)
SO HOOOTTT... I'M EXHAUSTED ...
HAA
HAA
GOOD WORK, KUU-CHAN.
IT'S HOT 'COS OF GLOBAL WARMING, Y'KNOW?
HUH? WEREN'T YOU GOING ON ABOUT AN ICE AGE LAST WINTER?
SHEESH!
I STILL AM!
MY BODY'S GOT LOCAL WARMING GOING ON.
SINCE I WAS RUNNING.
YOU KNOW, HINAKO.
YOU'RE KINDA DUMB WHEN YOU DON'T HAVE A CAR, YOU KNOW THAT?
HMPH.
WELL, OUR CAR'S TOTALED.
GO COMPLAIN TO THAT BIG GUY.
GRKK!
THANK YOU FOR WAITING.

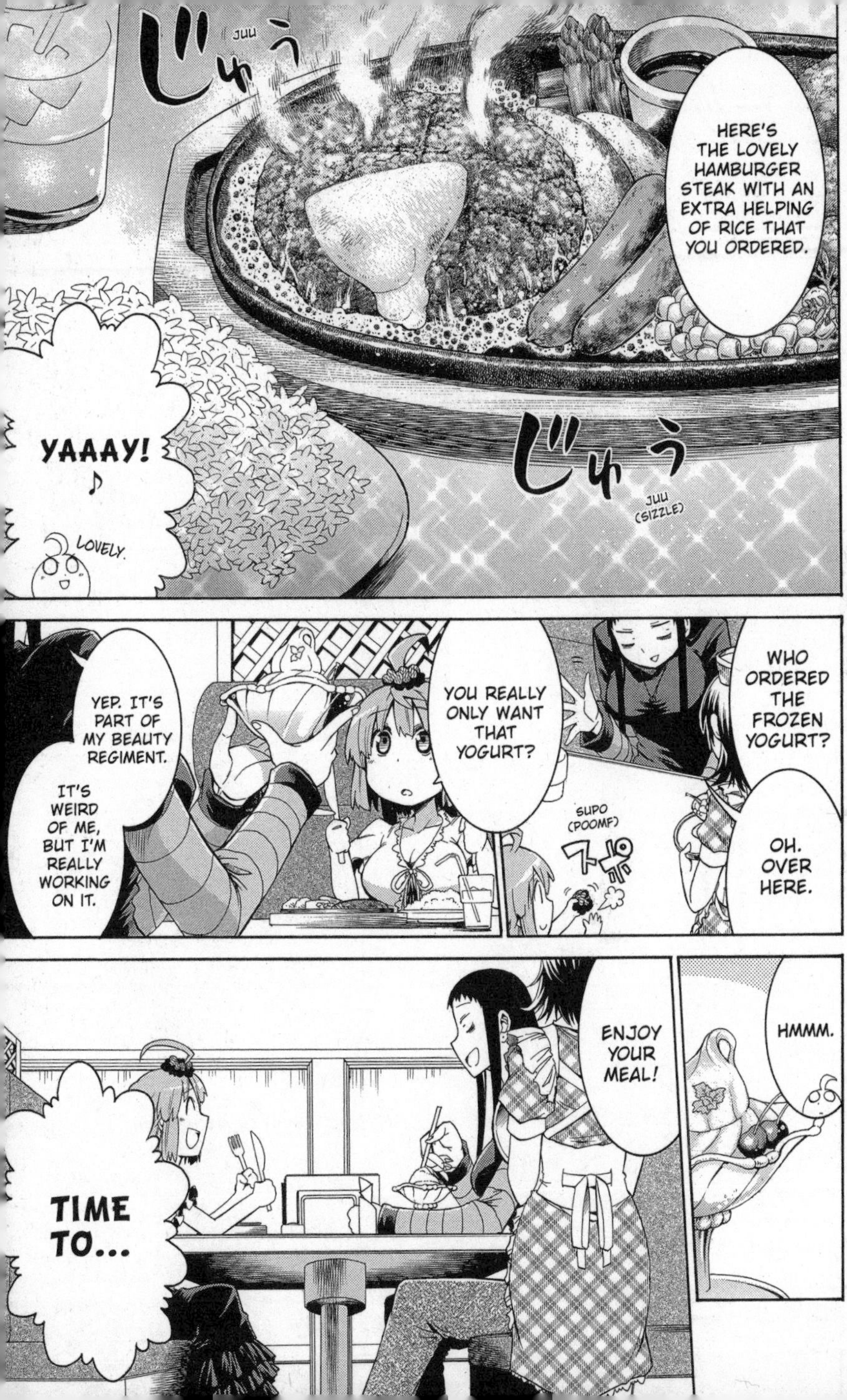
HERE'S THE LOVELY HAMBURGER STEAK WITH AN EXTRA HELPING OF RICE THAT YOU ORDERED.
じゅう
JUU
じゅう
JUU (SIZZLE)
YAAAY! ♪
LOVELY.
WHO ORDERED THE FROZEN YOGURT?
OH. OVER HERE.
スポ
SUPO (POOMF)
YOU REALLY ONLY WANT THAT YOGURT?
YEP. IT'S PART OF MY BEAUTY REGIMENT.
IT'S WEIRD OF ME, BUT I'M REALLY WORKING ON IT.
HMMM.
ENJOY YOUR MEAL!
TIME TO...

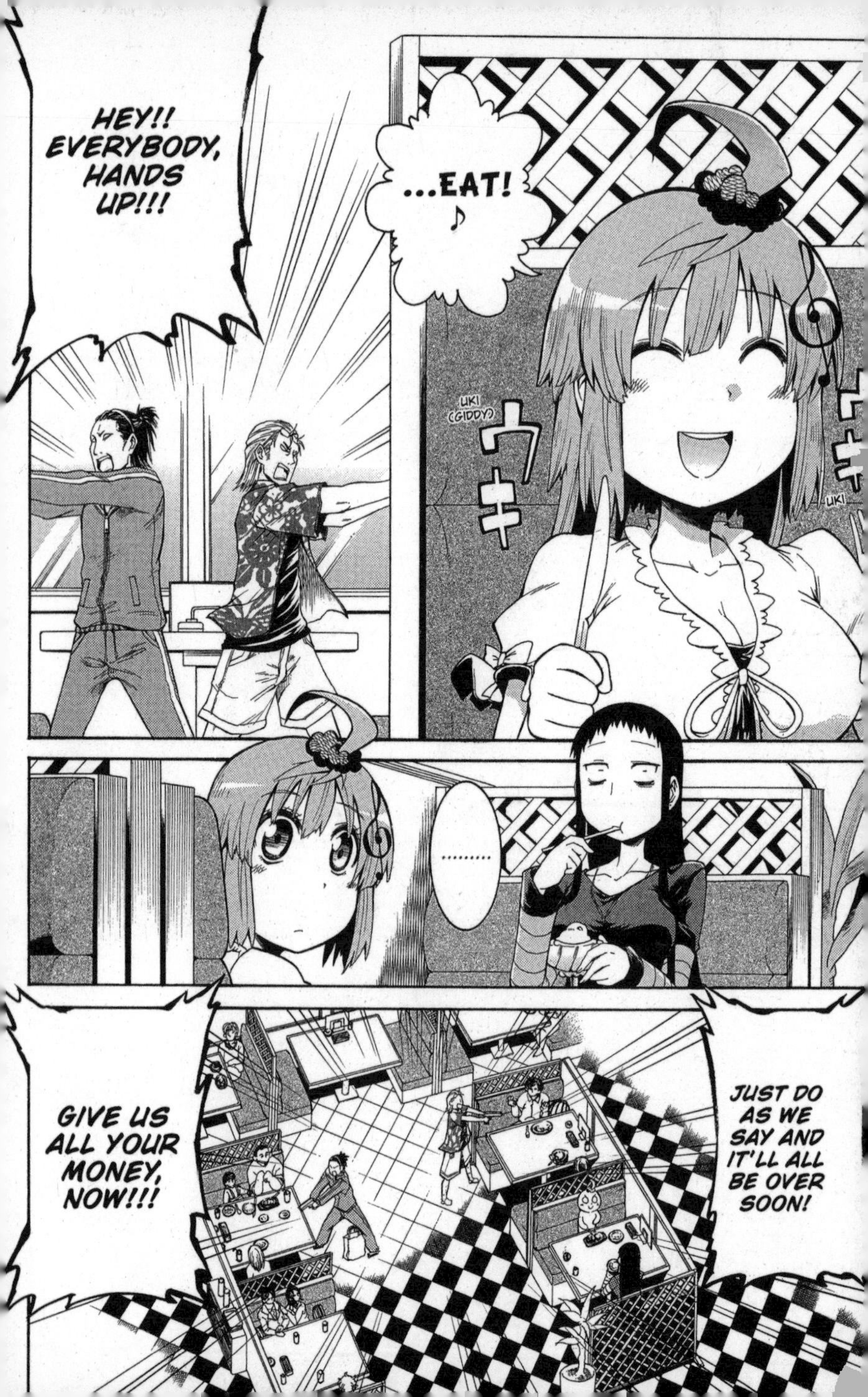
...EAT! ♪
UKI (GIDDY)
ウキ
UKI
HEY!! EVERYBODY, HANDS UP!!!
....
JUST DO AS WE SAY AND IT'LL ALL BE OVER SOON!
GIVE US ALL YOUR MONEY, NOW!!!

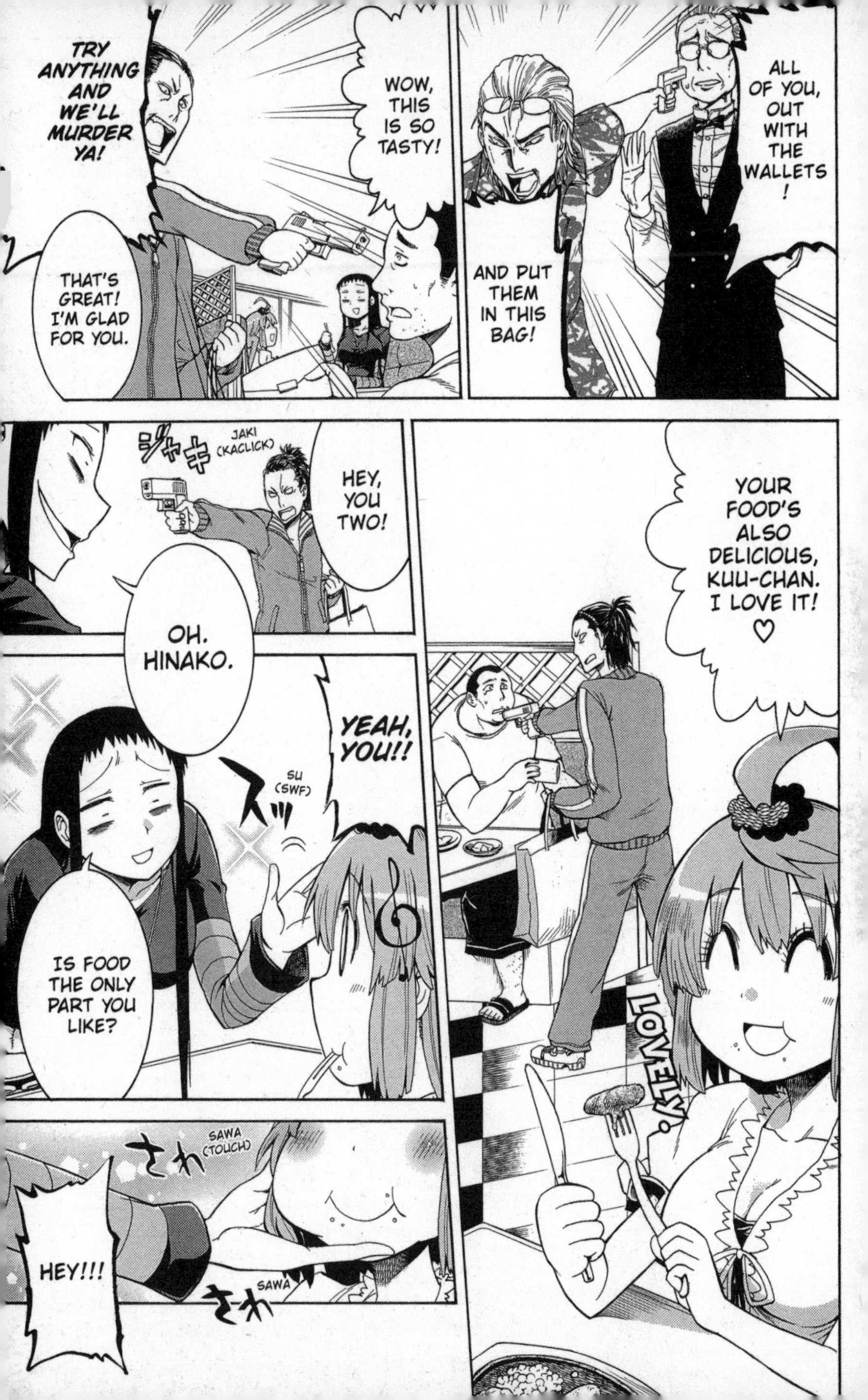
ALL OF YOU, OUT WITH THE WALLETS!
AND PUT THEM IN THIS BAG!
WOW, THIS IS SO TASTY!
TRY ANYTHING AND WE'LL MURDER YA!
THAT'S GREAT! I'M GLAD FOR YOU.
YOUR FOOD'S ALSO DELICIOUS, KUU-CHAN. I LOVE IT! ♡
LOVELY.
HEY, YOU TWO!
JAKI (KACLICK)
OH. HINAKO.
YEAH, YOU!!
SU (SWF)
IS FOOD THE ONLY PART YOU LIKE?
SAWA (TOUCH)
HEY!!!
SAWA

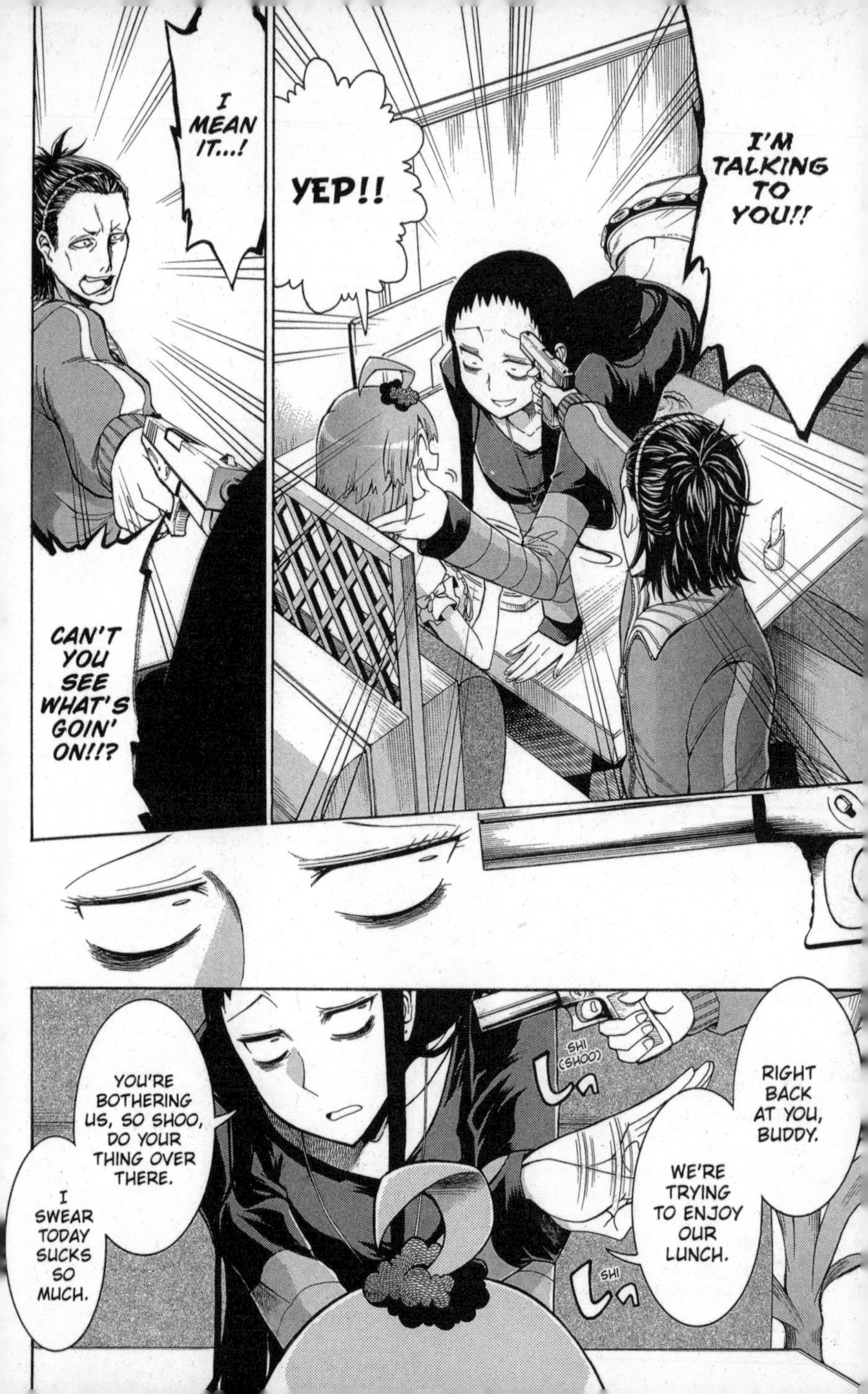
I'M TALKING TO YOU!!
YEP!!
I MEAN IT...!
CAN'T YOU SEE WHAT'S GOIN' ON!!?
RIGHT BACK AT YOU, BUDDY.
WE'RE TRYING TO ENJOY OUR LUNCH.
SHI (SHOO)
SHI
YOU'RE BOTHERING US, SO SHOO, DO YOUR THING OVER THERE.
I SWEAR TODAY SUCKS SO MUCH.

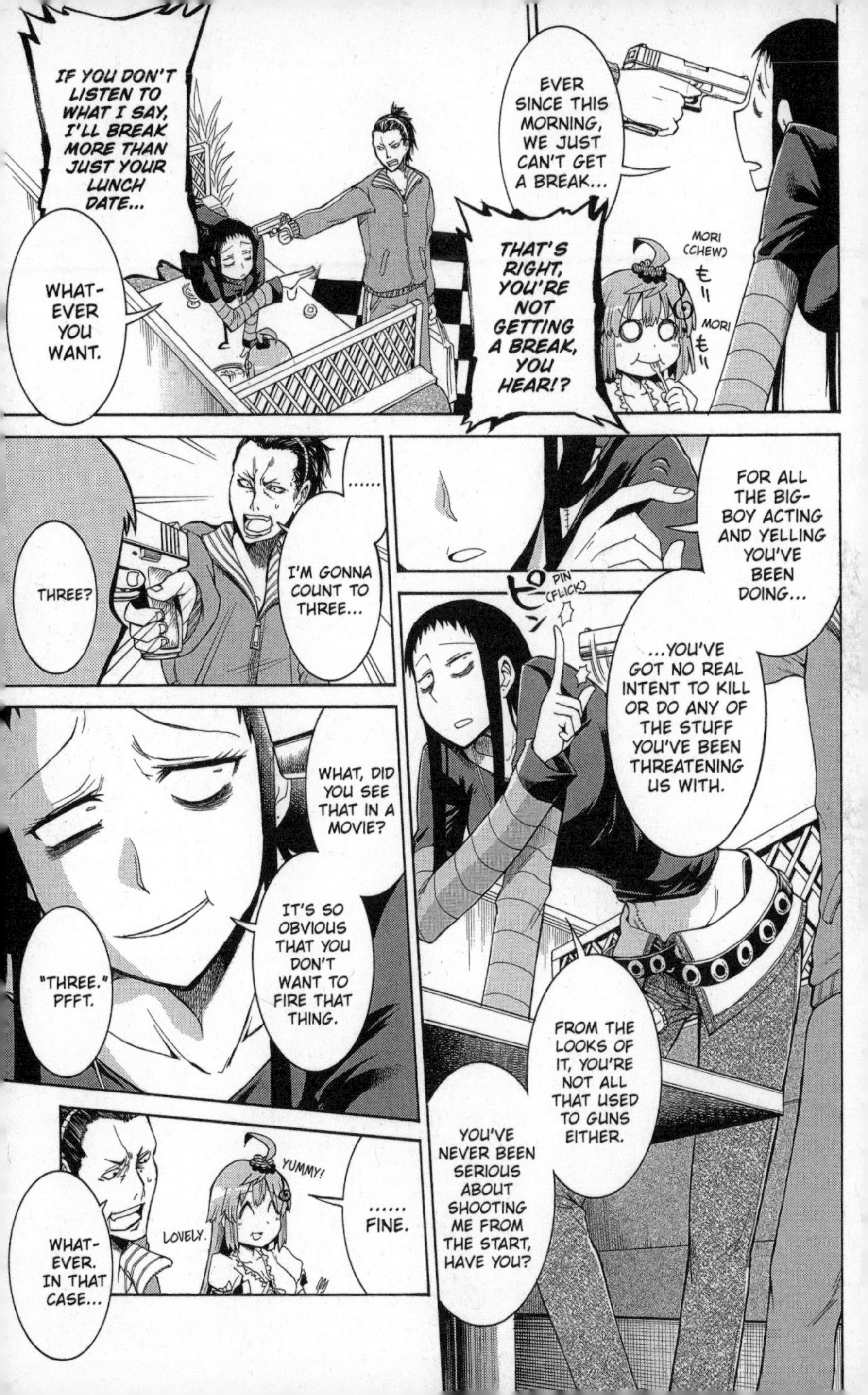
EVER SINCE THIS MORNING, WE JUST CAN'T GET A BREAK...
MORI (CHEW) もり
MORI もり
THAT'S RIGHT, YOU'RE NOT GETTING A BREAK, YOU HEAR!?
IF YOU DON'T LISTEN TO WHAT I SAY, I'LL BREAK MORE THAN JUST YOUR LUNCH DATE...
WHATEVER YOU WANT.
FOR ALL THE BIG-BOY ACTING AND YELLING YOU'VE BEEN DOING...
PIN (FLICK)
...YOU'VE GOT NO REAL INTENT TO KILL OR DO ANY OF THE STUFF YOU'VE BEEN THREATENING US WITH.
FROM THE LOOKS OF IT, YOU'RE NOT ALL THAT USED TO GUNS EITHER.
YOU'VE NEVER BEEN SERIOUS ABOUT SHOOTING ME FROM THE START, HAVE YOU?
......
I'M GONNA COUNT TO THREE...
THREE?
WHAT, DID YOU SEE THAT IN A MOVIE?
IT'S SO OBVIOUS THAT YOU DON'T WANT TO FIRE THAT THING.
"THREE." PFFT.
...... FINE.
YUMMY!
LOVELY.
WHATEVER. IN THAT CASE...

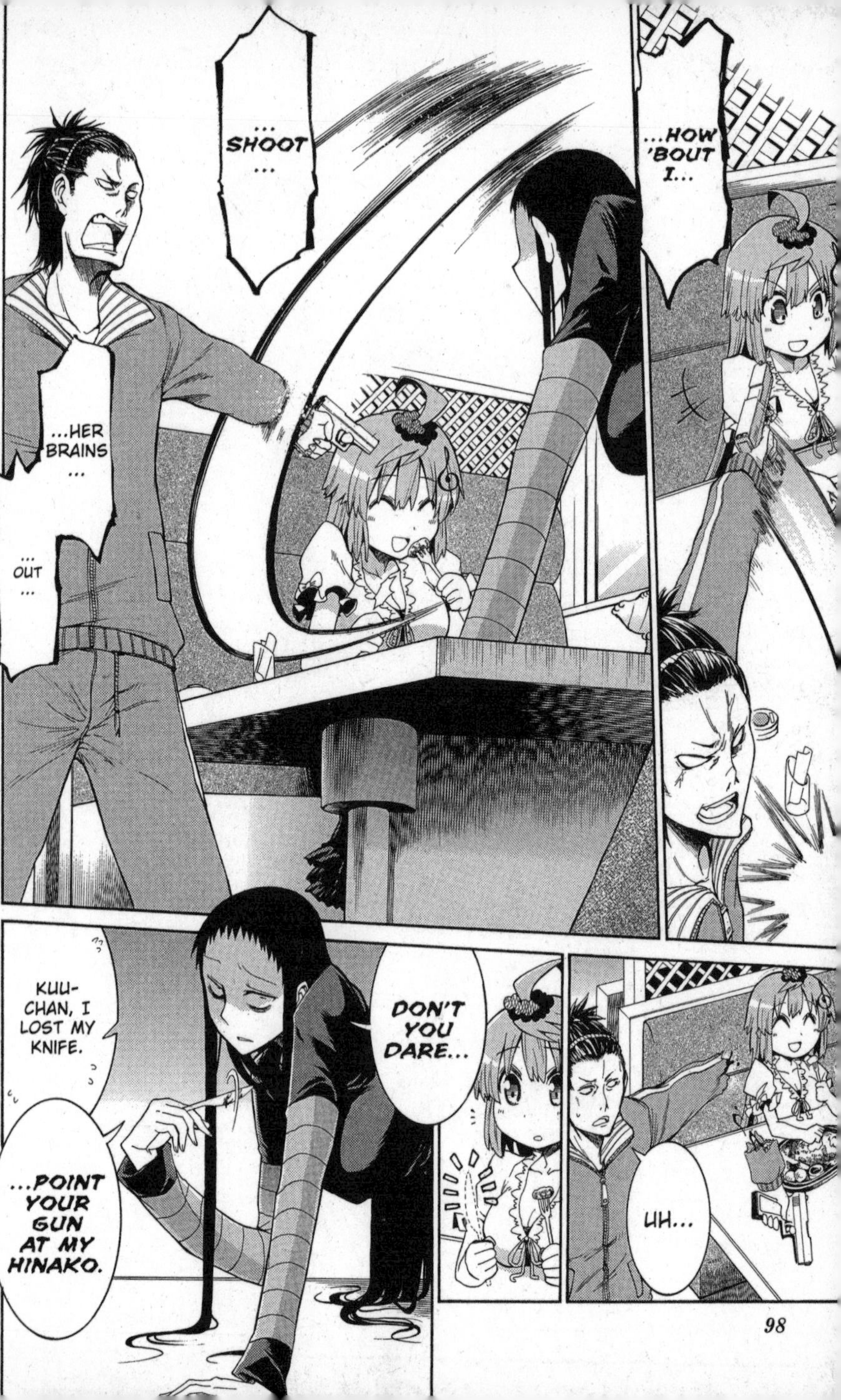

...HOW 'BOUT I...
...SHOOT...
...HER BRAINS...
...OUT...
UH...
DON'T YOU DARE...
KUU-CHAN, I LOST MY KNIFE.
...POINT YOUR GUN AT MY HINAKO.

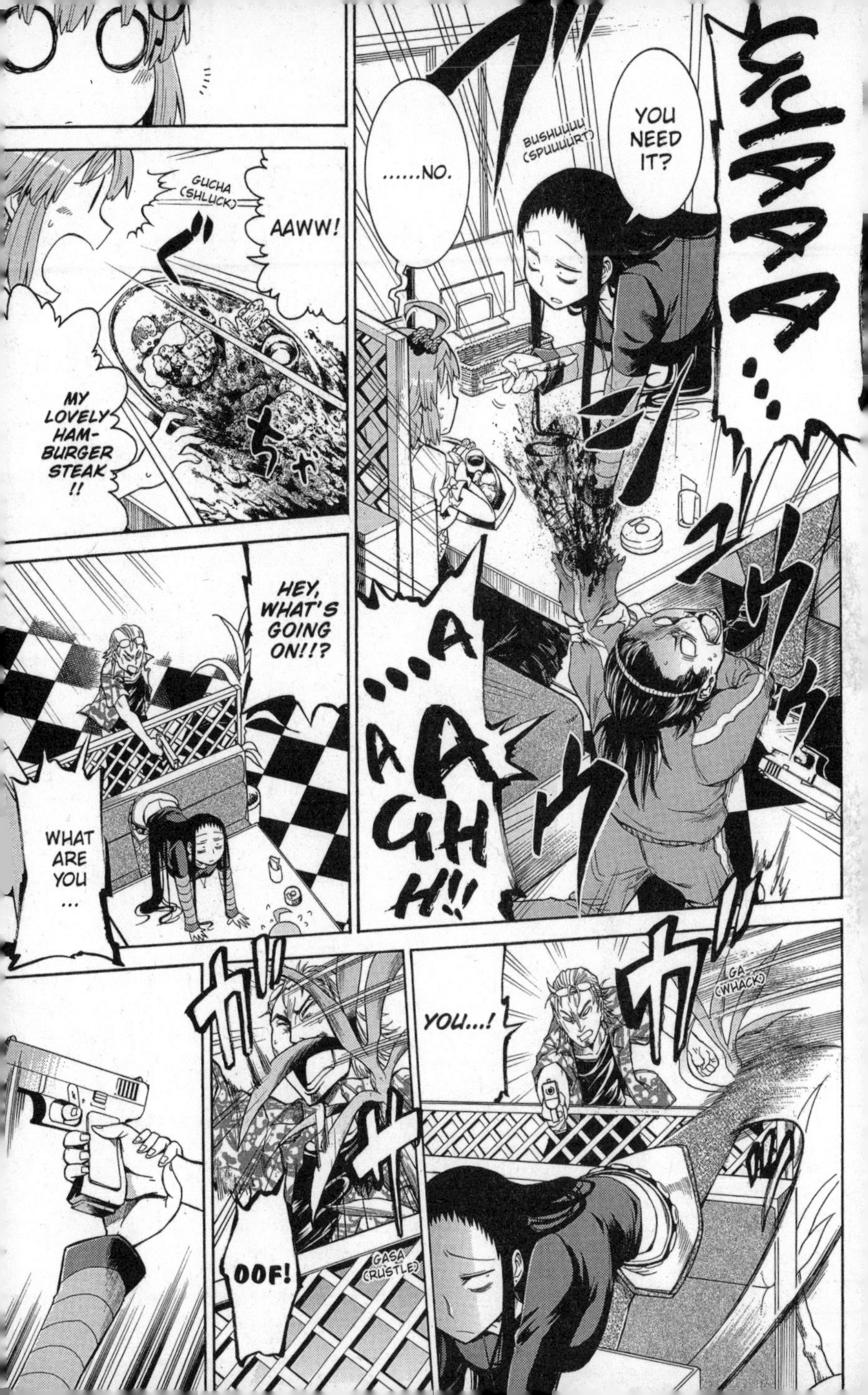

KYAAAA...
YOU NEED IT?
BUSHUUUU (SPUUUURT)
......NO.
...A AAGHH!!
GUCHA (SHLUCK)
AAWW!
MY LOVELY HAM-BURGER STEAK !!
HEY, WHAT'S GOING ON!!?
WHAT ARE YOU ...
GA (WHACK)
YOU...!
OOF!
GASA (RUSTLE)

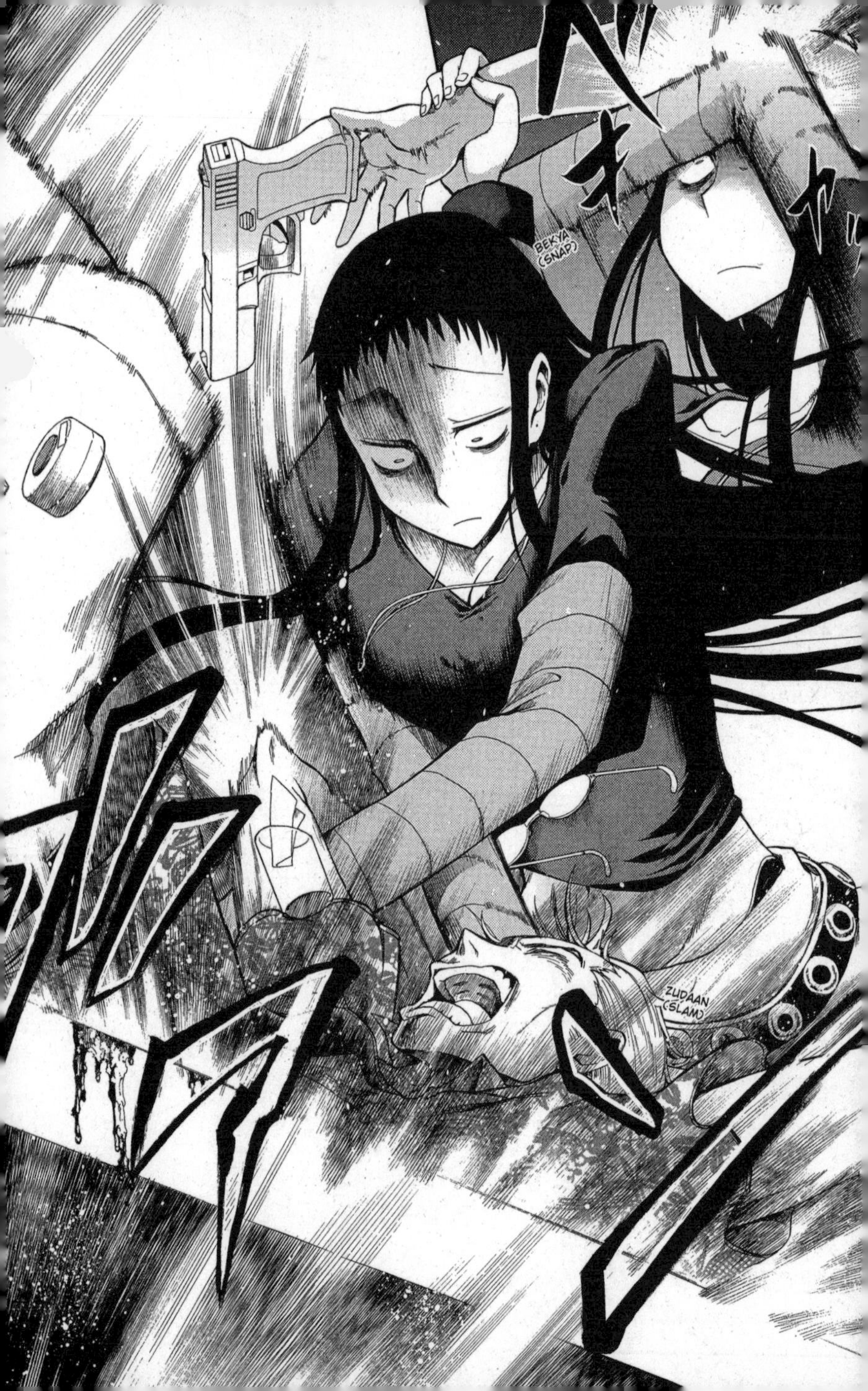
BEKYA (SNAP)
ZUDAAN (SLAM)

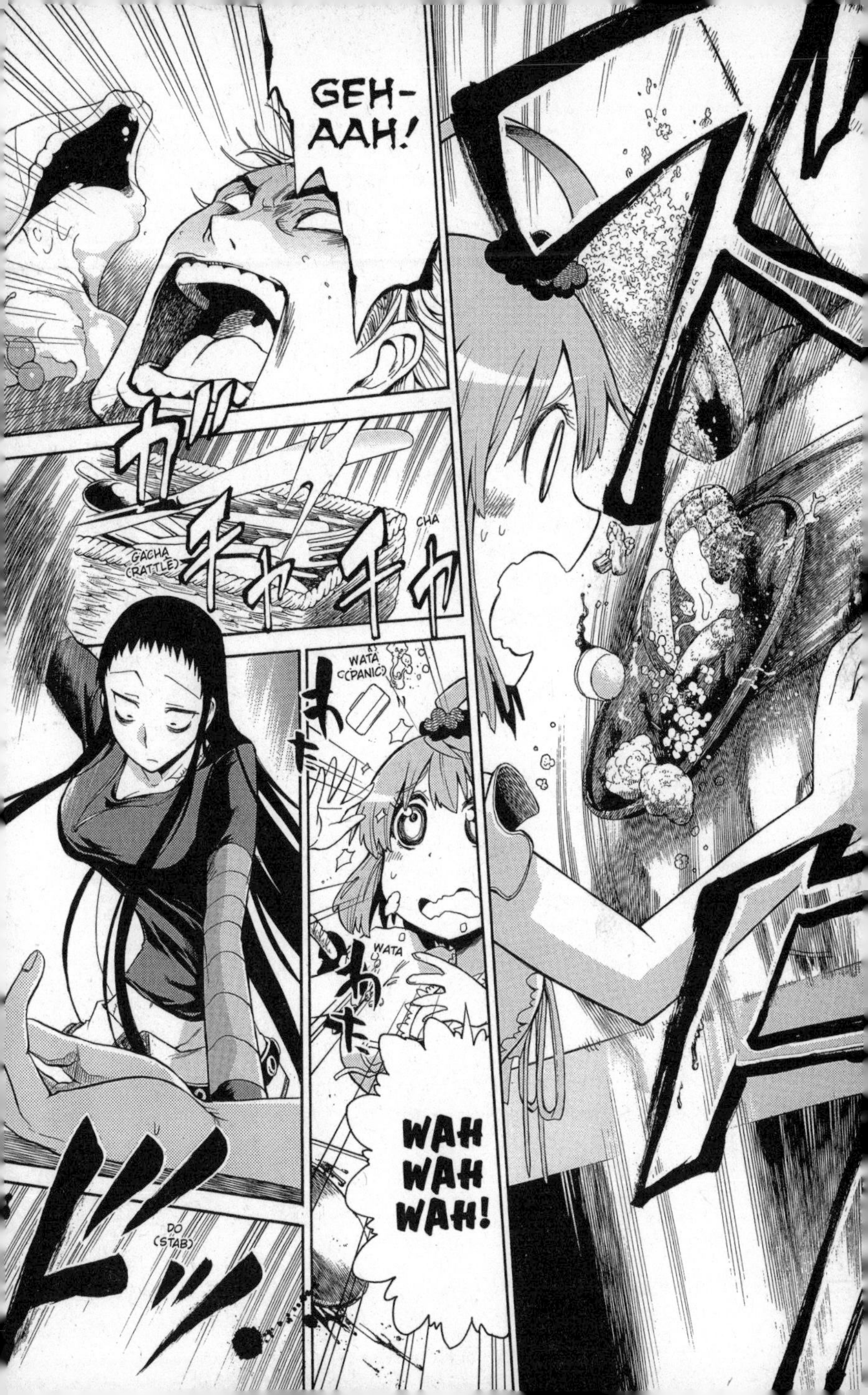
GEH-AAH!
GACHA (RATTLE)
CHA
WATA (PANIC)
WATA
WAH WAH WAH!
DO (STAB)

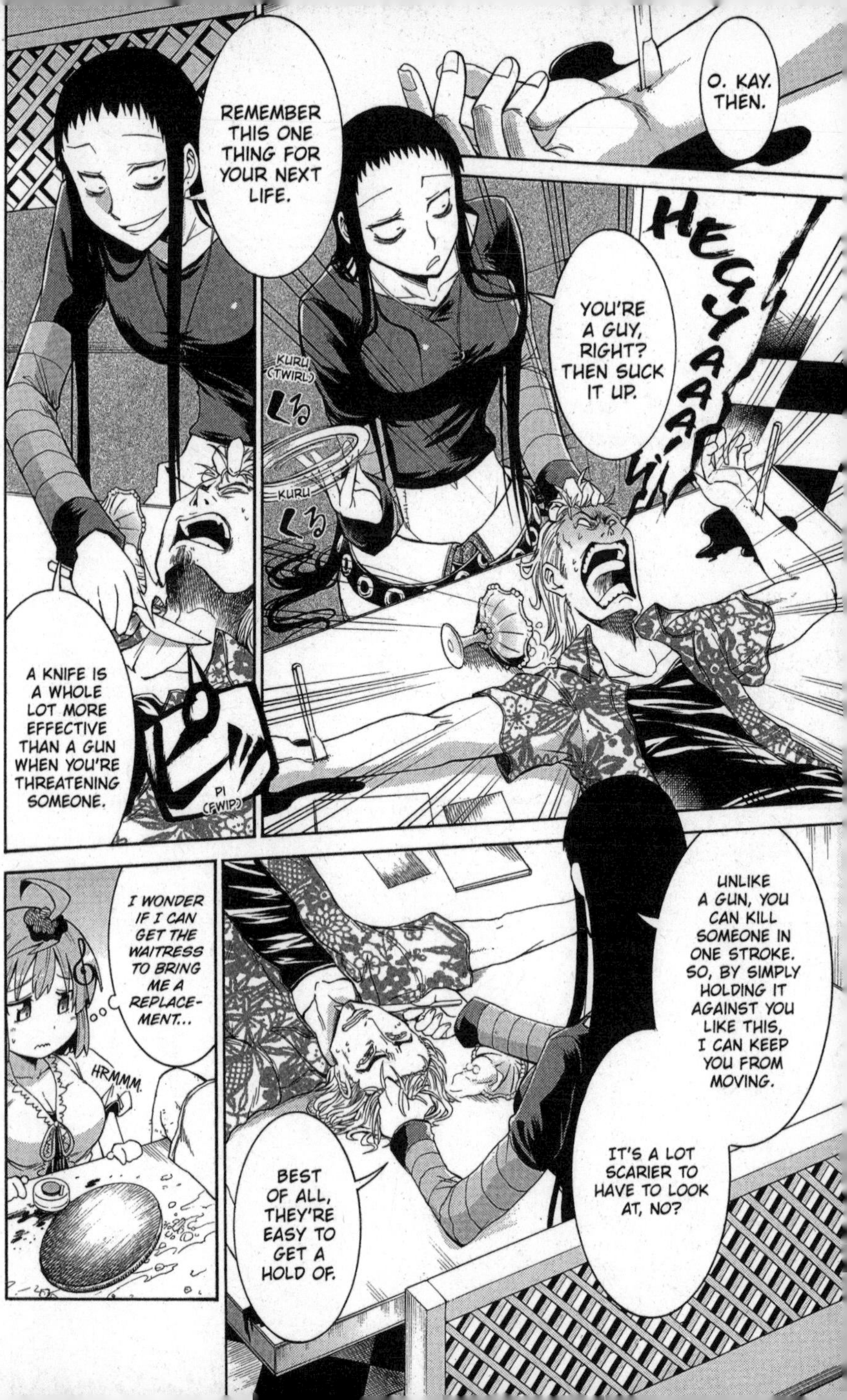
O. KAY. THEN.
HEGYAAAA-!!
YOU'RE A GUY, RIGHT? THEN SUCK IT UP.
KURU (TWIRL)
KURU
REMEMBER THIS ONE THING FOR YOUR NEXT LIFE.
A KNIFE IS A WHOLE LOT MORE EFFECTIVE THAN A GUN WHEN YOU'RE THREATENING SOMEONE.
PI (FWIP)
UNLIKE A GUN, YOU CAN KILL SOMEONE IN ONE STROKE. SO, BY SIMPLY HOLDING IT AGAINST YOU LIKE THIS, I CAN KEEP YOU FROM MOVING.
IT'S A LOT SCARIER TO HAVE TO LOOK AT, NO?
BEST OF ALL, THEY'RE EASY TO GET A HOLD OF.
I WONDER IF I CAN GET THE WAITRESS TO BRING ME A REPLACEMENT...
HRMMM.

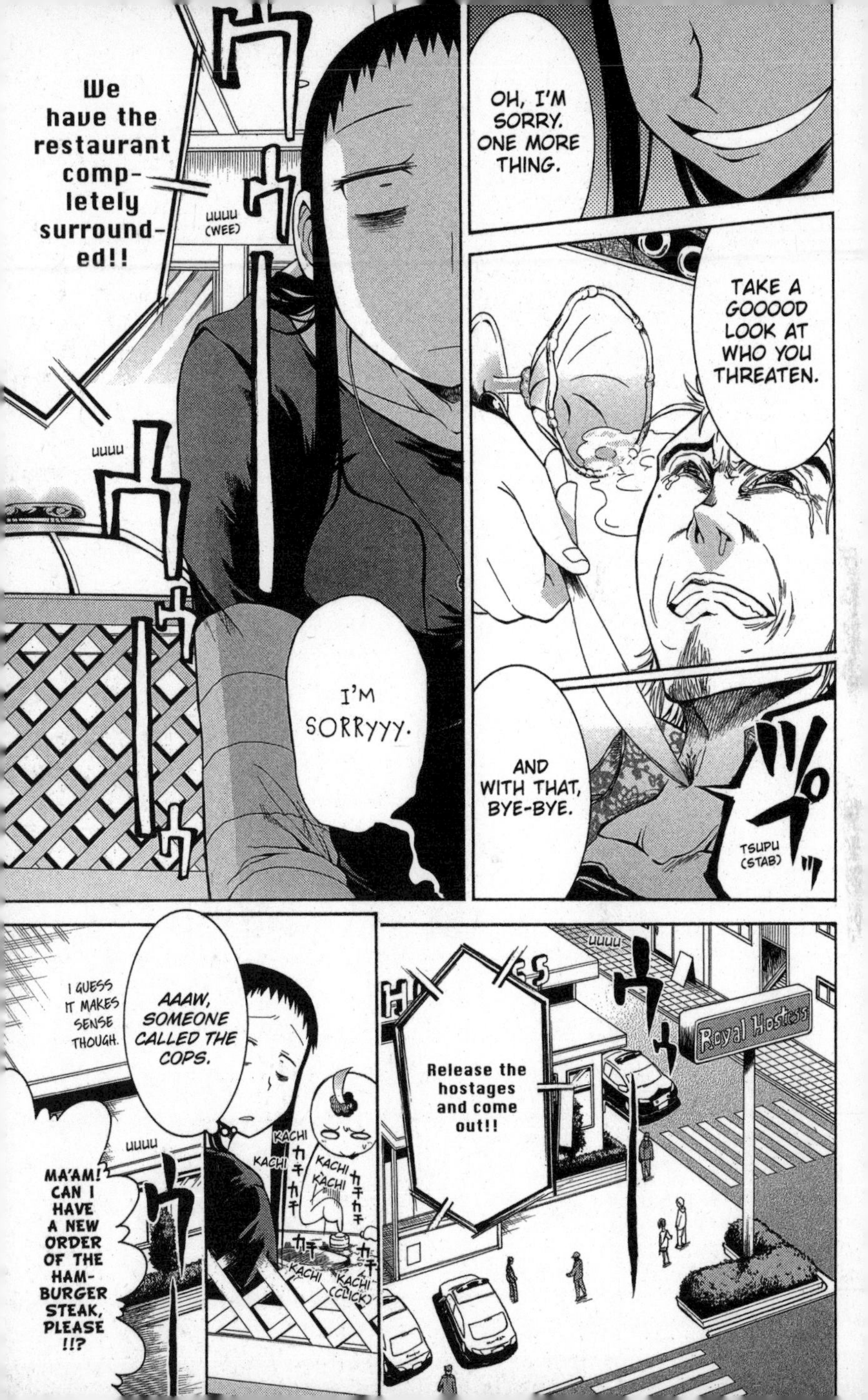
OH, I'M SORRY. ONE MORE THING.
TAKE A GOOOOD LOOK AT WHO YOU THREATEN.
AND WITH THAT, BYE-BYE.
TSUPU (STAB)
We have the restaurant comp-letely surround-ed!!
UUUU (WEE)
UUUU
I'M SORRYYY.
UUUU
Release the hostages and come out!!
Royal Hostess
AAAW, SOMEONE CALLED THE COPS.
I GUESS IT MAKES SENSE THOUGH.
KACHI KACHI KACHI KACHI
KACHI KACHI (CLICK)
UUUU
MA'AM! CAN I HAVE A NEW ORDER OF THE HAM-BURGER STEAK, PLEASE!!?

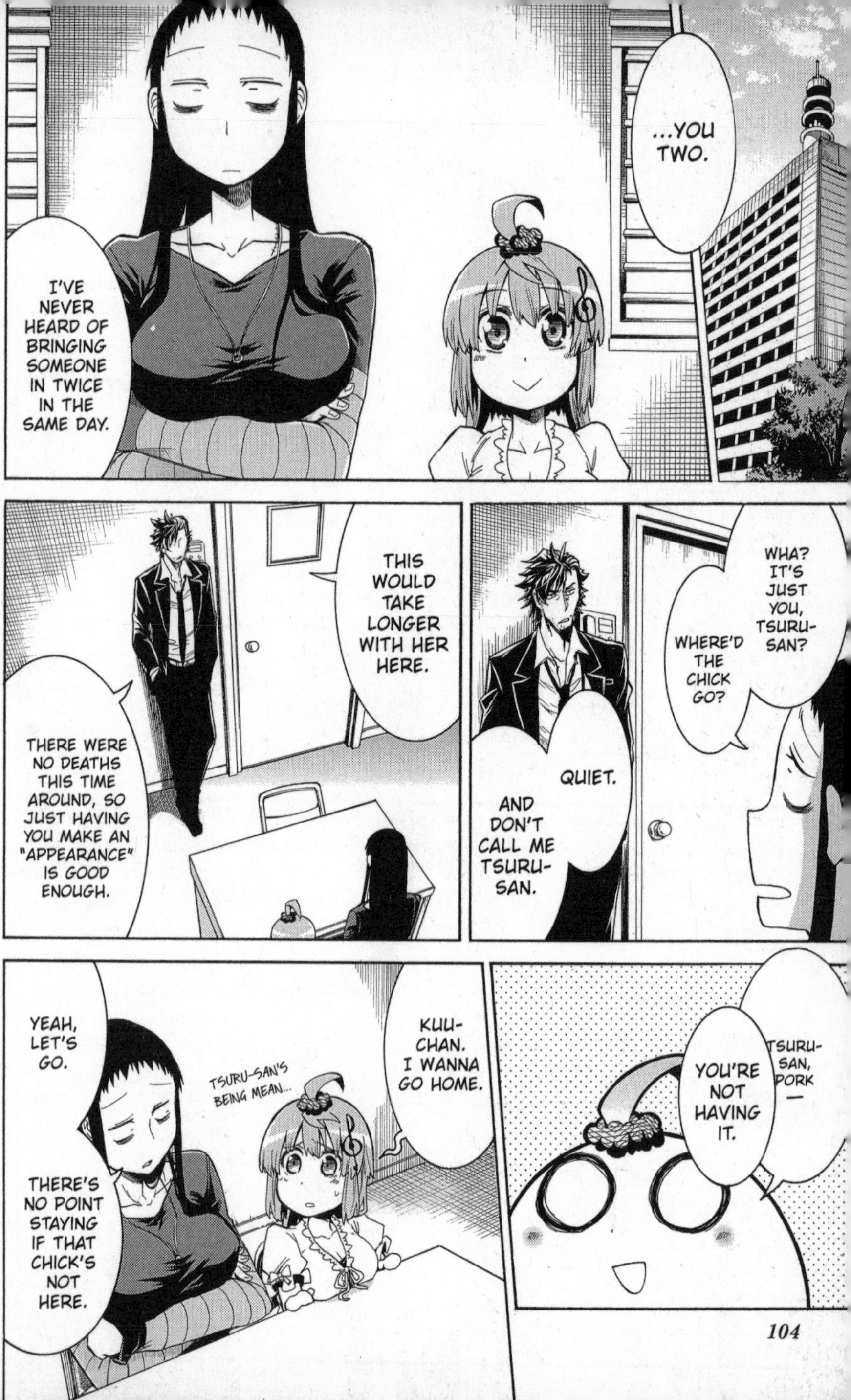
...YOU TWO.
I'VE NEVER HEARD OF BRINGING SOMEONE IN TWICE IN THE SAME DAY.
WHA? IT'S JUST YOU, TSURU-SAN?
WHERE'D THE CHICK GO?
QUIET.
AND DON'T CALL ME TSURU-SAN.
THIS WOULD TAKE LONGER WITH HER HERE.
THERE WERE NO DEATHS THIS TIME AROUND, SO JUST HAVING YOU MAKE AN "APPEARANCE" IS GOOD ENOUGH.
TSURU-SAN, PORK—
YOU'RE NOT HAVING IT.
KUU-CHAN. I WANNA GO HOME.
TSURU-SAN'S BEING MEAN...
YEAH, LET'S GO.
THERE'S NO POINT STAYING IF THAT CHICK'S NOT HERE.

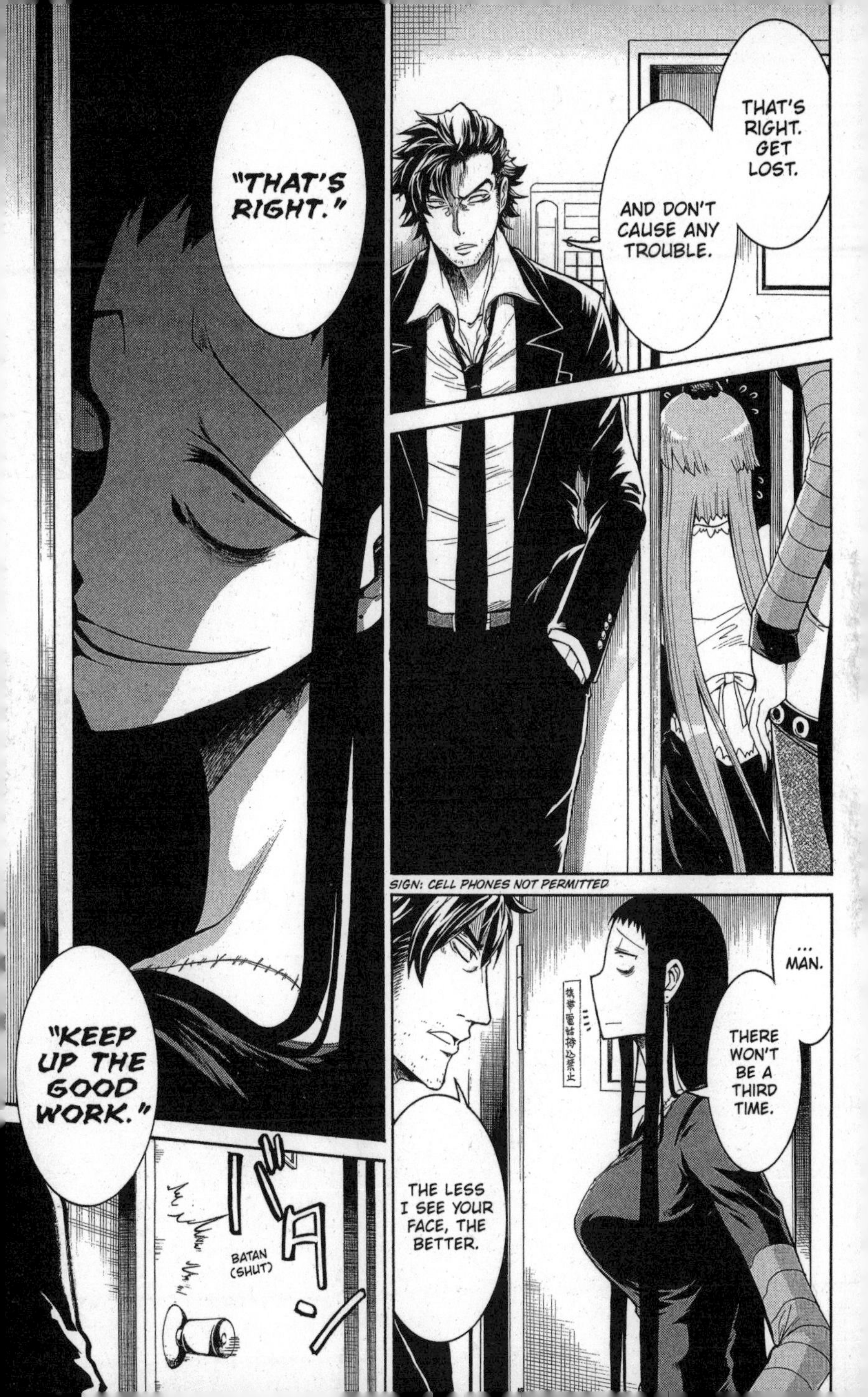
THAT'S RIGHT. GET LOST.
AND DON'T CAUSE ANY TROUBLE.
SIGN: CELL PHONES NOT PERMITTED
携帯電話持込禁止
...MAN.
THERE WON'T BE A THIRD TIME.
THE LESS I SEE YOUR FACE, THE BETTER.
"THAT'S RIGHT."
"KEEP UP THE GOOD WORK."
BATAN (SHUT)

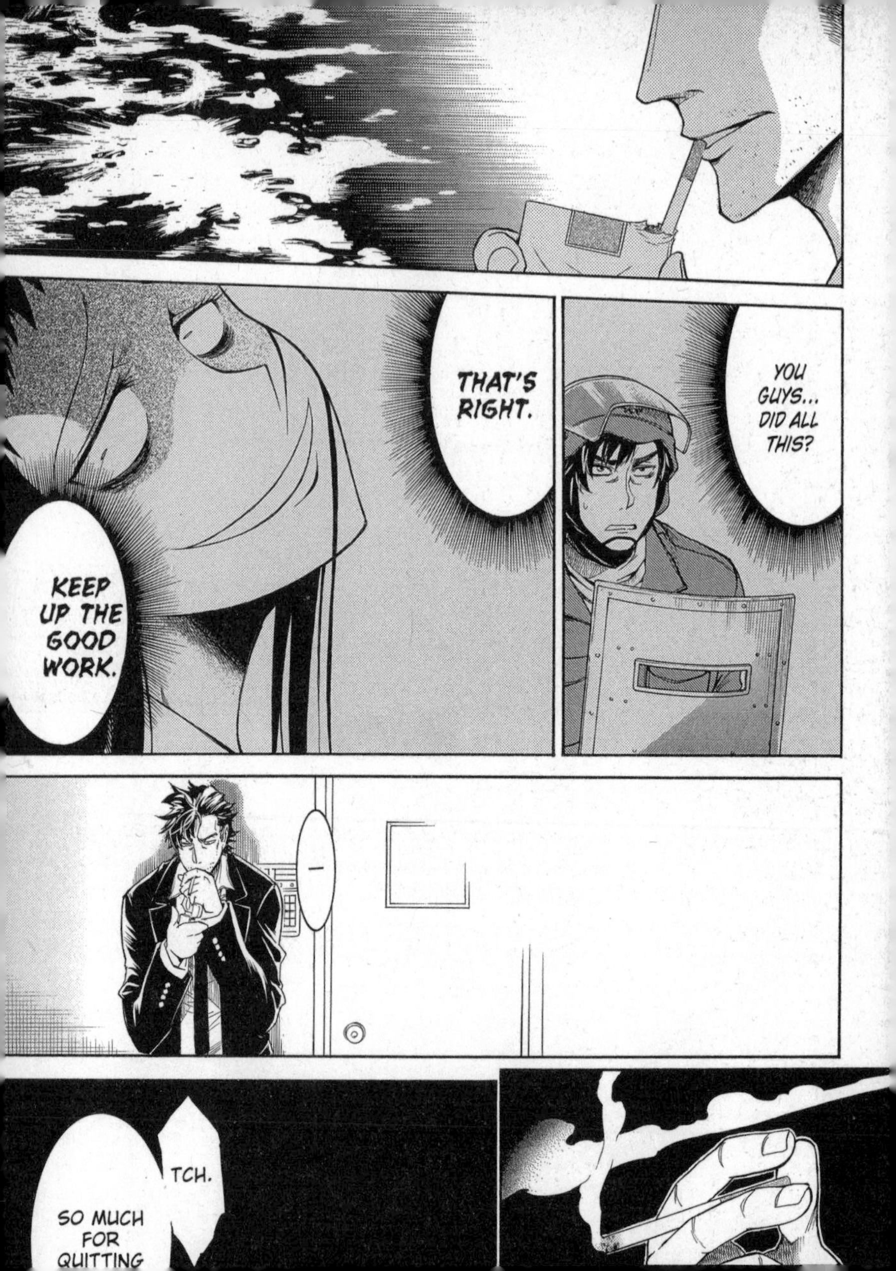
YOU GUYS... DID ALL THIS?
THAT'S RIGHT.
KEEP UP THE GOOD WORK.
—
TCH.
SO MUCH FOR QUITTING

MURCIÉLAGO

NOW LOADING

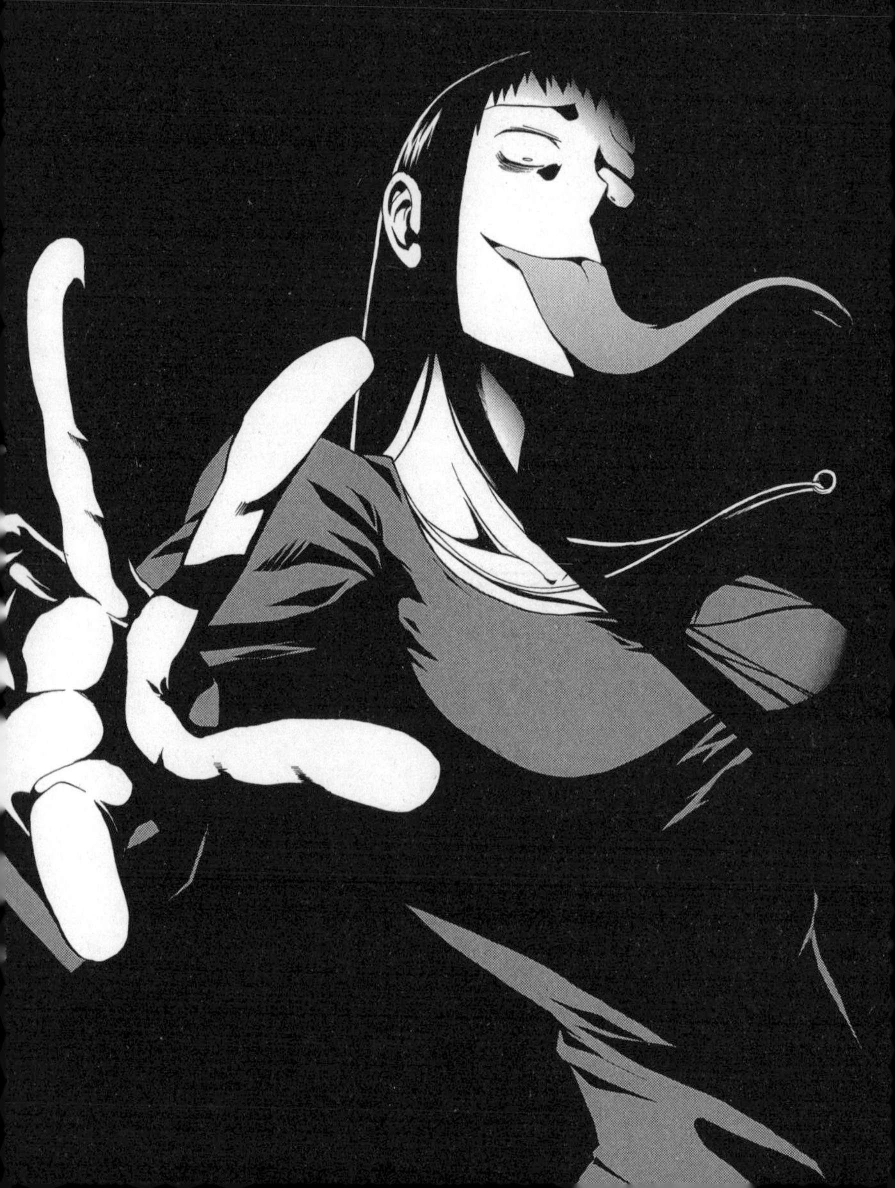

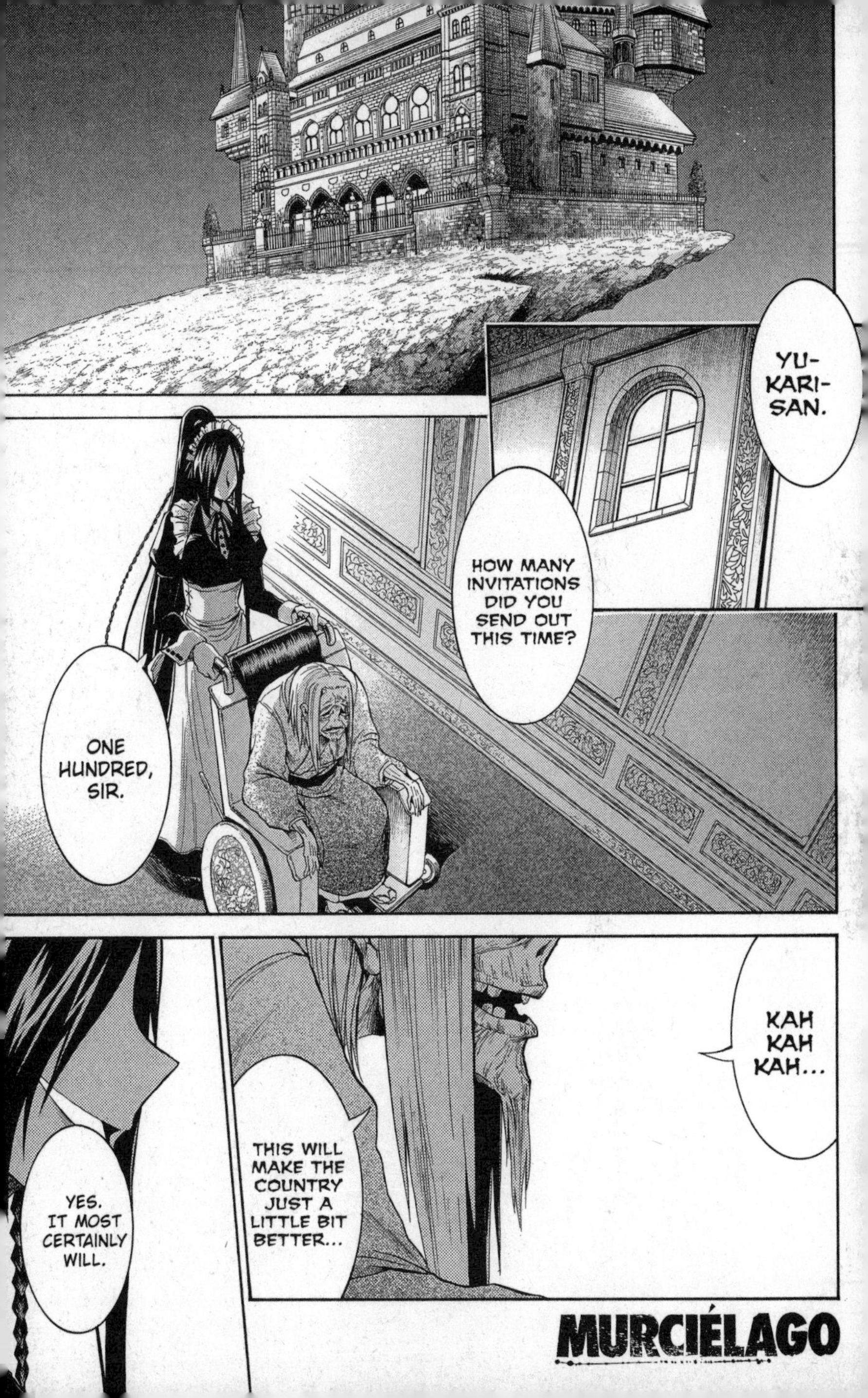
YU-KARI-SAN.
HOW MANY INVITATIONS DID YOU SEND OUT THIS TIME?
ONE HUNDRED, SIR.
KAH KAH KAH...
THIS WILL MAKE THE COUNTRY JUST A LITTLE BIT BETTER...
YES. IT MOST CERTAINLY WILL.
MURCIÉLAGO

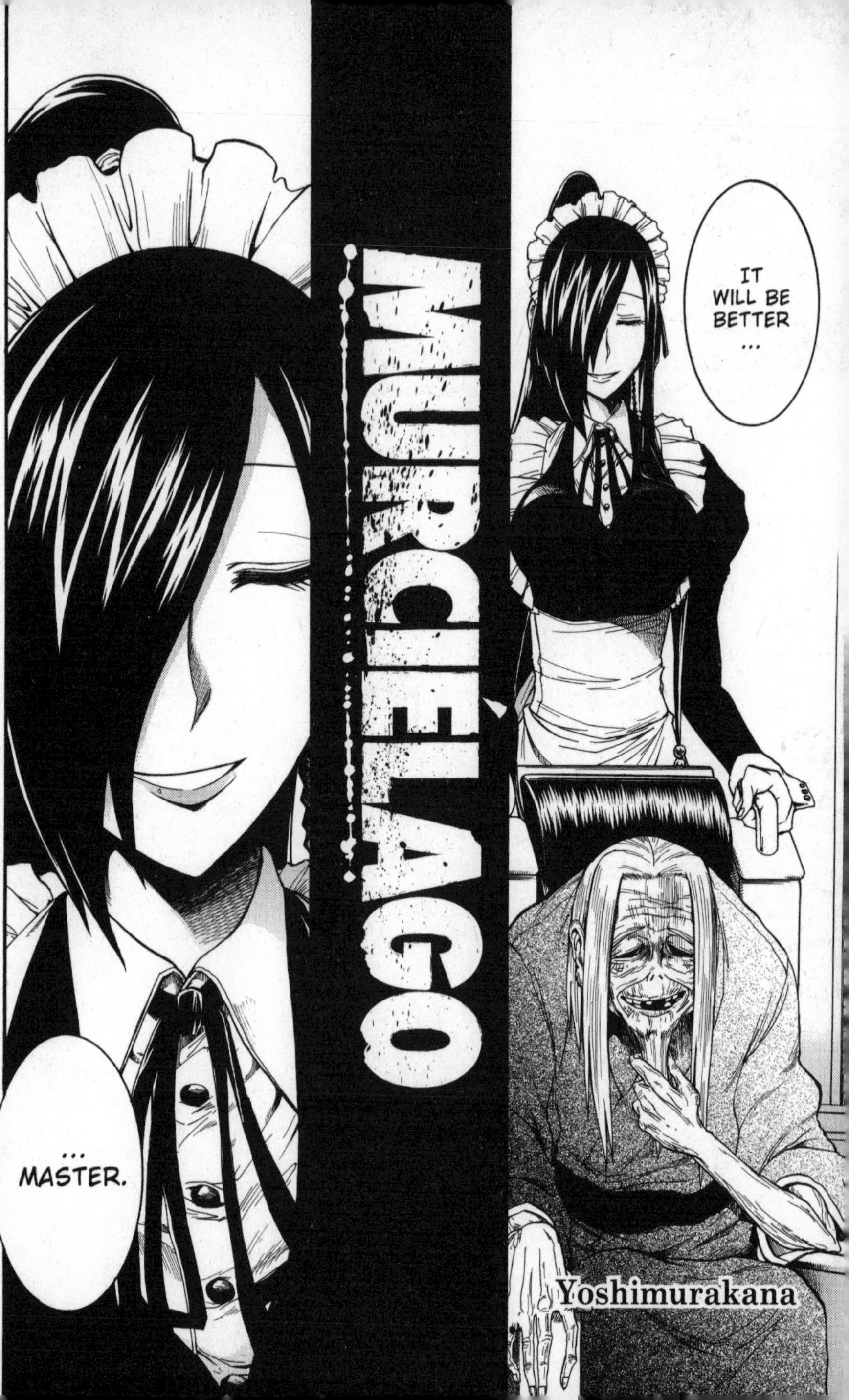
IT WILL BE BETTER ...
Yoshimurakana
MURCIÉLAGO
... MASTER.

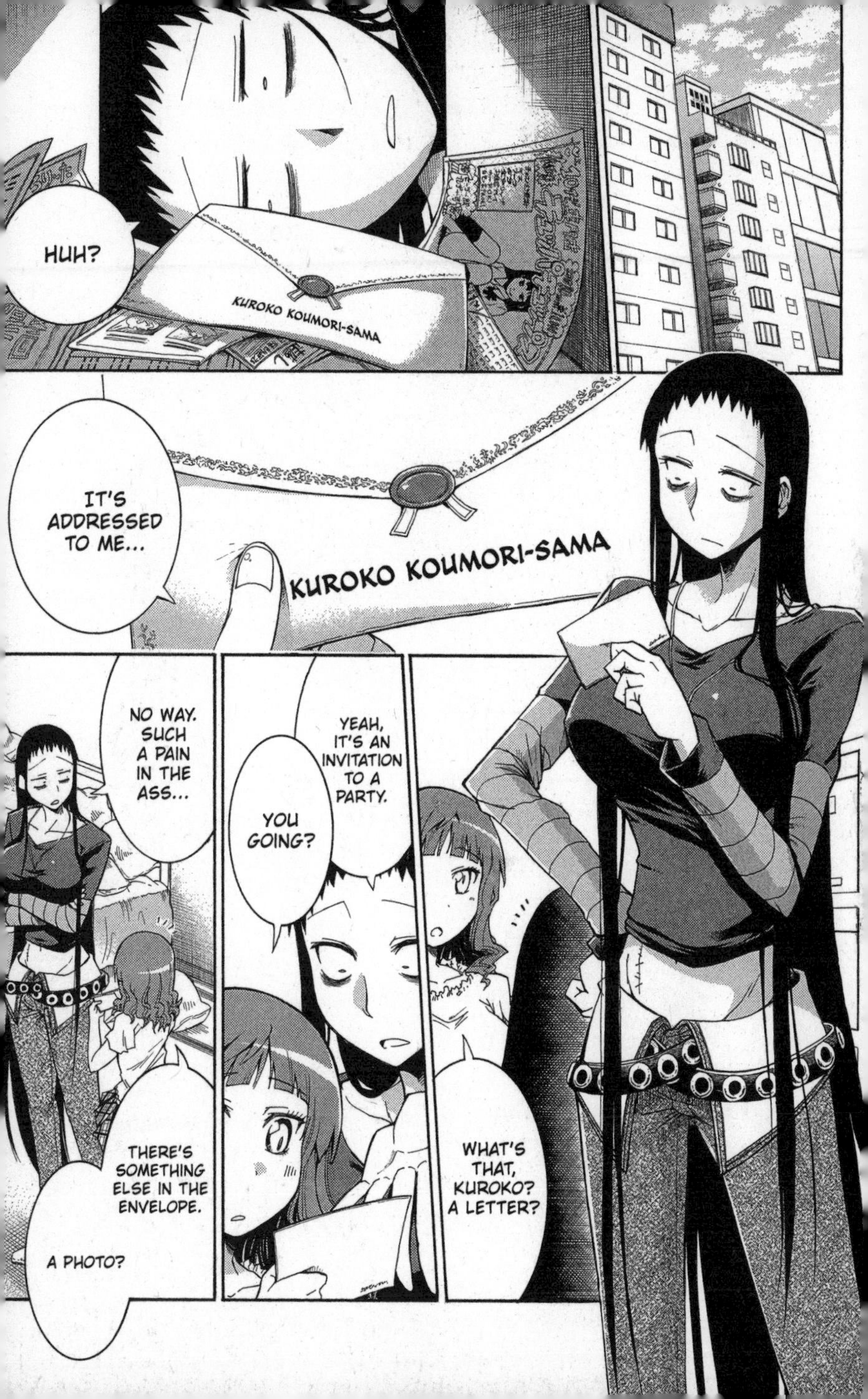

HUH?
KUROKO KOUMORI-SAMA
IT'S ADDRESSED TO ME...
KUROKO KOUMORI-SAMA
WHAT'S THAT, KUROKO? A LETTER?
YEAH, IT'S AN INVITATION TO A PARTY.
YOU GOING?
NO WAY. SUCH A PAIN IN THE ASS...
THERE'S SOMETHING ELSE IN THE ENVELOPE.
A PHOTO?

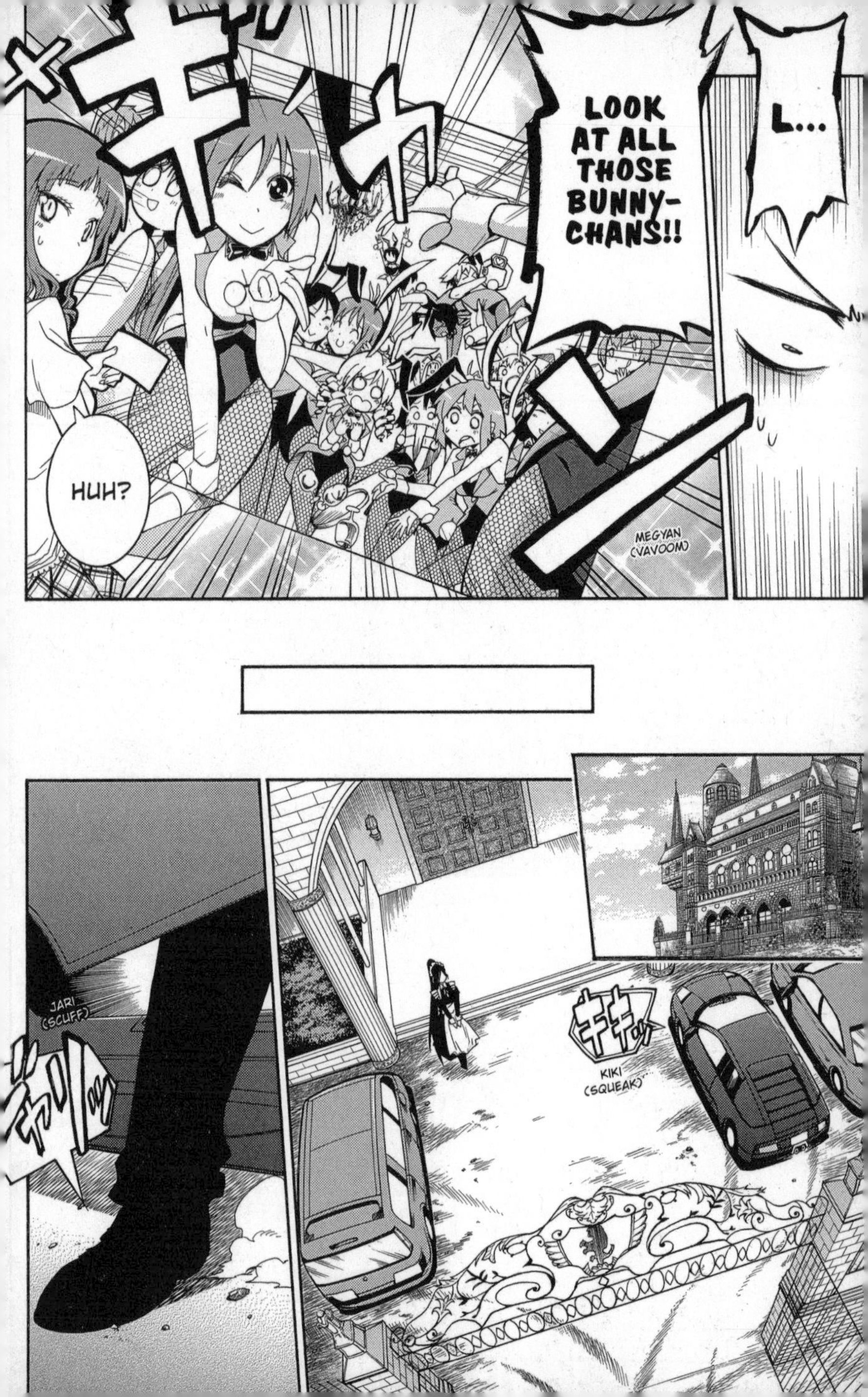
L...
LOOK AT ALL THOSE BUNNY-CHANS!!
HUH?
MEGYAN (VAVOOM)
KIKI (SQUEAK)
JARI (SCUFF)

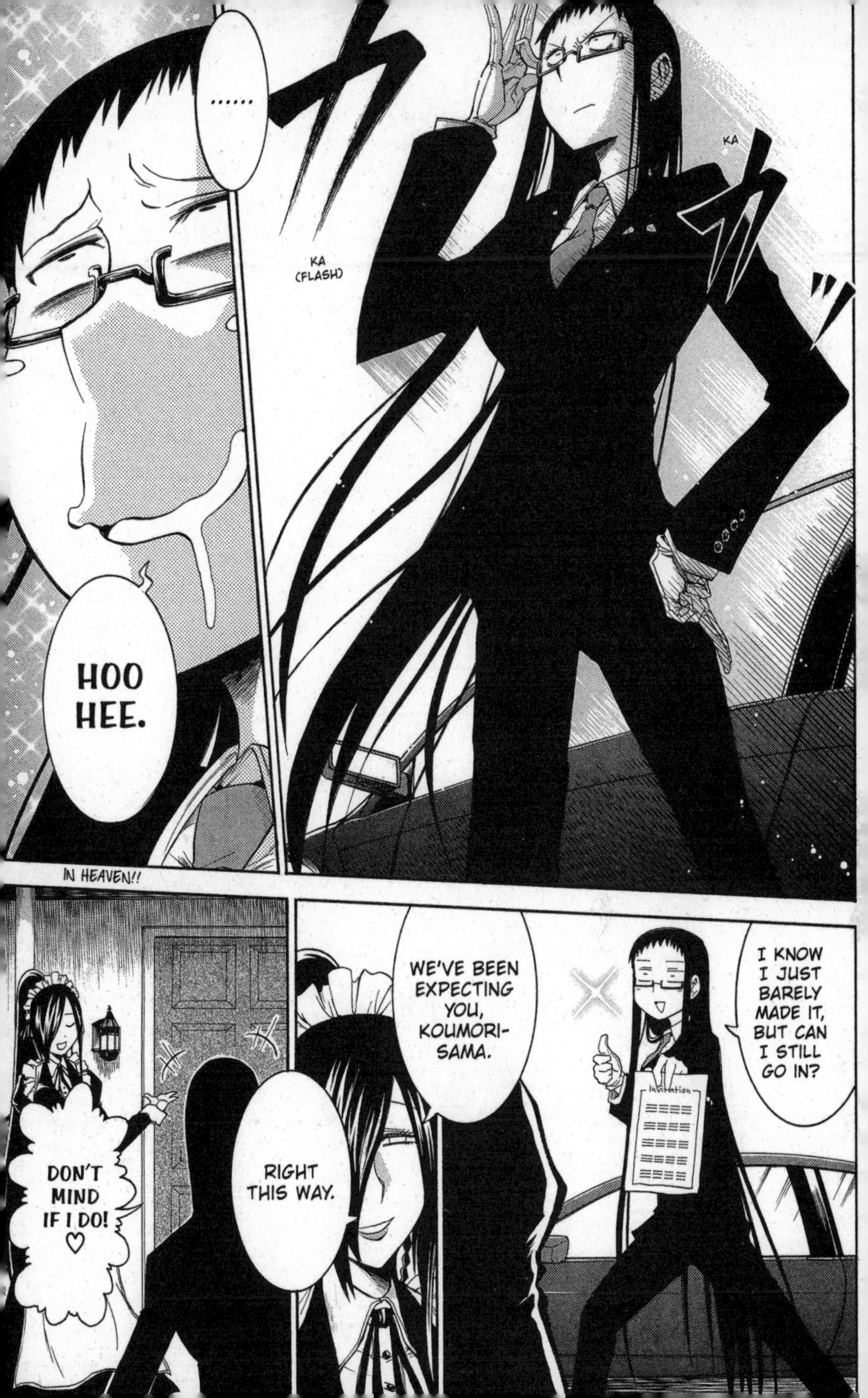
KA
KA (FLASH)
......
HOO HEE.
IN HEAVEN!!
I KNOW I JUST BARELY MADE IT, BUT CAN I STILL GO IN?
WE'VE BEEN EXPECTING YOU, KOUMORI-SAMA.
Invitation
RIGHT THIS WAY.
DON'T MIND IF I DO! ♡

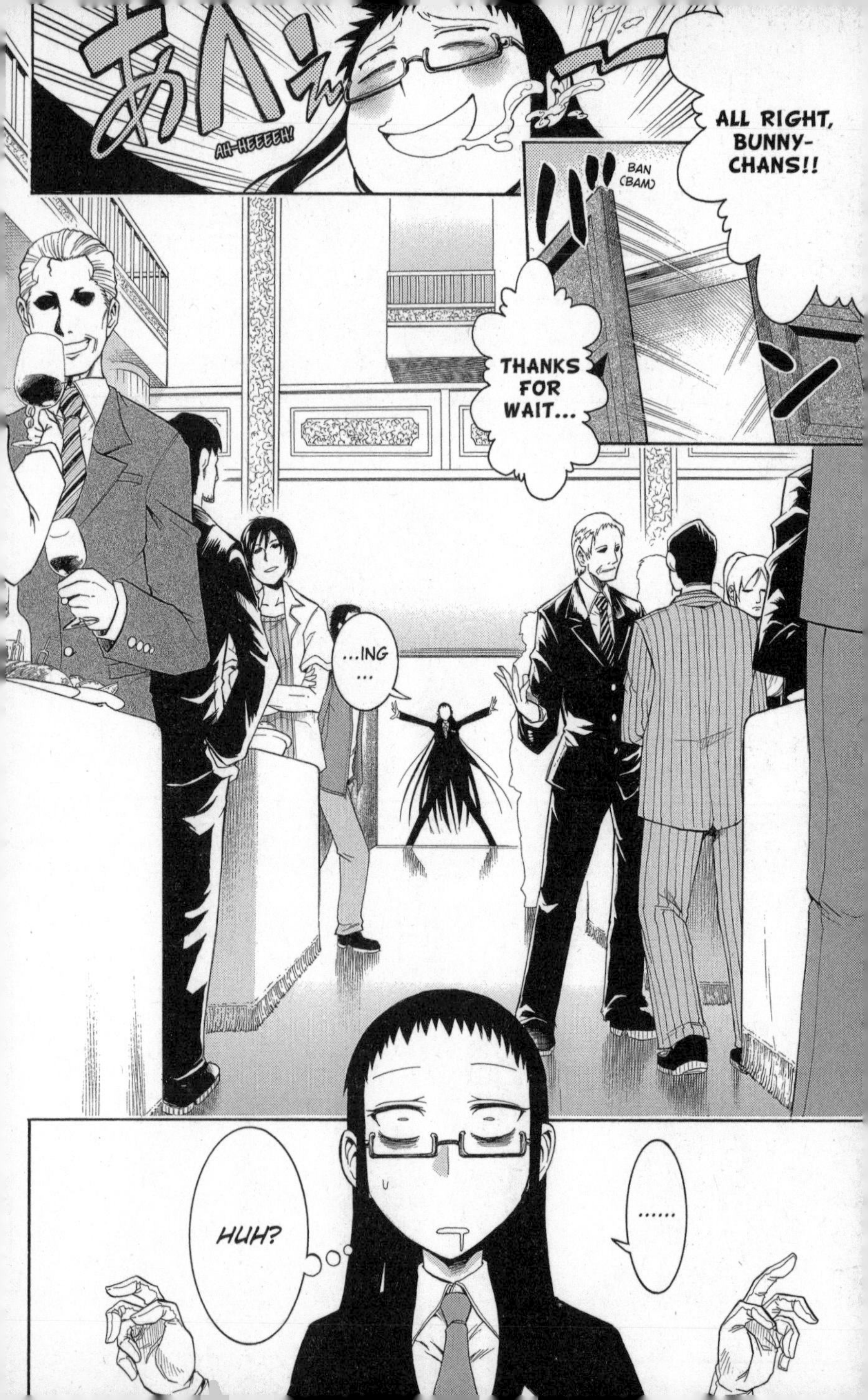
ALL RIGHT, BUNNY-CHANS!!
あへぇ
AH-HEEEEH!
バン
BAN (BAM)
THANKS FOR WAIT...
...ING ...
......
HUH?

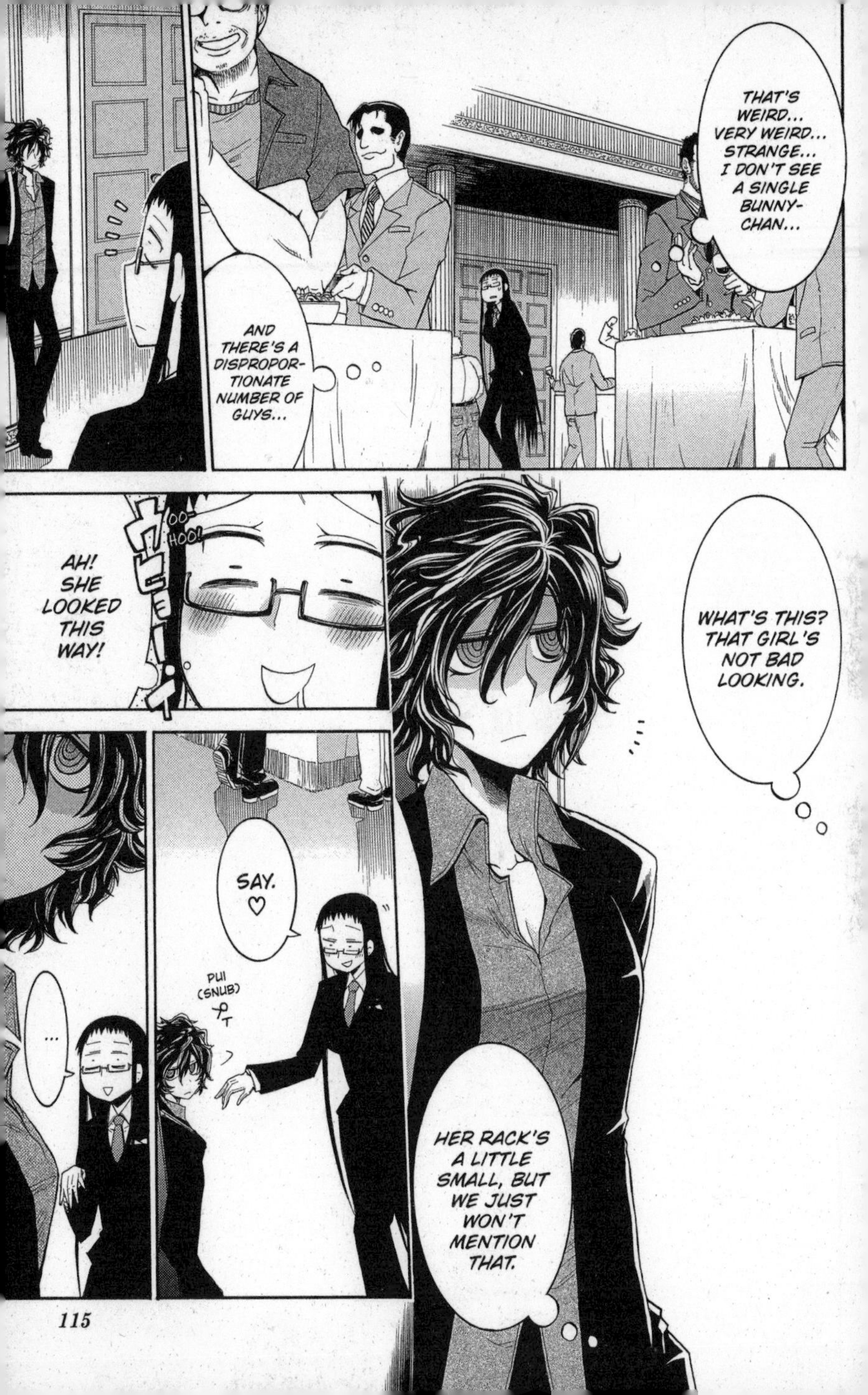
THAT'S WEIRD... VERY WEIRD... STRANGE... I DON'T SEE A SINGLE BUNNY-CHAN...
AND THERE'S A DISPROPORTIONATE NUMBER OF GUYS...
WHAT'S THIS? THAT GIRL'S NOT BAD LOOKING.
HER RACK'S A LITTLE SMALL, BUT WE JUST WON'T MENTION THAT.
OO-HOO!
AH! SHE LOOKED THIS WAY!
SAY. ♡
PUI (SNUB)
...

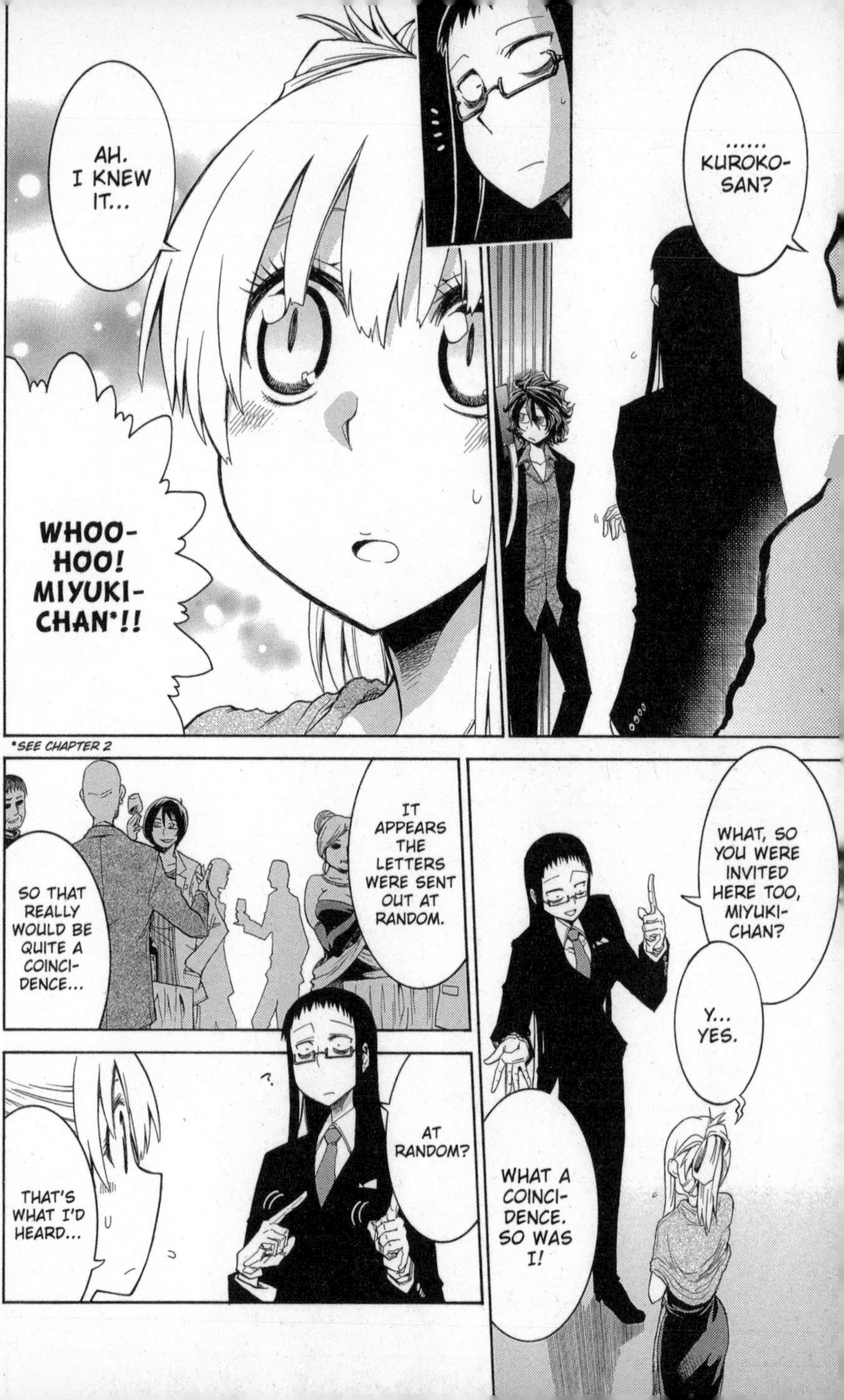
......KUROKO-SAN?
AH. I KNEW IT...
WHOO-HOO! MIYUKI-CHAN*!!
WHAT, SO YOU WERE INVITED HERE TOO, MIYUKI-CHAN?
Y... YES.
WHAT A COINCIDENCE. SO WAS I!
IT APPEARS THE LETTERS WERE SENT OUT AT RANDOM.
SO THAT REALLY WOULD BE QUITE A COINCIDENCE...
AT RANDOM?
THAT'S WHAT I'D HEARD...

*SEE CHAPTER 2

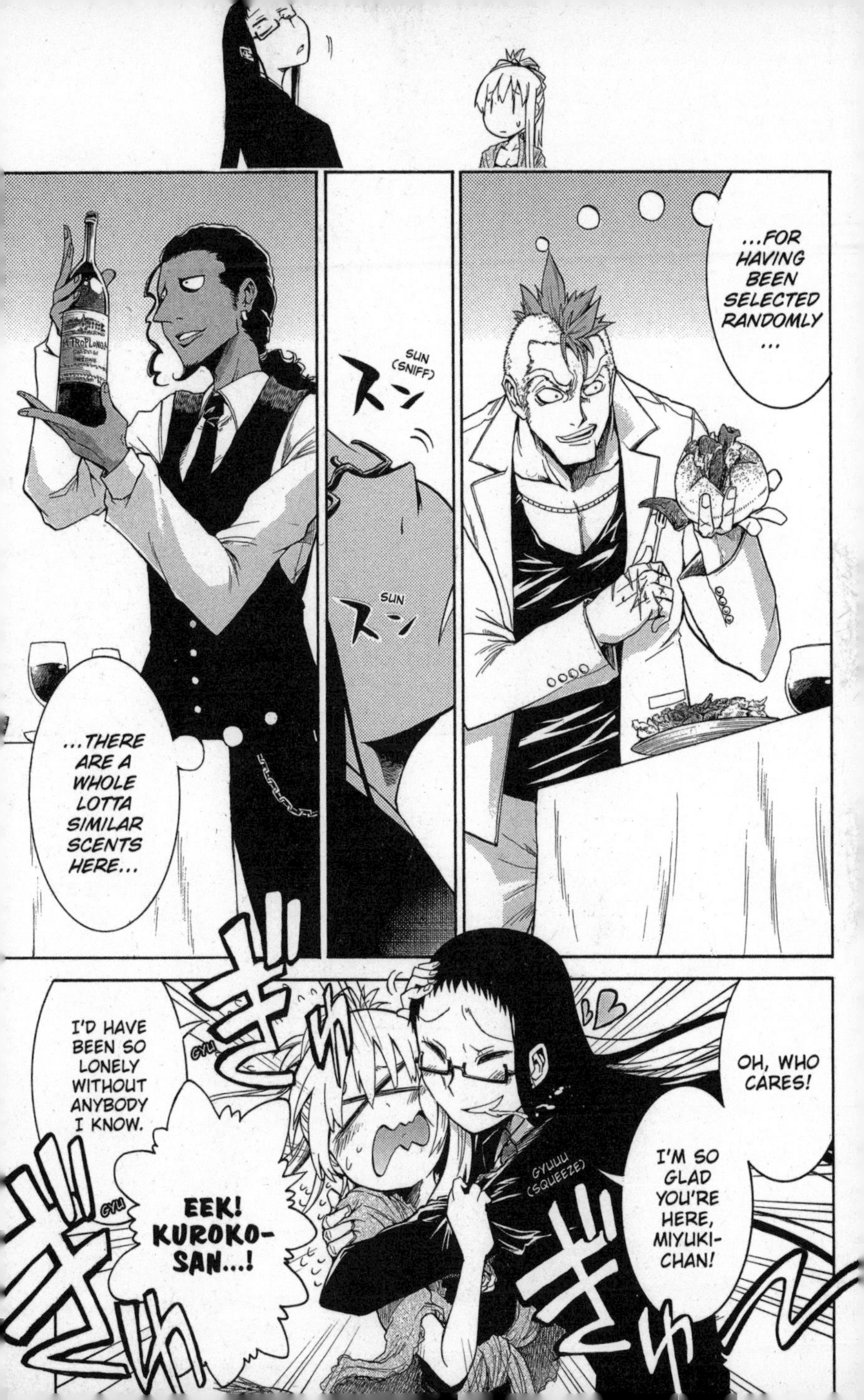
...FOR HAVING BEEN SELECTED RANDOMLY ...
SUN (SNIFF)
SUN
...THERE ARE A WHOLE LOTTA SIMILAR SCENTS HERE...
OH, WHO CARES!
I'M SO GLAD YOU'RE HERE, MIYUKI-CHAN!
GYUUU (SQUEEZE)
I'D HAVE BEEN SO LONELY WITHOUT ANYBODY I KNOW.
GYU
EEK! KUROKO-SAN...!
GYU

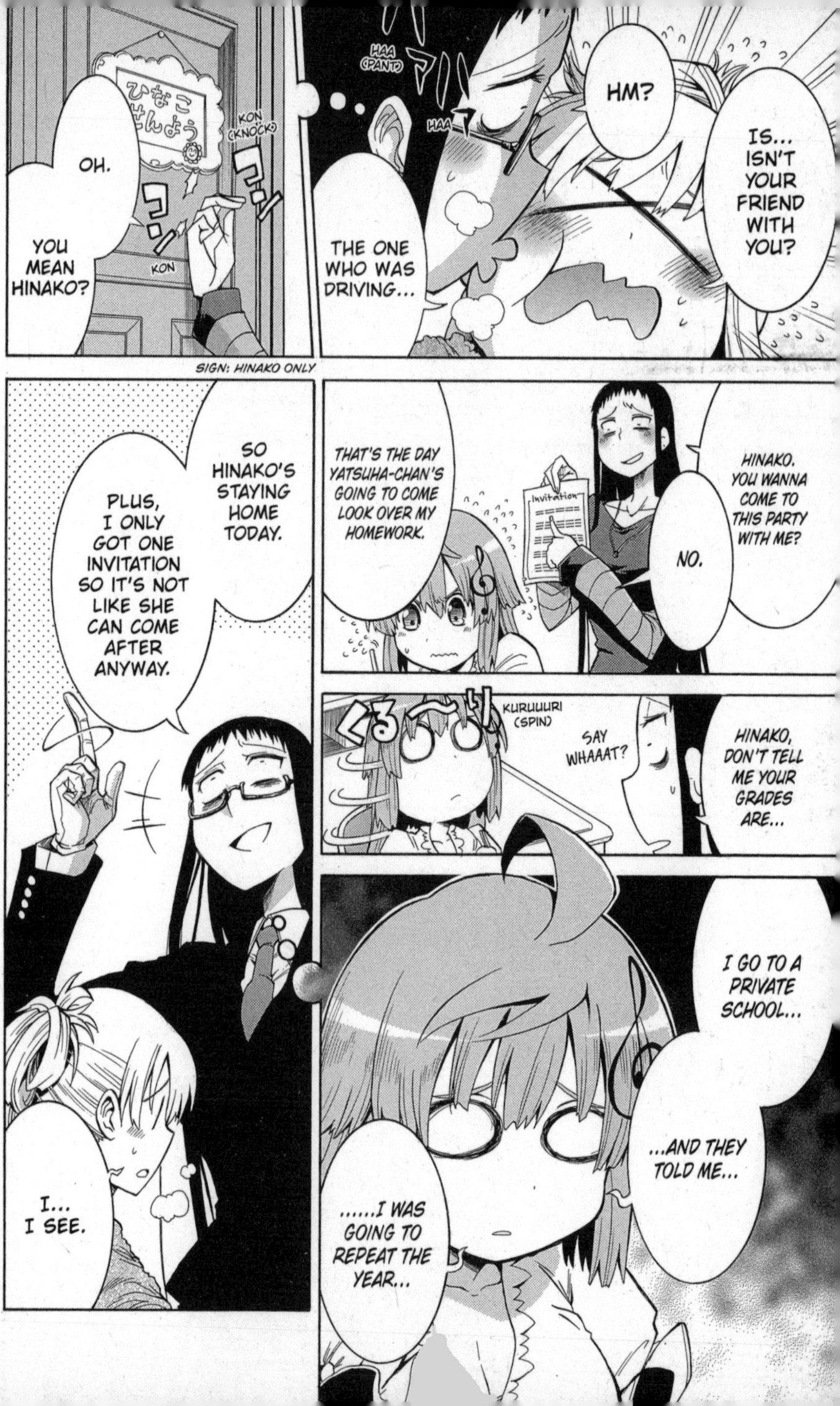
HM?
IS... ISN'T YOUR FRIEND WITH YOU?
HAA (PANT)
HAA
THE ONE WHO WAS DRIVING...
ひなこ せんよう
KON (KNOCK)
KON
OH.
YOU MEAN HINAKO?
SIGN: HINAKO ONLY
HINAKO. YOU WANNA COME TO THIS PARTY WITH ME?
NO.
THAT'S THE DAY YATSUHA-CHAN'S GOING TO COME LOOK OVER MY HOMEWORK.
Invitation
HINAKO, DON'T TELL ME YOUR GRADES ARE...
SAY WHAAAT?
くる〜り
KURUUURI (SPIN)
I GO TO A PRIVATE SCHOOL...
...AND THEY TOLD ME...
......I WAS GOING TO REPEAT THE YEAR...
SO HINAKO'S STAYING HOME TODAY.
PLUS, I ONLY GOT ONE INVITATION SO IT'S NOT LIKE SHE CAN COME AFTER ANYWAY.
I... I SEE.

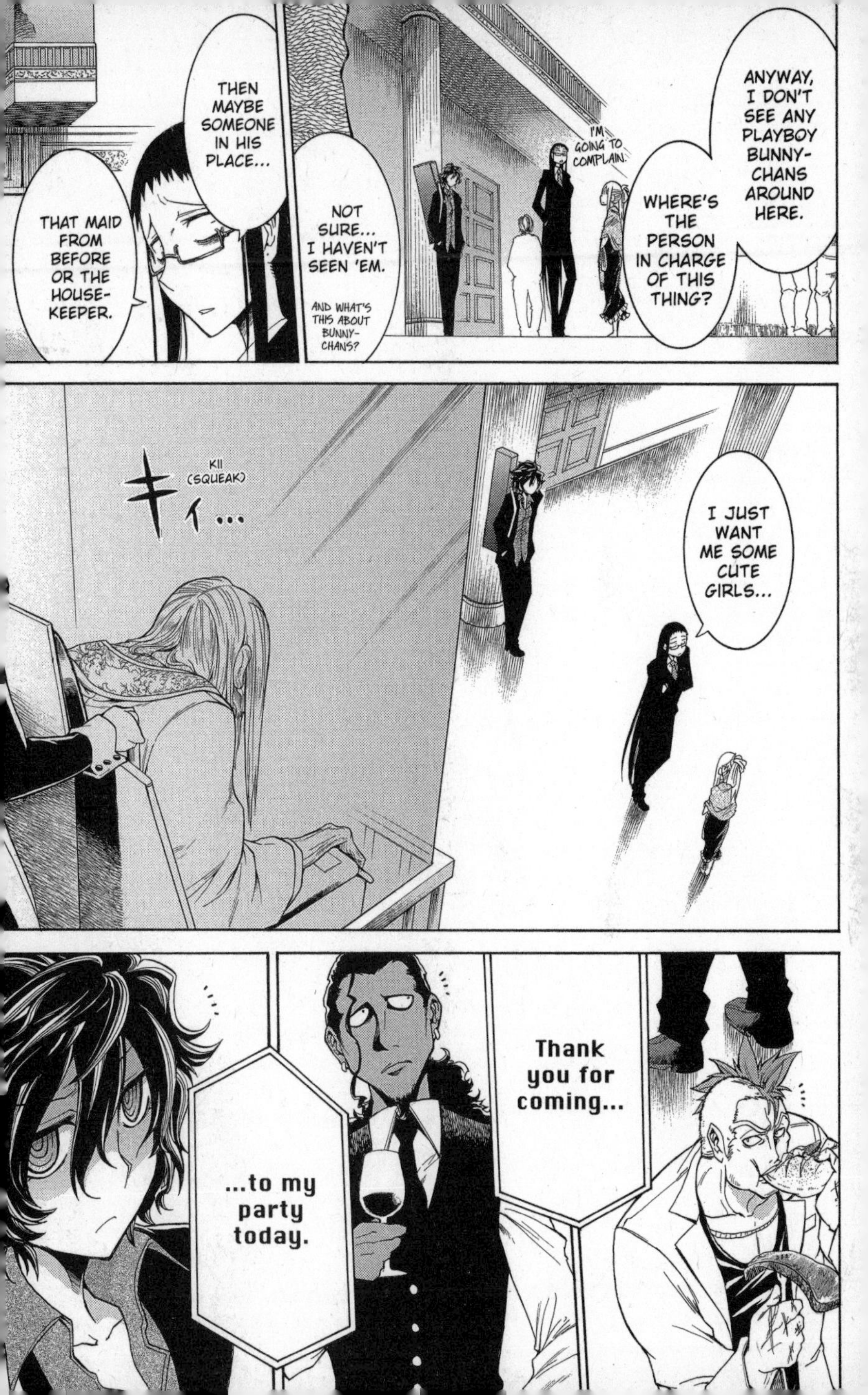
ANYWAY, I DON'T SEE ANY PLAYBOY BUNNY-CHANS AROUND HERE.
I'M GOING TO COMPLAIN.
WHERE'S THE PERSON IN CHARGE OF THIS THING?
NOT SURE... I HAVEN'T SEEN 'EM.
AND WHAT'S THIS ABOUT BUNNY-CHANS?
THEN MAYBE SOMEONE IN HIS PLACE...
THAT MAID FROM BEFORE OR THE HOUSE-KEEPER.
I JUST WANT ME SOME CUTE GIRLS...
KII (SQUEAK)
キィ...
Thank you for coming...
...to my party today.

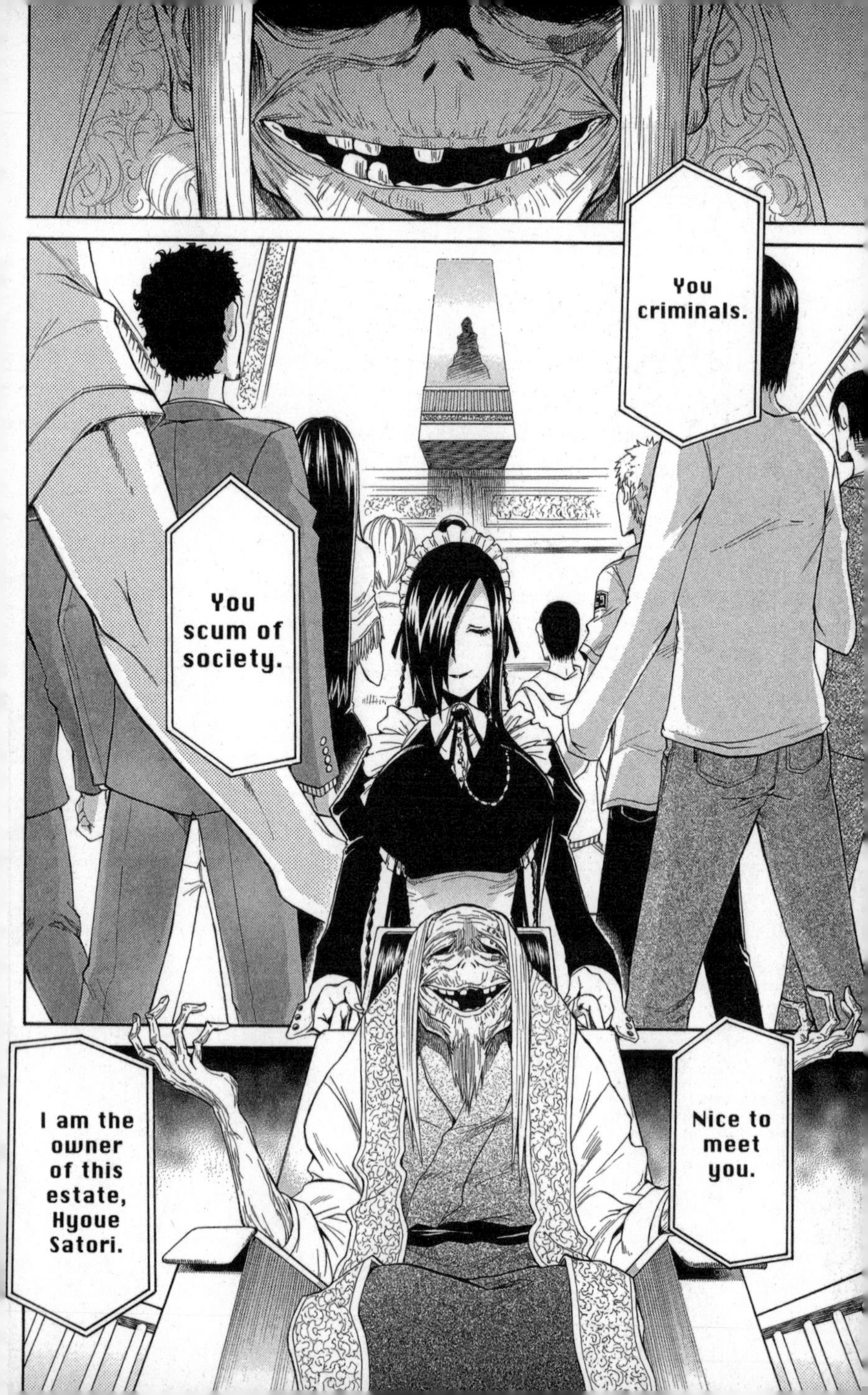
You criminals.
You scum of society.
Nice to meet you.
I am the owner of this estate, Hyoue Satori.

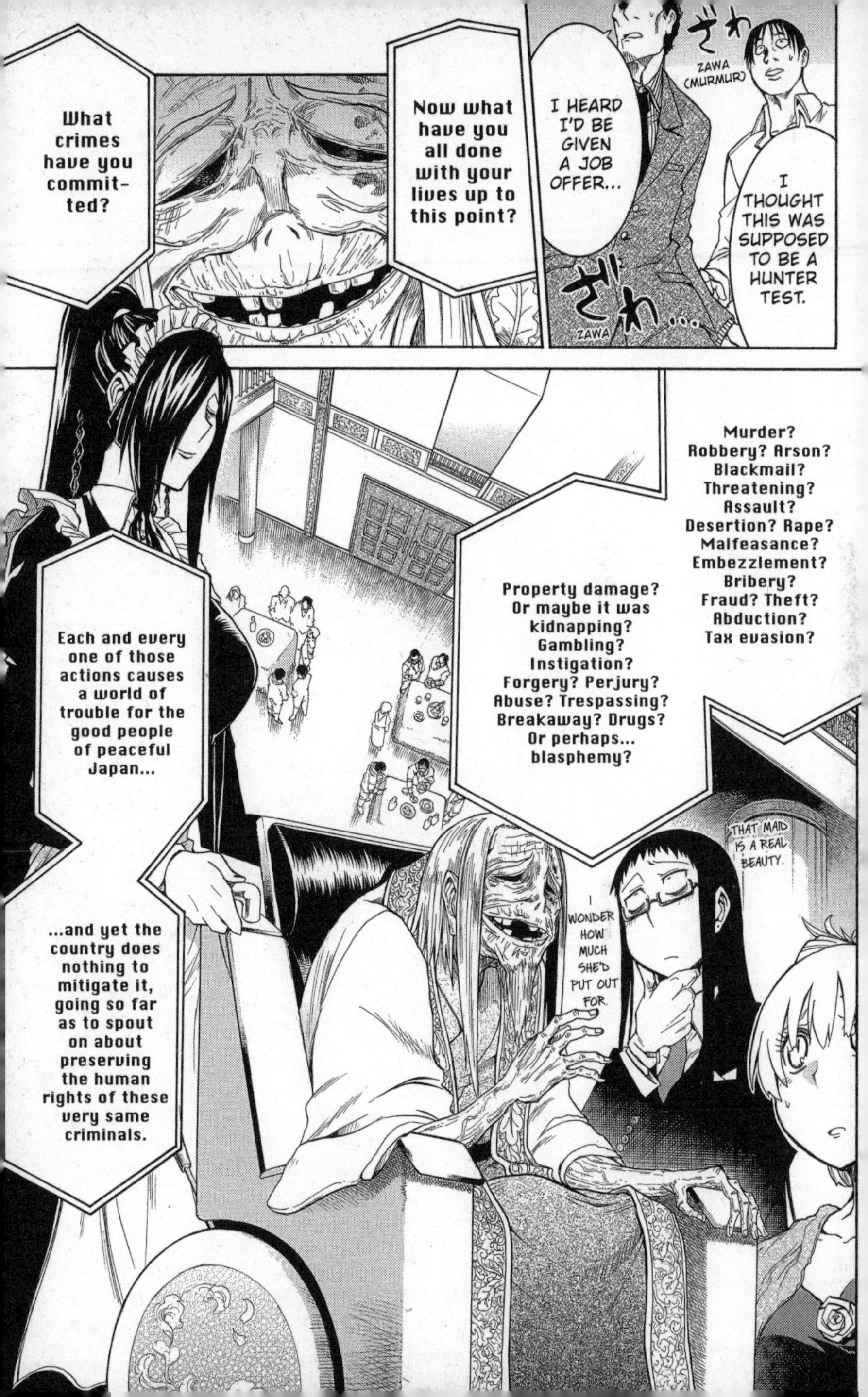
ざわ
ZAWA (MURMUR)
I THOUGHT THIS WAS SUPPOSED TO BE A HUNTER TEST.
I HEARD I'D BE GIVEN A JOB OFFER...
ざわ...
ZAWA
Now what have you all done with your lives up to this point?
What crimes have you commit-ted?
Murder? Robbery? Arson? Blackmail? Threatening? Assault? Desertion? Rape? Malfeasance? Embezzlement? Bribery? Fraud? Theft? Abduction? Tax evasion?
Property damage? Or maybe it was kidnapping? Gambling? Instigation? Forgery? Perjury? Abuse? Trespassing? Breakaway? Drugs? Or perhaps... blasphemy?
THAT MAID IS A REAL BEAUTY.
I WONDER HOW MUCH SHE'D PUT OUT FOR.
Each and every one of those actions causes a world of trouble for the good people of peaceful Japan...
...and yet the country does nothing to mitigate it, going so far as to spout on about preserving the human rights of these very same criminals.

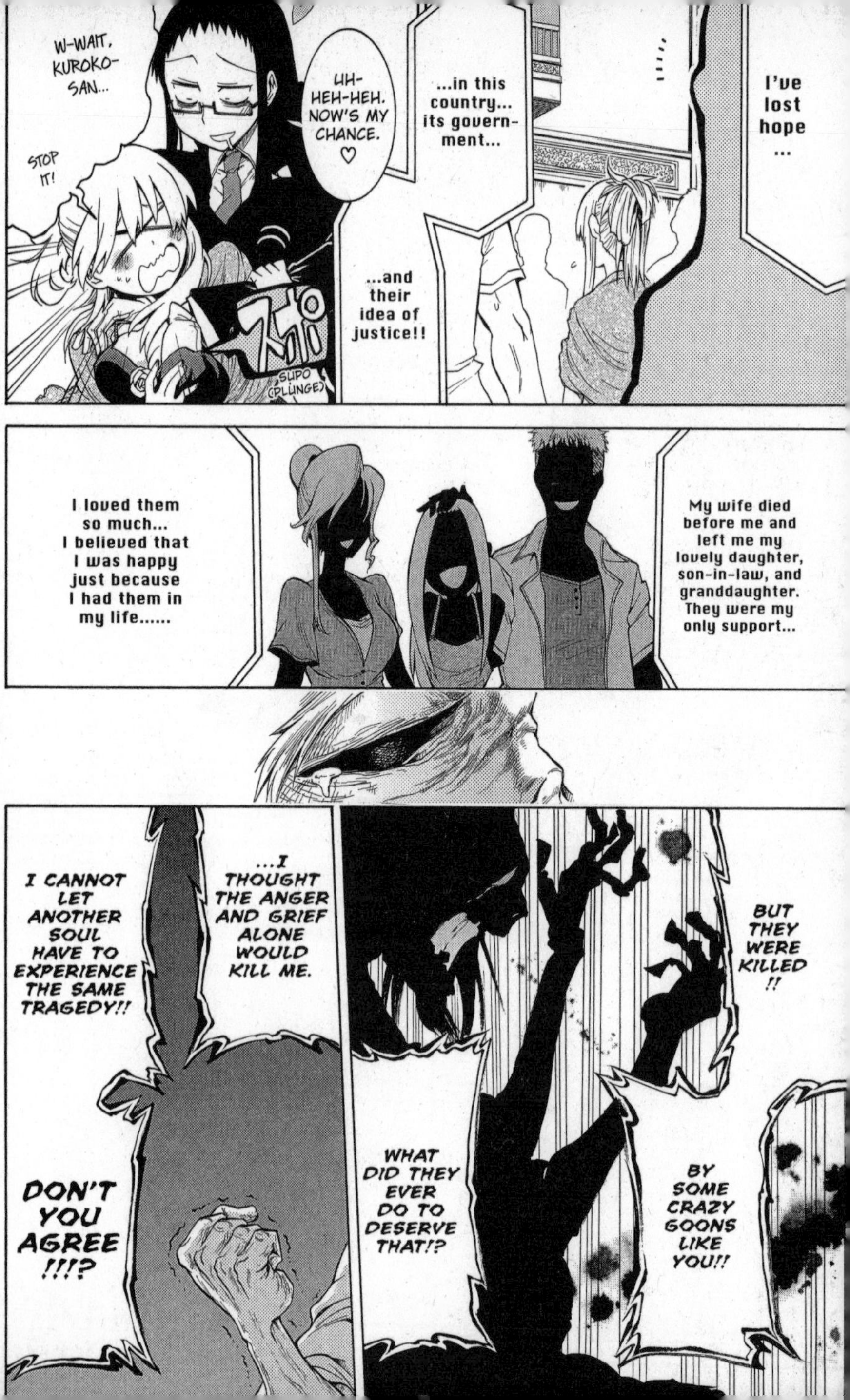
I've lost hope...
...in this country... its government...
...and their idea of justice!!
UH-HEH-HEH. NOW'S MY CHANCE. ♡
W-WAIT, KUROKO-SAN...
STOP IT!
SUPO (PLUNGE)
My wife died before me and left me my lovely daughter, son-in-law, and granddaughter. They were my only support...
I loved them so much... I believed that I was happy just because I had them in my life......
BUT THEY WERE KILLED!!
BY SOME CRAZY GOONS LIKE YOU!!
WHAT DID THEY EVER DO TO DESERVE THAT!?
...I THOUGHT THE ANGER AND GRIEF ALONE WOULD KILL ME.
I CANNOT LET ANOTHER SOUL HAVE TO EXPERIENCE THE SAME TRAGEDY!!
DON'T YOU AGREE!!!?

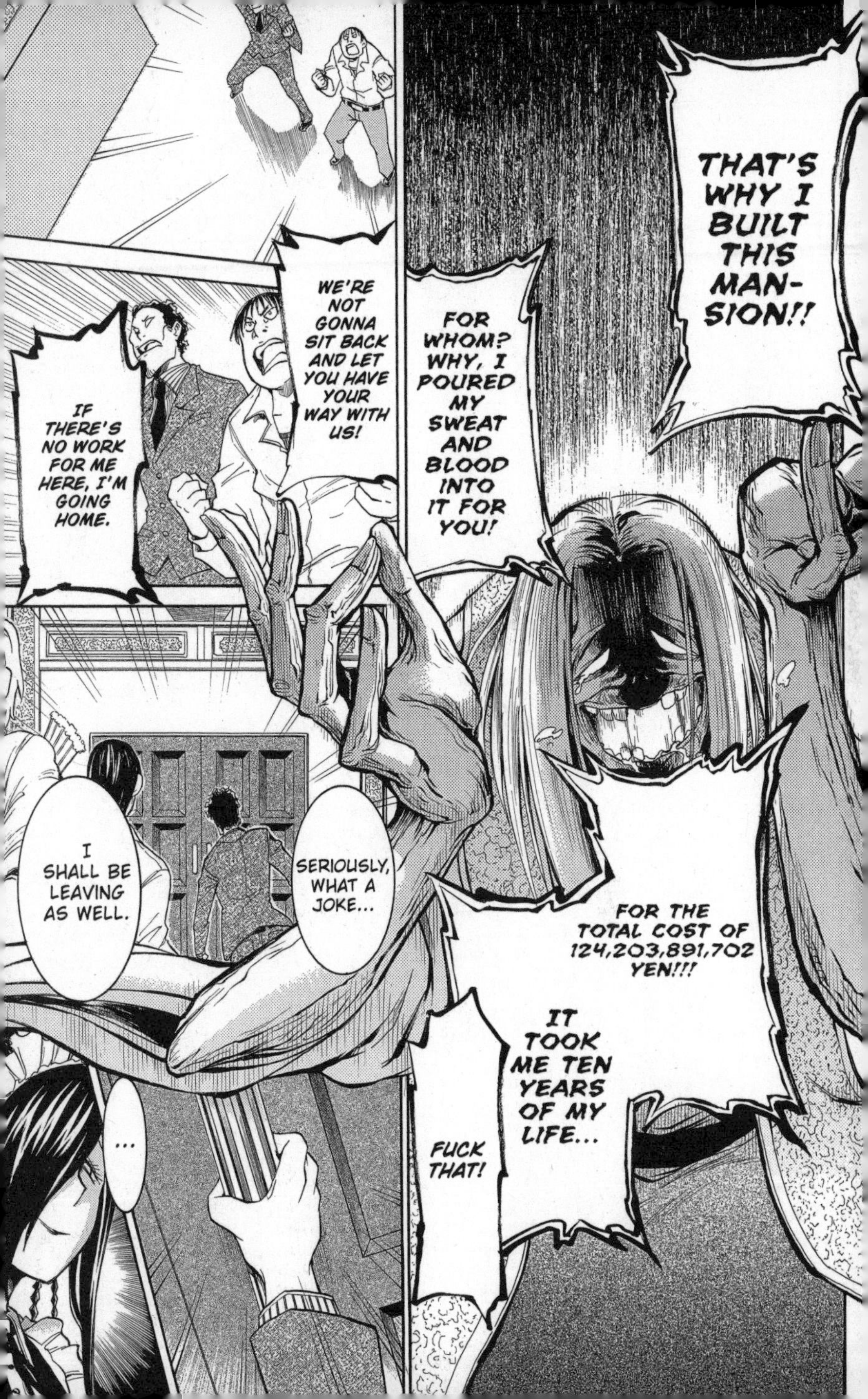
THAT'S WHY I BUILT THIS MAN-SION!!
FOR WHOM? WHY, I POURED MY SWEAT AND BLOOD INTO IT FOR YOU!
FOR THE TOTAL COST OF 124,203,891,702 YEN!!!
IT TOOK ME TEN YEARS OF MY LIFE...
FUCK THAT!
WE'RE NOT GONNA SIT BACK AND LET YOU HAVE YOUR WAY WITH US!
IF THERE'S NO WORK FOR ME HERE, I'M GOING HOME.
SERIOUSLY, WHAT A JOKE...
I SHALL BE LEAVING AS WELL.
...

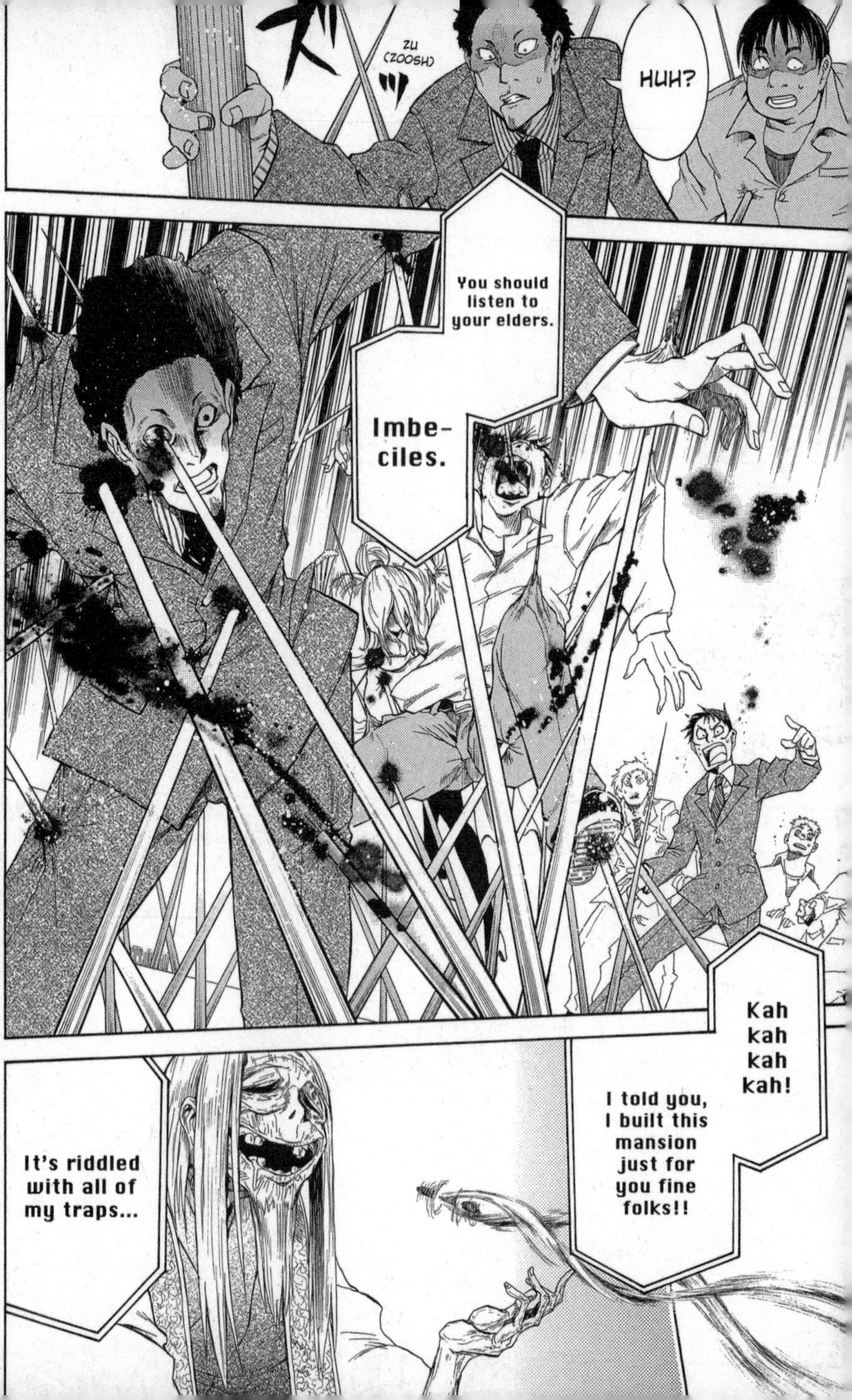
HUH?
ZU (ZOOSH)
You should listen to your elders.
Imbe-ciles.
Kah kah kah kah!
I told you, I built this mansion just for you fine folks!!
It's riddled with all of my traps...

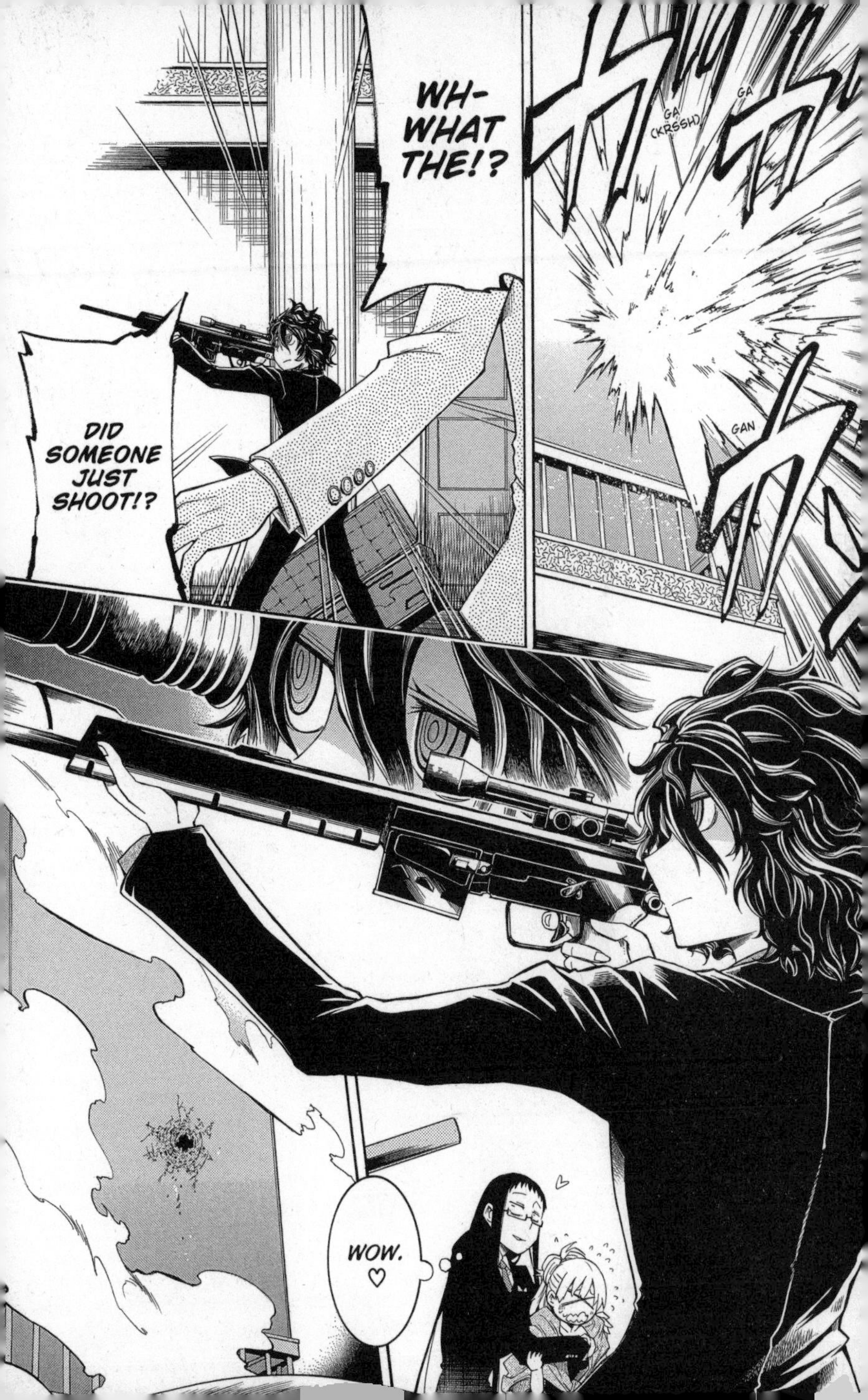
GA
GA (KRSSH)
GAN
WH- WHAT THE!?
DID SOMEONE JUST SHOOT!?
WOW. ♡

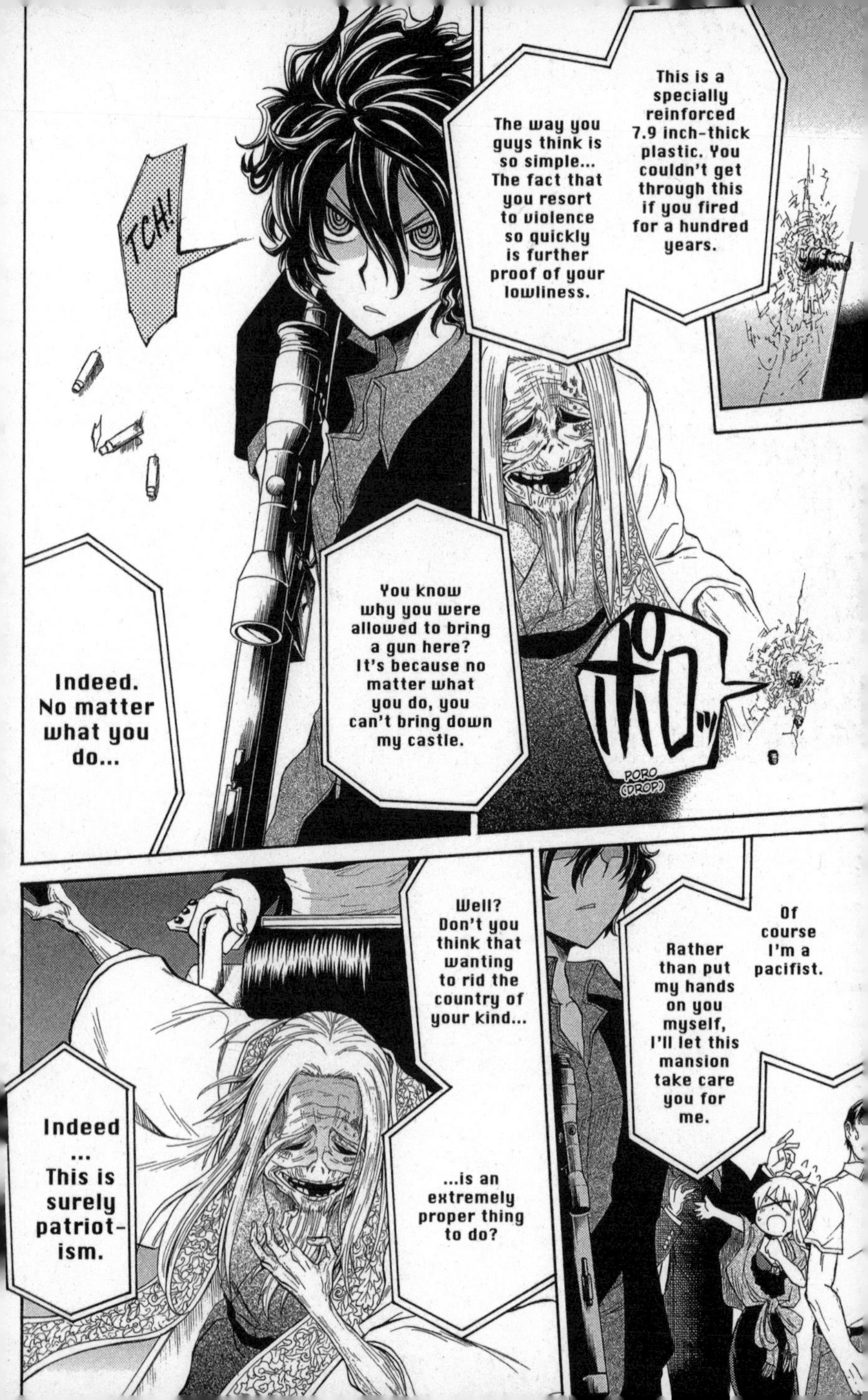
This is a specially reinforced 7.9 inch-thick plastic. You couldn't get through this if you fired for a hundred years.
The way you guys think is so simple... The fact that you resort to violence so quickly is further proof of your lowliness.
TCH!
ポロッ
PORO (DROP)
You know why you were allowed to bring a gun here? It's because no matter what you do, you can't bring down my castle.
Indeed. No matter what you do...
Of course I'm a pacifist.
Rather than put my hands on you myself, I'll let this mansion take care you for me.
Well? Don't you think that wanting to rid the country of your kind...
...is an extremely proper thing to do?
Indeed ... This is surely patriot-ism.

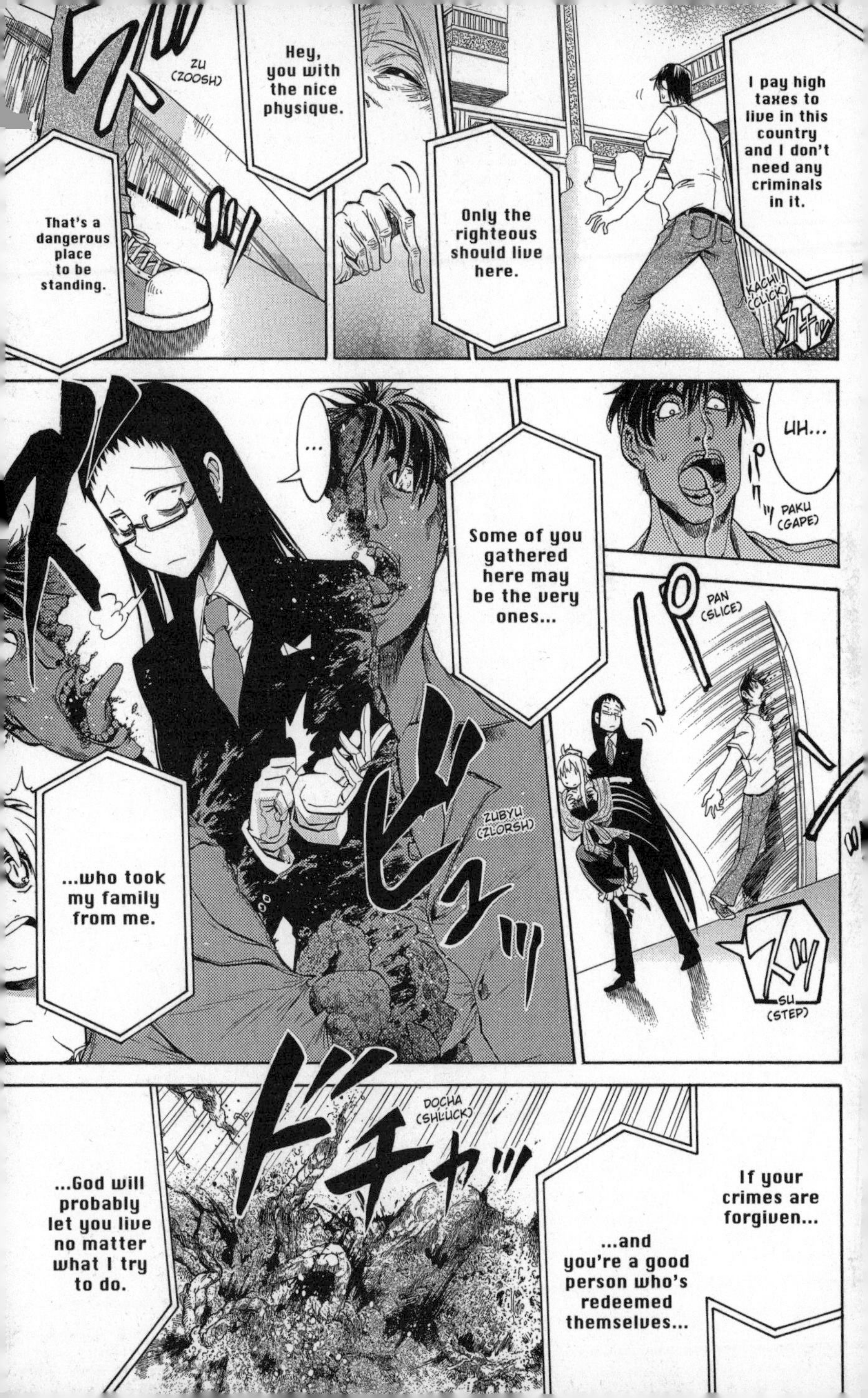
I pay high taxes to live in this country and I don't need any criminals in it.
KACHI (CLICK)
Only the righteous should live here.
Hey, you with the nice physique.
ZU (ZOOSH)
That's a dangerous place to be standing.
UH...
PAKU (GAPE)
PAN (SLICE)
SU (STEP)
Some of you gathered here may be the very ones...
...
ZUBYU (ZLORSH)
...who took my family from me.
If your crimes are forgiven...
...and you're a good person who's redeemed themselves...
DOCHA (SHLUCK)
...God will probably let you live no matter what I try to do.

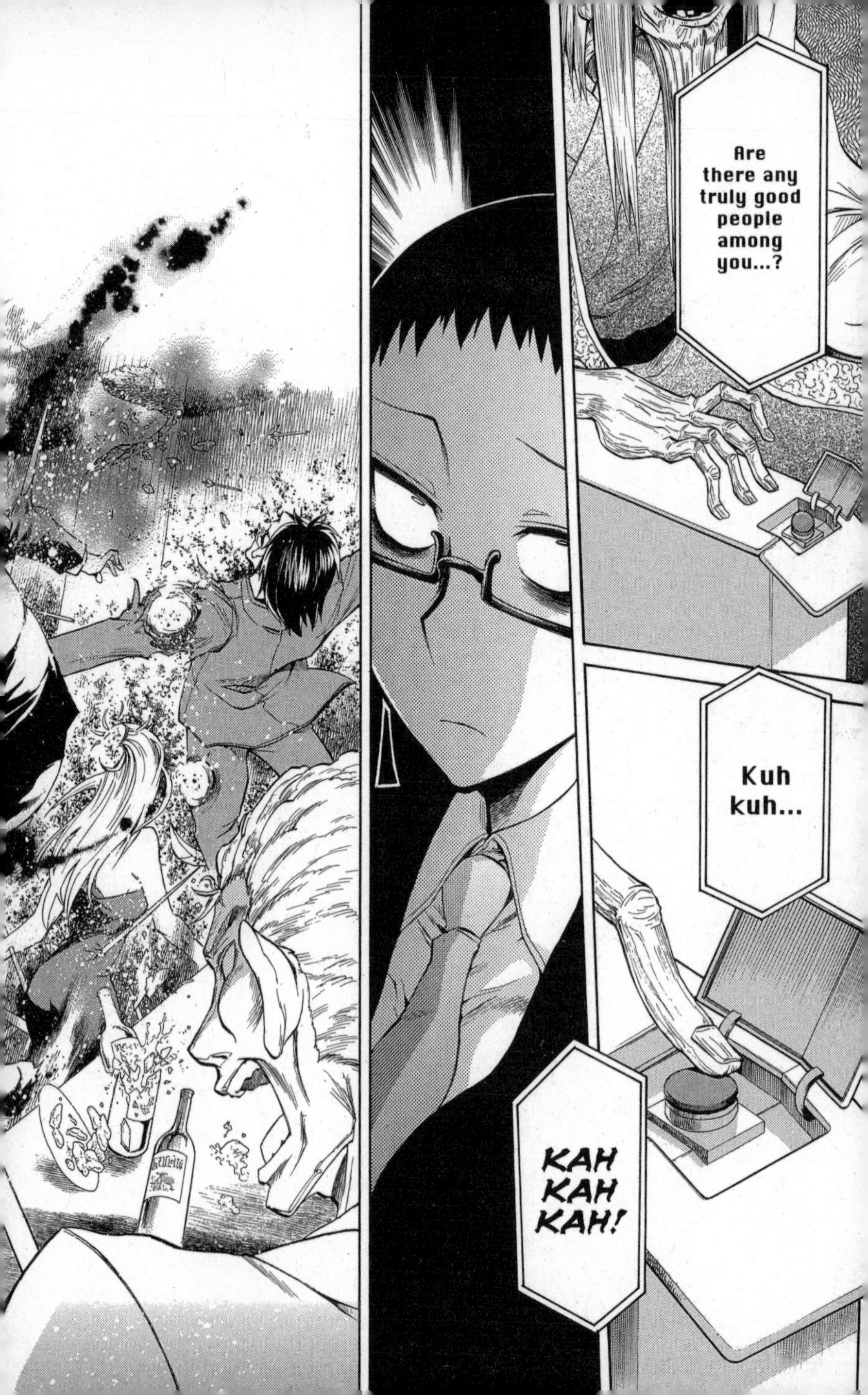
Are there any truly good people among you...?
Kuh kuh...
KAH KAH KAH!

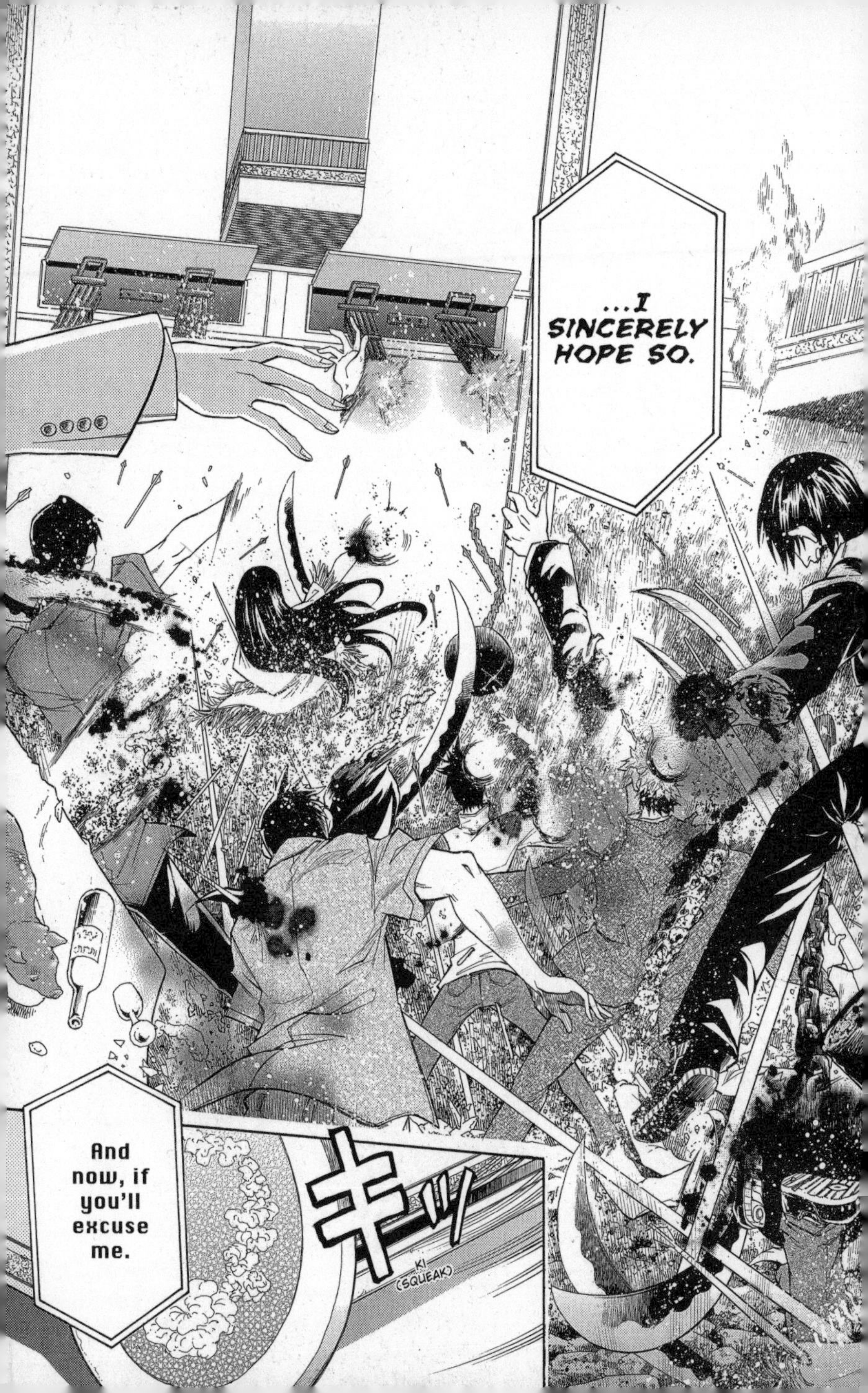
...I SINCERELY HOPE SO.
And now, if you'll excuse me.
キッ
KI (SQUEAK)

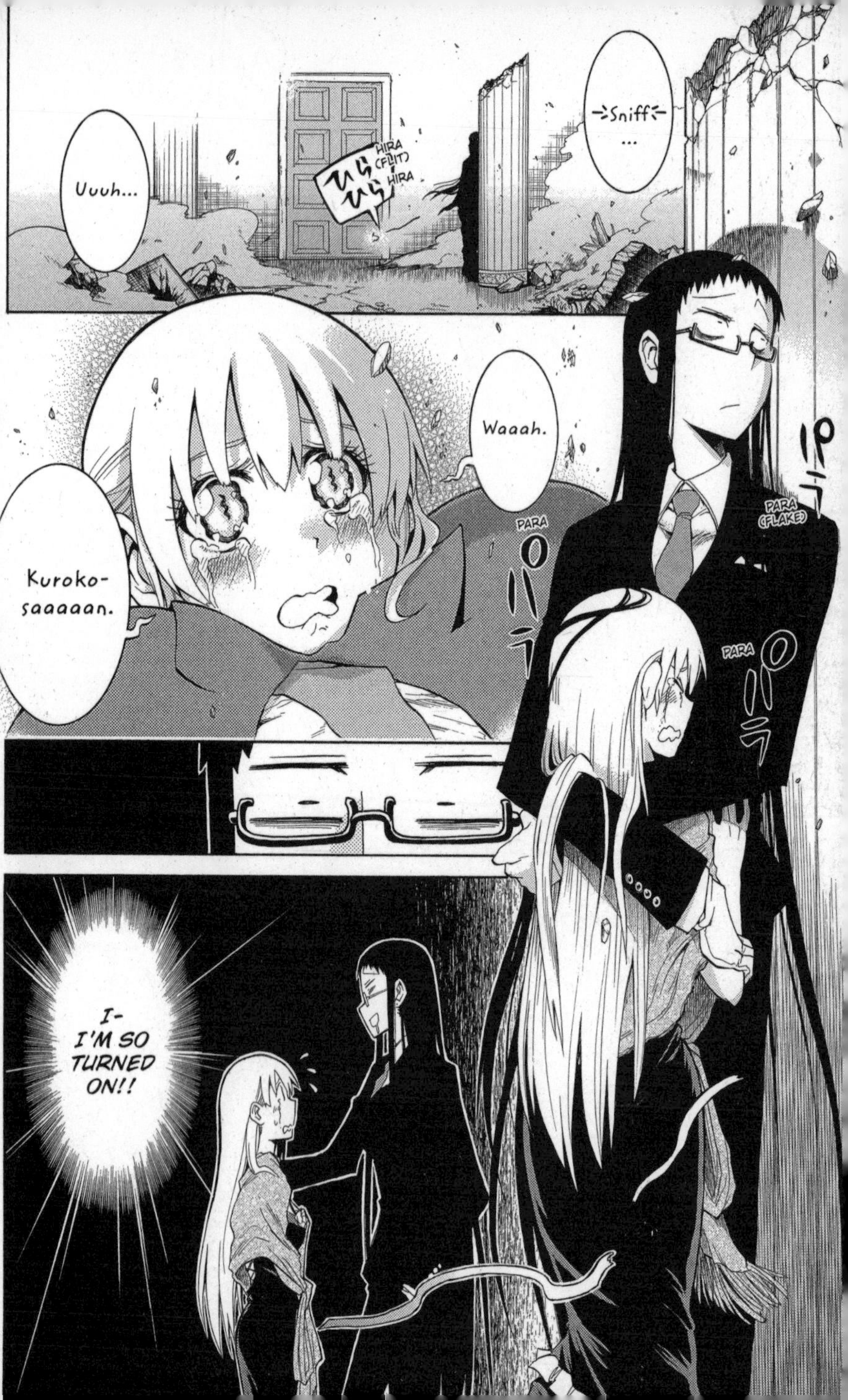
Sniff
...
ひら ひら
HIRA (FLIT) HIRA
Uuuh...
パラ
PARA (FLAKE)
PARA
パラ
PARA
パラ
Waaah.
Kuroko-saaaaan.
I- I'M SO TURNED ON!!

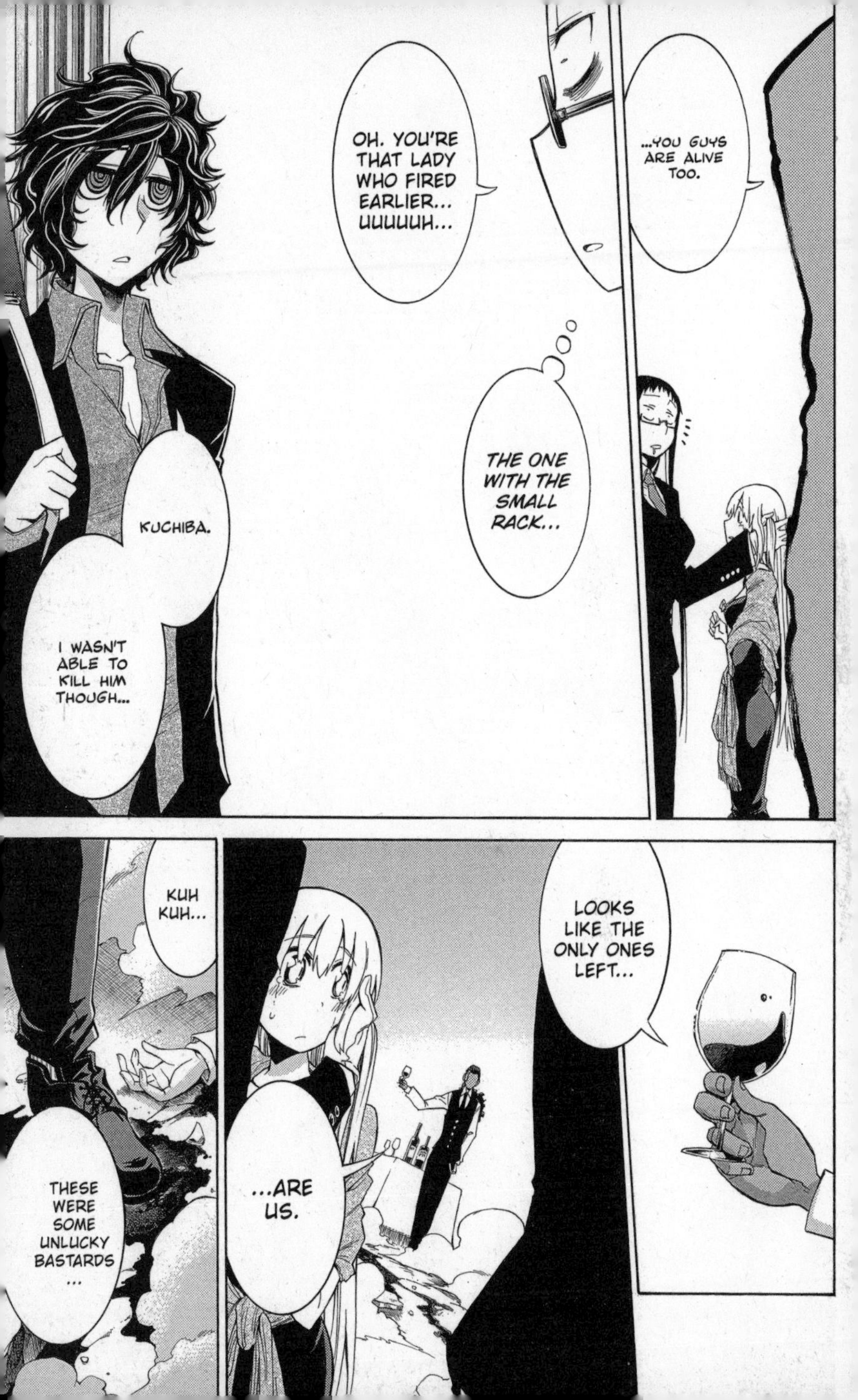
...YOU GUYS ARE ALIVE TOO.
OH. YOU'RE THAT LADY WHO FIRED EARLIER... UUUUUH...
THE ONE WITH THE SMALL RACK...
KUCHIBA.
I WASN'T ABLE TO KILL HIM THOUGH...
LOOKS LIKE THE ONLY ONES LEFT...
...ARE US.
KUH KUH...
THESE WERE SOME UNLUCKY BASTARDS ...

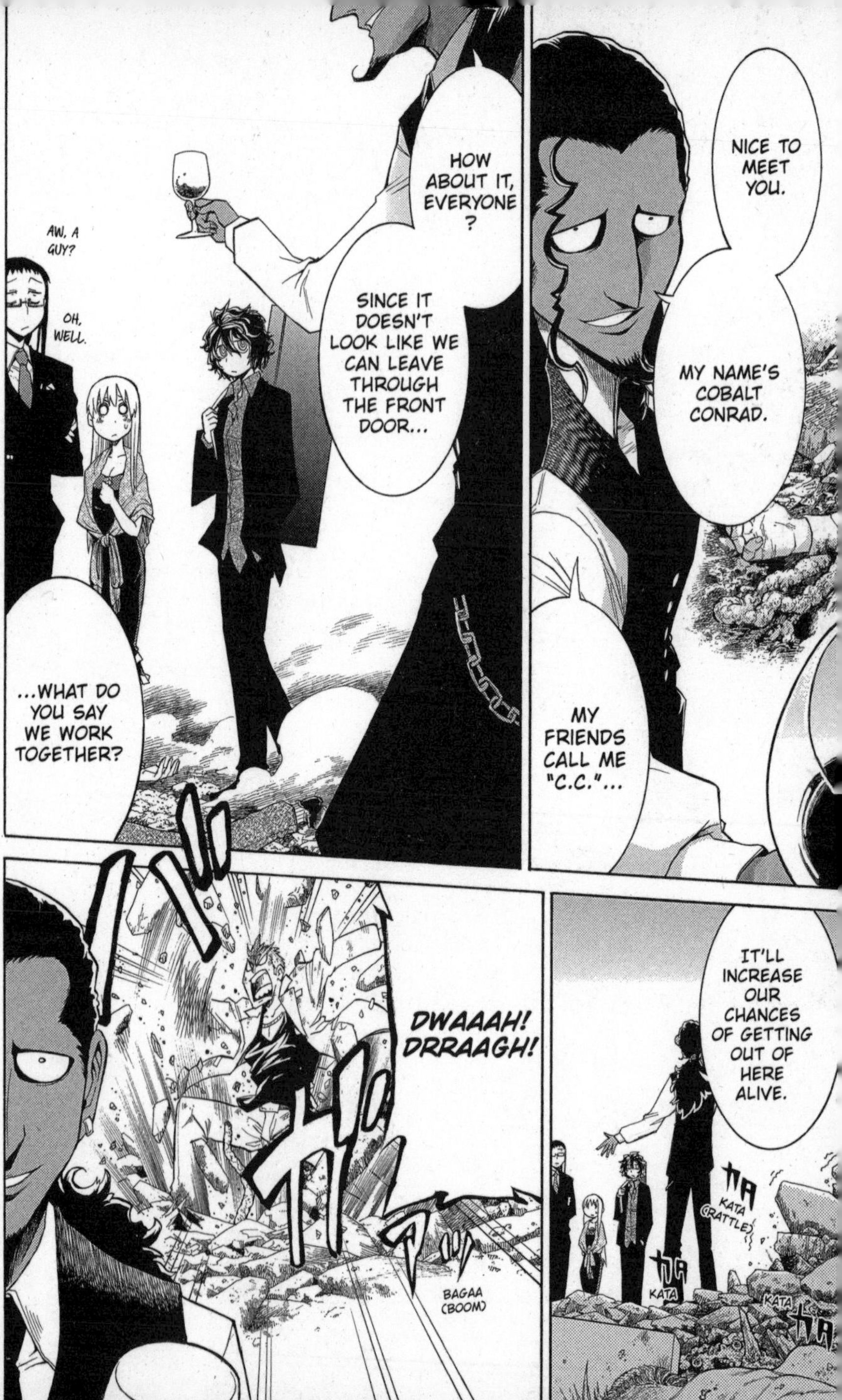
NICE TO MEET YOU.
MY NAME'S COBALT CONRAD.
MY FRIENDS CALL ME "C.C."...
HOW ABOUT IT, EVERYONE?
SINCE IT DOESN'T LOOK LIKE WE CAN LEAVE THROUGH THE FRONT DOOR...
...WHAT DO YOU SAY WE WORK TOGETHER?
AW, A GUY?
OH, WELL.
IT'LL INCREASE OUR CHANCES OF GETTING OUT OF HERE ALIVE.
KATA (RATTLE)
KATA
KATA
DWAAAH! DRRAAGH!
BAGAA (BOOM)

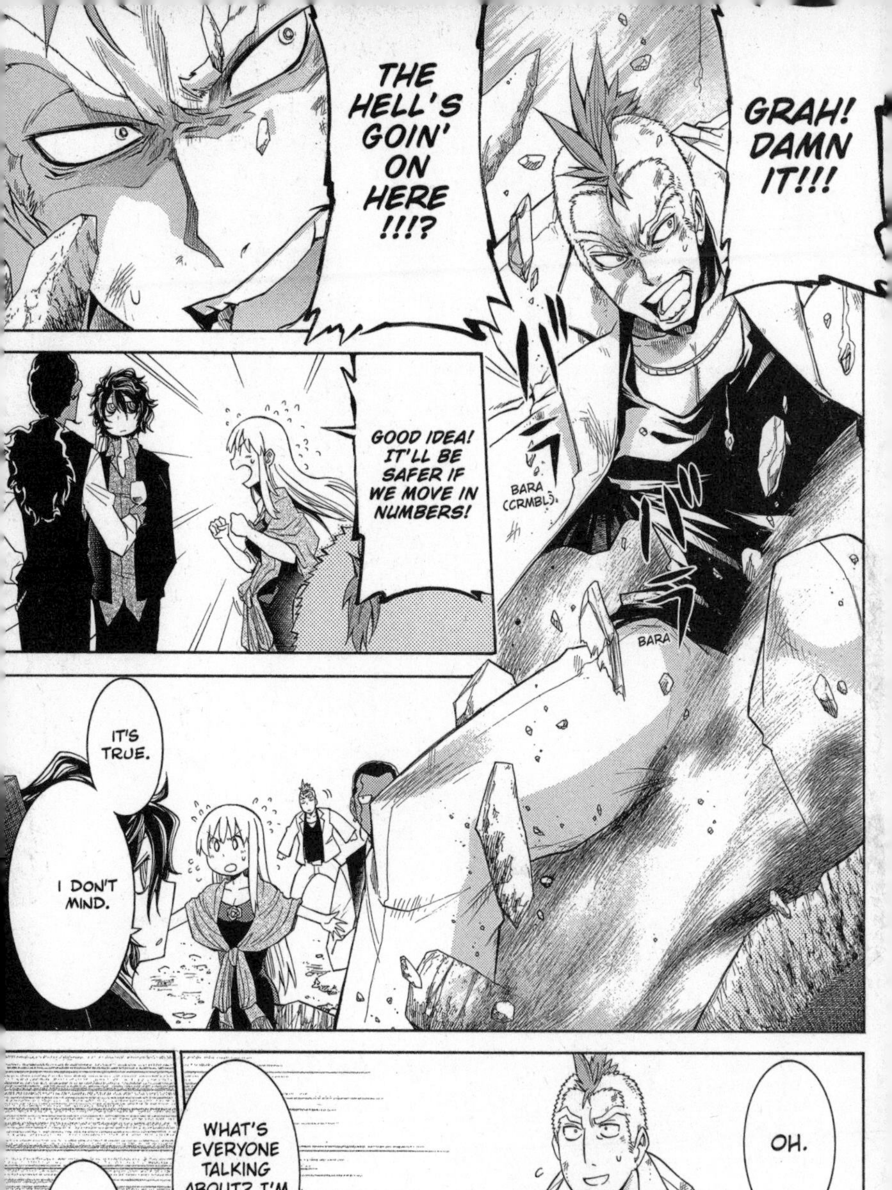
GRAH! DAMN IT!!!
BARA (CRMBL)
BARA
THE HELL'S GOIN' ON HERE!!!?
GOOD IDEA! IT'LL BE SAFER IF WE MOVE IN NUMBERS!
IT'S TRUE.
I DON'T MIND.
OH.
WHAT'S EVERYONE TALKING ABOUT? I'M A LITTLE BEHIND...
HEY.

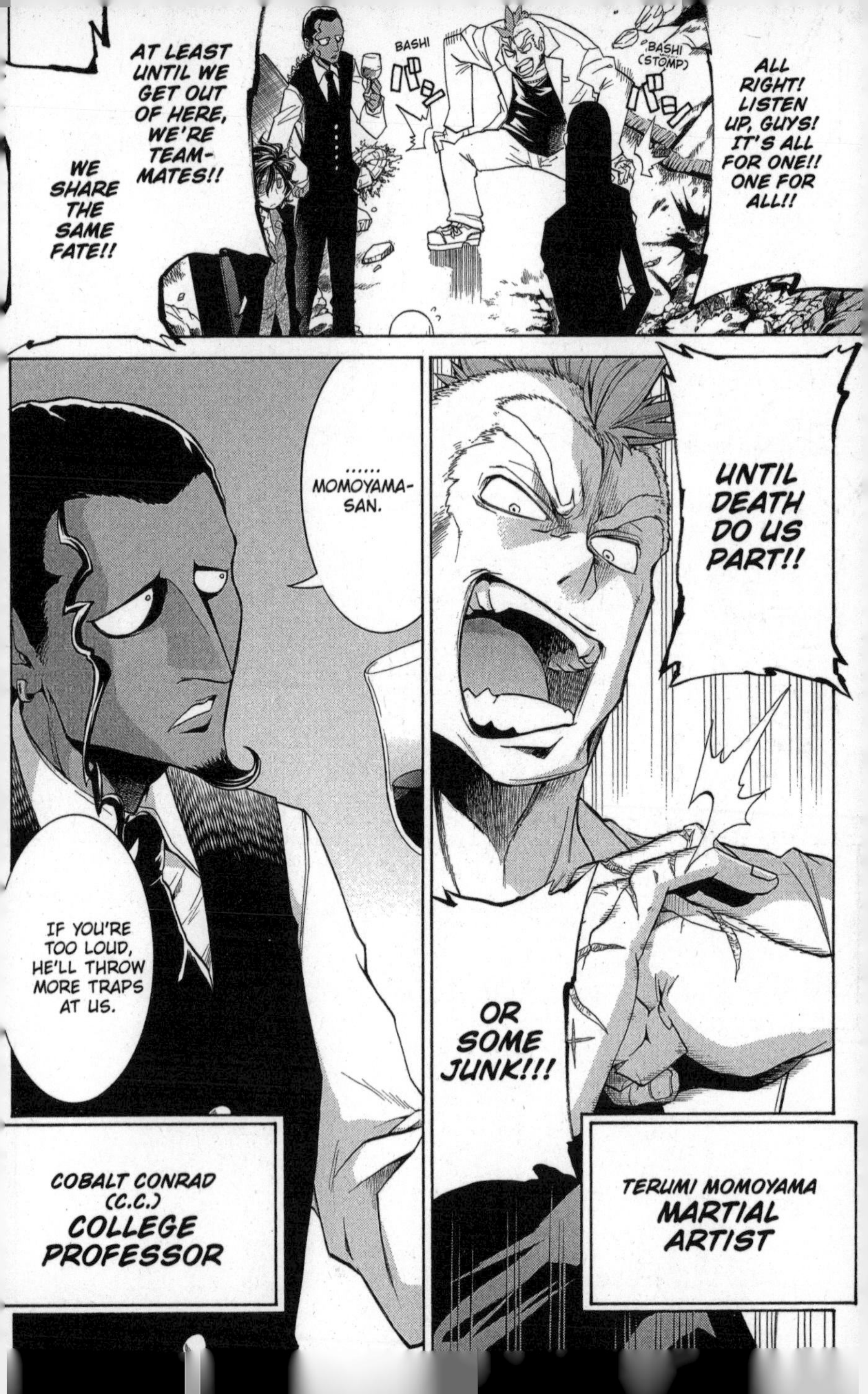

ALL RIGHT! LISTEN UP, GUYS! IT'S ALL FOR ONE!! ONE FOR ALL!!
BASHI (STOMP)
BASHI
AT LEAST UNTIL WE GET OUT OF HERE, WE'RE TEAM-MATES!!
WE SHARE THE SAME FATE!!
UNTIL DEATH DO US PART!!
OR SOME JUNK!!!
TERUMI MOMOYAMA MARTIAL ARTIST
...... MOMOYAMA-SAN.
IF YOU'RE TOO LOUD, HE'LL THROW MORE TRAPS AT US.
COBALT CONRAD (C.C.) COLLEGE PROFESSOR

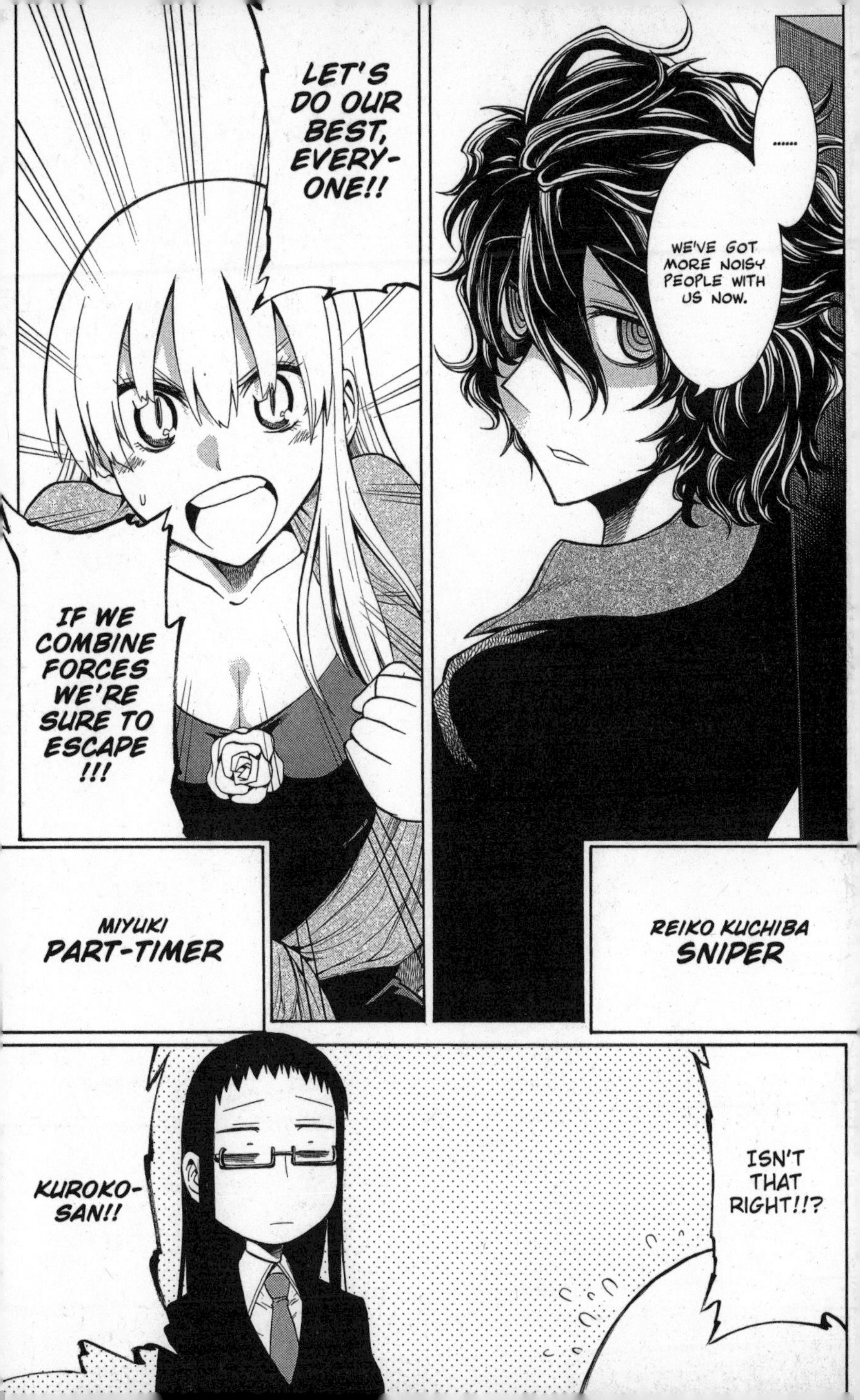
……
WE'VE GOT MORE NOISY PEOPLE WITH US NOW.
REIKO KUCHIBA
SNIPER
LET'S DO OUR BEST, EVERY-ONE!!
IF WE COMBINE FORCES WE'RE SURE TO ESCAPE !!!
MIYUKI
PART-TIMER
ISN'T THAT RIGHT!!?
KUROKO-SAN!!

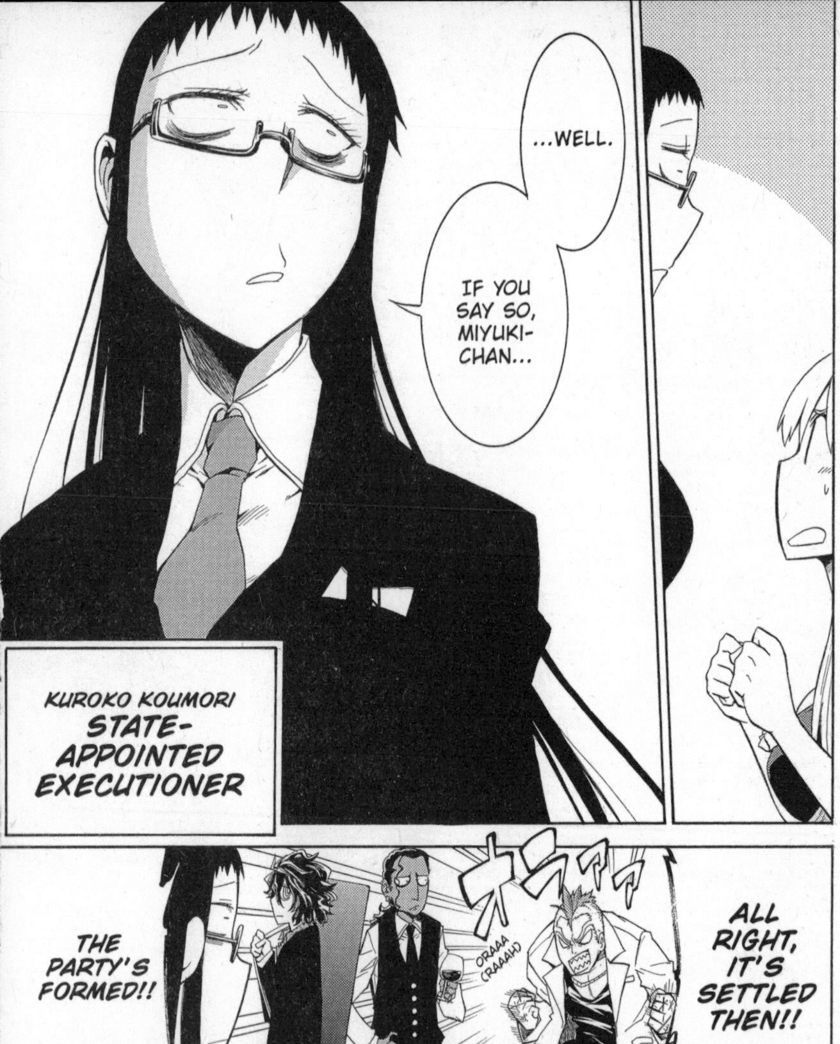
...WELL.
IF YOU SAY SO, MIYUKI-CHAN...
KUROKO KOUMORI STATE-APPOINTED EXECUTIONER
ALL RIGHT, IT'S SETTLED THEN!!
オラァァ
ORAAA (RAAAH)
THE PARTY'S FORMED!!
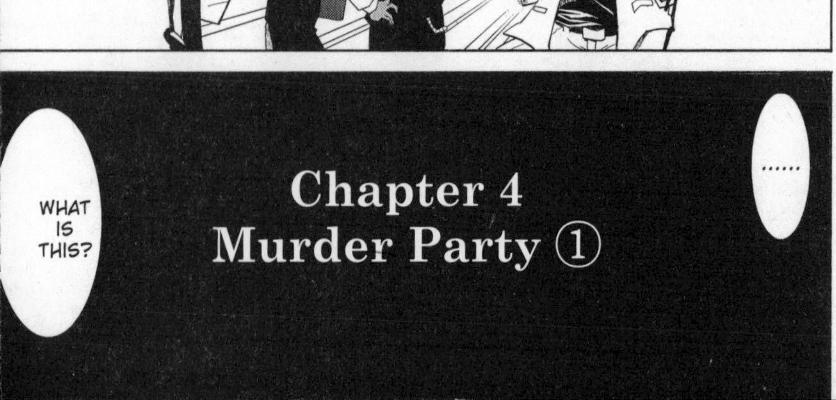
......
WHAT IS THIS?

Chapter 4 Murder Party ①

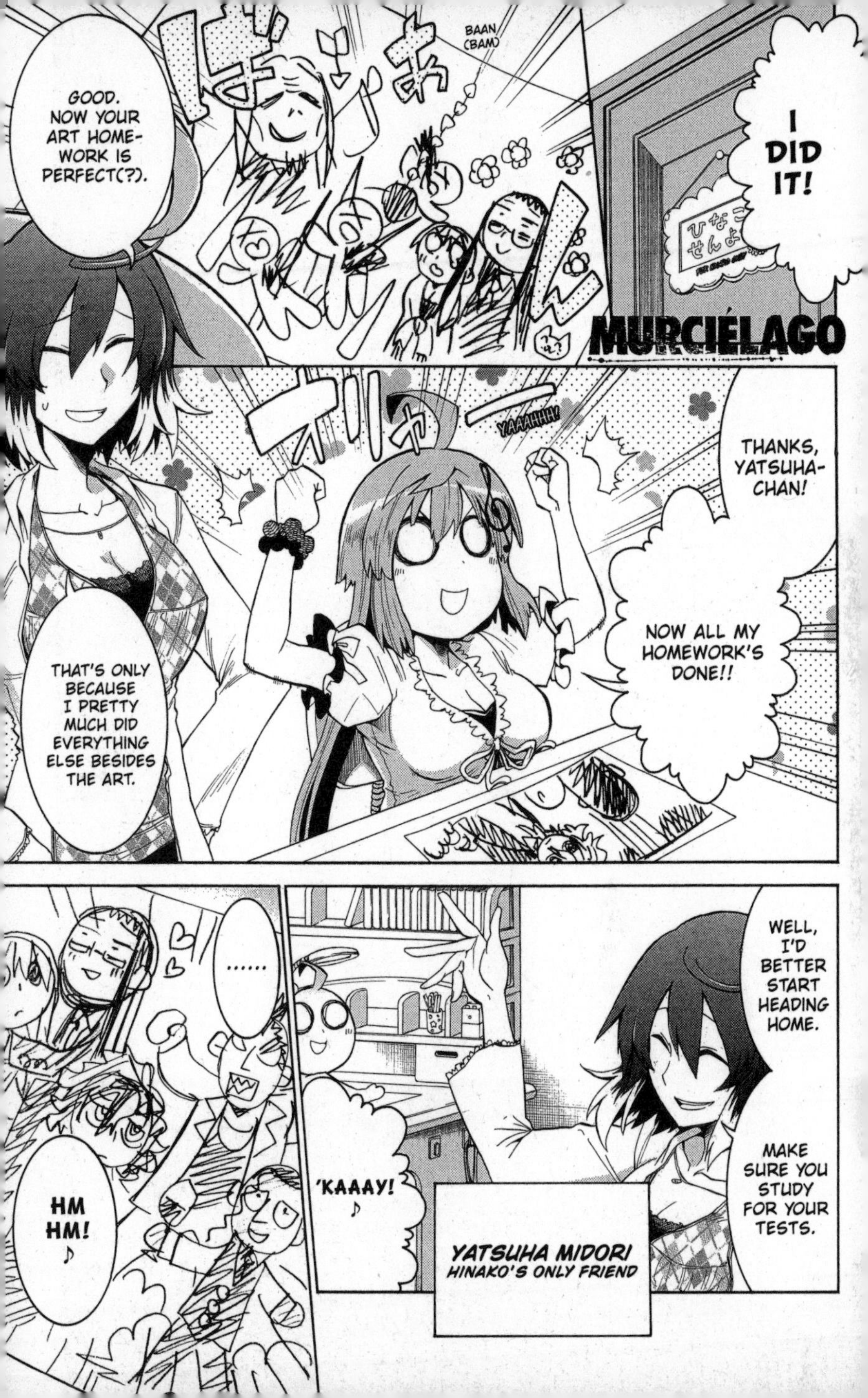
I DID IT!
BAAN (BAM)
GOOD. NOW YOUR ART HOMEWORK IS PERFECT(?).
MURCIÉLAGO
THANKS, YATSUHA-CHAN!
NOW ALL MY HOMEWORK'S DONE!!
YAAAHHH!
THAT'S ONLY BECAUSE I PRETTY MUCH DID EVERYTHING ELSE BESIDES THE ART.
WELL, I'D BETTER START HEADING HOME.
MAKE SURE YOU STUDY FOR YOUR TESTS.
'KAAAY! ♪
YATSUHA MIDORI
HINAKO'S ONLY FRIEND
......
HM HM! ♪

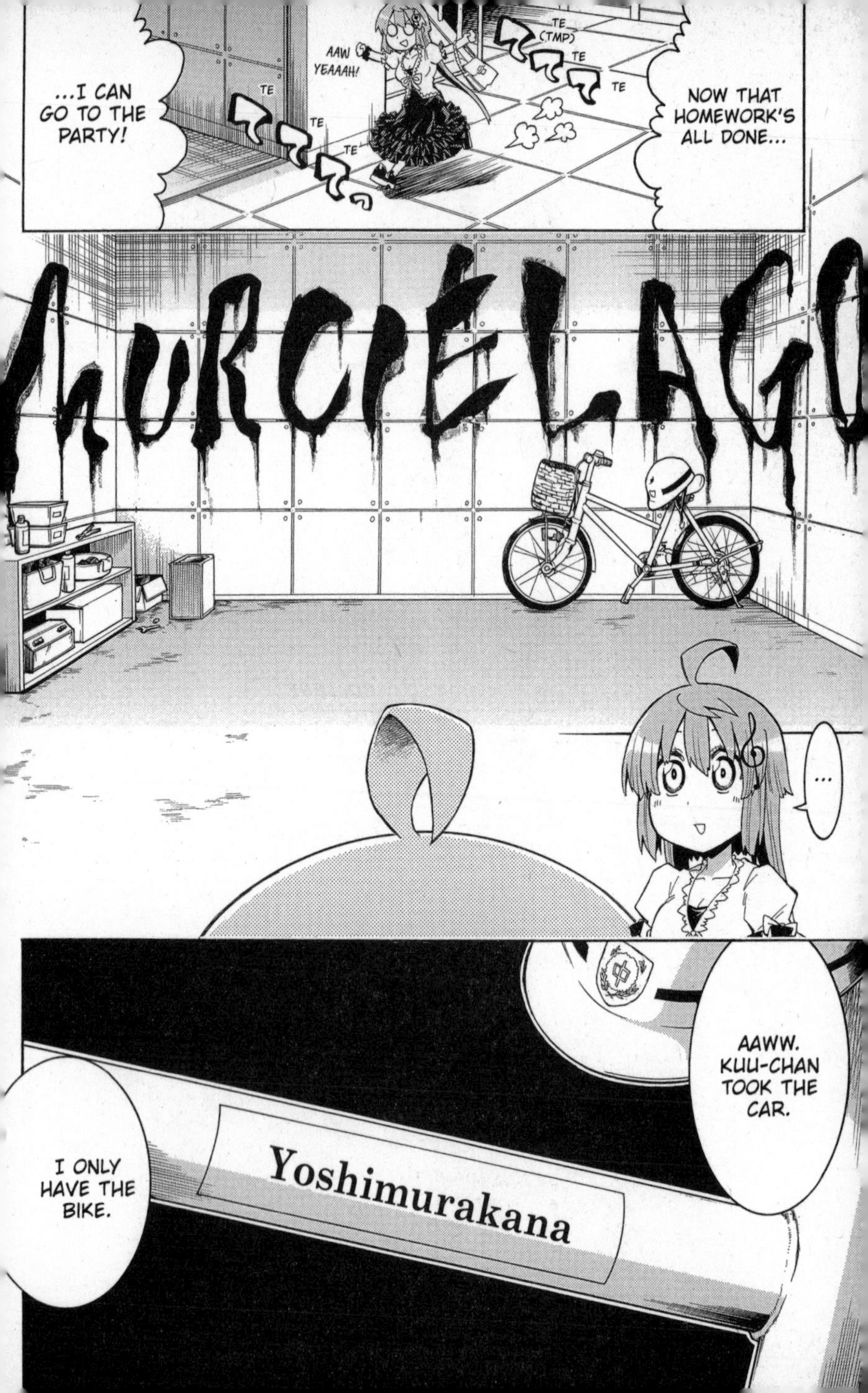
NOW THAT HOMEWORK'S ALL DONE...
TE (TMP)
TE
TE
AAW YEAAAH!
...I CAN GO TO THE PARTY!
TE
TE
TE
MURCIÉLAGO
...
AAWW. KUU-CHAN TOOK THE CAR.
Yoshimurakana
I ONLY HAVE THE BIKE.

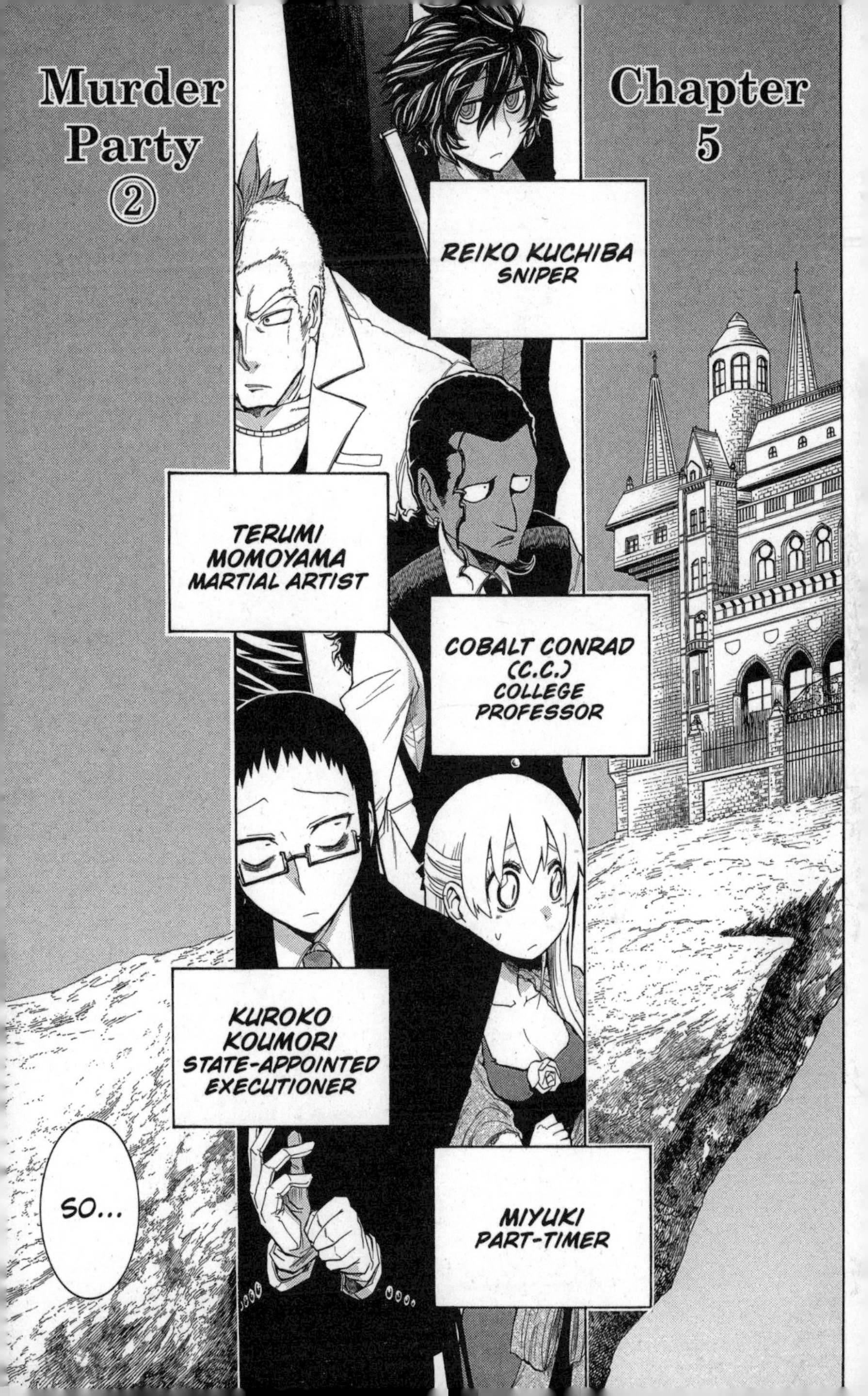
Chapter 5
Murder Party ②
REIKO KUCHIBA SNIPER
TERUMI MOMOYAMA MARTIAL ARTIST
COBALT CONRAD (C.C.) COLLEGE PROFESSOR
KUROKO KOUMORI STATE-APPOINTED EXECUTIONER
MIYUKI PART-TIMER
SO...

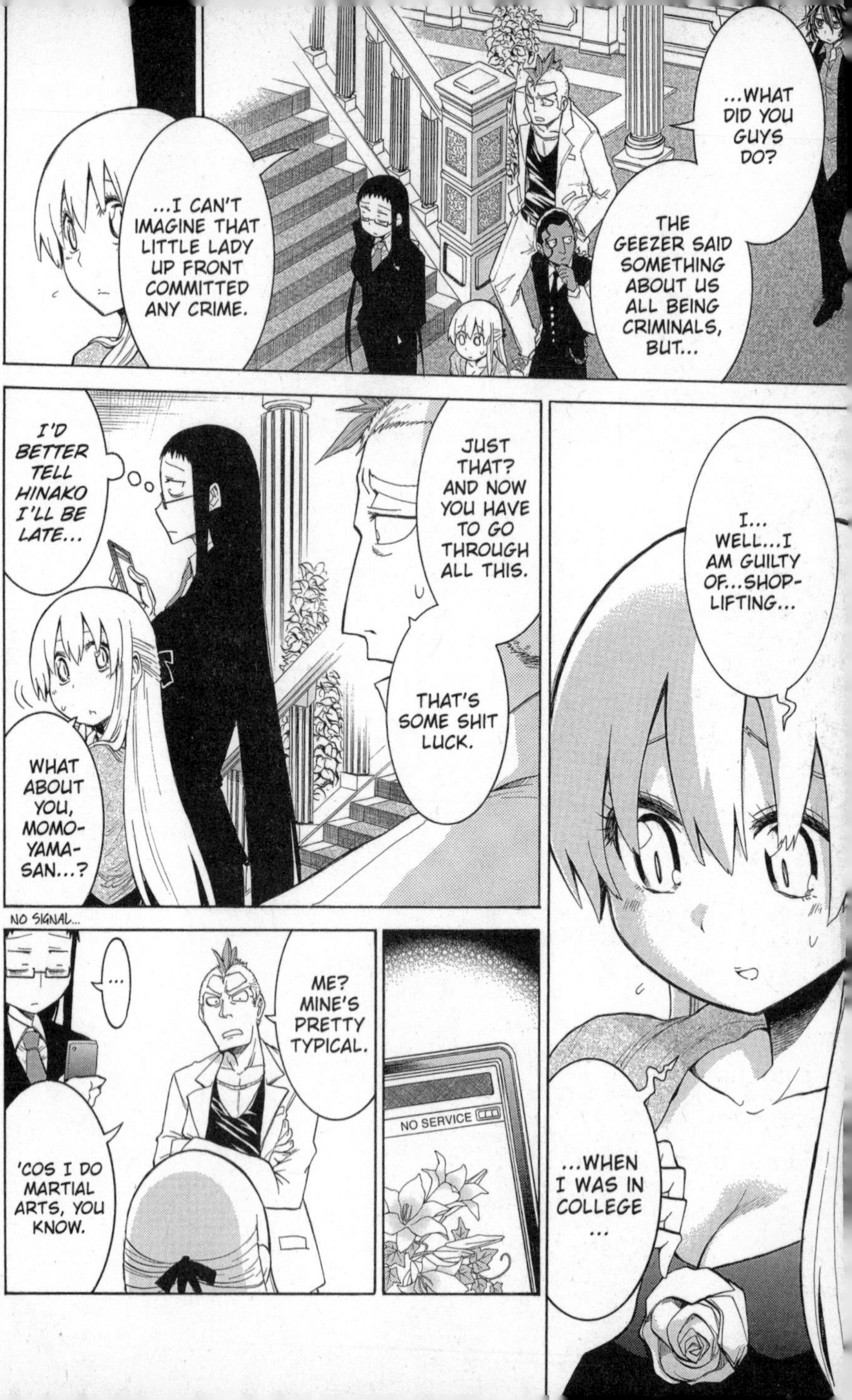
...WHAT DID YOU GUYS DO?
THE GEEZER SAID SOMETHING ABOUT US ALL BEING CRIMINALS, BUT...
...I CAN'T IMAGINE THAT LITTLE LADY UP FRONT COMMITTED ANY CRIME.
I... WELL...I AM GUILTY OF...SHOP-LIFTING...
...WHEN I WAS IN COLLEGE...
JUST THAT? AND NOW YOU HAVE TO GO THROUGH ALL THIS.
THAT'S SOME SHIT LUCK.
I'D BETTER TELL HINAKO I'LL BE LATE...
WHAT ABOUT YOU, MOMO-YAMA-SAN...?
NO SIGNAL...
NO SERVICE
ME? MINE'S PRETTY TYPICAL.
...
'COS I DO MARTIAL ARTS, YOU KNOW.

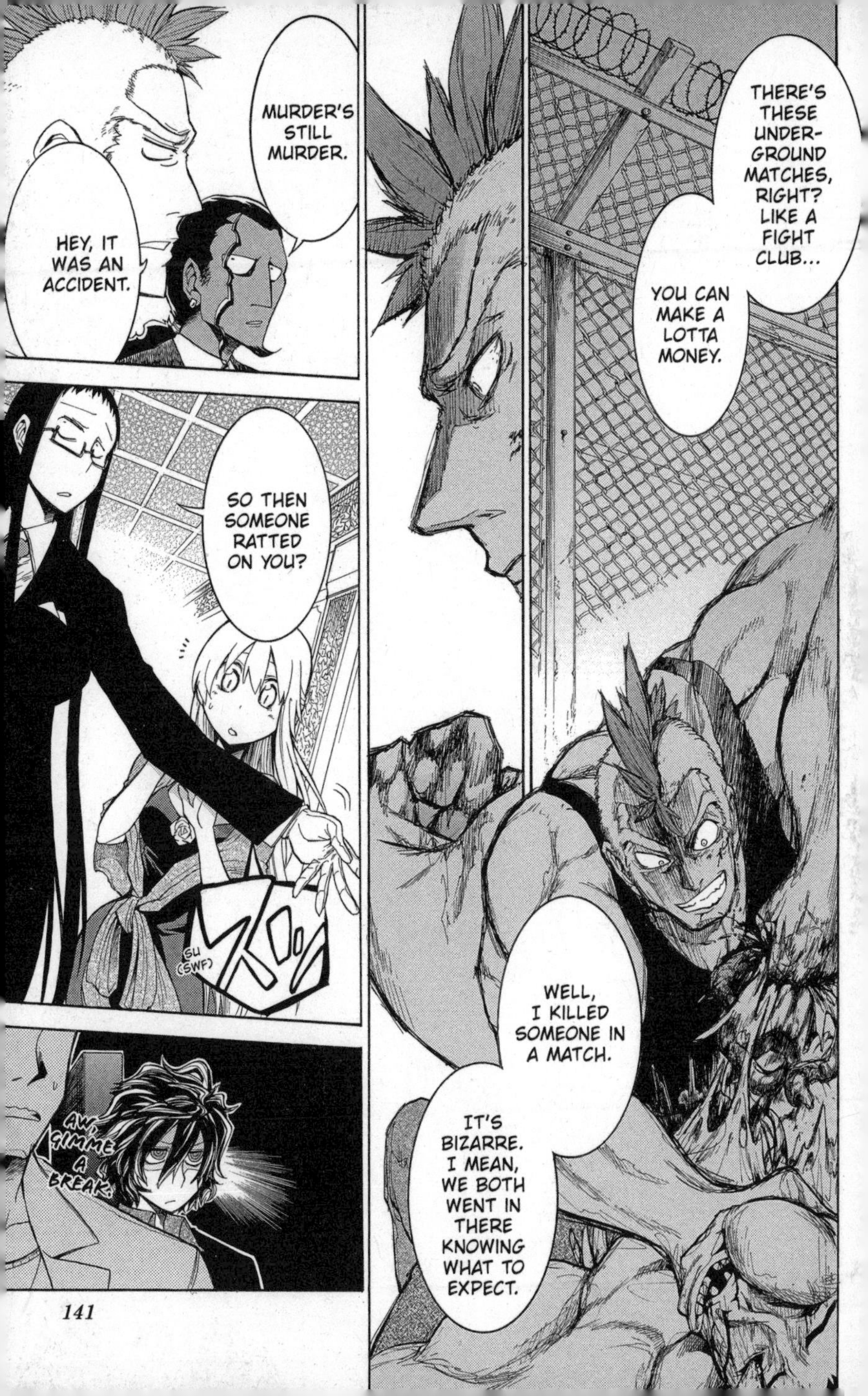
THERE'S THESE UNDER-GROUND MATCHES, RIGHT? LIKE A FIGHT CLUB...
YOU CAN MAKE A LOTTA MONEY.
WELL, I KILLED SOMEONE IN A MATCH.
IT'S BIZARRE. I MEAN, WE BOTH WENT IN THERE KNOWING WHAT TO EXPECT.
MURDER'S STILL MURDER.
HEY, IT WAS AN ACCIDENT.
SO THEN SOMEONE RATTED ON YOU?
SU (SWF)
AW, GIMME A BREAK.

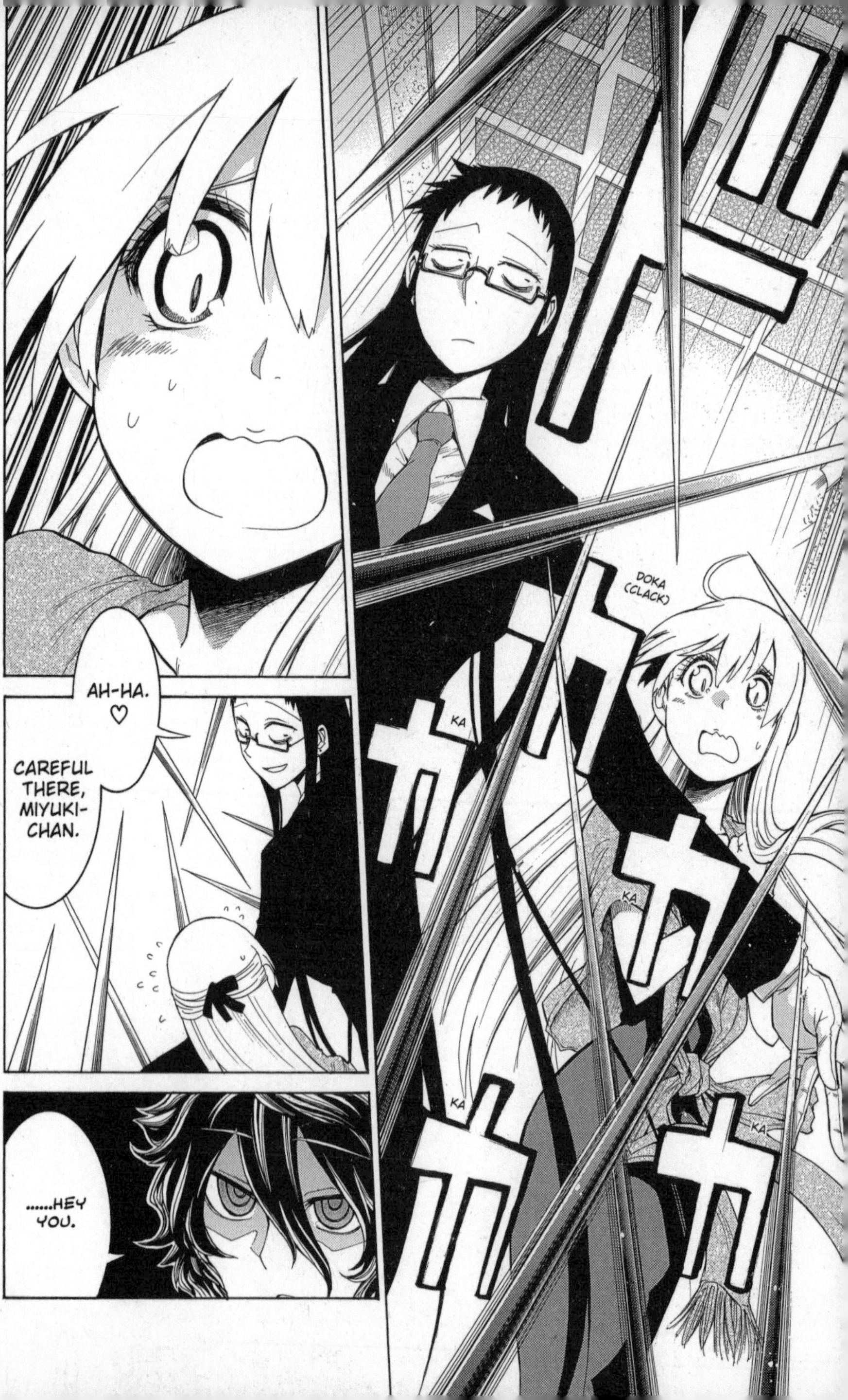
DOKA (CLACK)
KA
KA
KA
KA
AH-HA. ♡
CAREFUL THERE, MIYUKI-CHAN.
......HEY YOU.

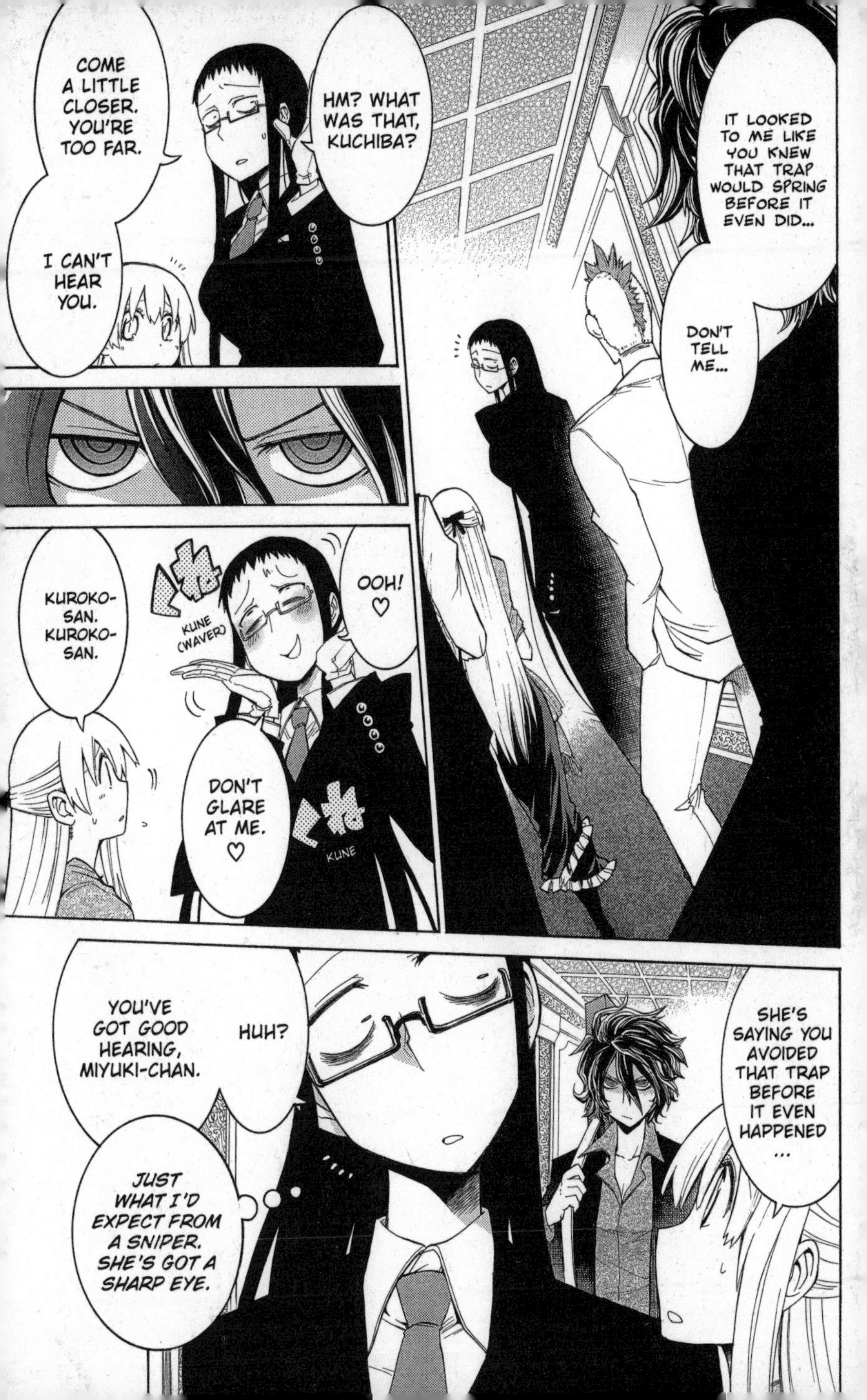
IT LOOKED TO ME LIKE YOU KNEW THAT TRAP WOULD SPRING BEFORE IT EVEN DID...
DON'T TELL ME...
HM? WHAT WAS THAT, KUCHIBA?
COME A LITTLE CLOSER. YOU'RE TOO FAR.
I CAN'T HEAR YOU.
OOH! ♡
KUNE (WAVER)
KUROKO-SAN. KUROKO-SAN.
DON'T GLARE AT ME. ♡
KUNE
SHE'S SAYING YOU AVOIDED THAT TRAP BEFORE IT EVEN HAPPENED...
HUH?
YOU'VE GOT GOOD HEARING, MIYUKI-CHAN.
JUST WHAT I'D EXPECT FROM A SNIPER. SHE'S GOT A SHARP EYE.

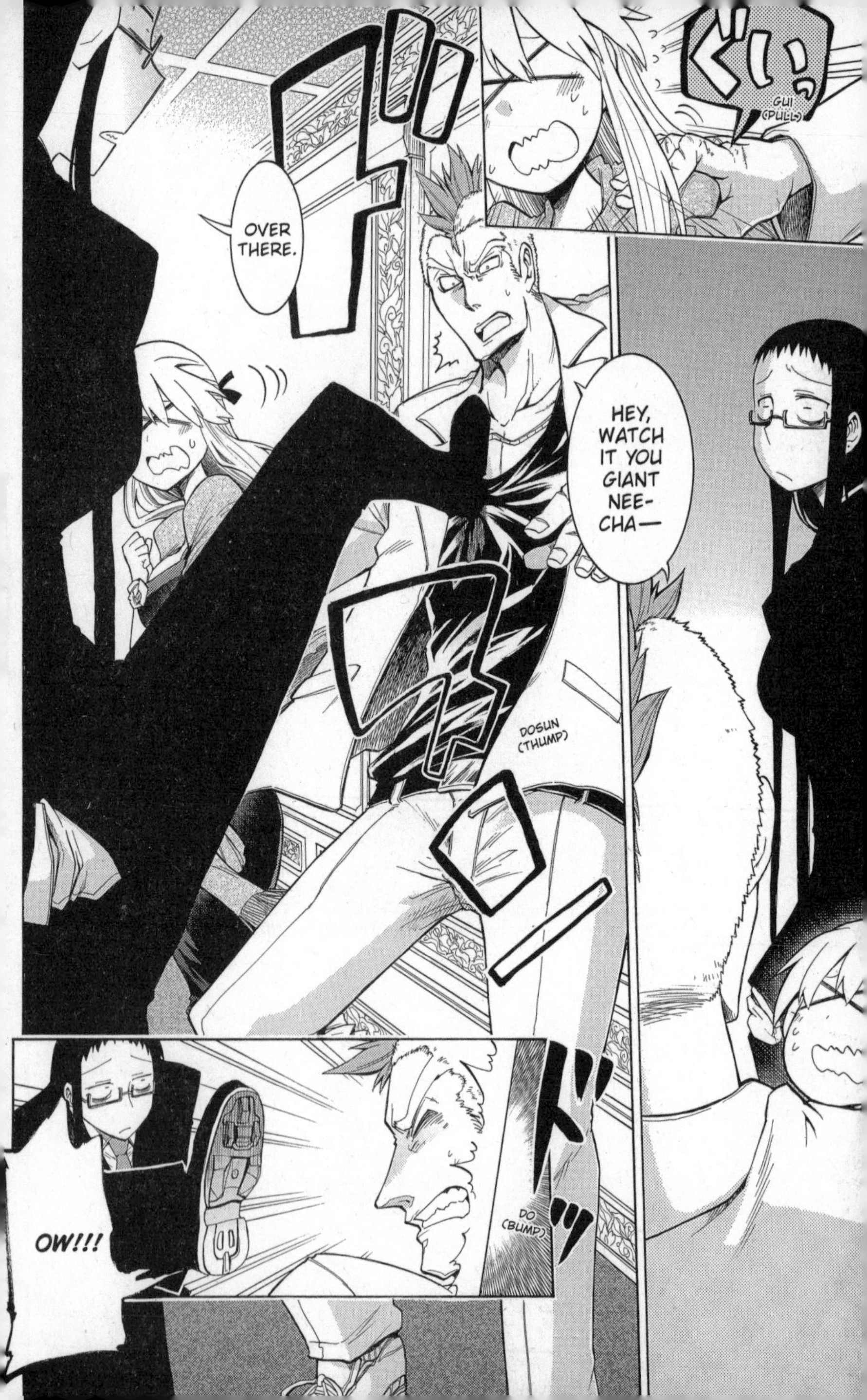
GUI (PULL)
OVER THERE.
HEY, WATCH IT YOU GIANT NEE-CHA—
DOSUN (THUMP)
DO (BUMP)
OW!!!

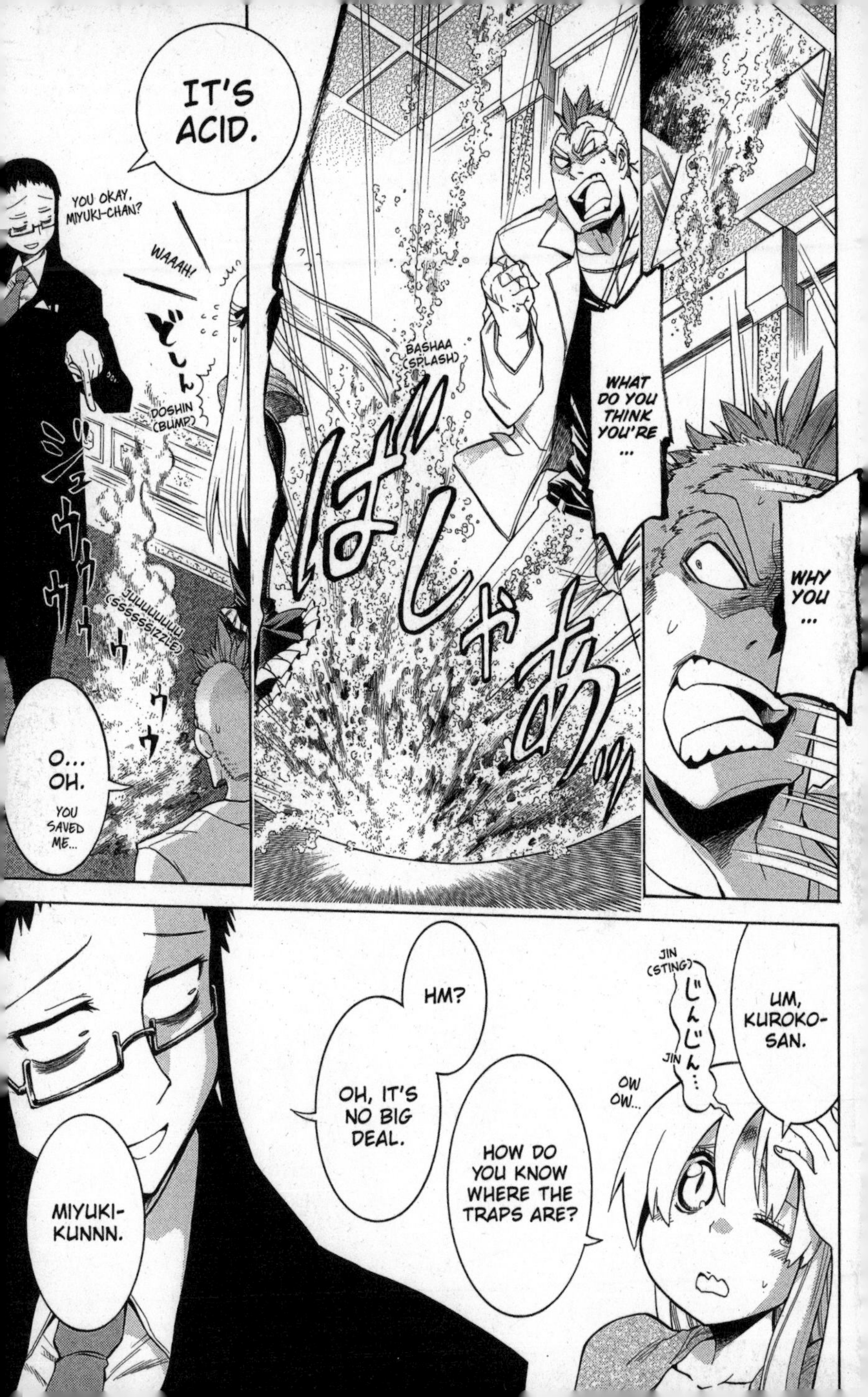
WHAT DO YOU THINK YOU'RE ...
WHY YOU ...
BASHAA (SPLASH)
ばしゃあ
IT'S ACID.
WAAAH!
YOU OKAY, MIYUKI-CHAN?
どしん
DOSHIN (BUMP)
JUUUUUUU (SSSSSSIZZLE)
O... OH.
YOU SAVED ME...
UM, KUROKO-SAN.
JIN (STING)
じんじん…
JIN
OW OW...
HM?
HOW DO YOU KNOW WHERE THE TRAPS ARE?
OH, IT'S NO BIG DEAL.
MIYUKI-KUNNN.

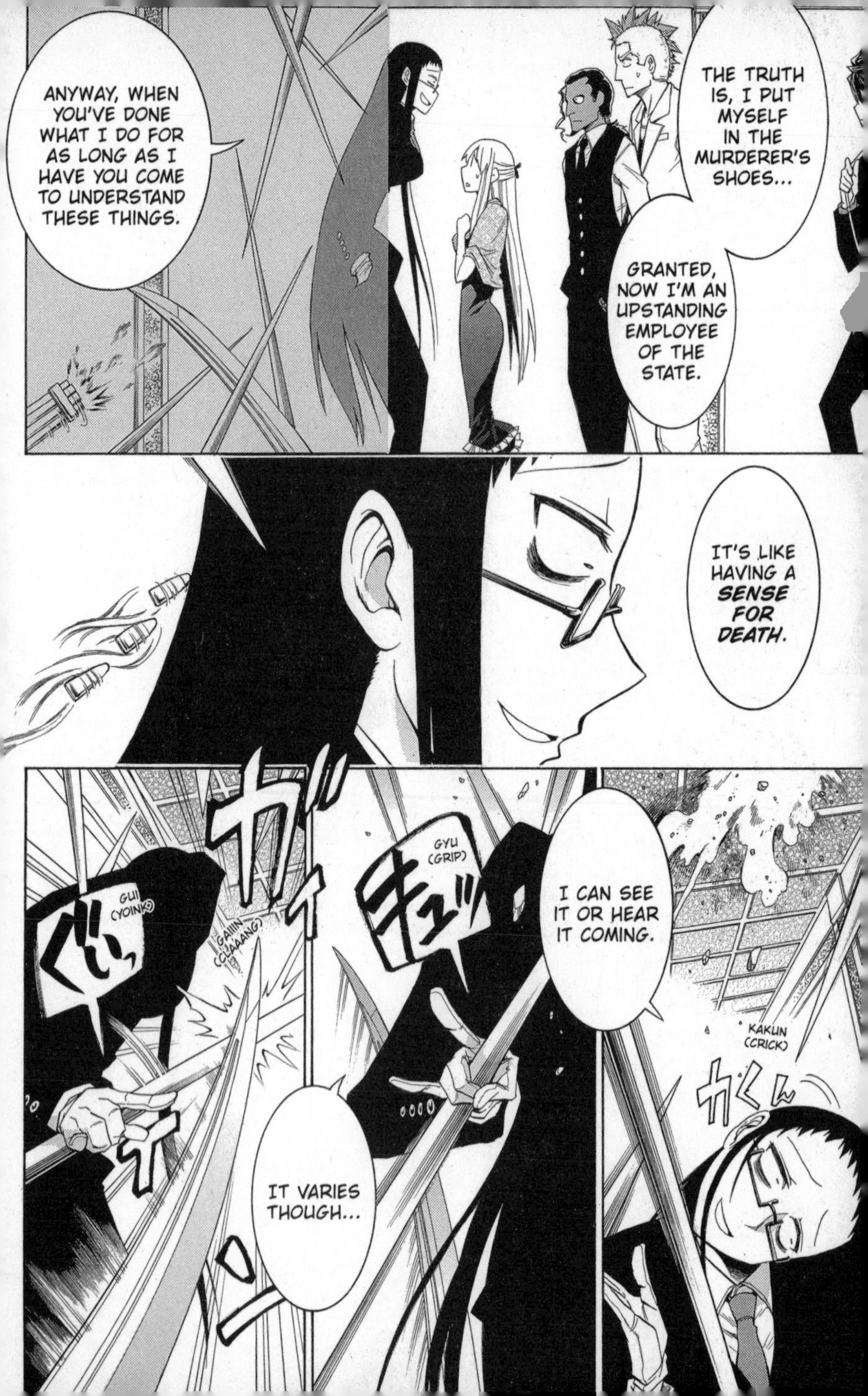
THE TRUTH IS, I PUT MYSELF IN THE MURDERER'S SHOES...
GRANTED, NOW I'M AN UPSTANDING EMPLOYEE OF THE STATE.
ANYWAY, WHEN YOU'VE DONE WHAT I DO FOR AS LONG AS I HAVE YOU COME TO UNDERSTAND THESE THINGS.
IT'S LIKE HAVING A SENSE FOR DEATH.
I CAN SEE IT OR HEAR IT COMING.
KAKUN (CRICK)
GYU (GRIP)
IT VARIES THOUGH...
GUI (YOINK)
GAIIN (CLAAANG)

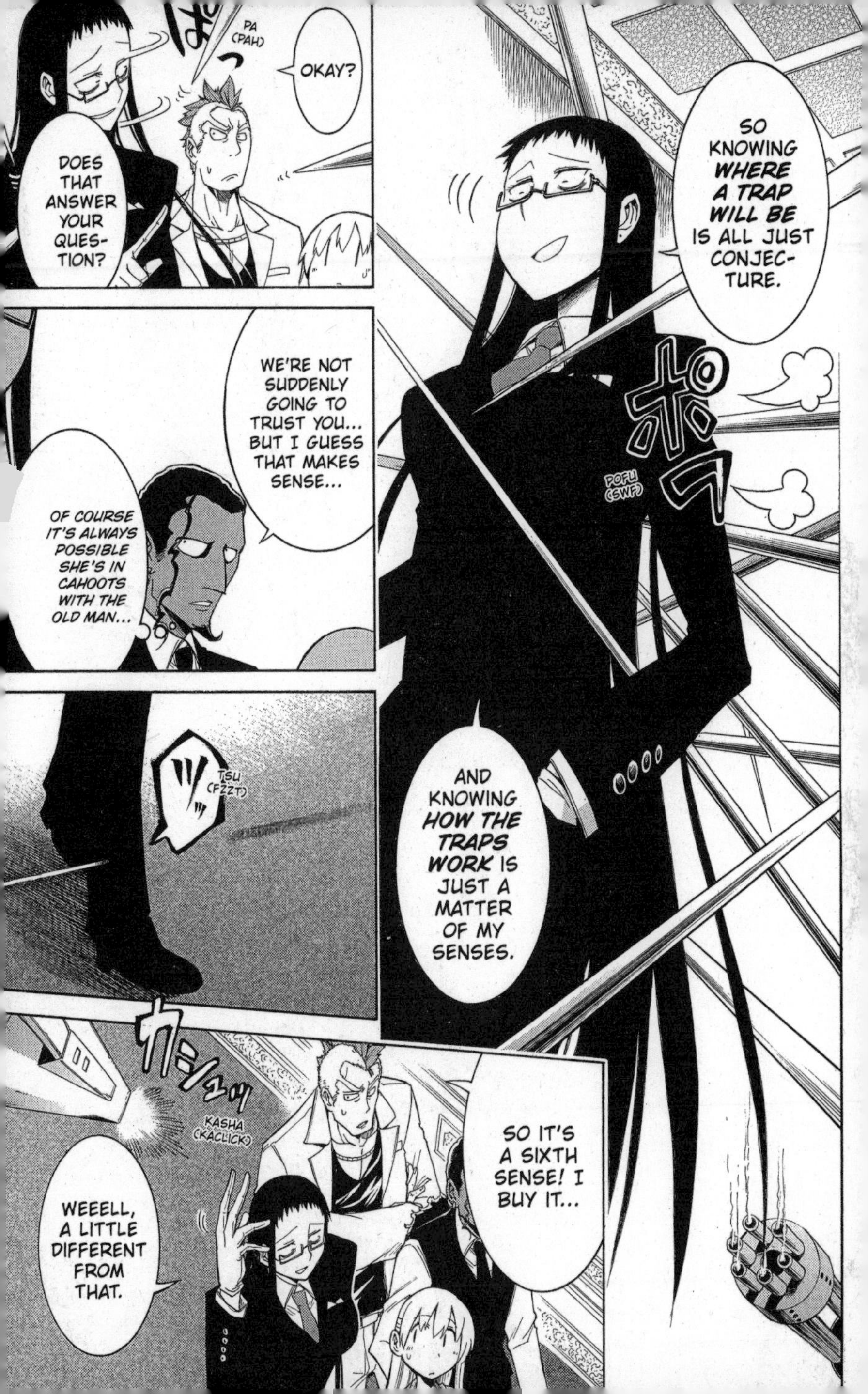
SO KNOWING ***WHERE A TRAP WILL BE*** IS ALL JUST CONJECTURE.
POFU (SWF)
AND KNOWING ***HOW THE TRAPS WORK*** IS JUST A MATTER OF MY SENSES.
PA (PAH)
OKAY?
DOES THAT ANSWER YOUR QUESTION?
WE'RE NOT SUDDENLY GOING TO TRUST YOU... BUT I GUESS THAT MAKES SENSE...
OF COURSE IT'S ALWAYS POSSIBLE SHE'S IN CAHOOTS WITH THE OLD MAN...
TSU (FZZT)
KASHA (KACLICK)
SO IT'S A SIXTH SENSE! I BUY IT...
WEEELL, A LITTLE DIFFERENT FROM THAT.

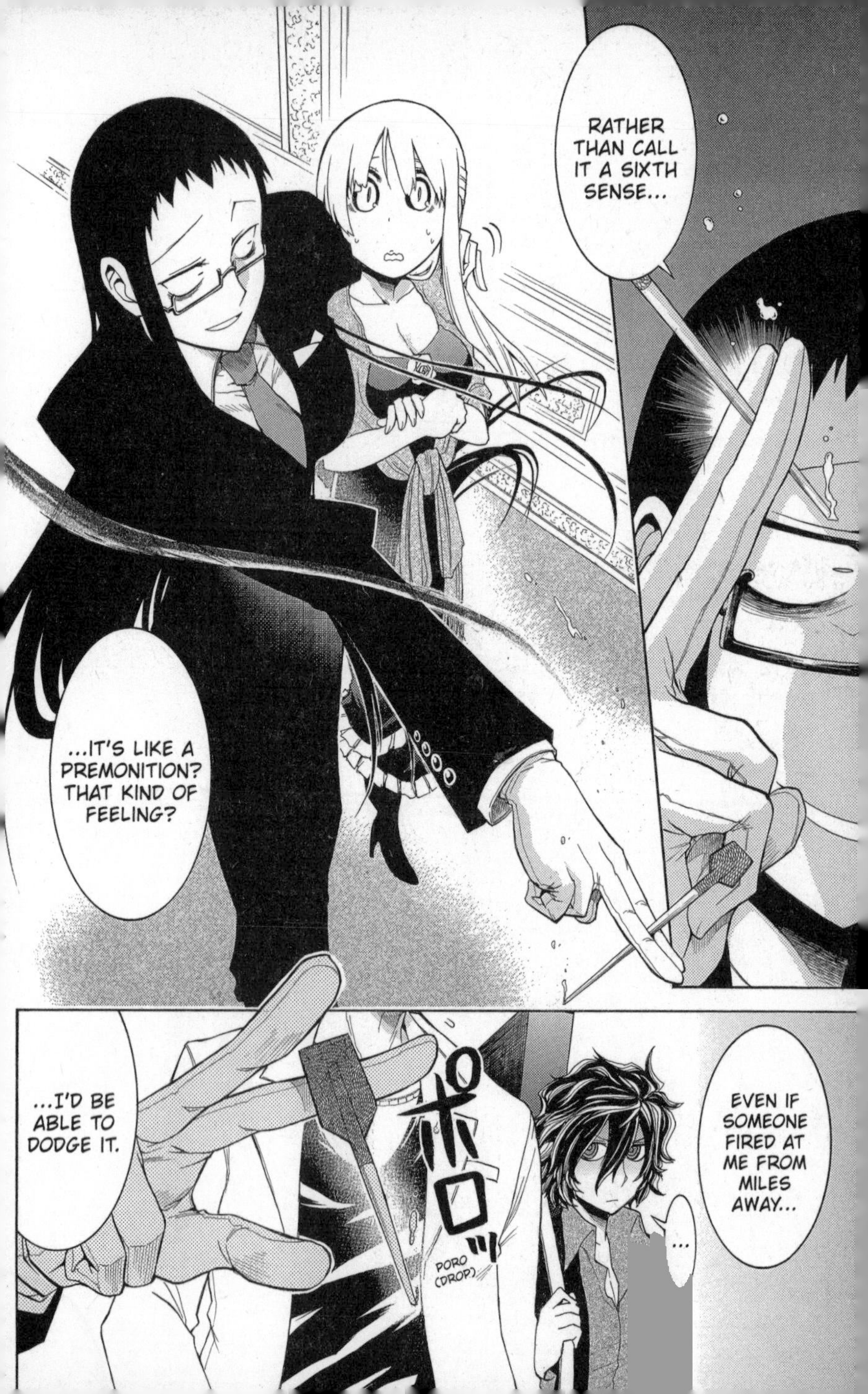
RATHER THAN CALL IT A SIXTH SENSE...
...IT'S LIKE A PREMONITION? THAT KIND OF FEELING?
EVEN IF SOMEONE FIRED AT ME FROM MILES AWAY...
...
PORO (DROP)
...I'D BE ABLE TO DODGE IT.

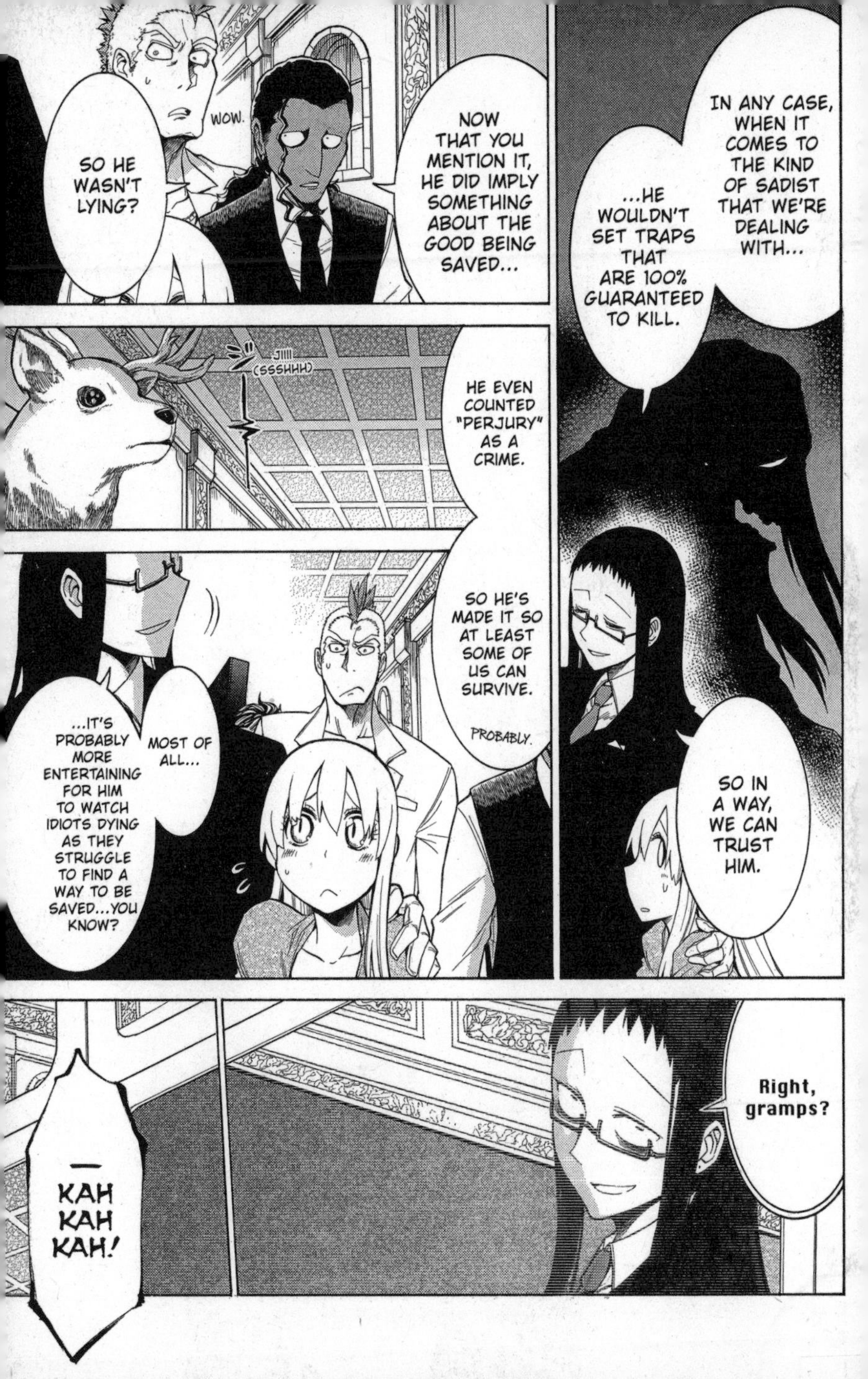
IN ANY CASE, WHEN IT COMES TO THE KIND OF SADIST THAT WE'RE DEALING WITH...
...HE WOULDN'T SET TRAPS THAT ARE 100% GUARANTEED TO KILL.
SO IN A WAY, WE CAN TRUST HIM.
NOW THAT YOU MENTION IT, HE DID IMPLY SOMETHING ABOUT THE GOOD BEING SAVED...
WOW.
SO HE WASN'T LYING?
HE EVEN COUNTED "PERJURY" AS A CRIME.
JIIII (SSSHHH)
SO HE'S MADE IT SO AT LEAST SOME OF US CAN SURVIVE.
PROBABLY.
MOST OF ALL...
...IT'S PROBABLY MORE ENTERTAINING FOR HIM TO WATCH IDIOTS DYING AS THEY STRUGGLE TO FIND A WAY TO BE SAVED...YOU KNOW?
Right, gramps?
—KAH KAH KAH!

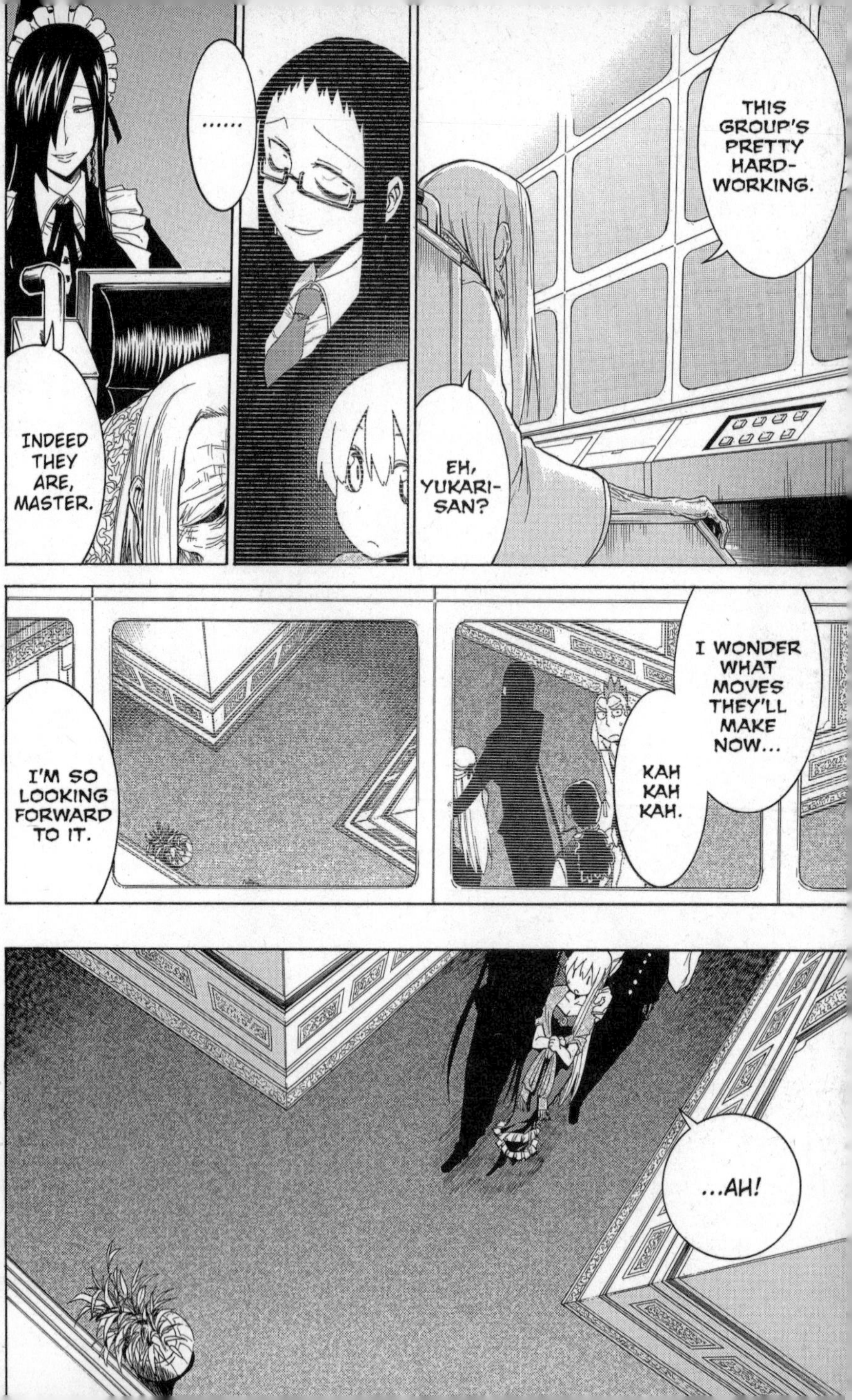
THIS GROUP'S PRETTY HARD-WORKING.
EH, YUKARI-SAN?
......
INDEED THEY ARE, MASTER.
I WONDER WHAT MOVES THEY'LL MAKE NOW...
KAH KAH KAH.
I'M SO LOOKING FORWARD TO IT.
...AH!

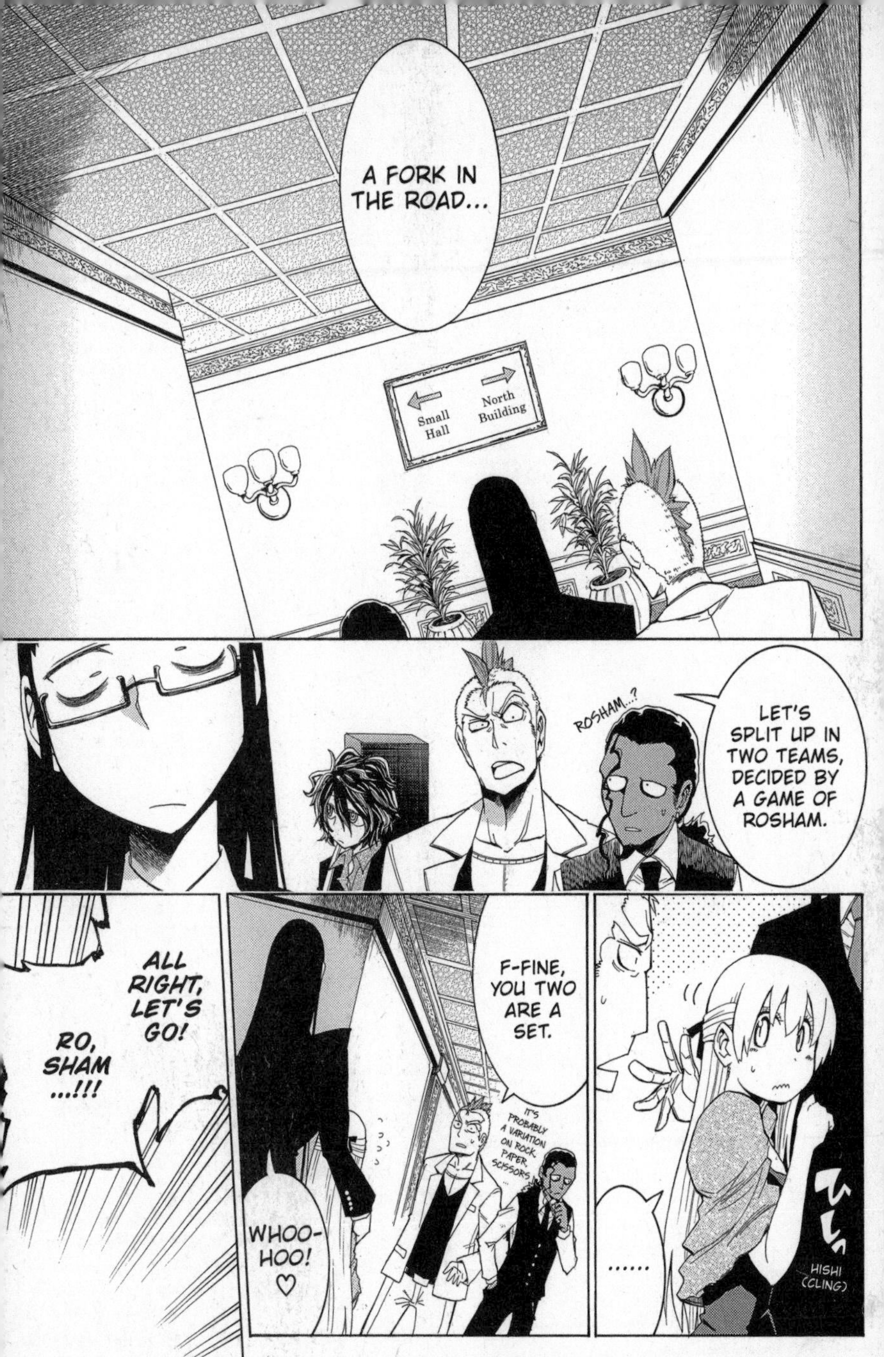
A FORK IN THE ROAD...
North Building
Small Hall
LET'S SPLIT UP IN TWO TEAMS, DECIDED BY A GAME OF ROSHAM.
ROSHAM...?
......
HISHI (CLING)
F-FINE, YOU TWO ARE A SET.
IT'S PROBABLY A VARIATION ON ROCK, PAPER, SCISSORS...
WHOO-HOO! ♡
ALL RIGHT, LET'S GO!
RO, SHAM ...!!!

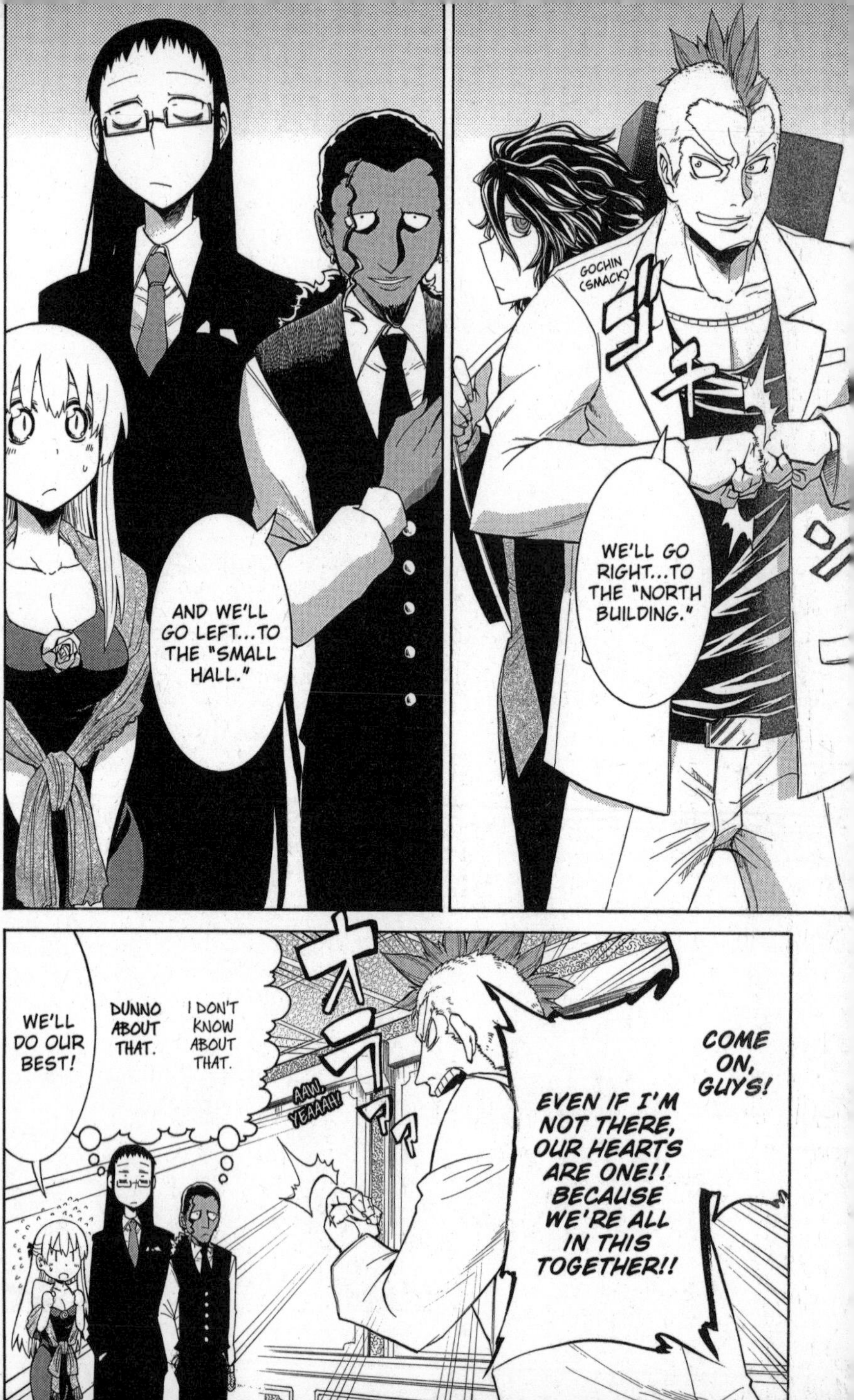
GOCHIN (SMACK)
WE'LL GO RIGHT...TO THE "NORTH BUILDING."
AND WE'LL GO LEFT...TO THE "SMALL HALL."
COME ON, GUYS!
EVEN IF I'M NOT THERE, OUR HEARTS ARE ONE!! BECAUSE WE'RE ALL IN THIS TOGETHER!!
AAW. YEAAAH!
I DON'T KNOW ABOUT THAT.
DUNNO ABOUT THAT.
WE'LL DO OUR BEST!

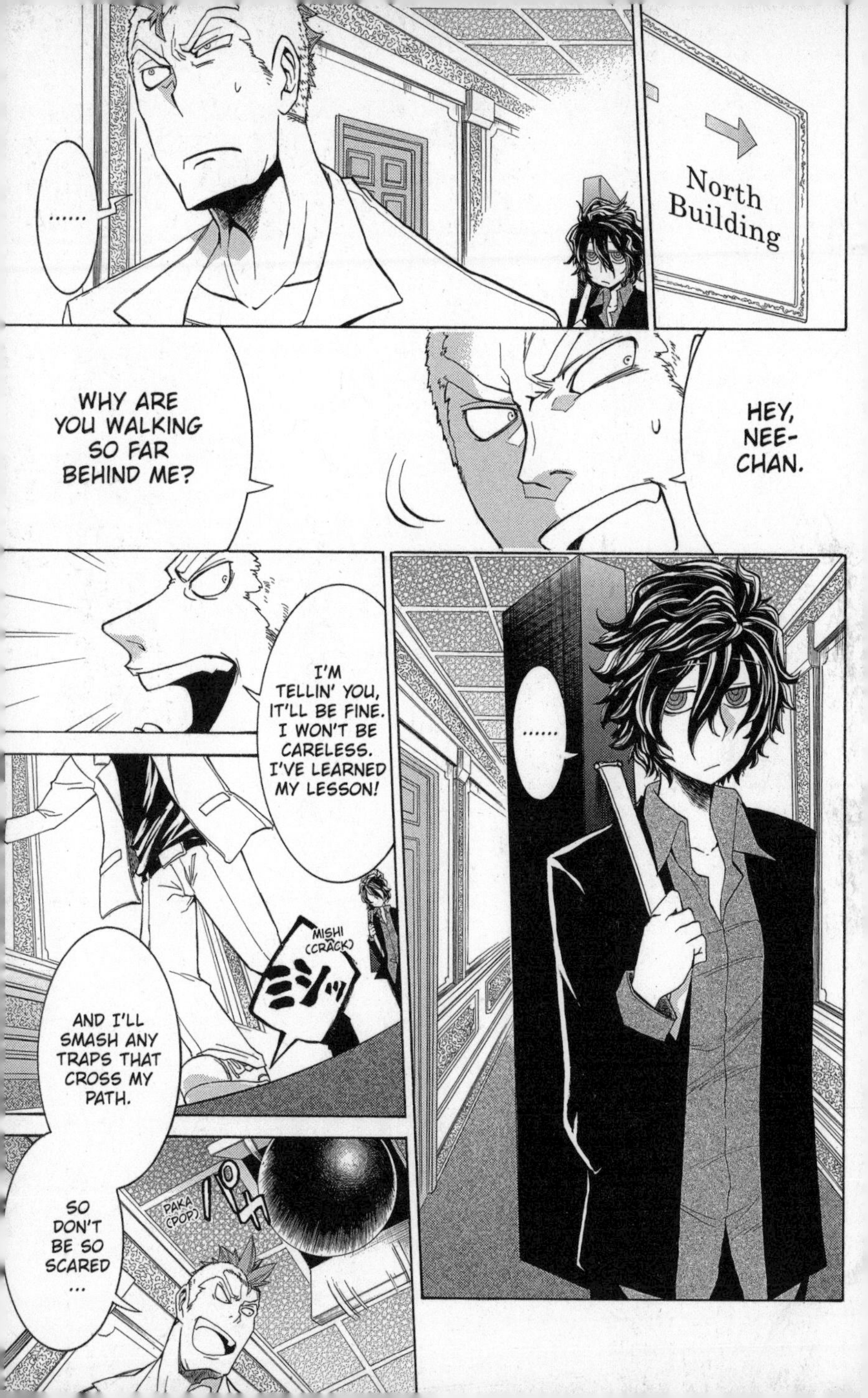
North Building
......
HEY, NEE-CHAN.
WHY ARE YOU WALKING SO FAR BEHIND ME?
......
I'M TELLIN' YOU, IT'LL BE FINE. I WON'T BE CARELESS. I'VE LEARNED MY LESSON!
ミシッ
MISHI (CRACK)
AND I'LL SMASH ANY TRAPS THAT CROSS MY PATH.
パカ
PAKA (POP)
SO DON'T BE SO SCARED ...

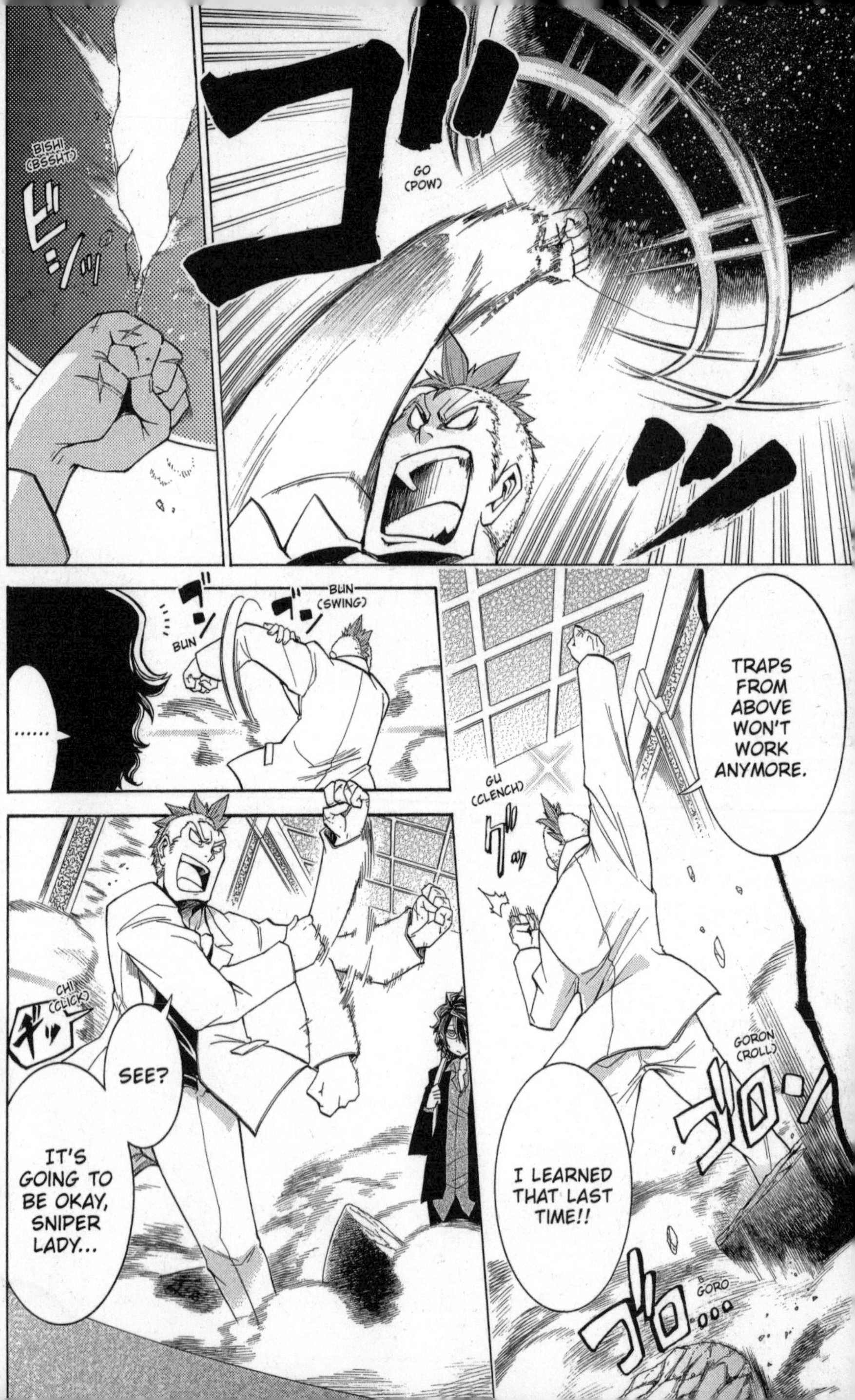
GO (POW)
BISHI (BSSHT)
TRAPS FROM ABOVE WON'T WORK ANYMORE.
GU (CLENCH)
GORON (ROLL)
I LEARNED THAT LAST TIME!!
GORO
BUN (SWING)
BUN
......
CHI (CLICK)
SEE?
IT'S GOING TO BE OKAY, SNIPER LADY...

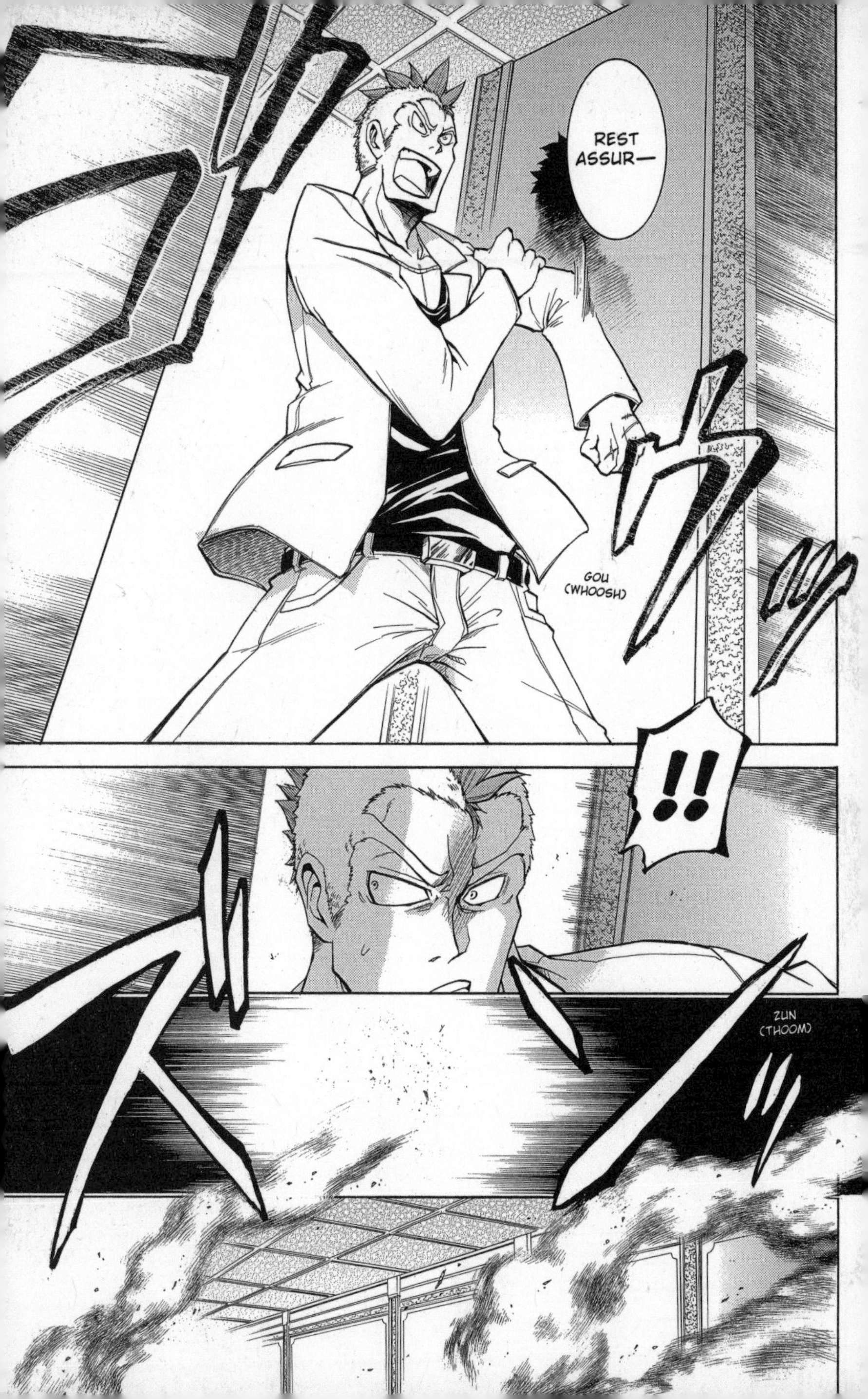
REST ASSUR—
GOU (WHOOSH)
!!
ZUN (THOOM)

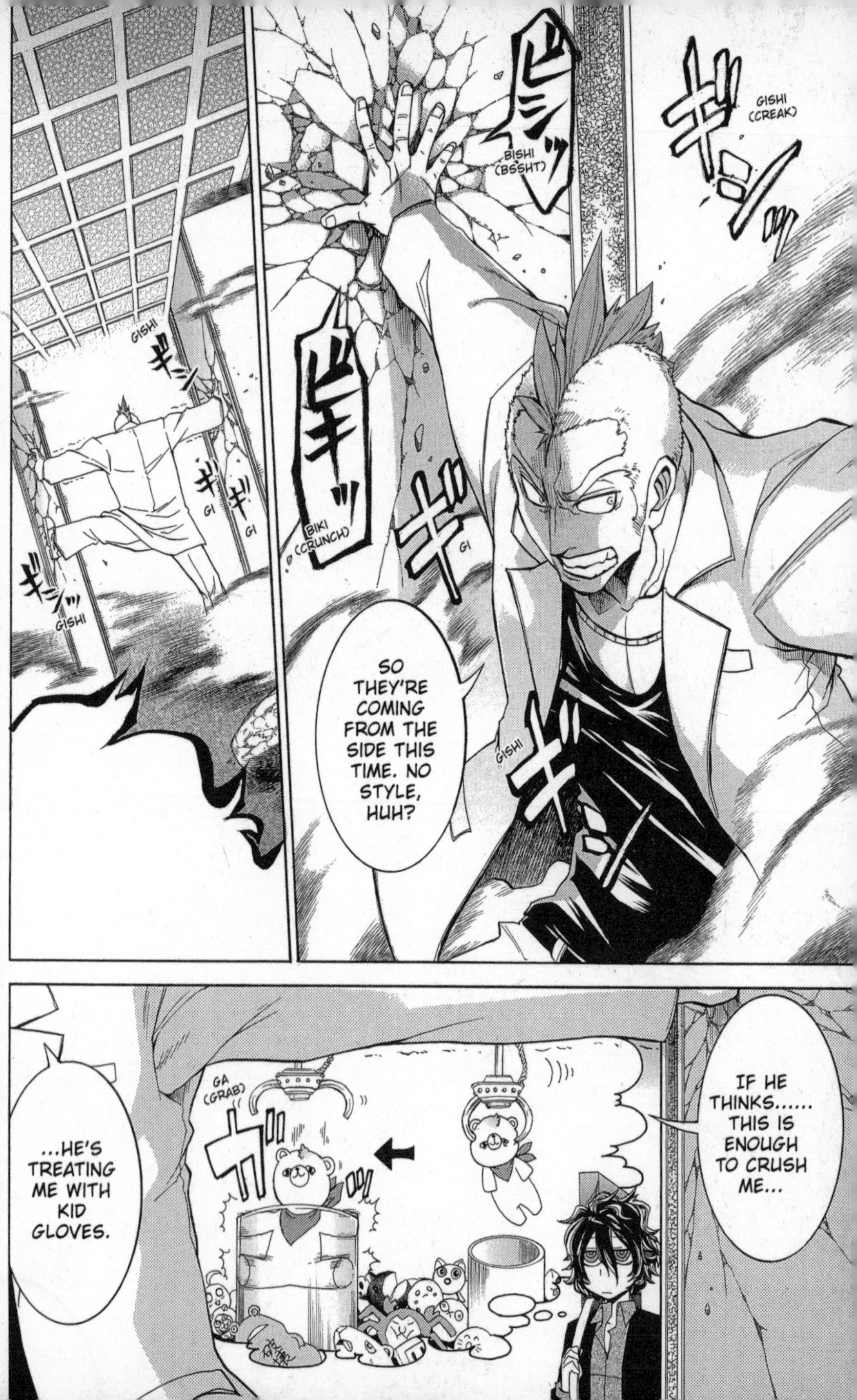
GISHI (CREAK)
BISHI (BSSHT)
BIKI (CRUNCH)
GI
GISHI
SO THEY'RE COMING FROM THE SIDE THIS TIME. NO STYLE, HUH?
GISHI
GI
GI
GISHI
IF HE THINKS...... THIS IS ENOUGH TO CRUSH ME...
GA (GRAB)
...HE'S TREATING ME WITH KID GLOVES.

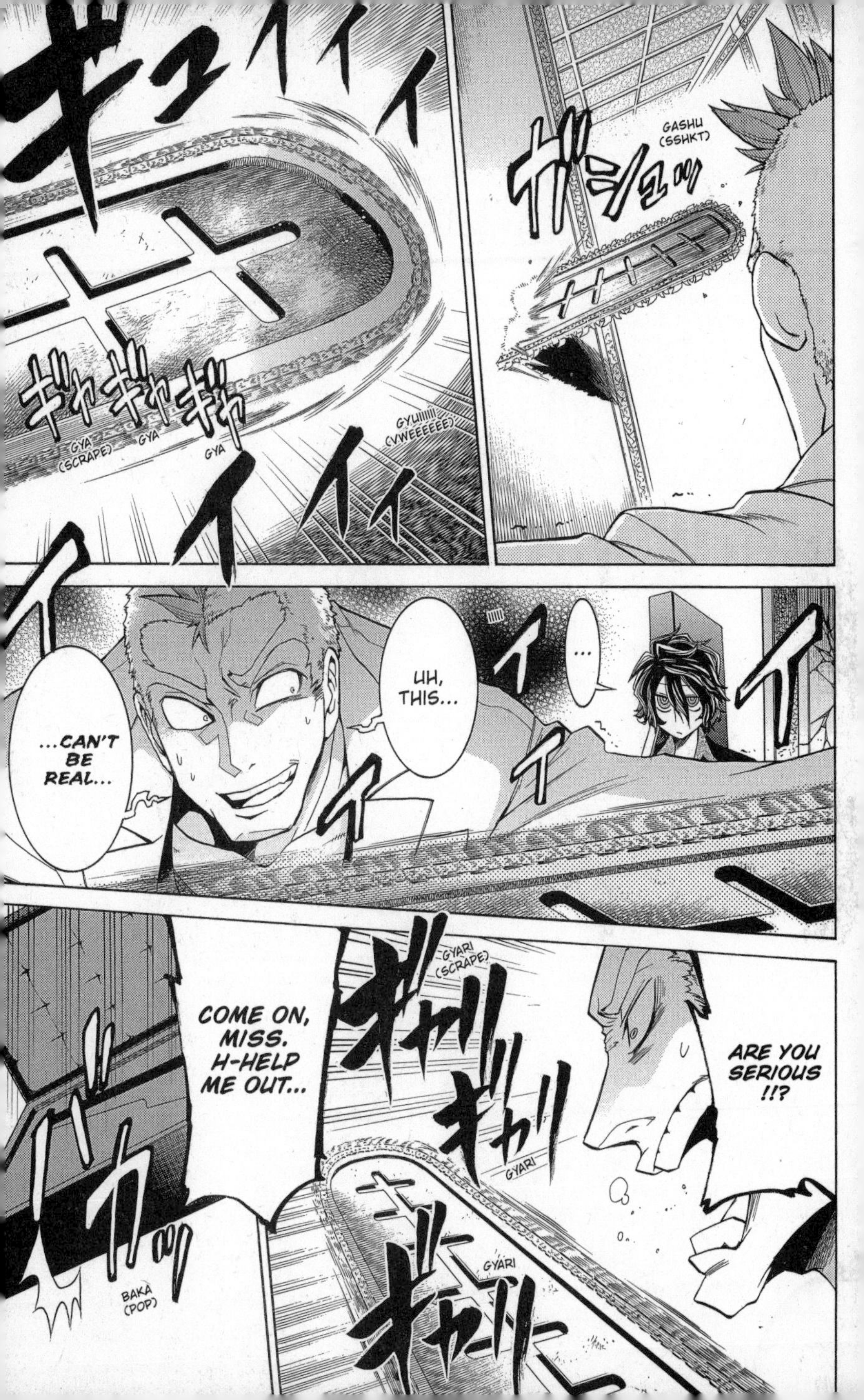
GASHU (SSHKT)
GYA (SCRAPE)
GYA
GYA
GYUIIIIIII (VWEEEEEEE)
...
UH, THIS...
...CAN'T BE REAL...
ARE YOU SERIOUS !!?
GYARI (SCRAPE)
GYARI
GYARI
COME ON, MISS. H-HELP ME OUT...
BAKA (POP)

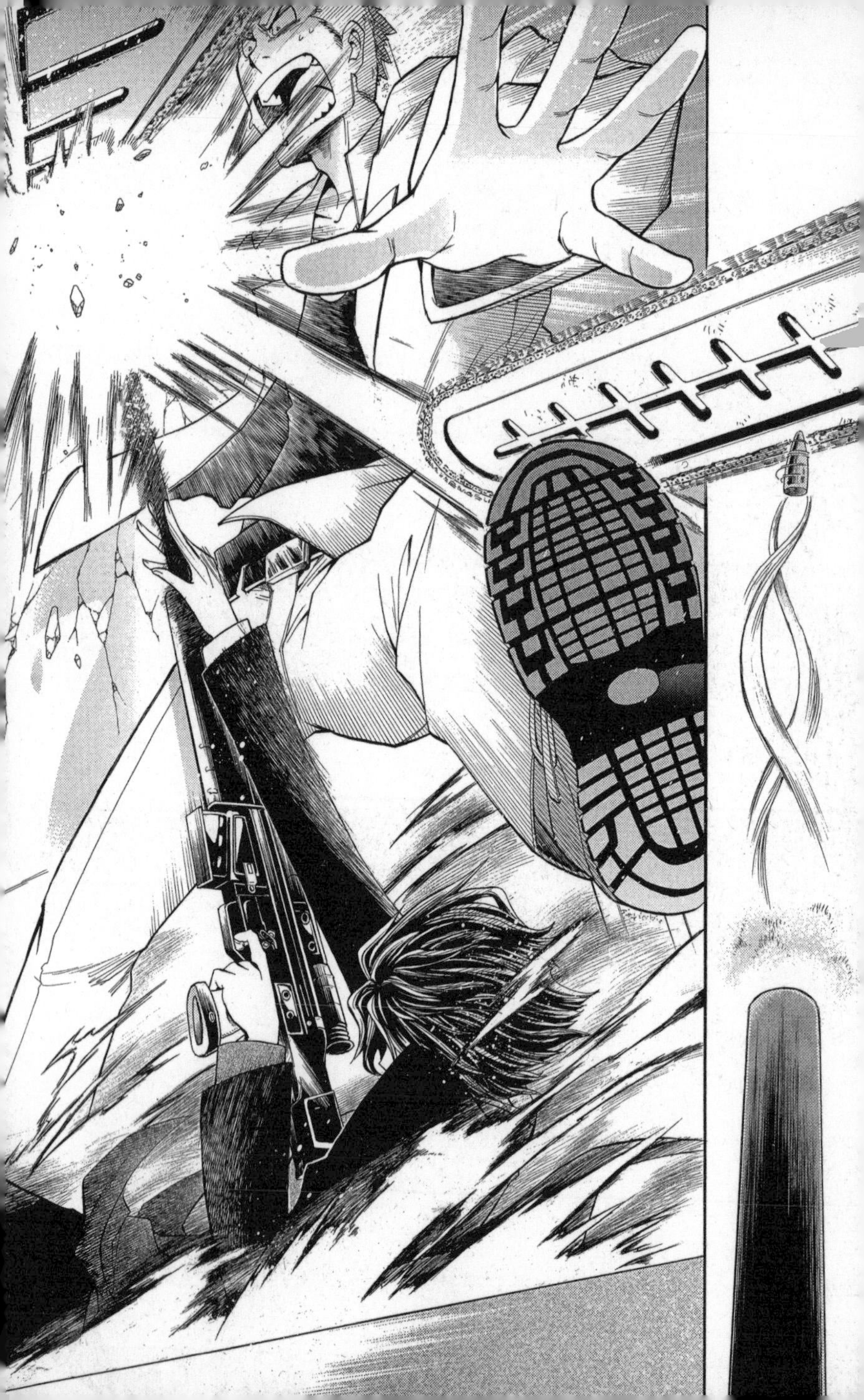

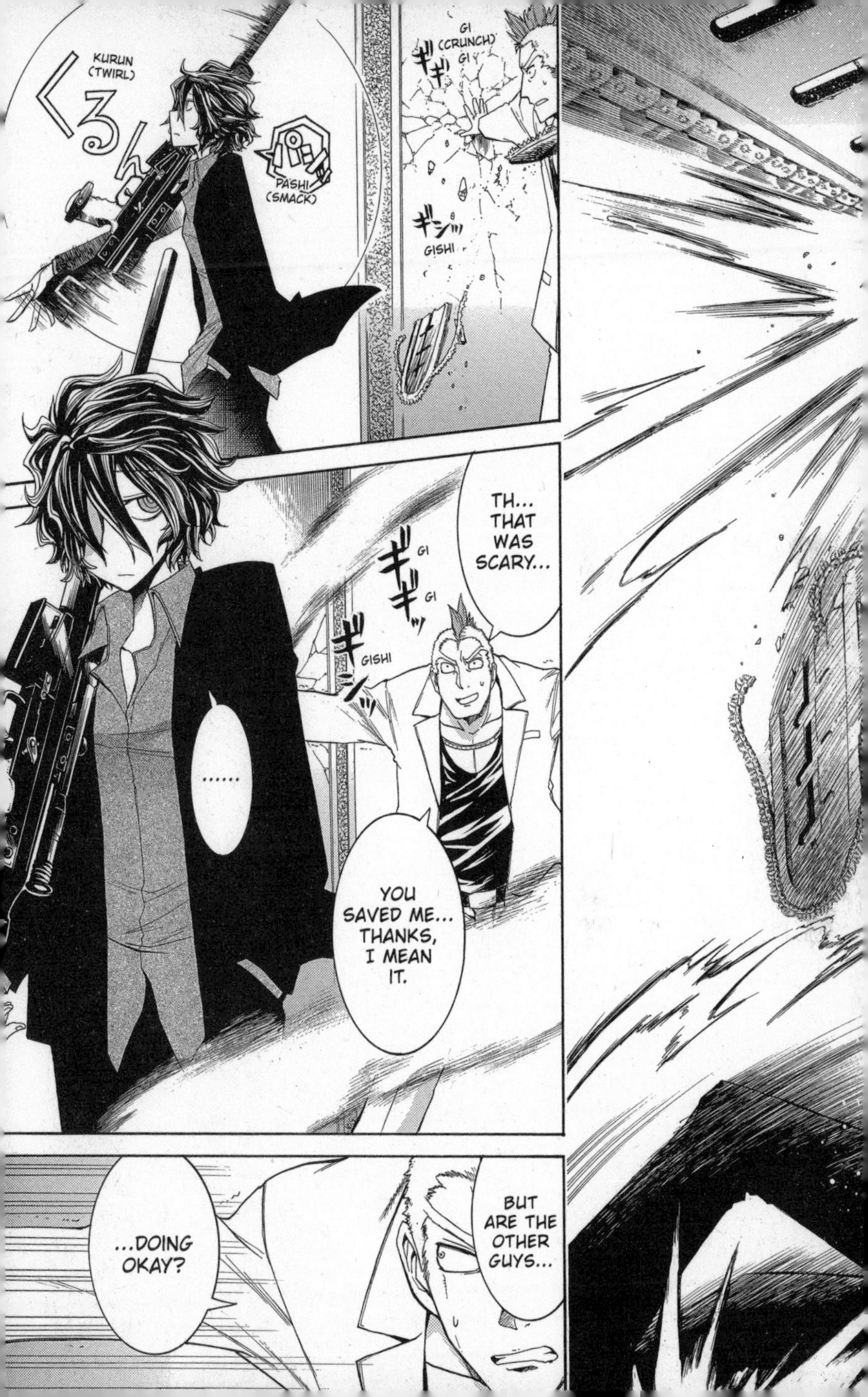
ギ GI (CRUNCH)
ギ GI
ギシッ GISHI
くるん KURUN (TWIRL)
パシ PA'SHI (SMACK)
TH... THAT WAS SCARY...
ギ GI
ギッ GI
ギシッ GISHI
......
YOU SAVED ME... THANKS, I MEAN IT.
BUT ARE THE OTHER GUYS...
...DOING OKAY?

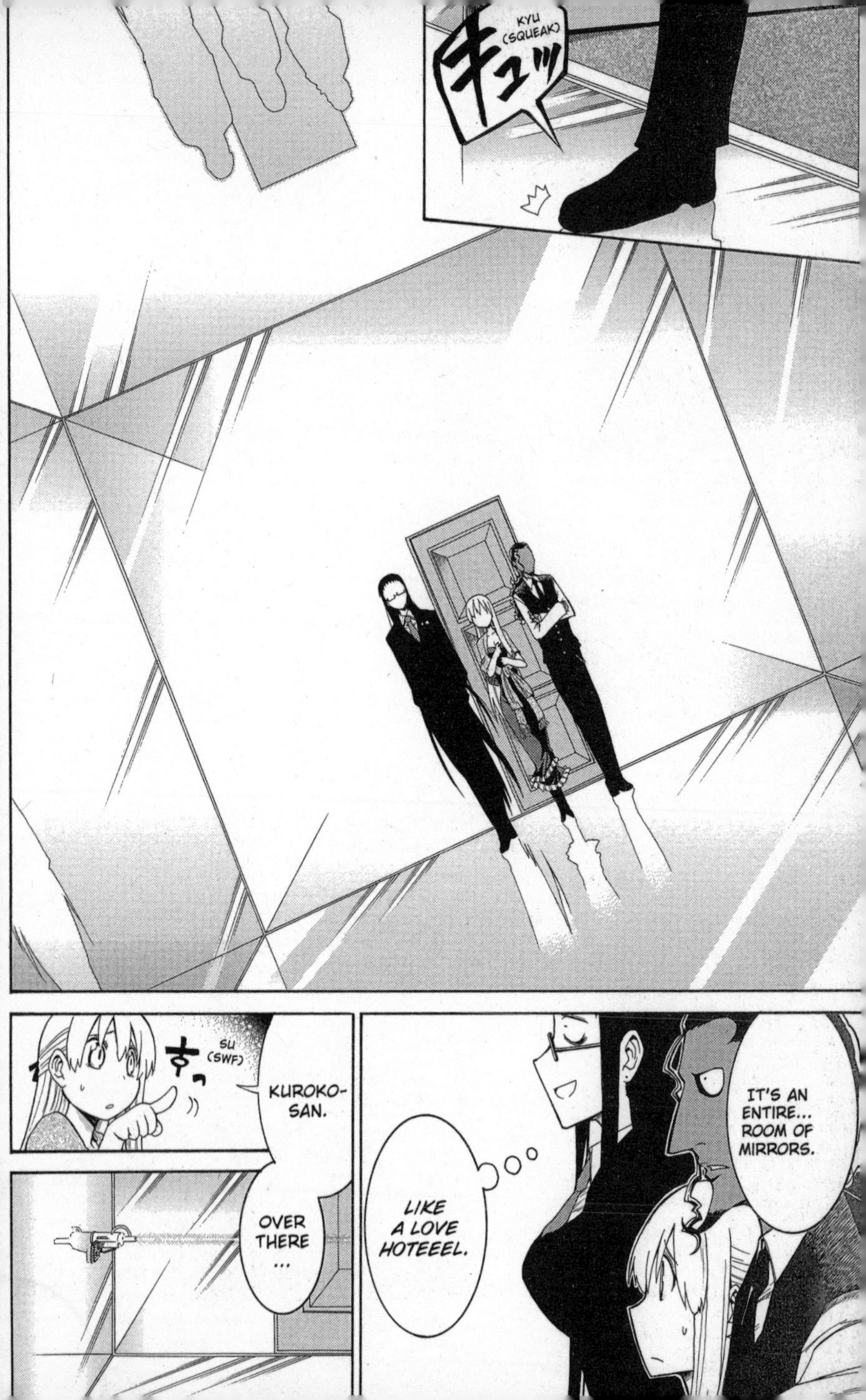

キュッ
KYU (SQUEAK)
IT'S AN ENTIRE... ROOM OF MIRRORS.
LIKE A LOVE HOTEEEL.
スッ
SU (SWF)
KUROKO-SAN.
OVER THERE ...

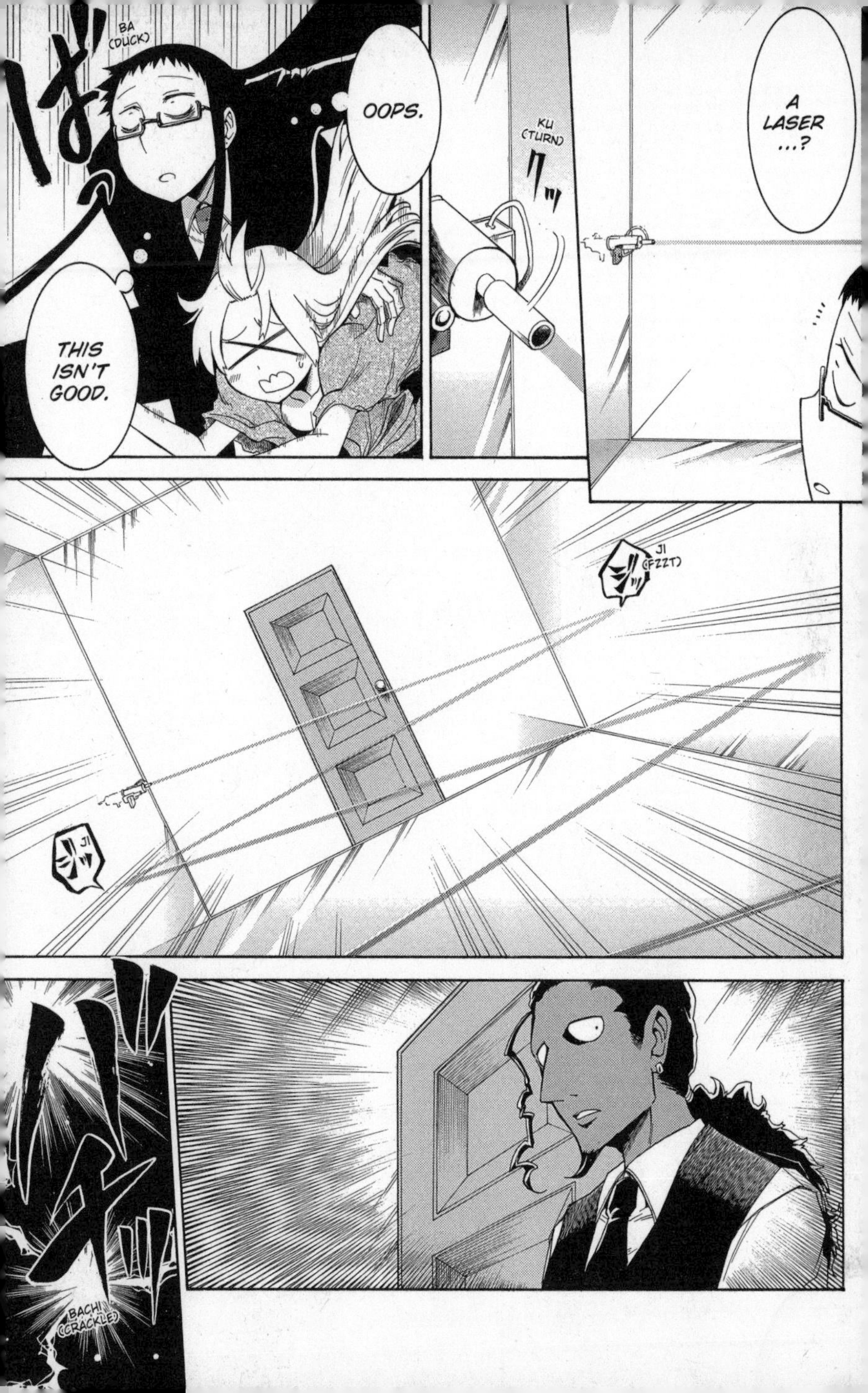
A LASER ...?
...
KU (TURN)
OOPS.
BA (DUCK)
THIS ISN'T GOOD.
JI (FZZT)
JI
BACHI (CRACKLE)

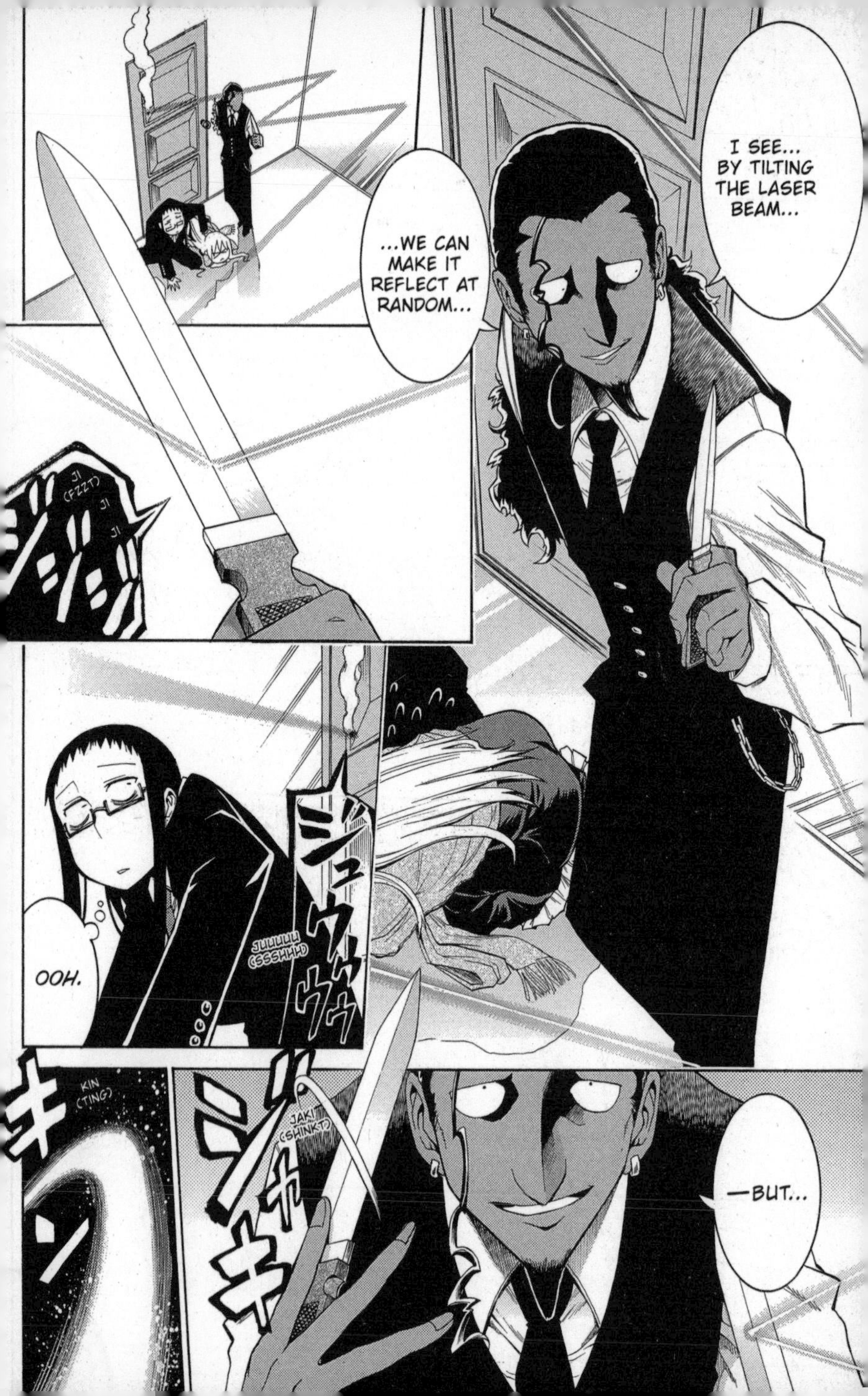
I SEE... BY TILTING THE LASER BEAM...
...WE CAN MAKE IT REFLECT AT RANDOM...
JI (FZZT) JI JI
JUUUUUU (SSSHHH)
OOH.
—BUT...
JAKI (SHINK!)
KIN (TING)

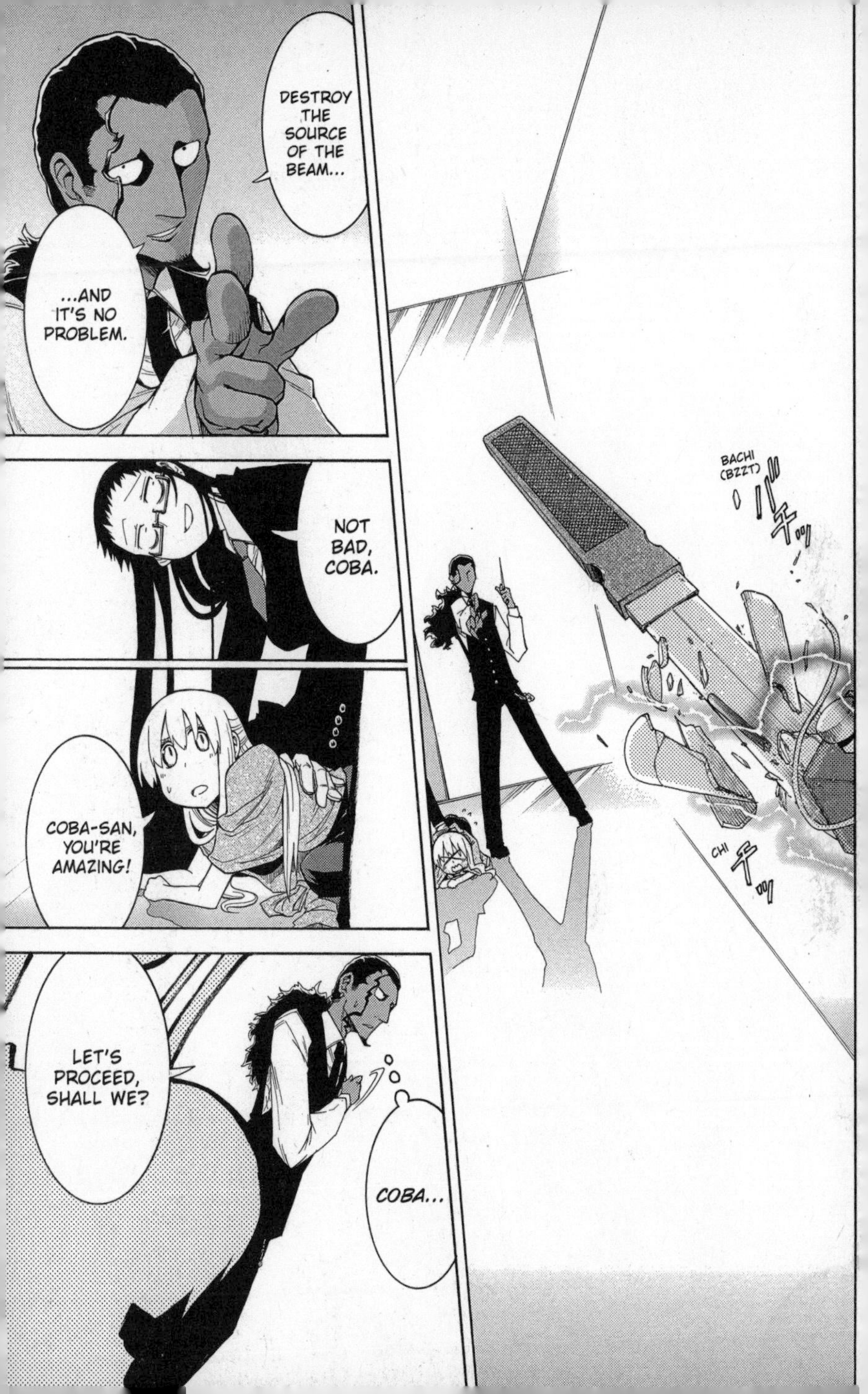
BACHI (BZZT)
CHI
DESTROY THE SOURCE OF THE BEAM...
...AND IT'S NO PROBLEM.
NOT BAD, COBA.
COBA-SAN, YOU'RE AMAZING!
LET'S PROCEED, SHALL WE?
COBA...

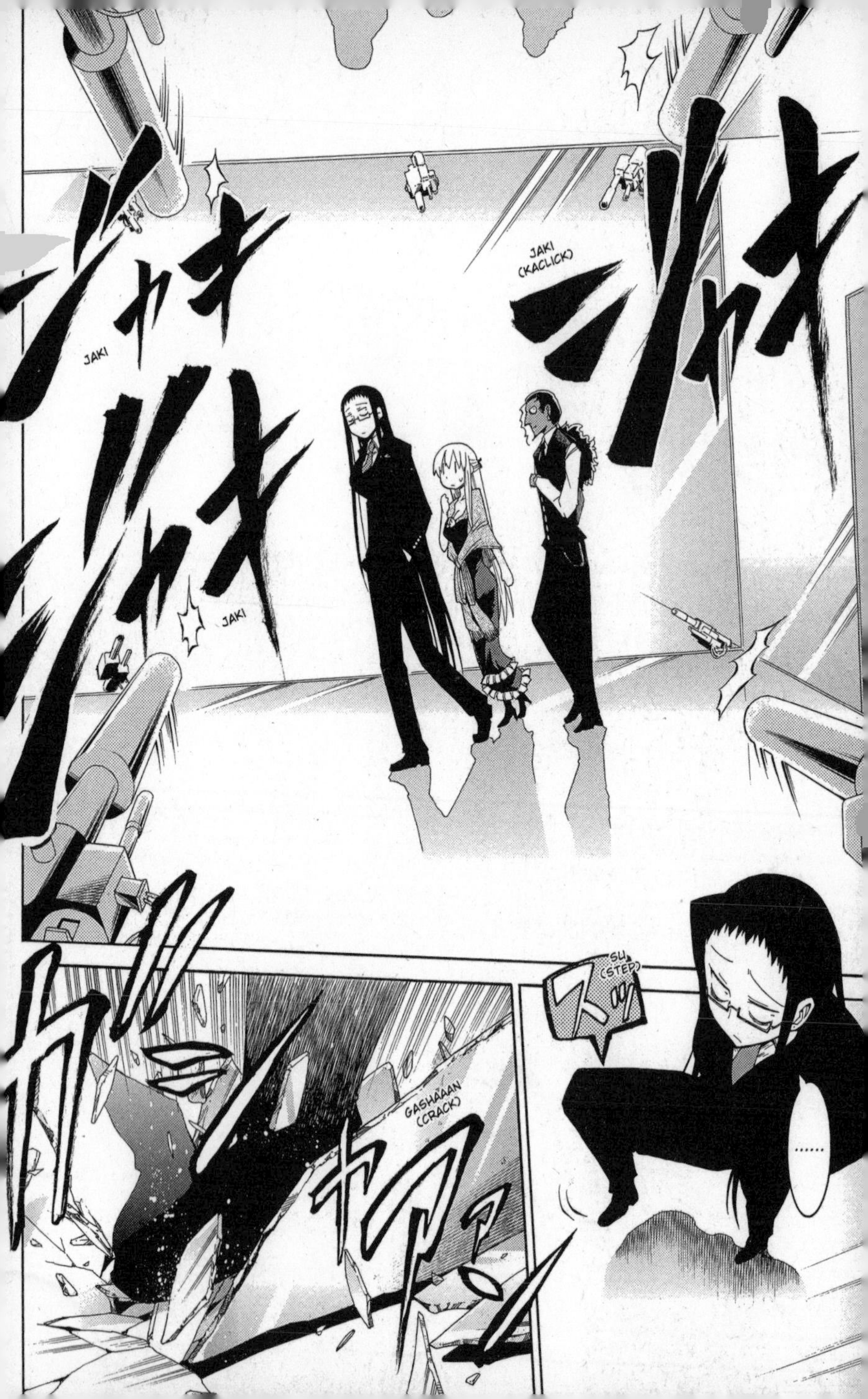

ジャキ
JAKI (KACLICK)
ジャキ
JAKI
ジャキ
ジャキ
JAKI
スッ
SU (STEP)
……
ガシャアァン
GASHAAAN (CRACK)

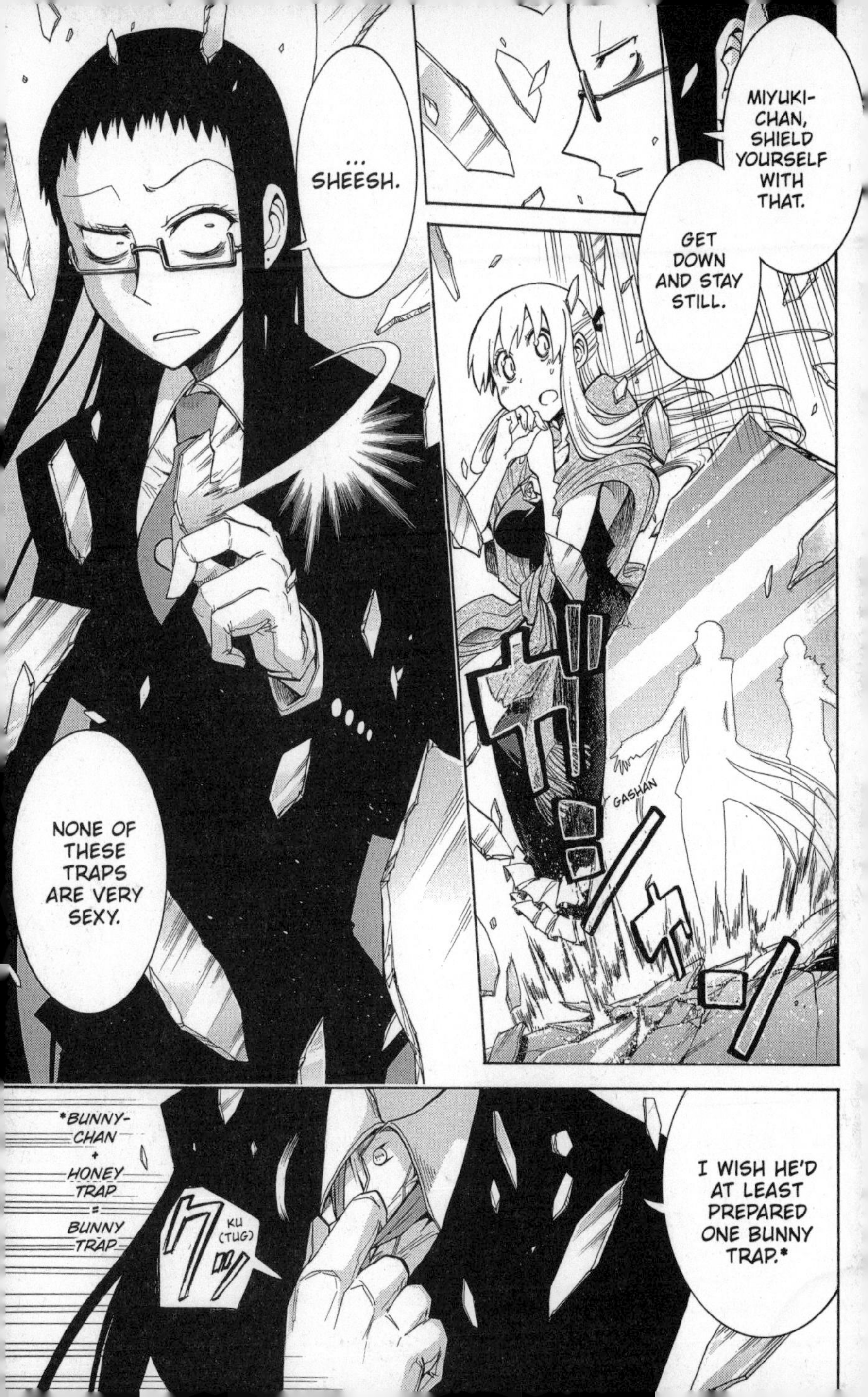
MIYUKI-CHAN, SHIELD YOURSELF WITH THAT.
GET DOWN AND STAY STILL.
GASHAN
...SHEESH.
NONE OF THESE TRAPS ARE VERY SEXY.
I WISH HE'D AT LEAST PREPARED ONE BUNNY TRAP.*
KU (TUG)
*BUNNY-CHAN + HONEY TRAP = BUNNY TRAP

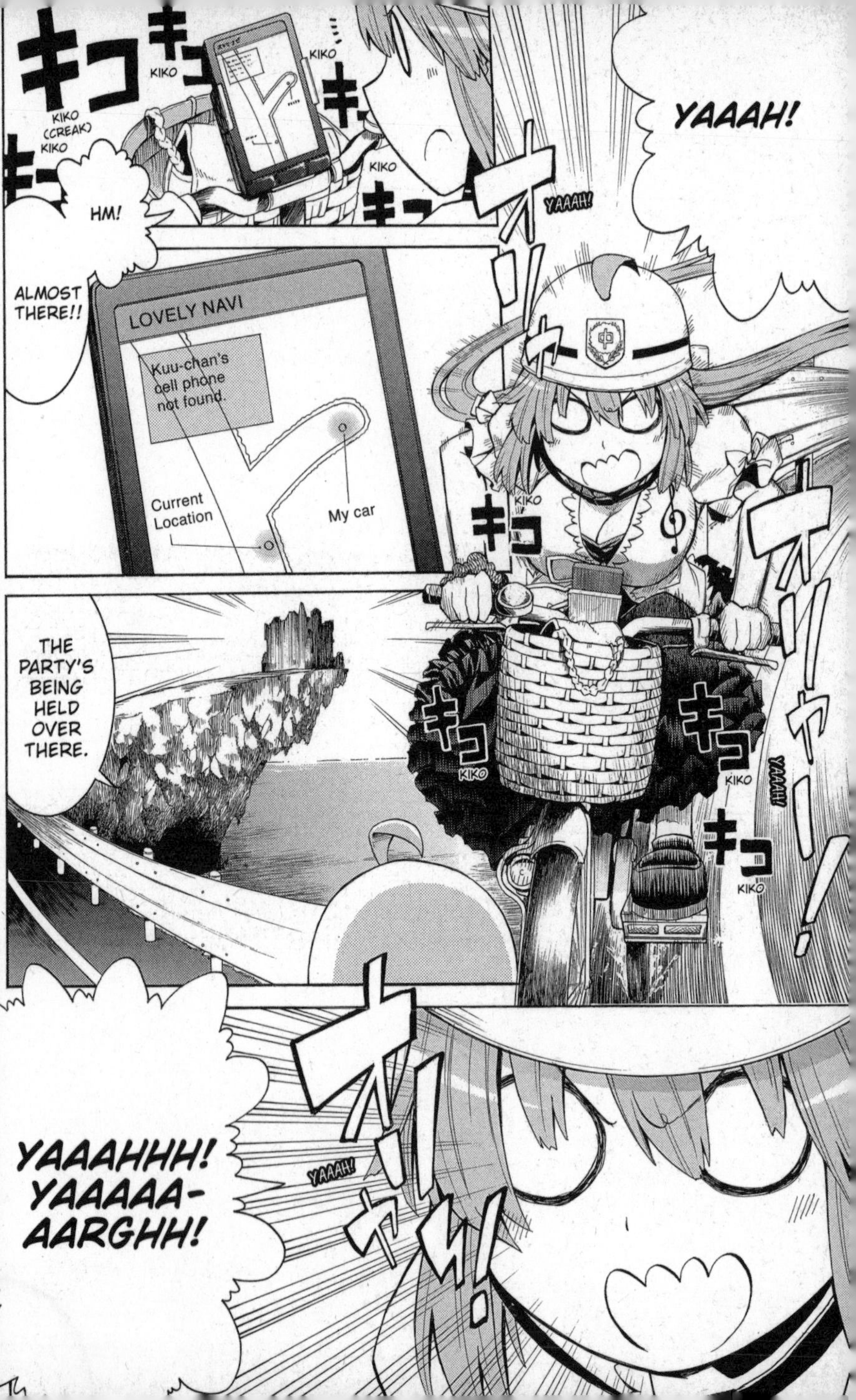
YAAAH!
YAAAH!
KIKO
KIKO
YAAAH!
KIKO
KIKO
KIKO
KIKO
KIKO (CREAK) KIKO
KIKO
HM!
ALMOST THERE!!
LOVELY NAVI
Kuu-chan's cell phone not found.
My car
Current Location
THE PARTY'S BEING HELD OVER THERE.
YAAAH!
YAAAHHH! YAAAAA-AARGHH!

MURCIÉLAGO

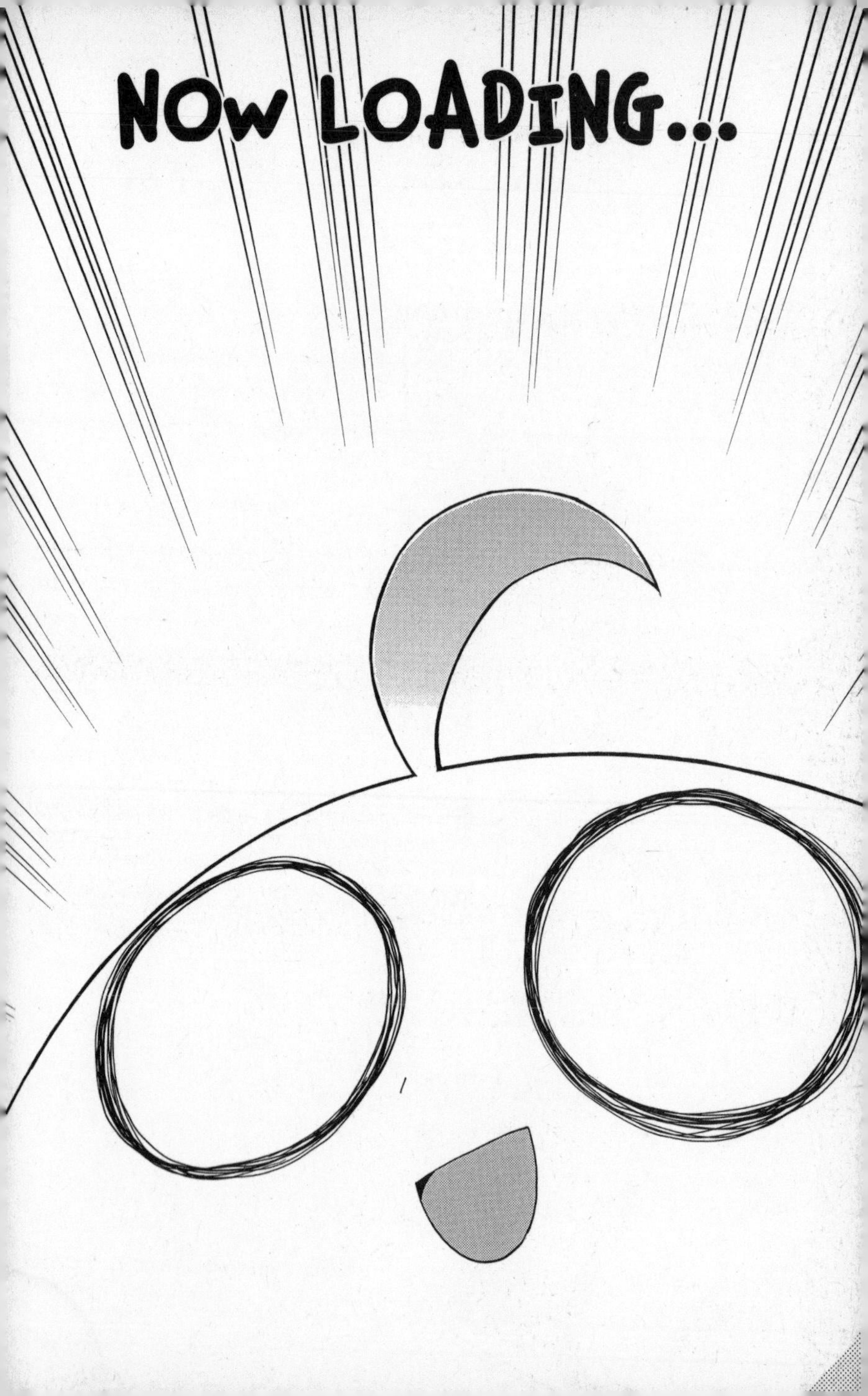
NOW LOADING...

Pilot film of MURCIÉLAGO

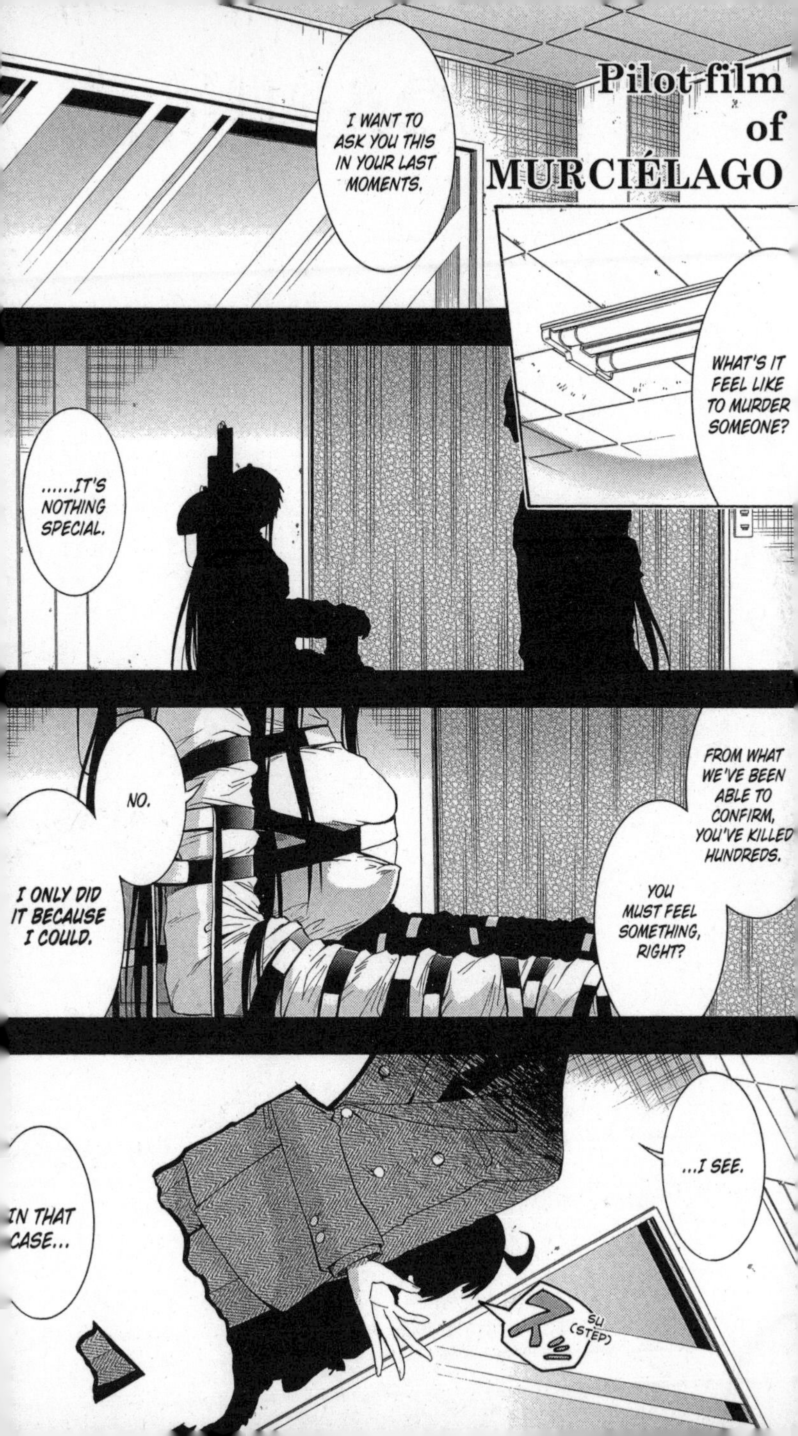
I WANT TO ASK YOU THIS IN YOUR LAST MOMENTS.
WHAT'S IT FEEL LIKE TO MURDER SOMEONE?
......IT'S NOTHING SPECIAL.
FROM WHAT WE'VE BEEN ABLE TO CONFIRM, YOU'VE KILLED HUNDREDS.
YOU MUST FEEL SOMETHING, RIGHT?
NO.
I ONLY DID IT BECAUSE I COULD.
...I SEE.
IN THAT CASE...
SU (STEP)

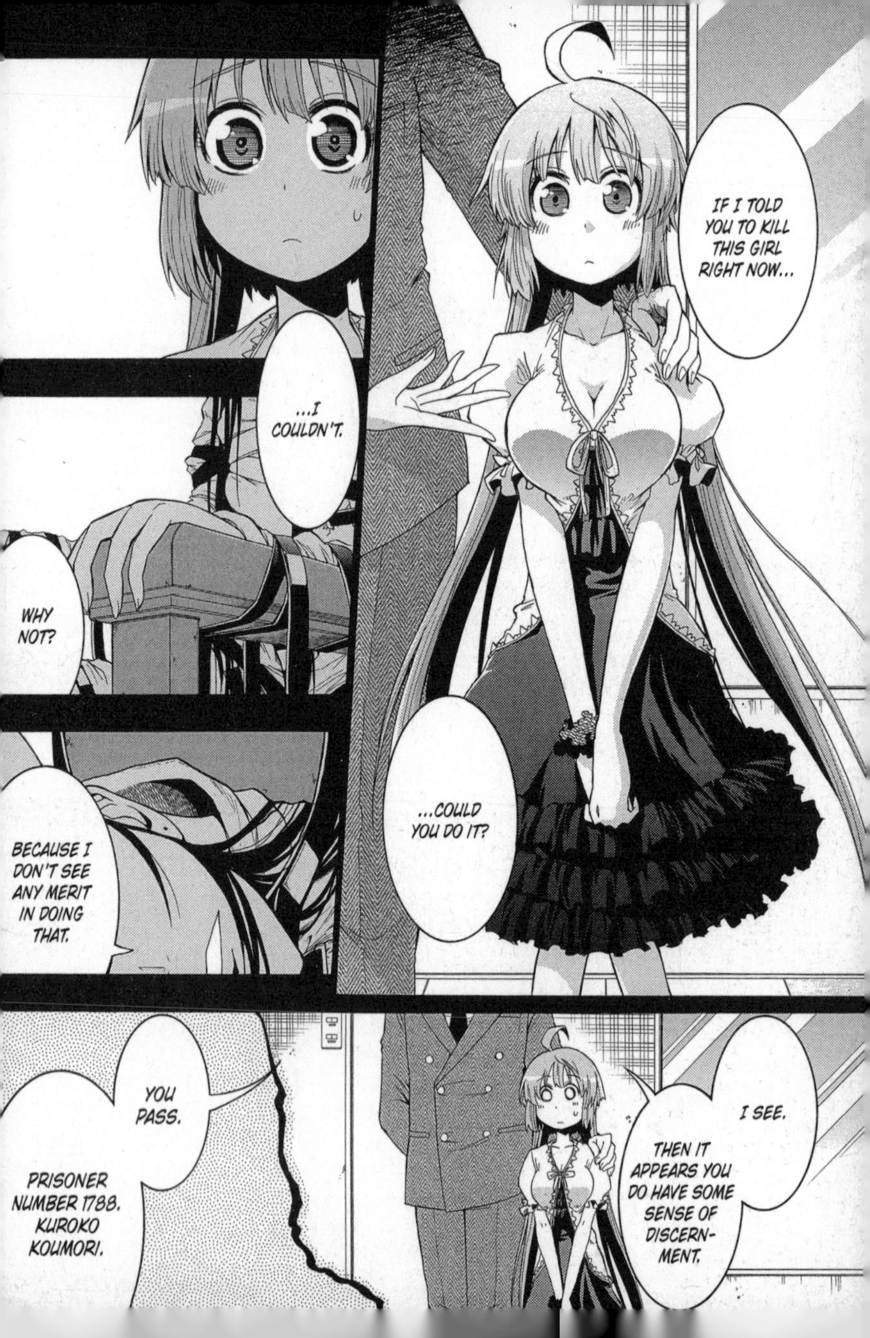
IF I TOLD YOU TO KILL THIS GIRL RIGHT NOW...
...COULD YOU DO IT?
...I COULDN'T.
WHY NOT?
BECAUSE I DON'T SEE ANY MERIT IN DOING THAT.
I SEE.
THEN IT APPEARS YOU DO HAVE SOME SENSE OF DISCERN-MENT.
YOU PASS.
PRISONER NUMBER 1788. KUROKO KOUMORI.

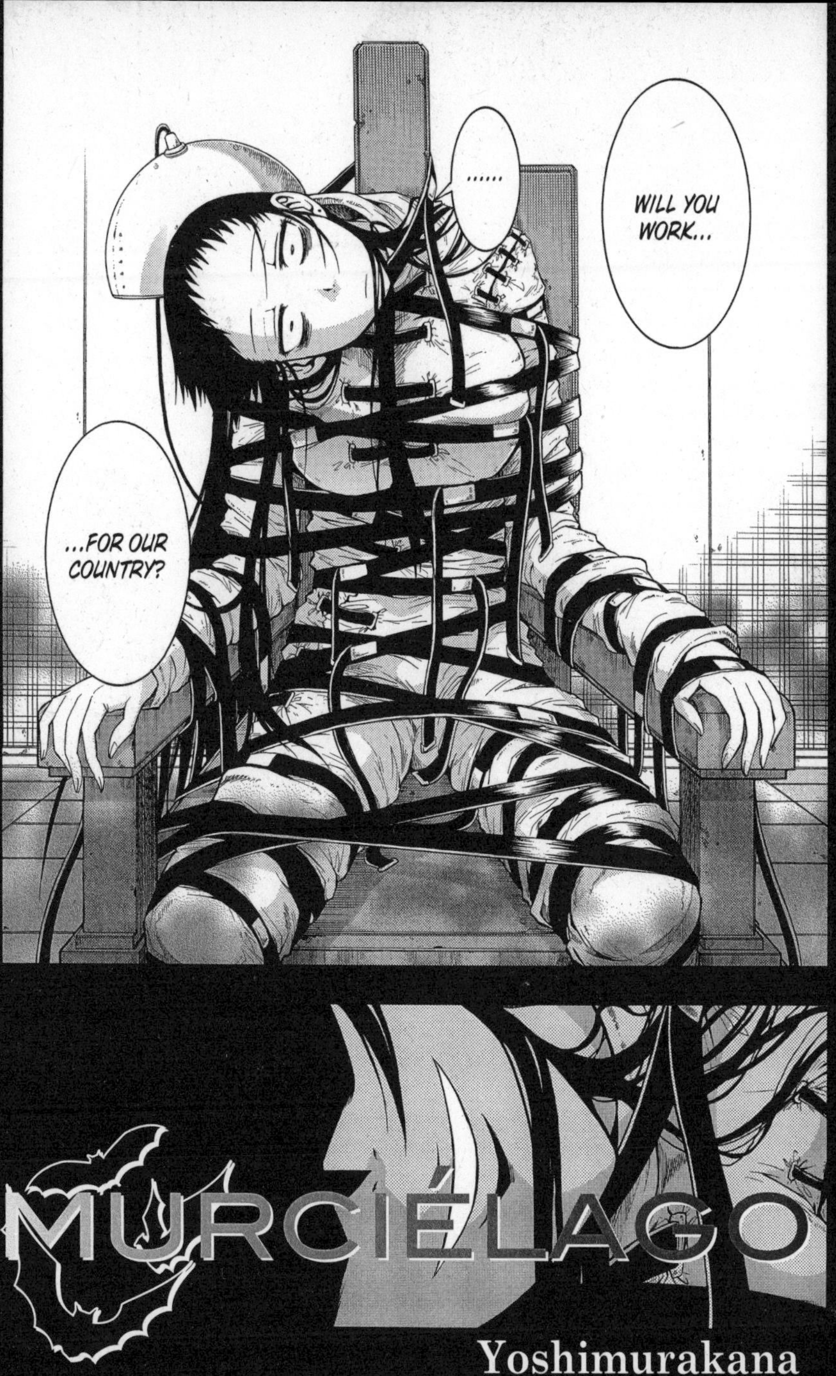
WILL YOU WORK...
......
...FOR OUR COUNTRY?
MURCIÉLAGO
Yoshimurakana

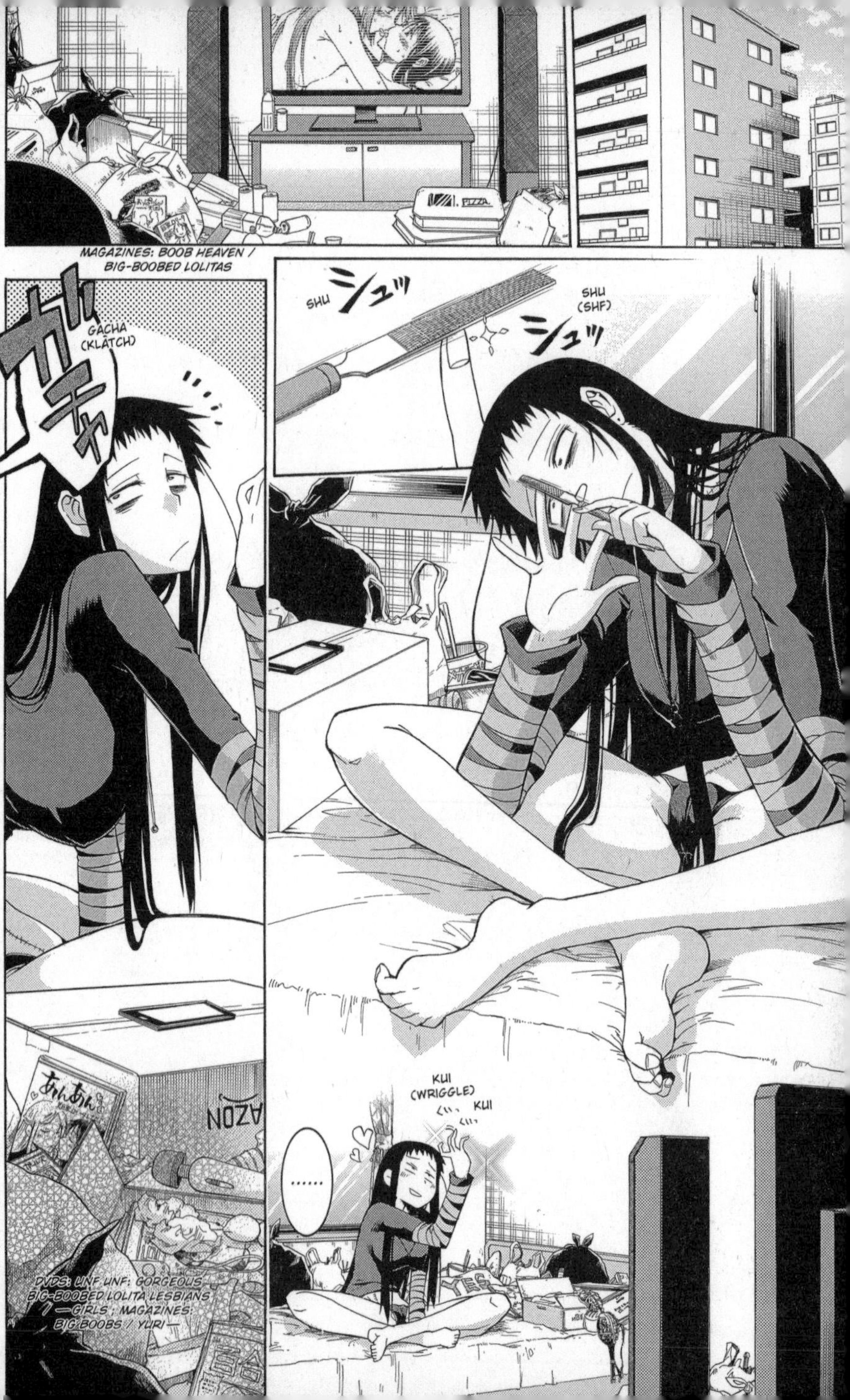
MAGAZINES: BOOB HEAVEN / BIG-BOOBED LOLITAS
SHU
シュッ
SHU (SHF)
シュッ
ガチャ
GACHA (KLÂTCH)
KUI (WRIGGLE)
くい、 KUI
くい
......
DVDS: UNF UNF: GORGEOUS BIG-BOOBED LOLITA LESBIANS / —GIRLS ; MAGAZINES: BIG BOOBS / YURI—

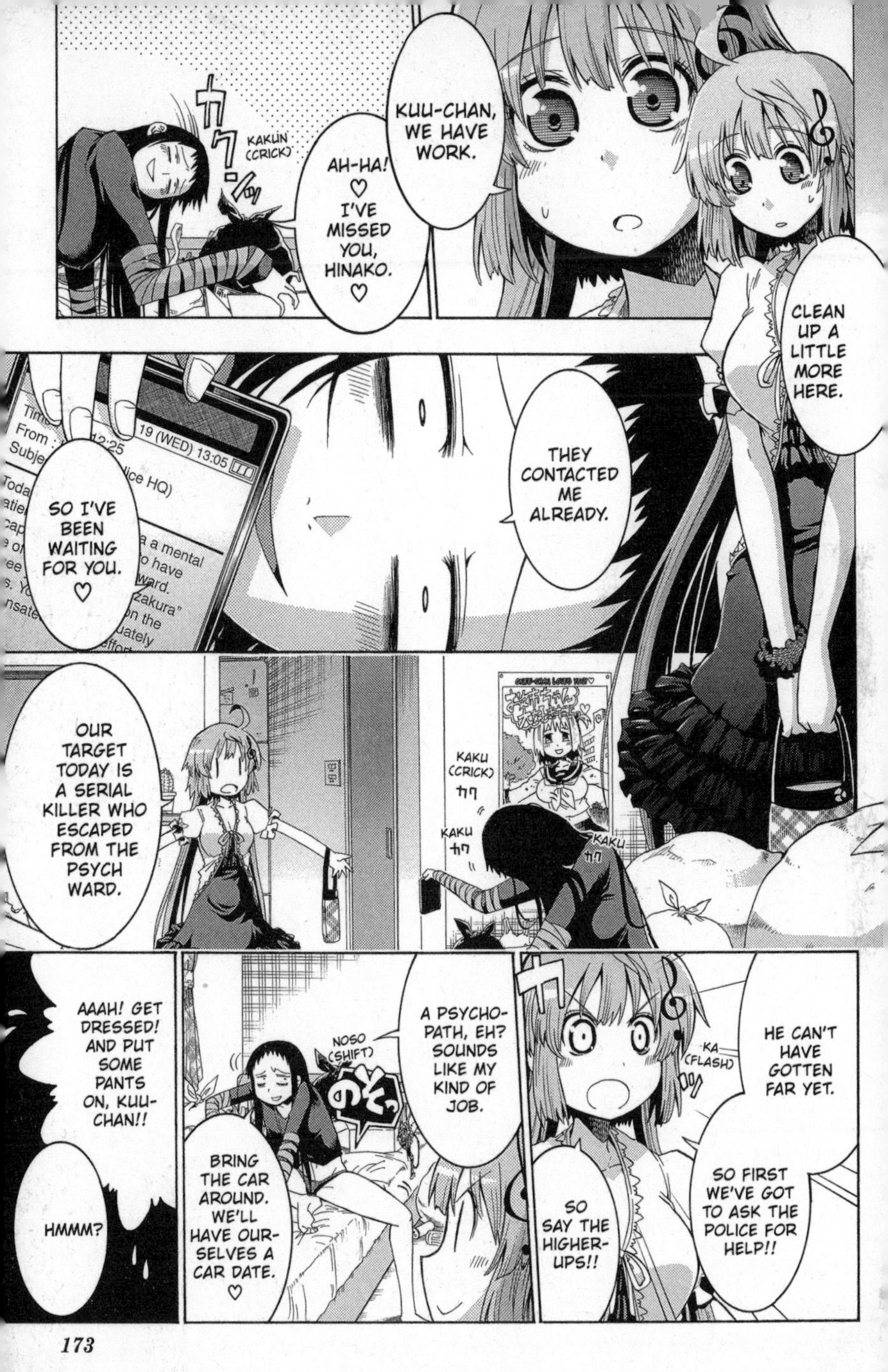

KUU-CHAN, WE HAVE WORK.
KAKUN (CRICK)
AH-HA! ♡ I'VE MISSED YOU, HINAKO. ♡
CLEAN UP A LITTLE MORE HERE.
THEY CONTACTED ME ALREADY.
19 (WED) 13:05
SO I'VE BEEN WAITING FOR YOU. ♡
OUR TARGET TODAY IS A SERIAL KILLER WHO ESCAPED FROM THE PSYCH WARD.
KAKU (CRICK)
KAKU
KAKU
HE CAN'T HAVE GOTTEN FAR YET.
SO FIRST WE'VE GOT TO ASK THE POLICE FOR HELP!!
KA (FLASH)
SO SAY THE HIGHER-UPS!!
A PSYCHO-PATH, EH? SOUNDS LIKE MY KIND OF JOB.
NOSO (SHIFT)
BRING THE CAR AROUND. WE'LL HAVE OURSELVES A CAR DATE. ♡
AAAH! GET DRESSED! AND PUT SOME PANTS ON, KUU-CHAN!!
HMMM?

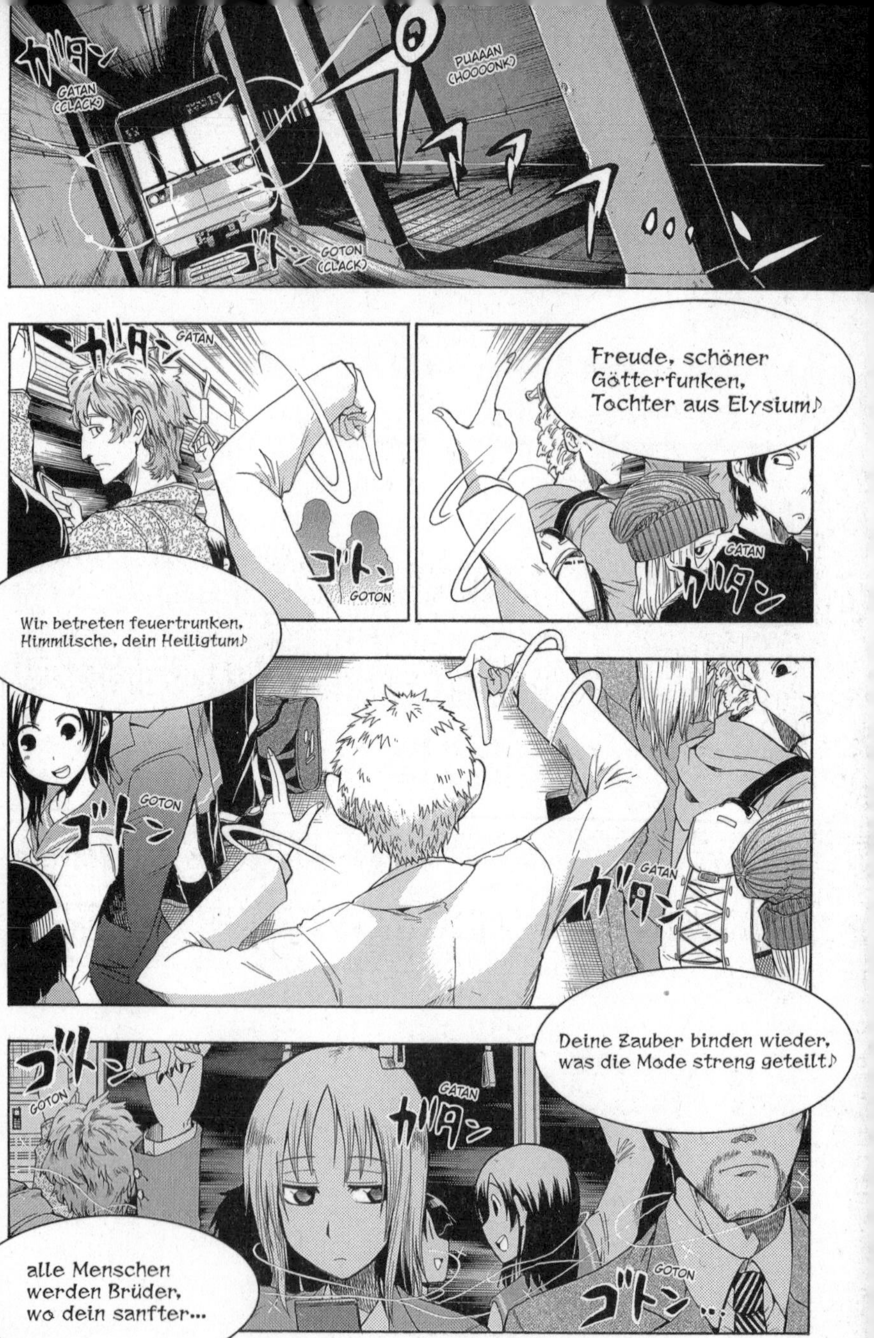
PUAAAN (HOOOONK)
GATAN (CLACK)
GOTON (CLACK)
Freude, schöner Götterfunken, Tochter aus Elysium♪
GATAN
GATAN
GOTON
Wir betreten feuertrunken, Himmlische, dein Heiligtum♪
GATAN
GOTON
Deine Zauber binden wieder, was die Mode streng geteilt♪
GOTON
GATAN
alle Menschen werden Brüder, wo dein sanfter...
GOTON

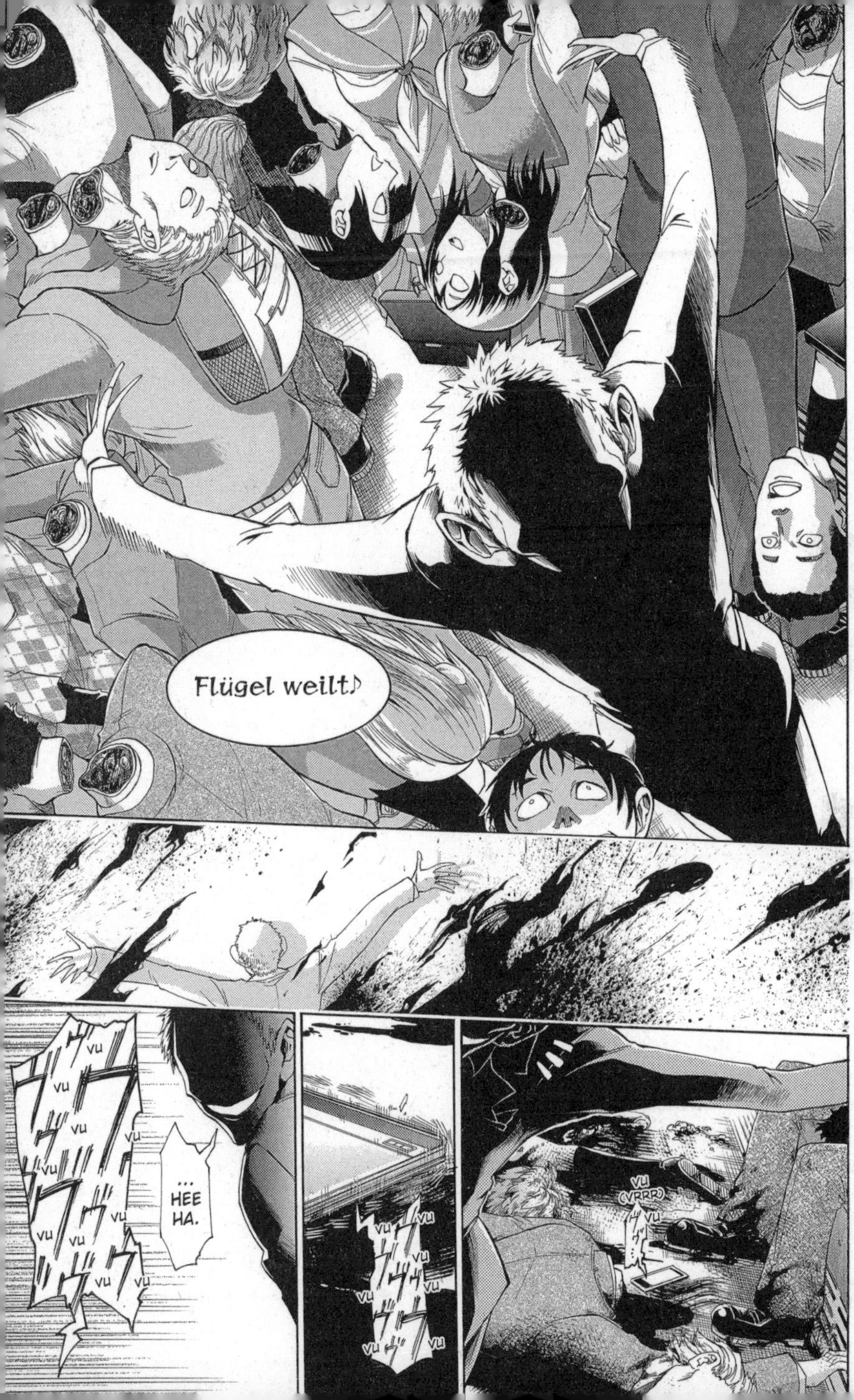
Flügel weilt♪
VU (VRRR)
VU
VU VU VU VU VU VU
... HEE HA.
VU VU VU VU VU VU VU VU VU VU

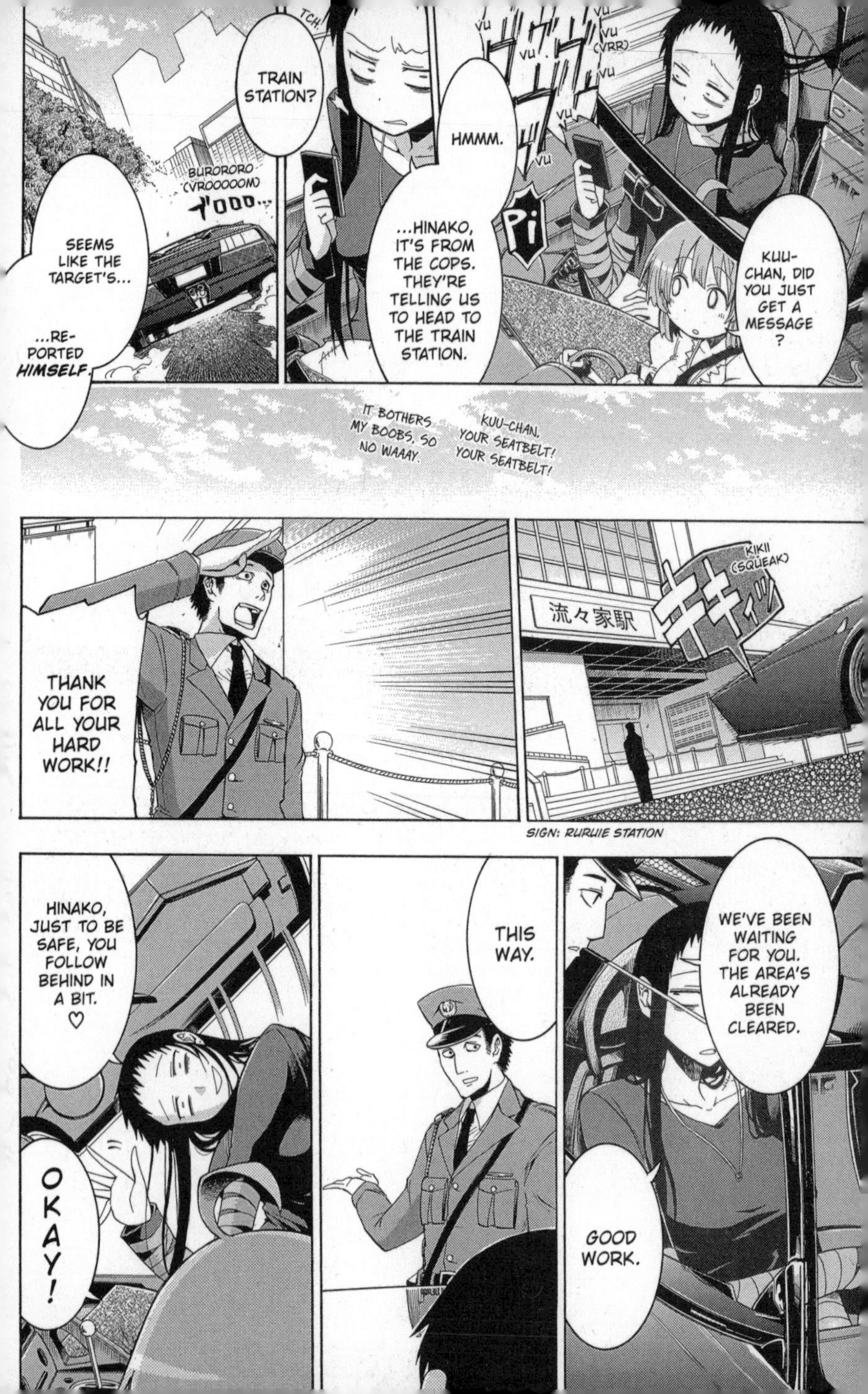
KUU-CHAN, DID YOU JUST GET A MESSAGE?
VU VU VU VU VU VU (VRR)
Pi
HMMM.
...HINAKO, IT'S FROM THE COPS. THEY'RE TELLING US TO HEAD TO THE TRAIN STATION.
TCH.
TRAIN STATION?
BURORORO (VROOOOOM)
SEEMS LIKE THE TARGET'S...
...RE-PORTED HIMSELF.
KUU-CHAN, YOUR SEATBELT! YOUR SEATBELT!
IT BOTHERS MY BOOBS, SO NO WAAAY.
KIKII (SQUEAK)
流々家駅
SIGN: RURUIE STATION
THANK YOU FOR ALL YOUR HARD WORK!!
WE'VE BEEN WAITING FOR YOU. THE AREA'S ALREADY BEEN CLEARED.
GOOD WORK.
THIS WAY.
HINAKO, JUST TO BE SAFE, YOU FOLLOW BEHIND IN A BIT. ♡
OKAY!

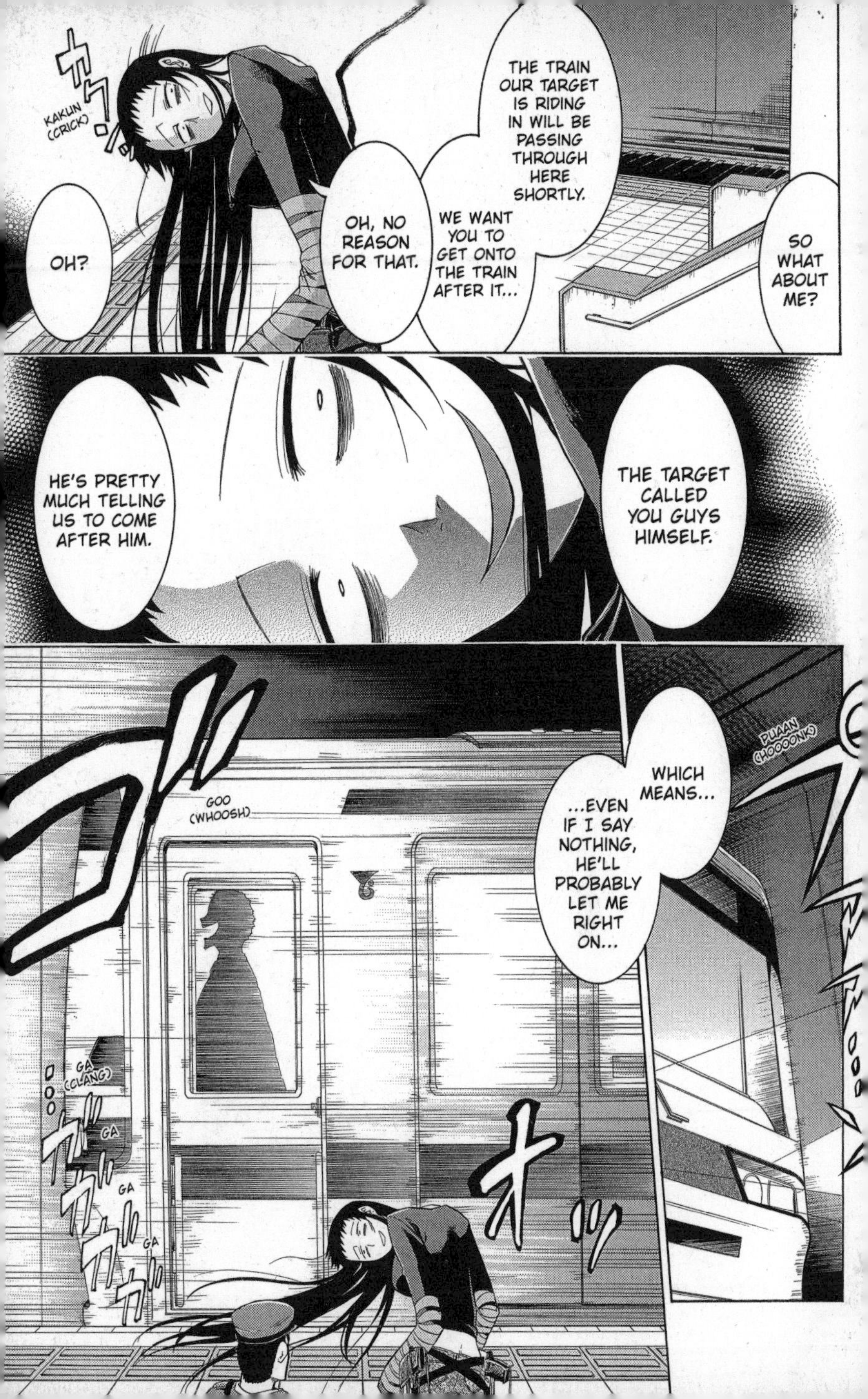
SO WHAT ABOUT ME?
THE TRAIN OUR TARGET IS RIDING IN WILL BE PASSING THROUGH HERE SHORTLY.
WE WANT YOU TO GET ONTO THE TRAIN AFTER IT...
OH, NO REASON FOR THAT.
KAKUN (CRICK)
OH?
THE TARGET CALLED YOU GUYS HIMSELF.
HE'S PRETTY MUCH TELLING US TO COME AFTER HIM.
PUAAN (HOOOONK)
WHICH MEANS...
...EVEN IF I SAY NOTHING, HE'LL PROBABLY LET ME RIGHT ON...
GOO (WHOOSH)
GA (CLANG)
GA
GA
GA

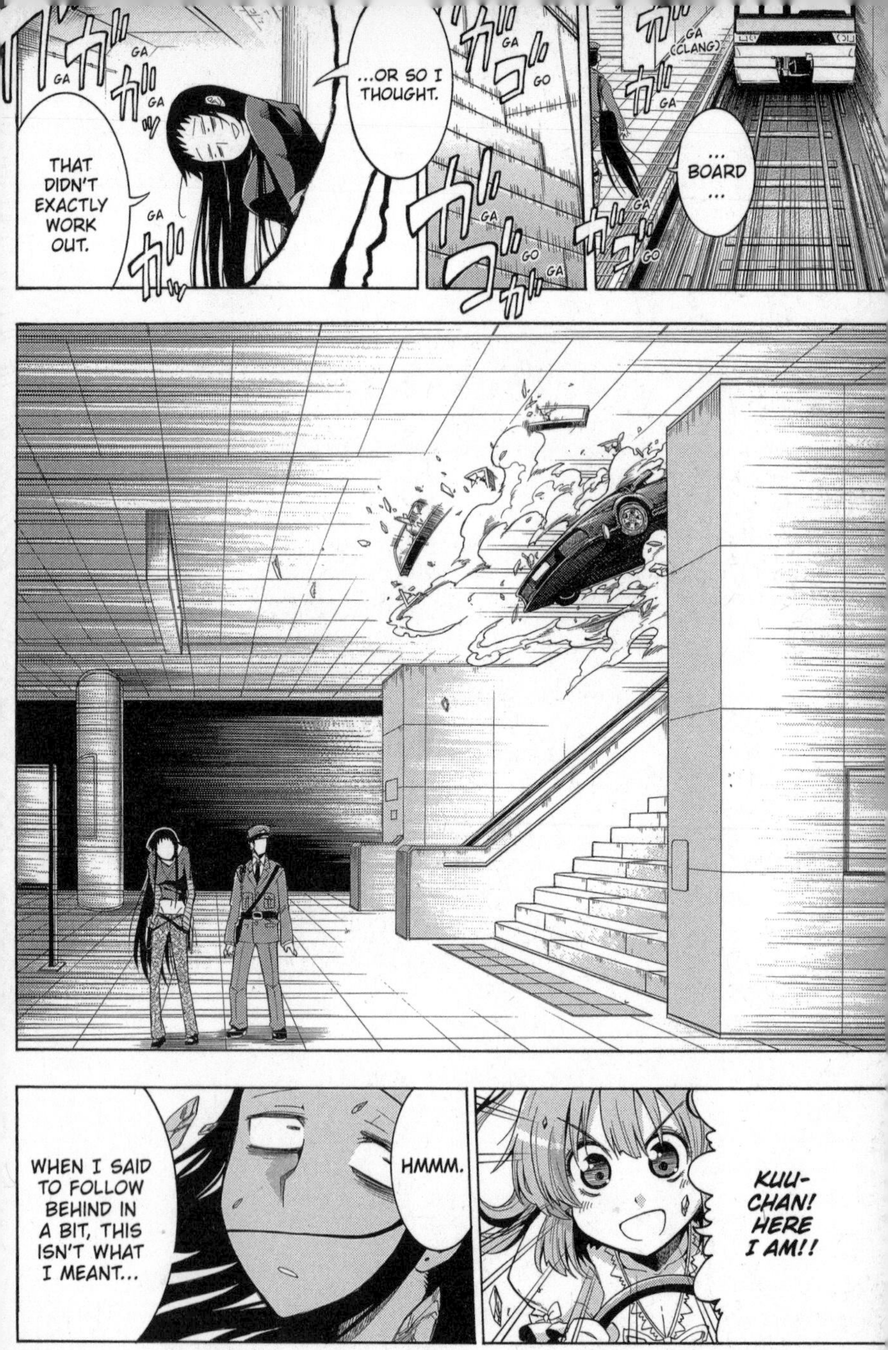
GA (CLANG)
GA
...BOARD...
GA
GO
GA
GO
GA
GO
GA
GA
GO
...OR SO I THOUGHT.
GA
GA
GA
THAT DIDN'T EXACTLY WORK OUT.
GA
KUU-CHAN! HERE I AM!!
HMMM.
WHEN I SAID TO FOLLOW BEHIND IN A BIT, THIS ISN'T WHAT I MEANT...

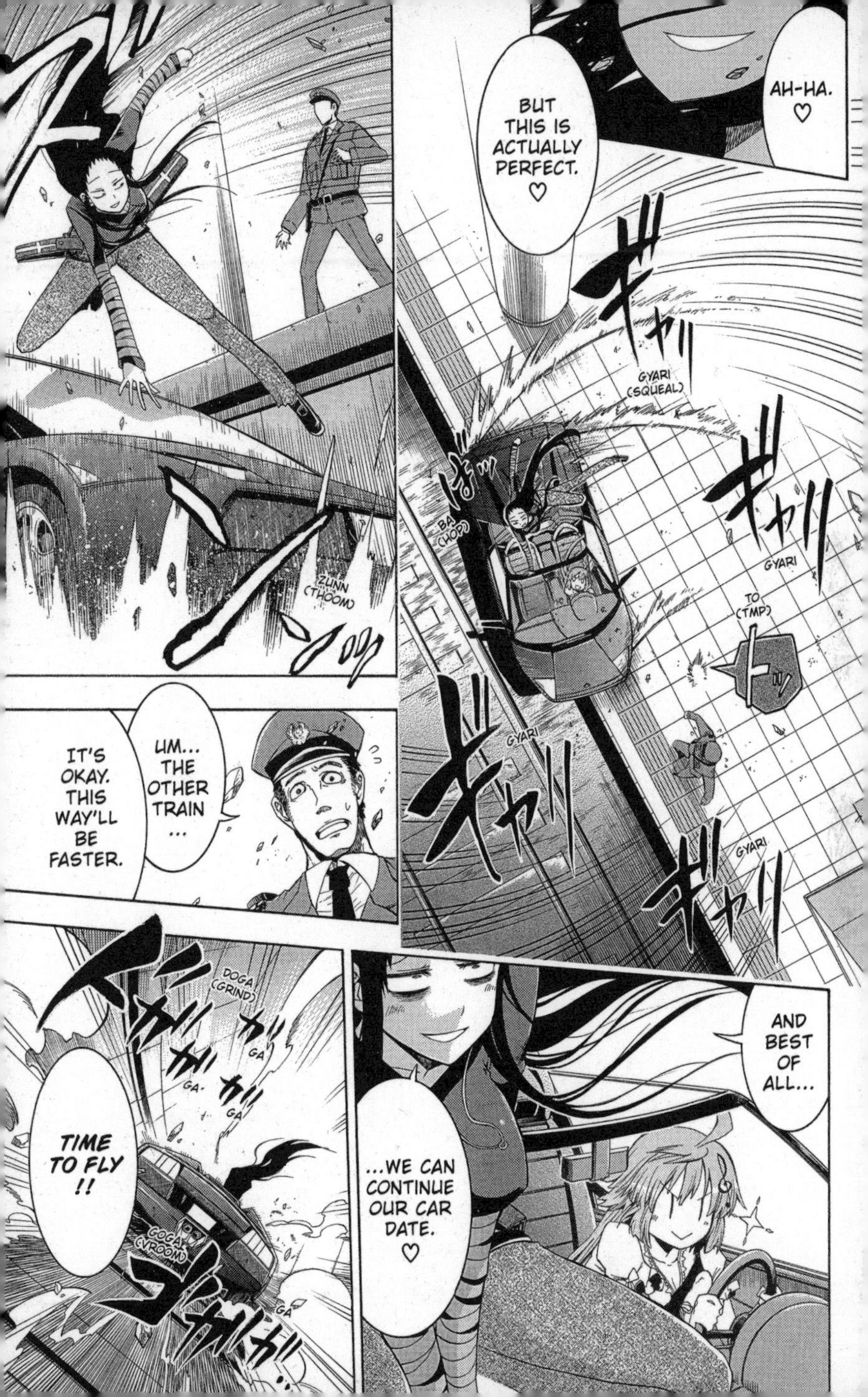

AH-HA. ♡
BUT THIS IS ACTUALLY PERFECT. ♡
GYARI (SQUEAL)
GYARI
BA (HOP)
TO (TMP)
GYARI
GYARI
ZUNN (THOOM)
UM... THE OTHER TRAIN ...
IT'S OKAY. THIS WAY'LL BE FASTER.
AND BEST OF ALL...
...WE CAN CONTINUE OUR CAR DATE. ♡
DOGA (GRIND)
GA
GA
GA
TIME TO FLY !!
GOGA (VROOM)
GA

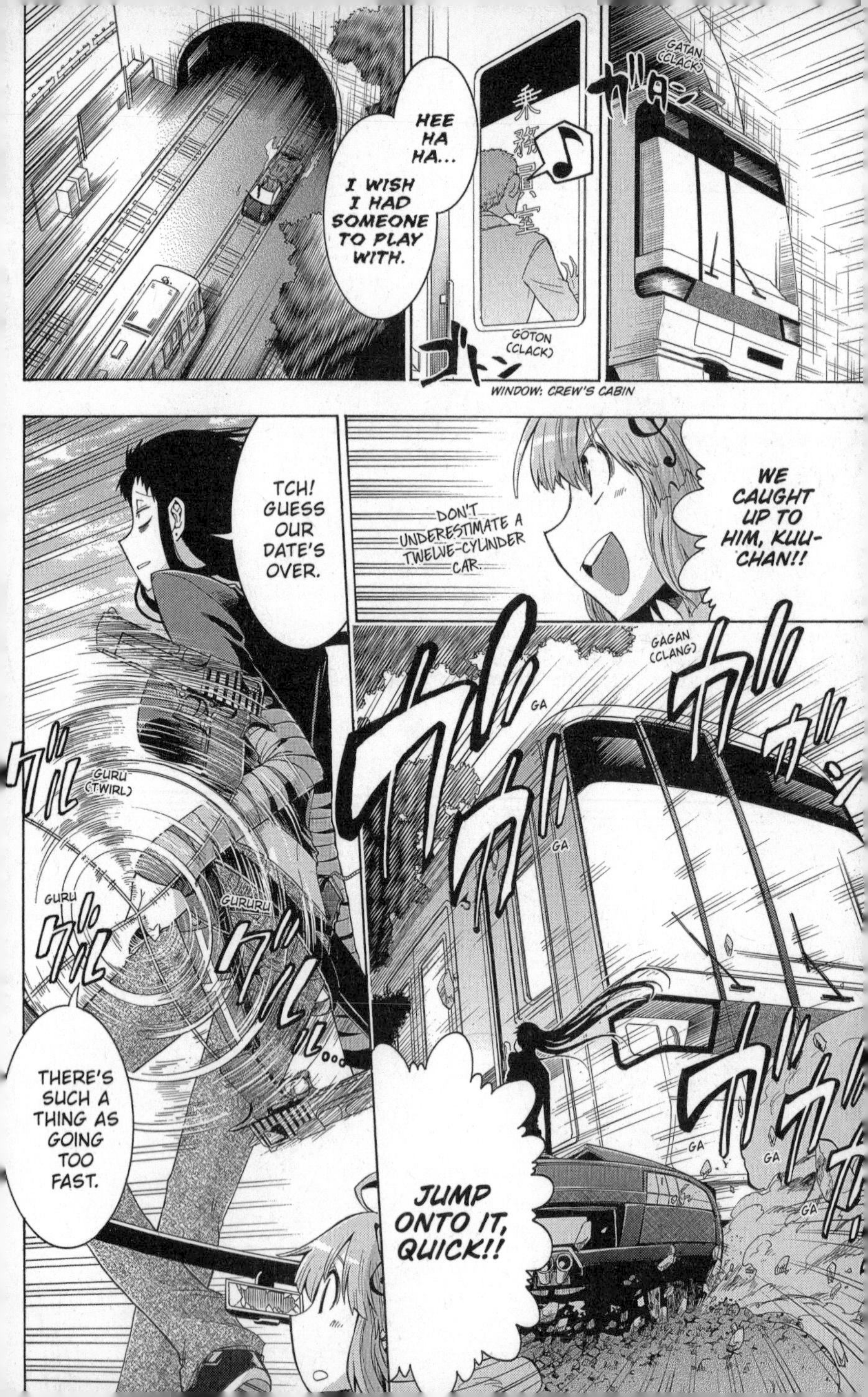
GATAN (CLACK)
HEE HA HA... I WISH I HAD SOMEONE TO PLAY WITH.
GOTON (CLACK)
WINDOW: CREW'S CABIN
WE CAUGHT UP TO HIM, KUU-CHAN!!
DON'T UNDERESTIMATE A TWELVE-CYLINDER CAR.
TCH! GUESS OUR DATE'S OVER.
GAGAN (CLANG)
GA
GA
GA
GA
GA
JUMP ONTO IT, QUICK!!
GURU (TWIRL)
GURU
GURURU
THERE'S SUCH A THING AS GOING TOO FAST.

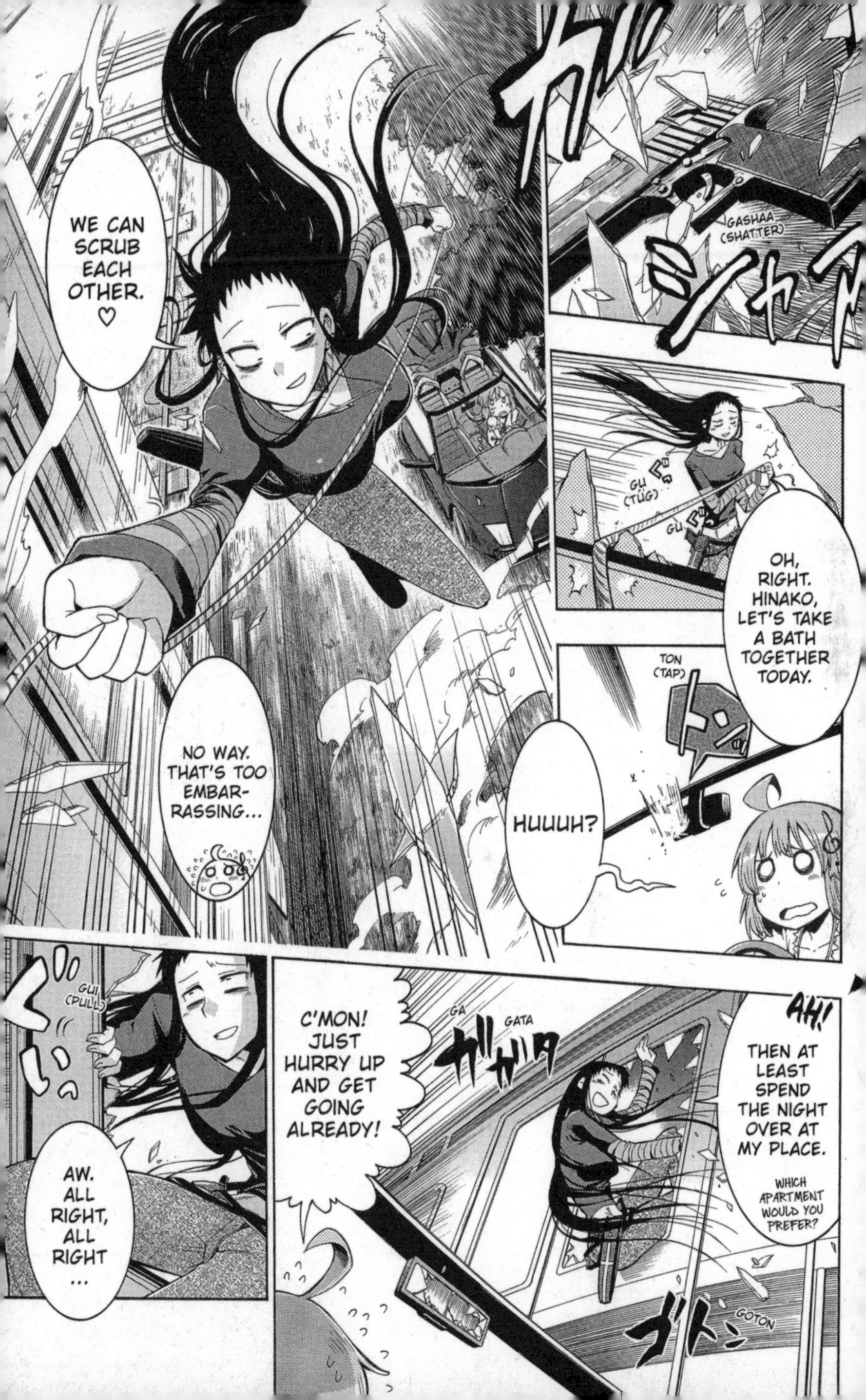
GASHAA (SHATTER)
GU (TUG)
GU
OH, RIGHT. HINAKO, LET'S TAKE A BATH TOGETHER TODAY.
TON (TAP)
HUUUH?
WE CAN SCRUB EACH OTHER. ♡
NO WAY. THAT'S TOO EMBAR-RASSING...
AH!
THEN AT LEAST SPEND THE NIGHT OVER AT MY PLACE.
WHICH APARTMENT WOULD YOU PREFER?
C'MON! JUST HURRY UP AND GET GOING ALREADY!
GA GATA
GOTON
GUI (PULL)
AW. ALL RIGHT, ALL RIGHT...

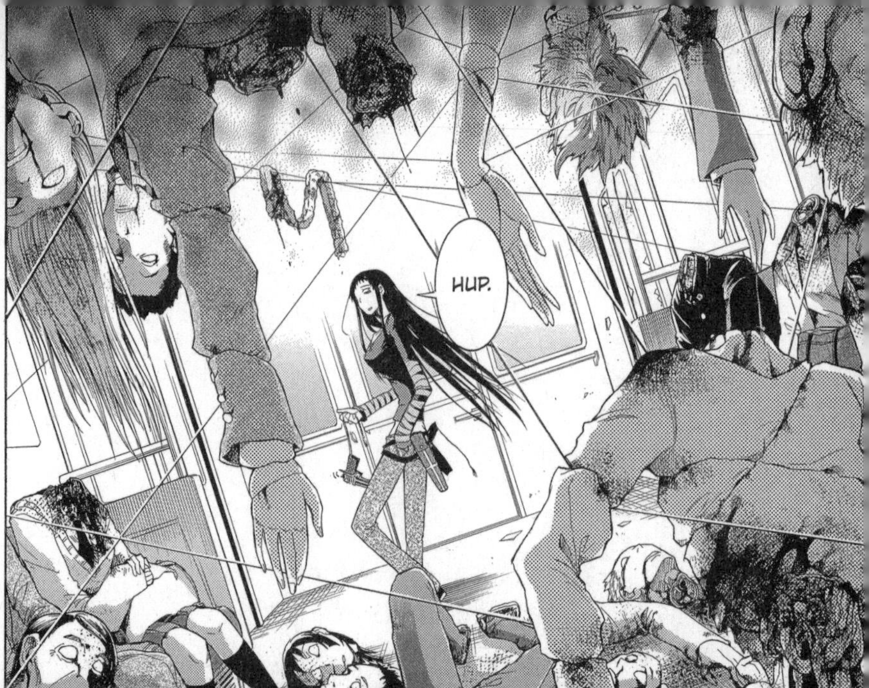
HUP.
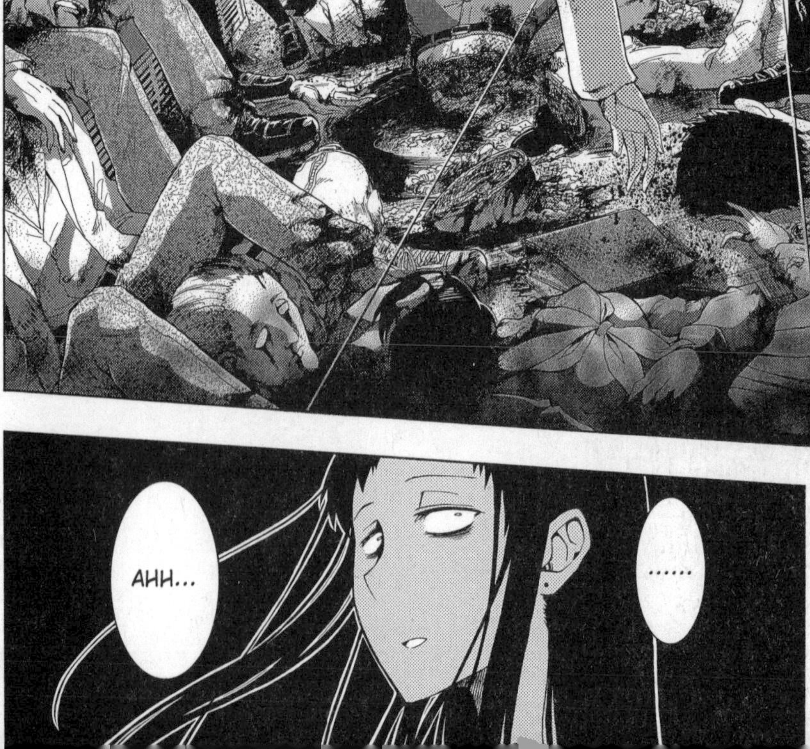
......
AHH...

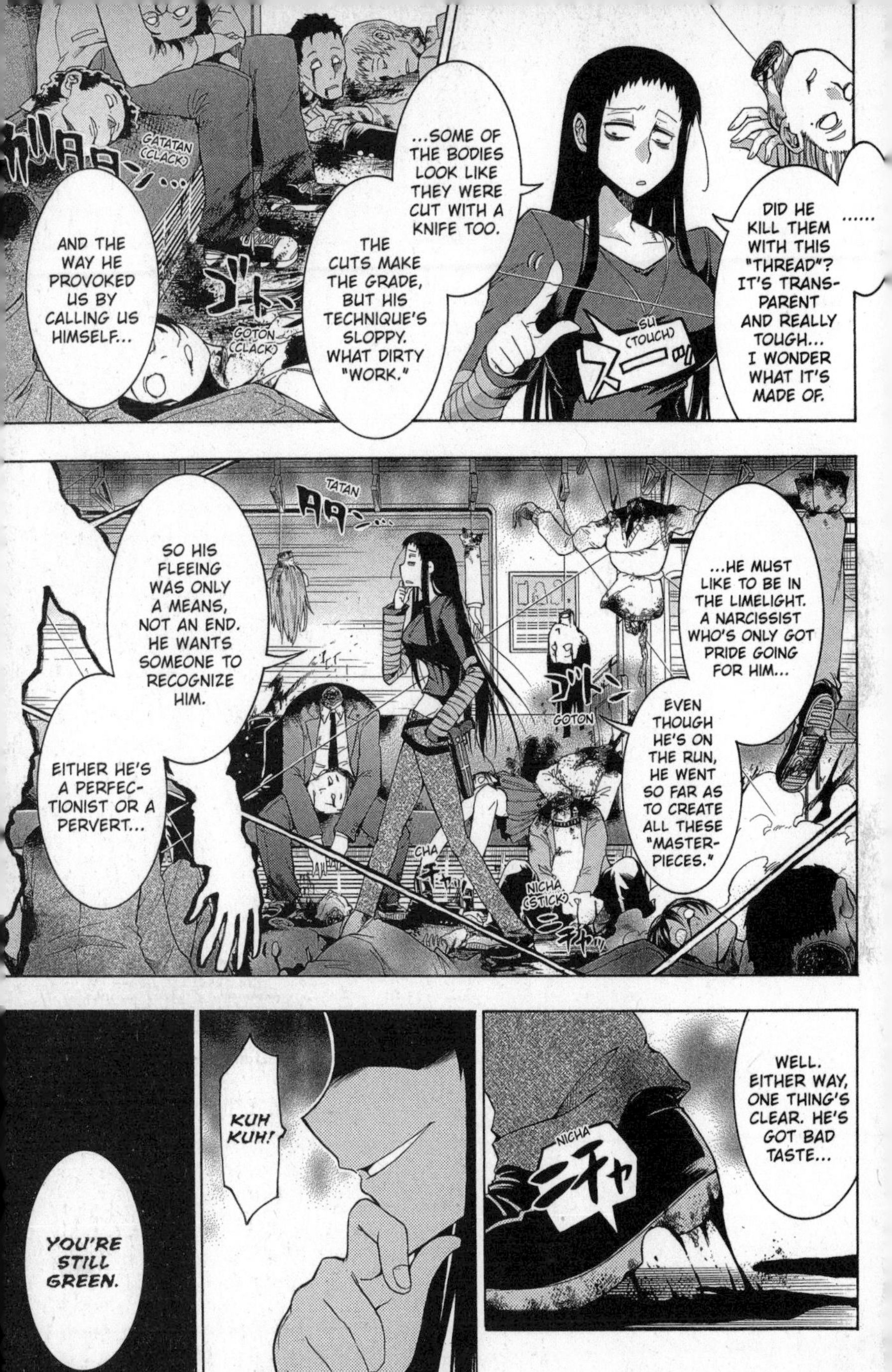
......
DID HE KILL THEM WITH THIS "THREAD"? IT'S TRANSPARENT AND REALLY TOUGH... I WONDER WHAT IT'S MADE OF.
SU (TOUCH)
...SOME OF THE BODIES LOOK LIKE THEY WERE CUT WITH A KNIFE TOO.
THE CUTS MAKE THE GRADE, BUT HIS TECHNIQUE'S SLOPPY. WHAT DIRTY "WORK."
GOTON (CLACK)
AND THE WAY HE PROVOKED US BY CALLING US HIMSELF...
GATATAN (CLACK)
...HE MUST LIKE TO BE IN THE LIMELIGHT. A NARCISSIST WHO'S ONLY GOT PRIDE GOING FOR HIM...
EVEN THOUGH HE'S ON THE RUN, HE WENT SO FAR AS TO CREATE ALL THESE "MASTERPIECES."
GOTON
TATAN
SO HIS FLEEING WAS ONLY A MEANS, NOT AN END. HE WANTS SOMEONE TO RECOGNIZE HIM.
EITHER HE'S A PERFECTIONIST OR A PERVERT...
NICHA (STICK)
CHA
WELL. EITHER WAY, ONE THING'S CLEAR. HE'S GOT BAD TASTE...
NICHA
KUH KUH!
YOU'RE STILL GREEN.

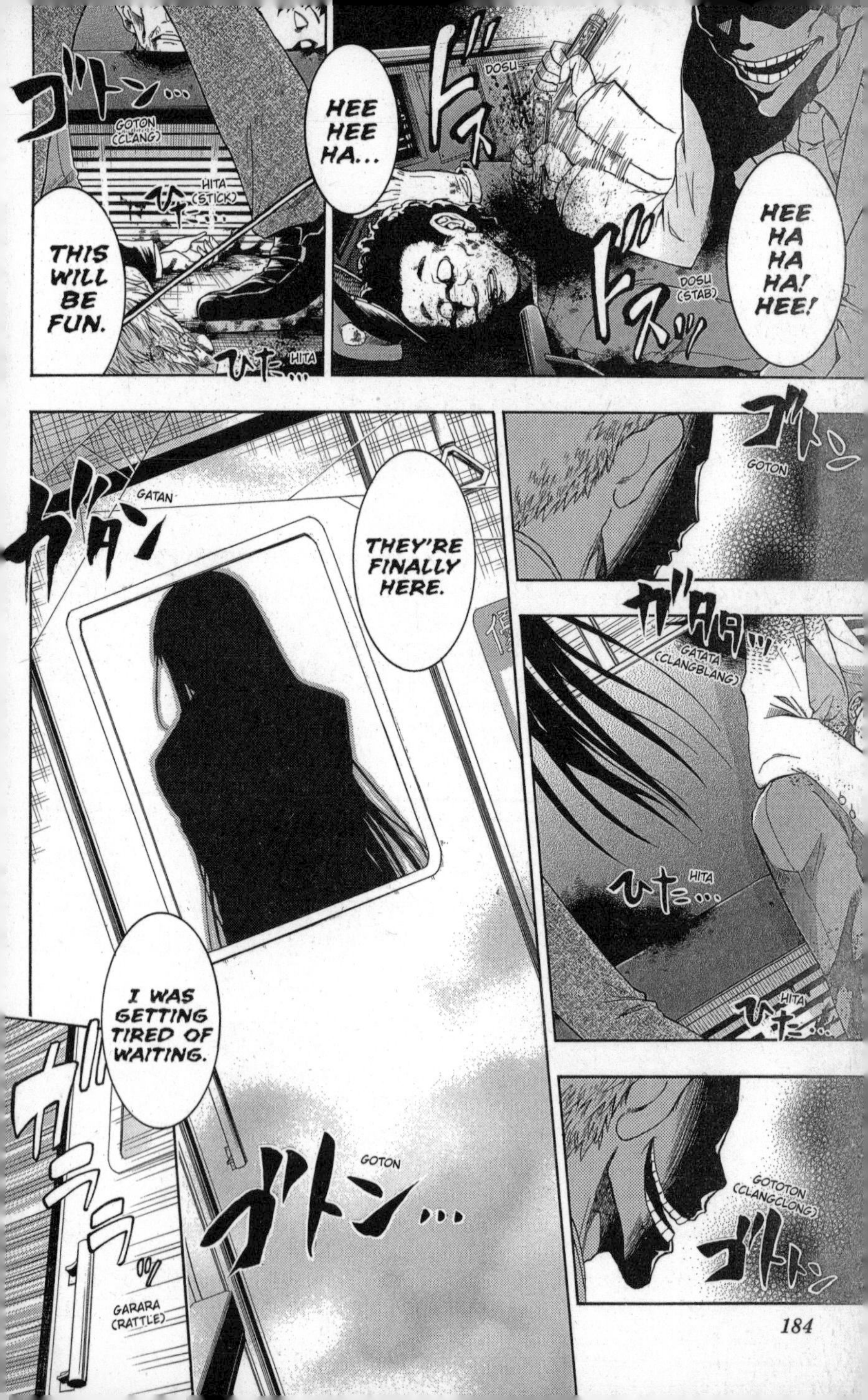
HEE HA HA HA! HEE!
DOSU (STAB)
DOSU
HEE HEE HA...
GOTON (CLANG)
HITA (STICK)
THIS WILL BE FUN.
HITA
GOTON
GATATA (CLANGBLANG)
HITA
HITA
GOTOTON (CLANGCLONG)
GATAN
THEY'RE FINALLY HERE.
I WAS GETTING TIRED OF WAITING.
GOTON
GARARA (RATTLE)

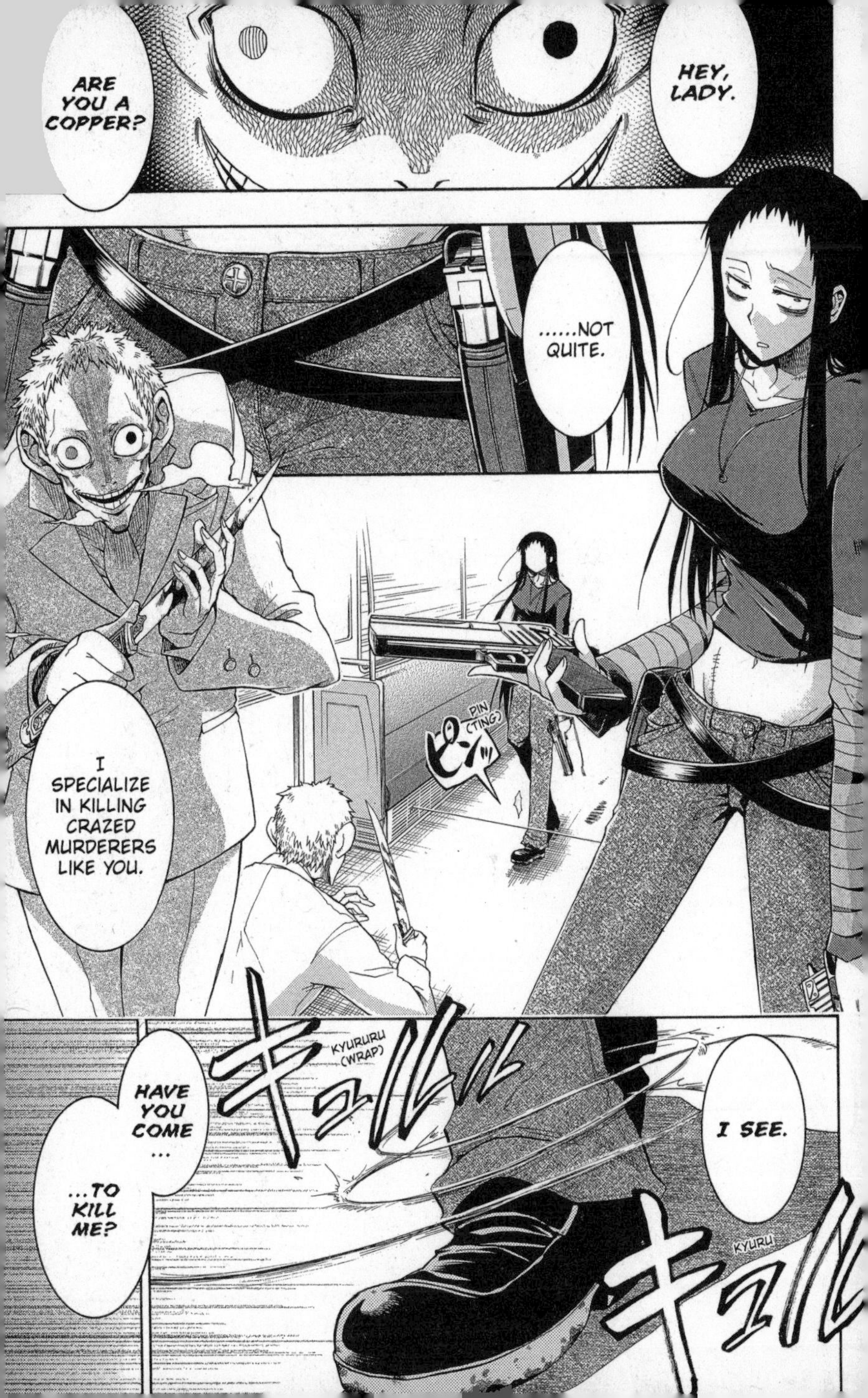
HEY, LADY.
ARE YOU A COPPER?
......NOT QUITE.
PIN (TING)
I SPECIALIZE IN KILLING CRAZED MURDERERS LIKE YOU.
I SEE.
KYURURU (WRAP)
HAVE YOU COME ...
...TO KILL ME?
KYURU

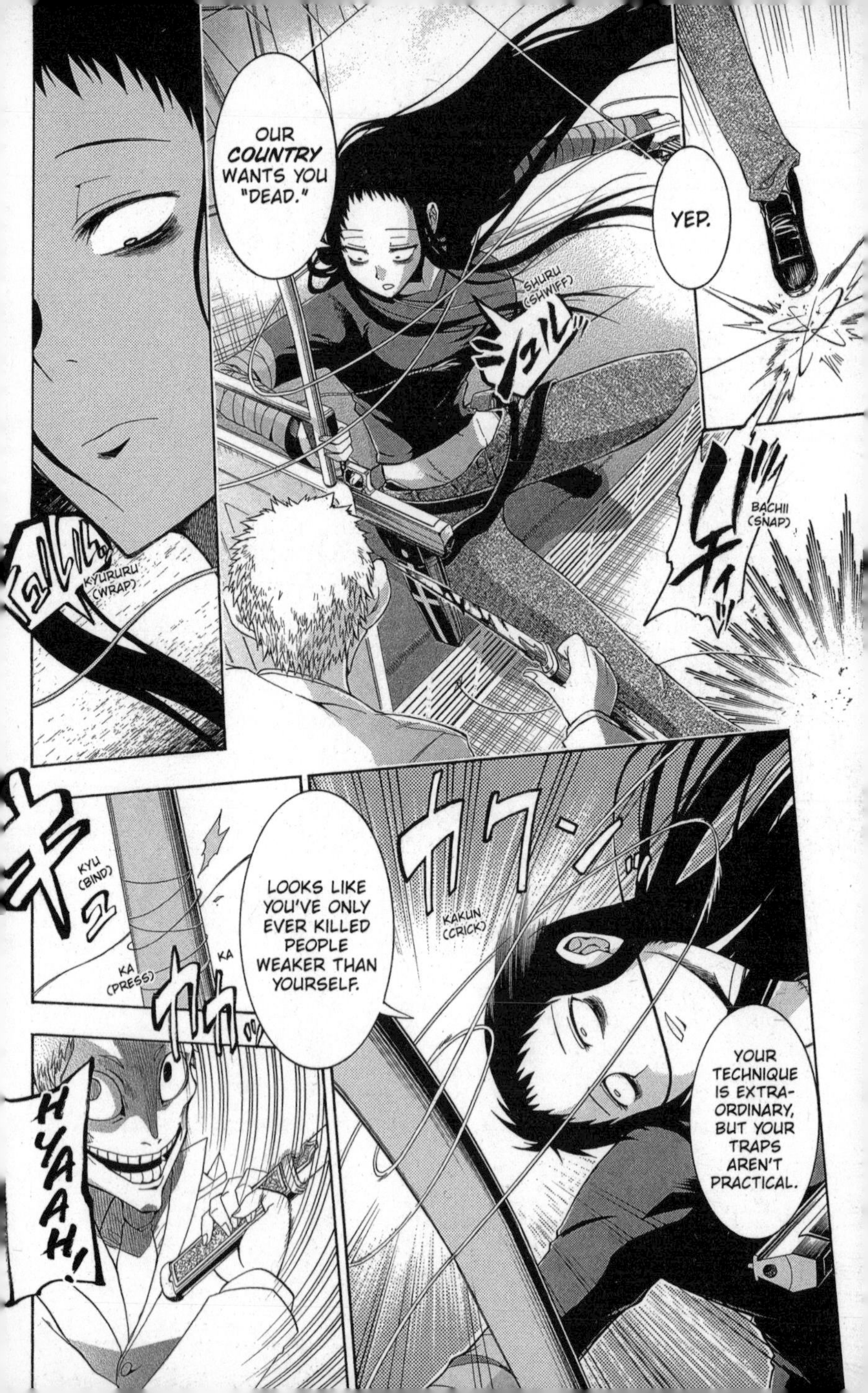
OUR COUNTRY WANTS YOU "DEAD."
YEP.
SHURU (SHWIFF)
BACHII (SNAP)
KYURURU (WRAP)
LOOKS LIKE YOU'VE ONLY EVER KILLED PEOPLE WEAKER THAN YOURSELF.
KAKUN (CRICK)
YOUR TECHNIQUE IS EXTRA-ORDINARY, BUT YOUR TRAPS AREN'T PRACTICAL.
KYU (BIND)
KA
KA (PRESS)
HYAAAH!

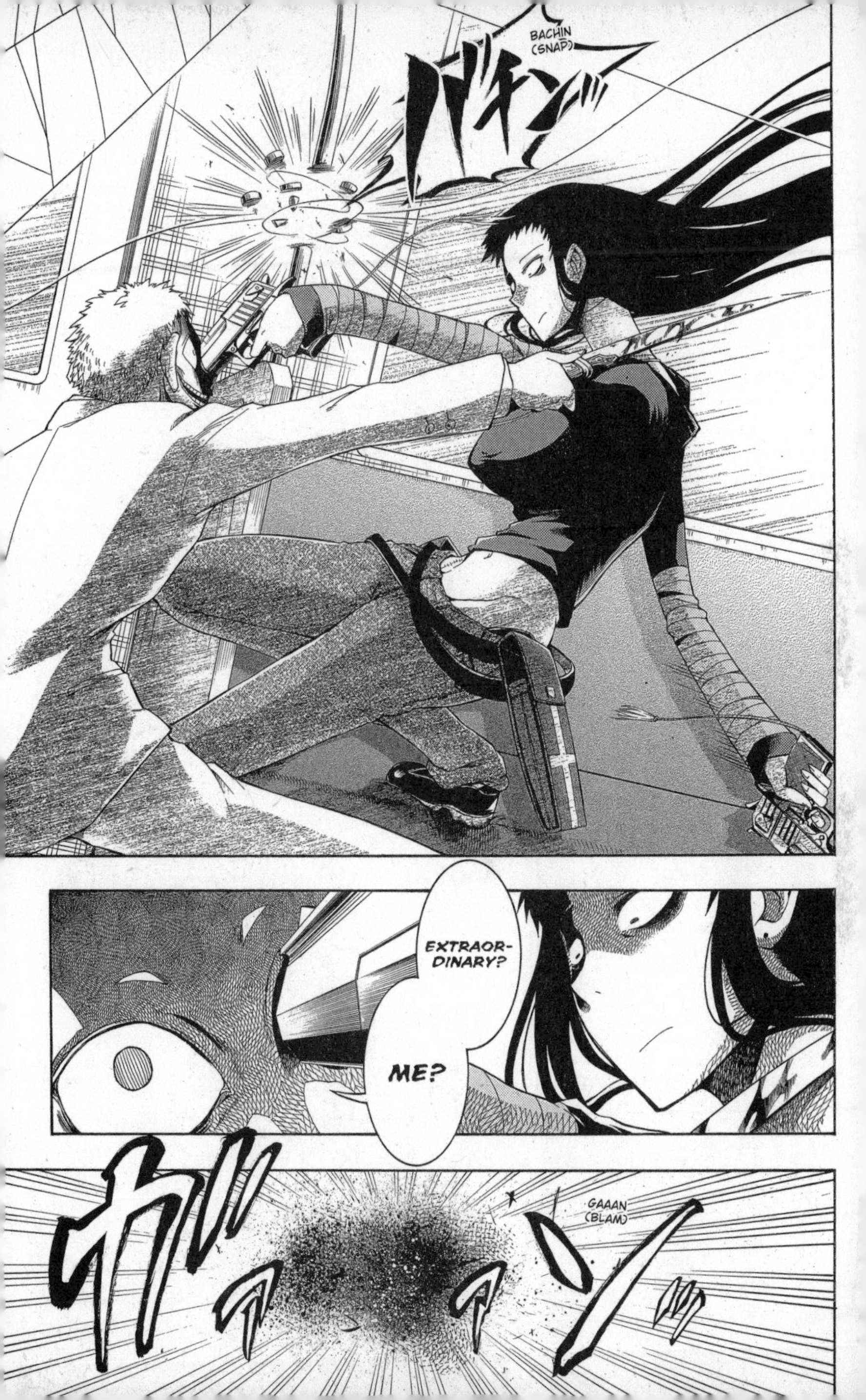
BACHIN (SNAP)
EXTRAOR-DINARY?
ME?
GAAAN (BLAM)

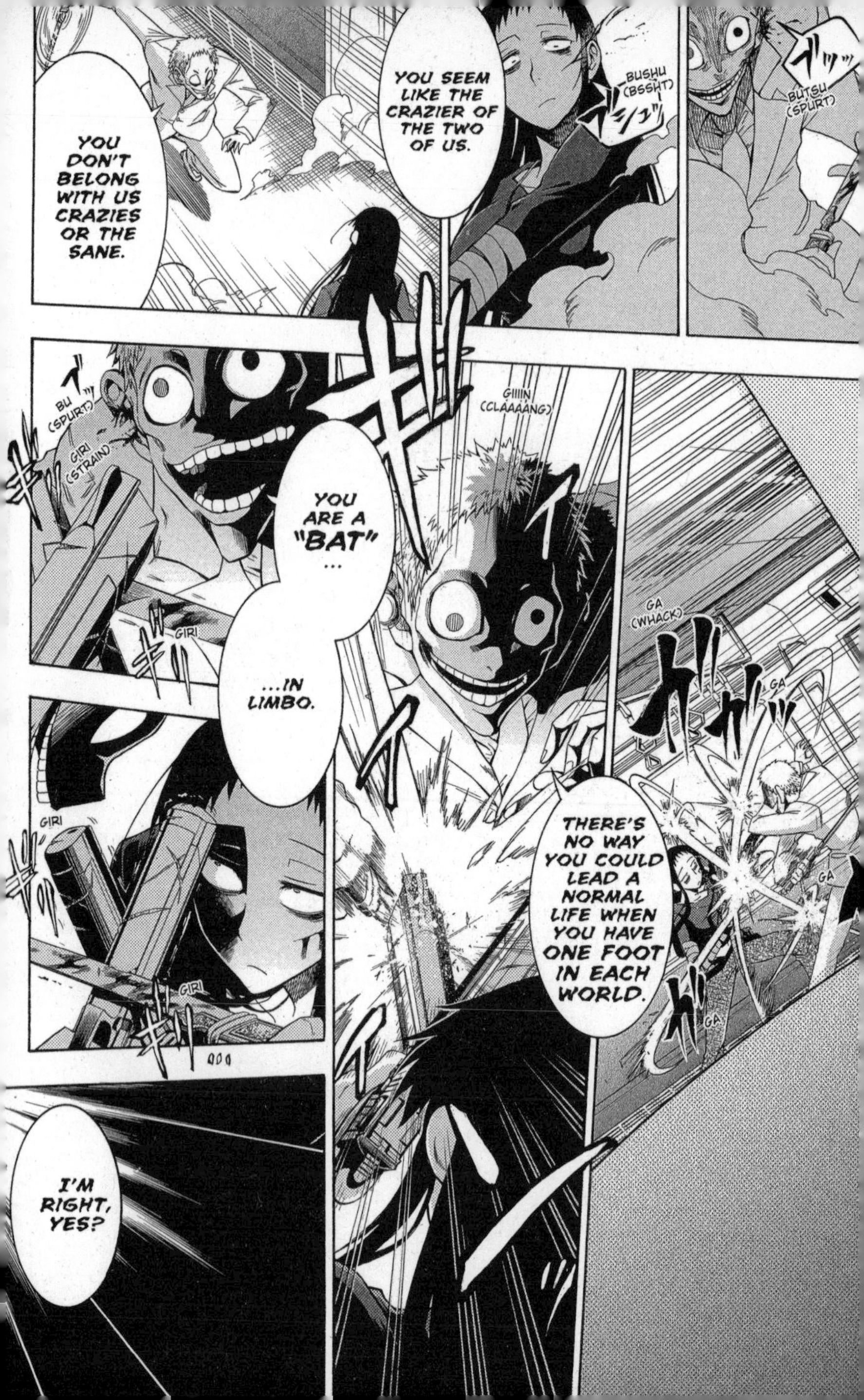

BUTSU (SPURT)
BUSHU (BSSHT)
YOU SEEM LIKE THE CRAZIER OF THE TWO OF US.
YOU DON'T BELONG WITH US CRAZIES OR THE SANE.
GA (WHACK)
GA
THERE'S NO WAY YOU COULD LEAD A NORMAL LIFE WHEN YOU HAVE ONE FOOT IN EACH WORLD.
GA
GA
GIIIN (CLAAAANG)
YOU ARE A "BAT"...
...IN LIMBO.
BU (SPURT)
GIRI (STRAIN)
GIRI
GIRI
GIRI
I'M RIGHT, YES?

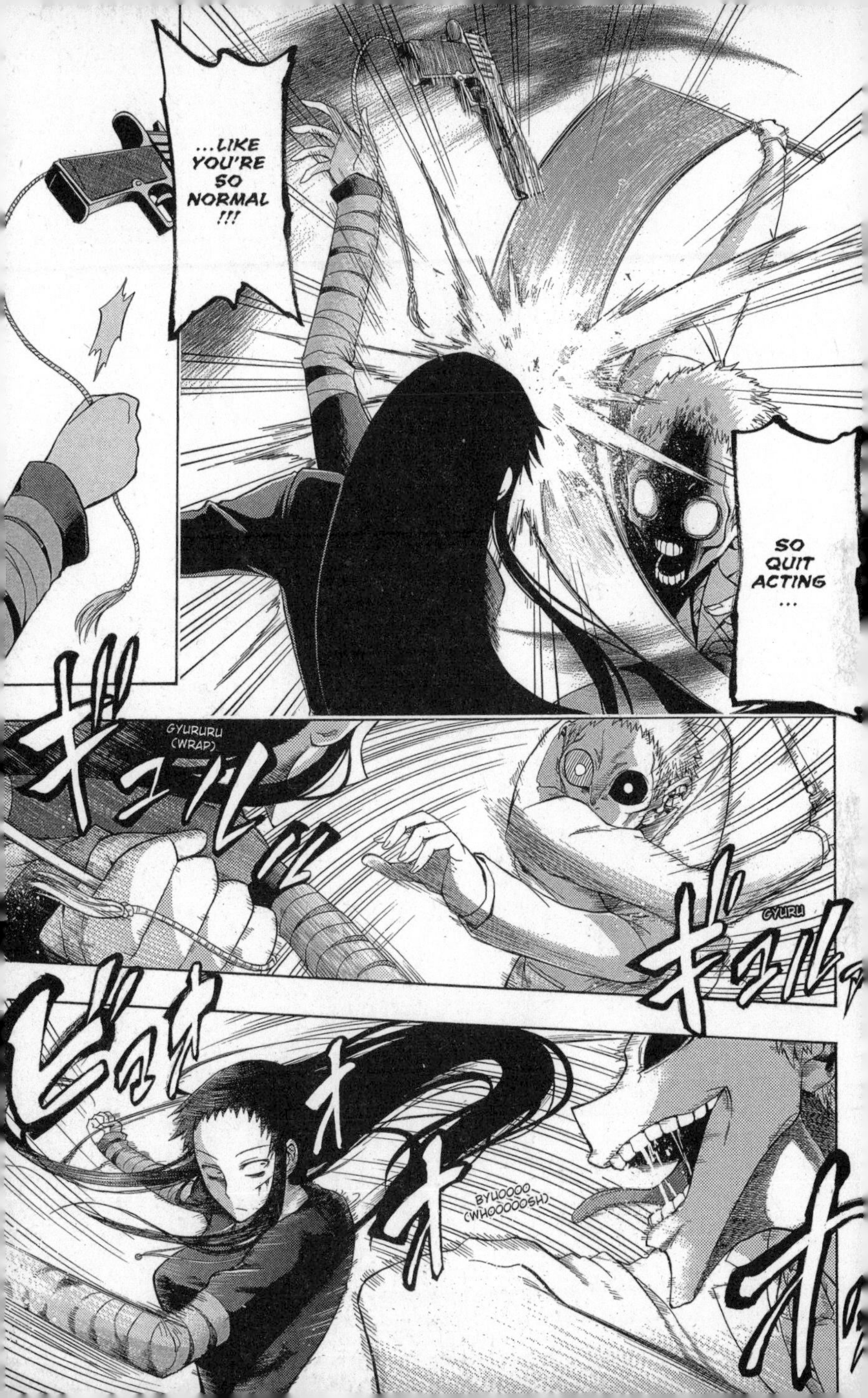
SO QUIT ACTING ...
...LIKE YOU'RE SO NORMAL !!!
GYURU
GYURURU (WRAP)
BYUOOOO (WHOOOOOSH)

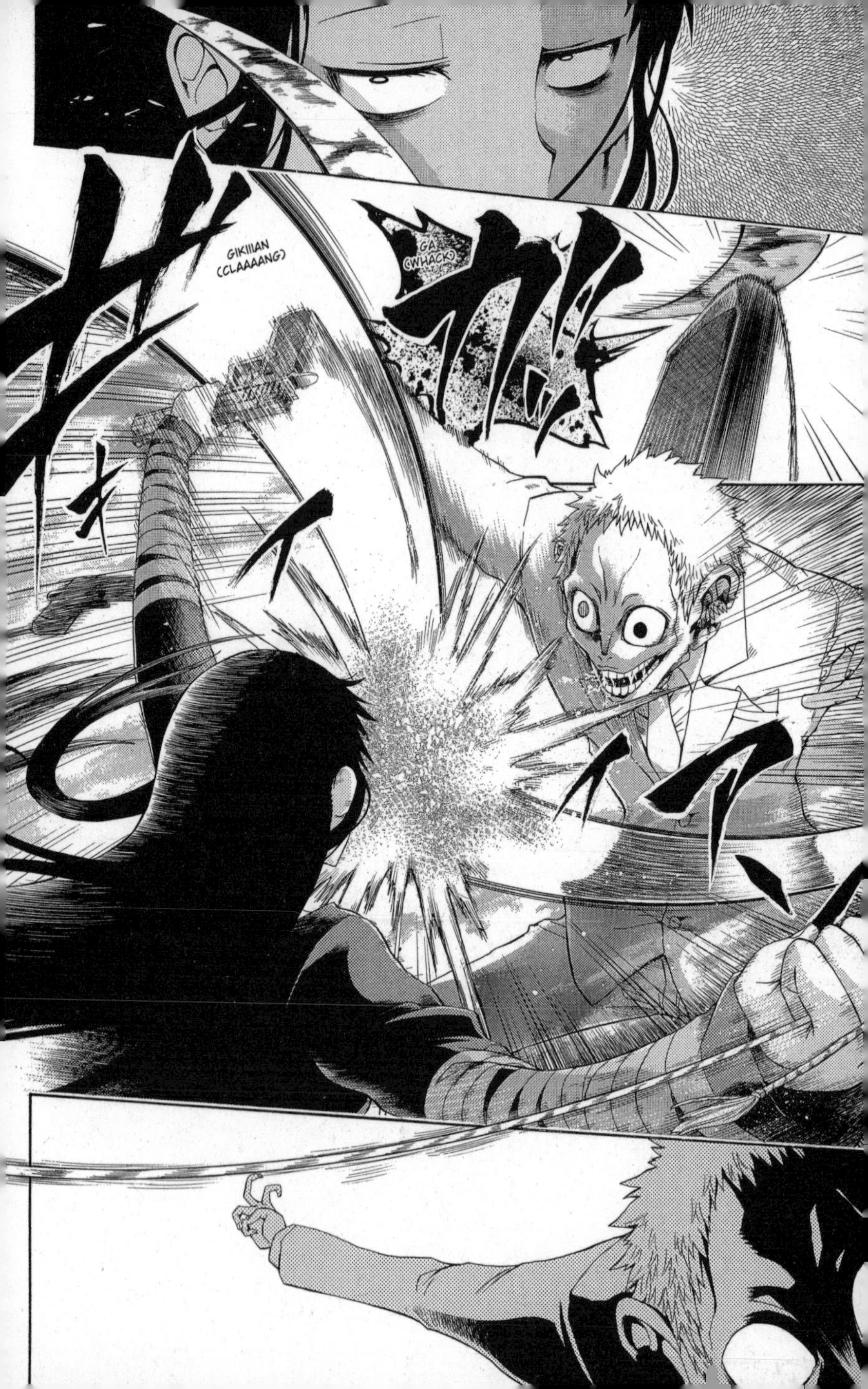
GA (WHACK)
GIKIIIAN (CLAAAANG)

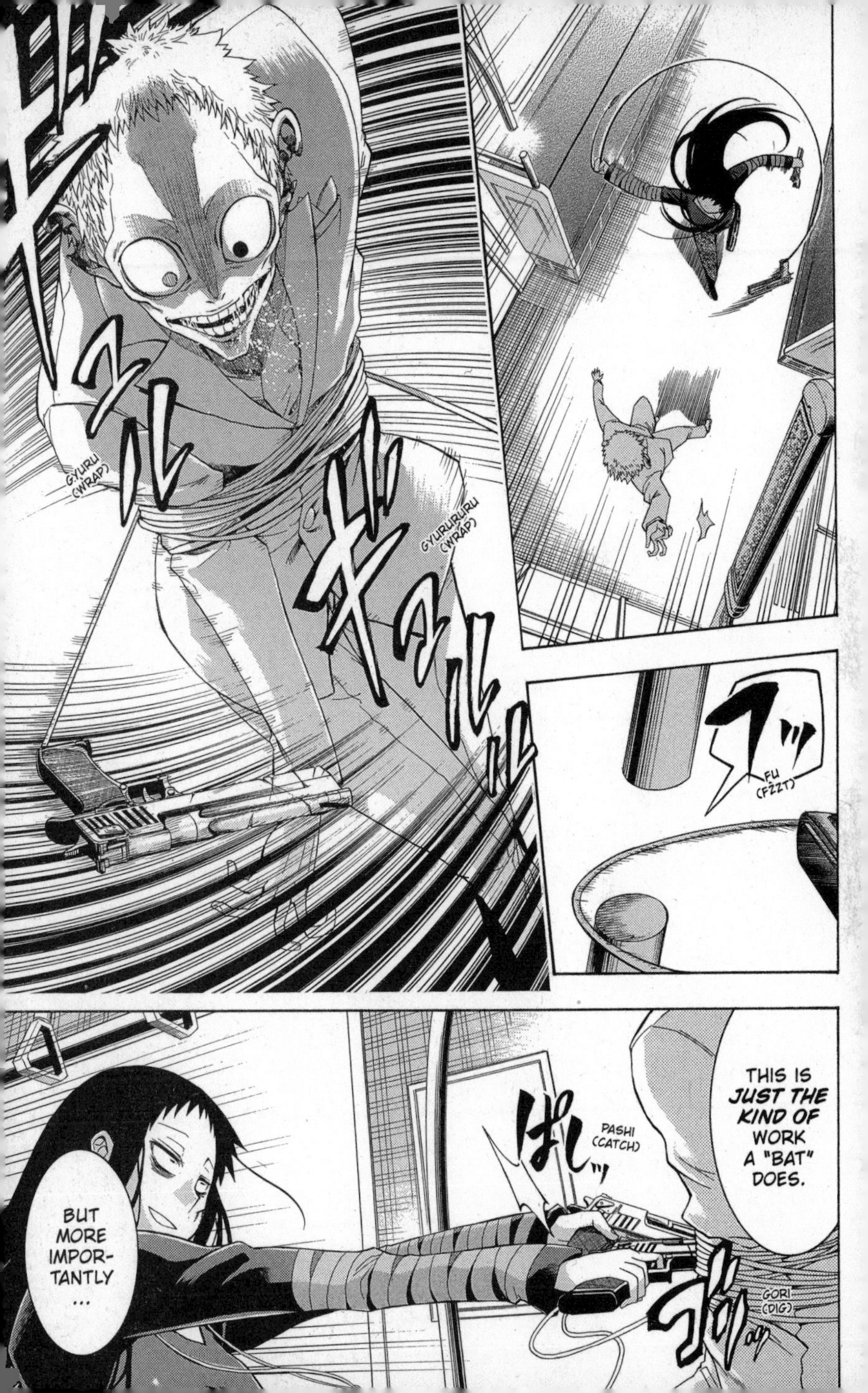
FU (FZZT)
GYURU (WRAP)
GYURURURU (WRAP)
THIS IS *JUST THE* KIND OF WORK A "BAT" DOES.
GORI (DIG)
PASHI (CATCH)
BUT MORE IMPORTANTLY ...

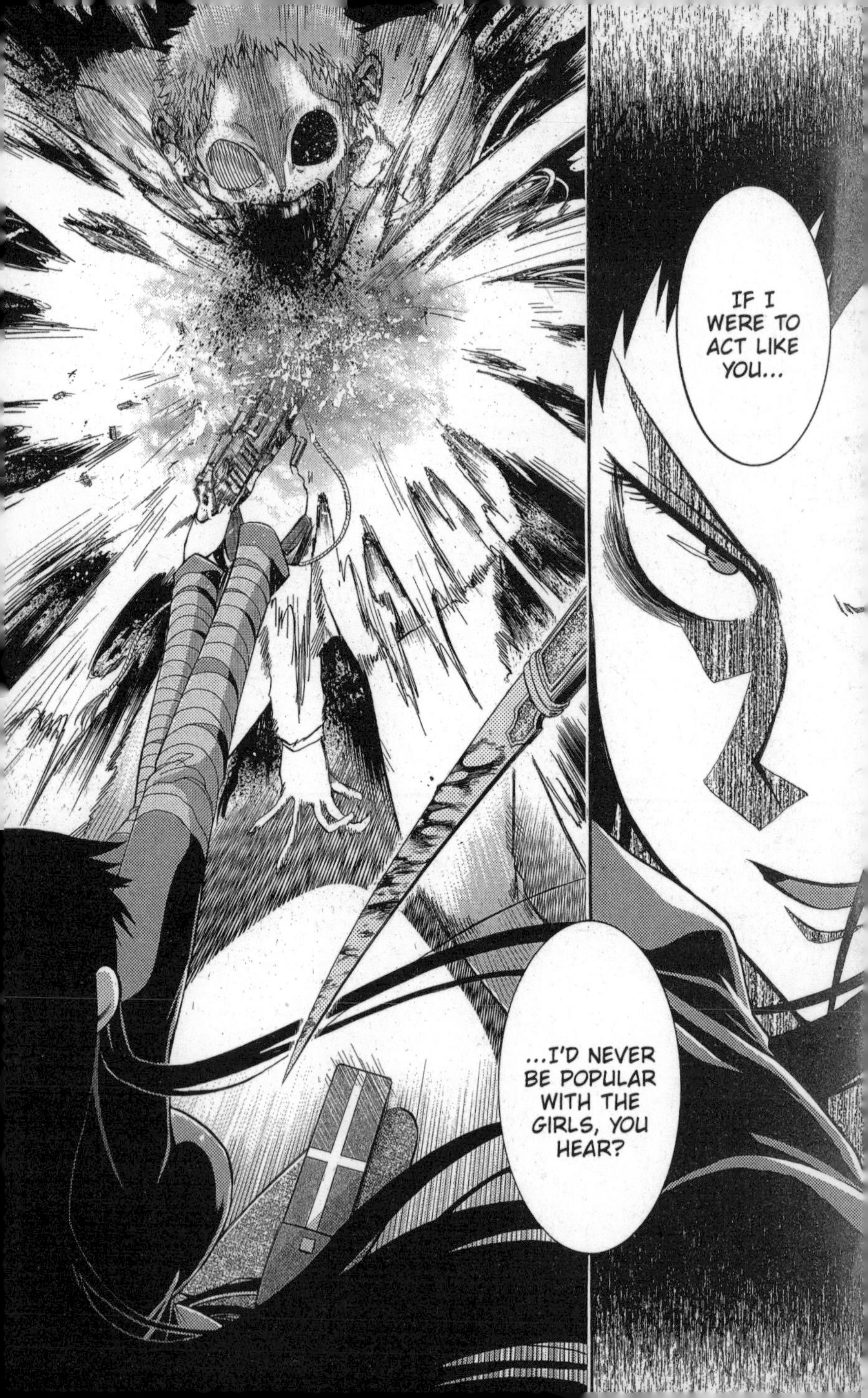
IF I WERE TO ACT LIKE YOU...
...I'D NEVER BE POPULAR WITH THE GIRLS, YOU HEAR?

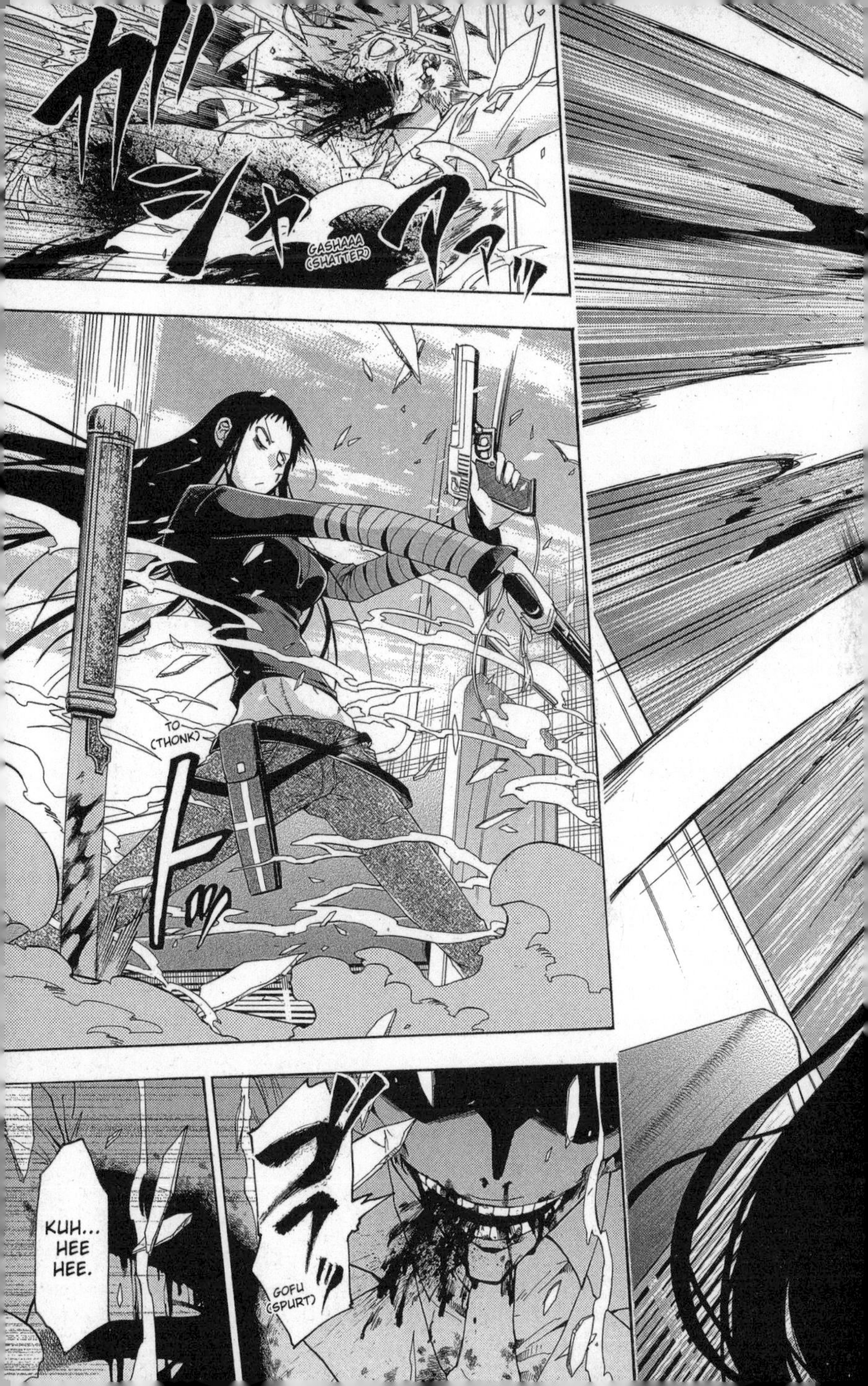
GASHAAA (SHATTER)
TO (THONK)
GOFU (SPURT)
KUH... HEE HEE.

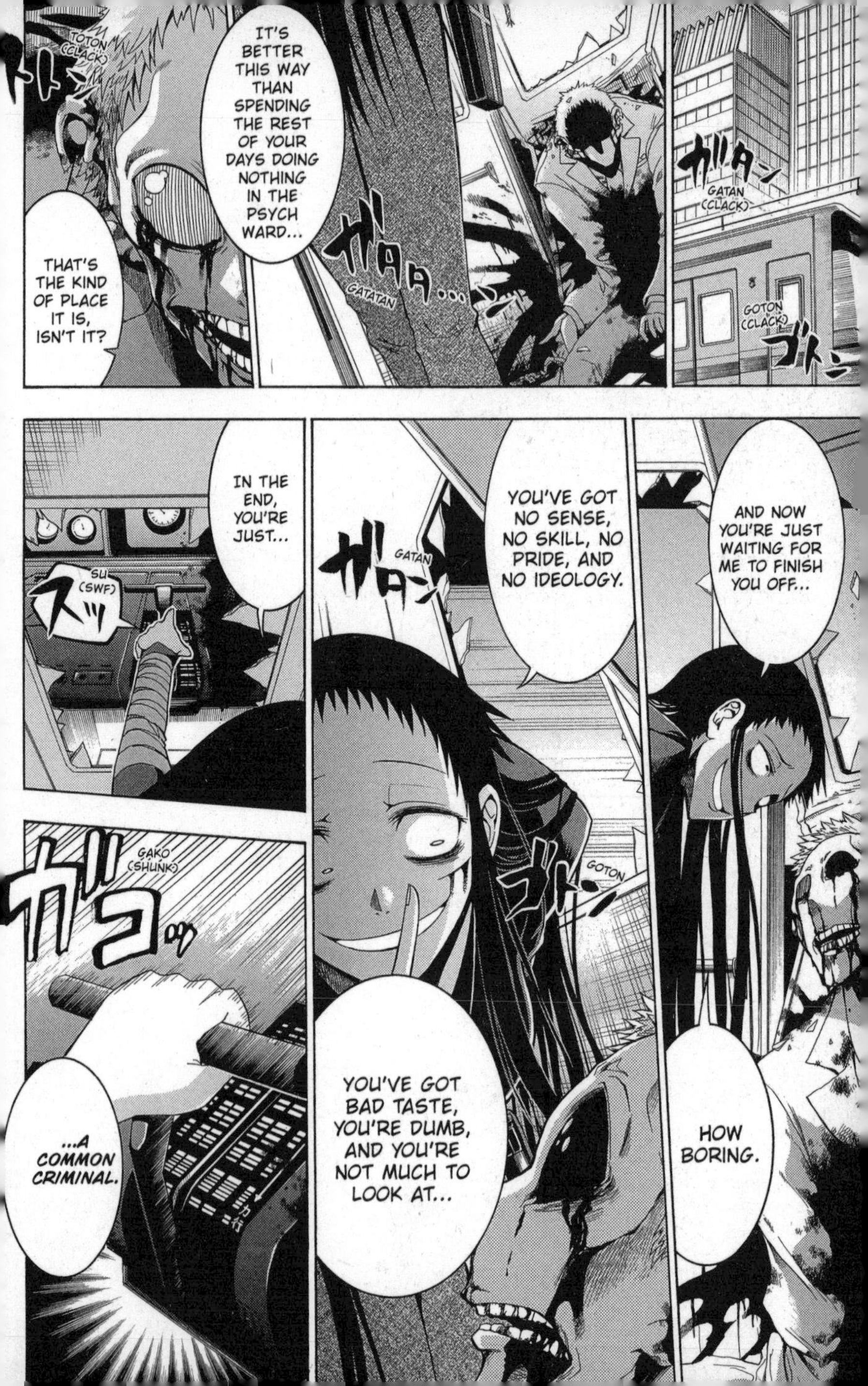

GATAN (CLACK)
GOTON (CLACK)
GATATAN
TOTON (CLACK)
IT'S BETTER THIS WAY THAN SPENDING THE REST OF YOUR DAYS DOING NOTHING IN THE PSYCH WARD...
THAT'S THE KIND OF PLACE IT IS, ISN'T IT?
AND NOW YOU'RE JUST WAITING FOR ME TO FINISH YOU OFF...
HOW BORING.
GATAN
YOU'VE GOT NO SENSE, NO SKILL, NO PRIDE, AND NO IDEOLOGY.
GOTON
YOU'VE GOT BAD TASTE, YOU'RE DUMB, AND YOU'RE NOT MUCH TO LOOK AT...
IN THE END, YOU'RE JUST...
SU (SWF)
GAKO (SHUNK)
...A COMMON CRIMINAL.

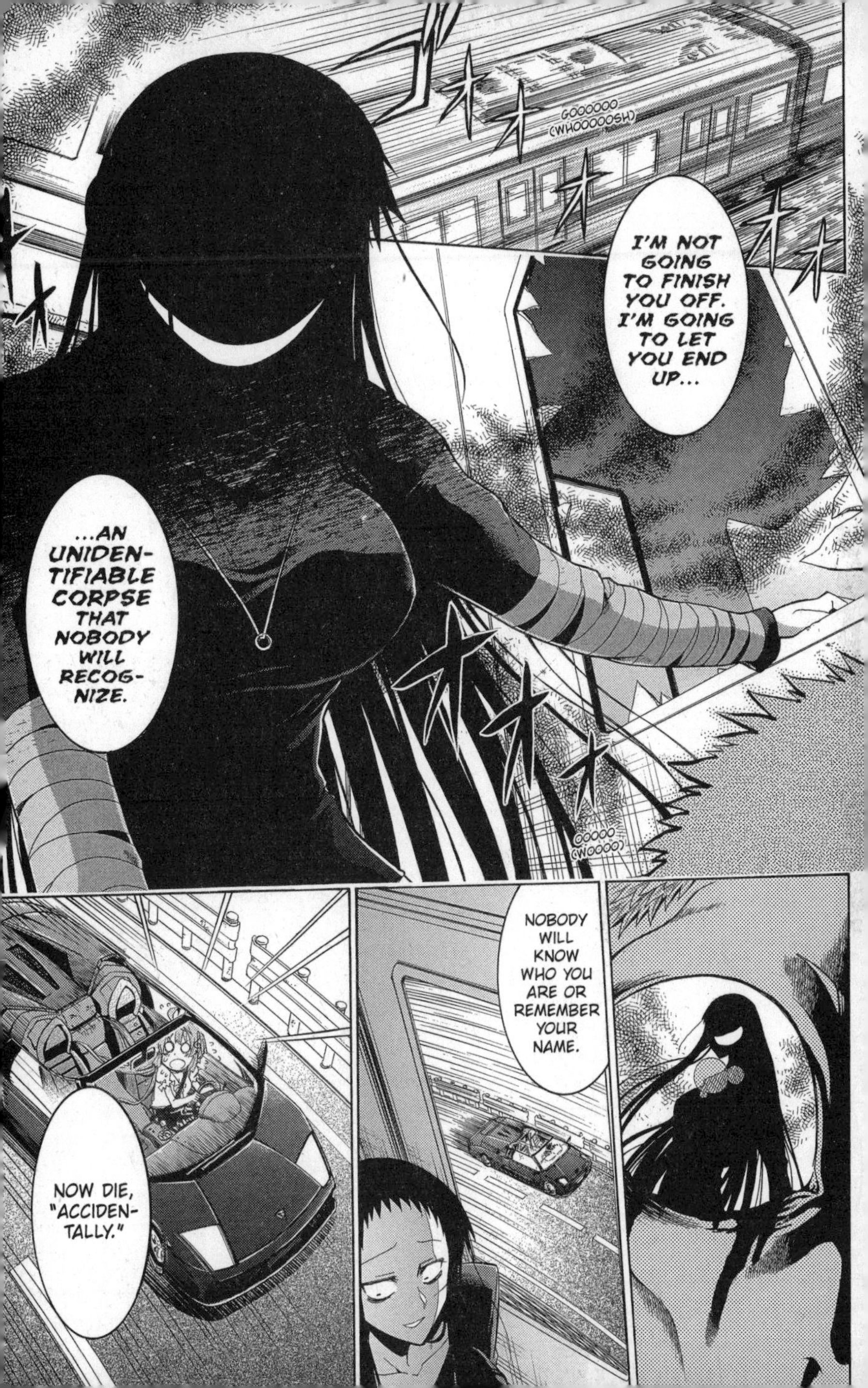
GOOOOOO (WHOOOOOSH)
I'M NOT GOING TO FINISH YOU OFF. I'M GOING TO LET YOU END UP...
...AN UNIDEN-TIFIABLE CORPSE THAT NOBODY WILL RECOG-NIZE.
OOOOO (WOOOO)
NOBODY WILL KNOW WHO YOU ARE OR REMEMBER YOUR NAME.
NOW DIE, "ACCIDEN-TALLY."

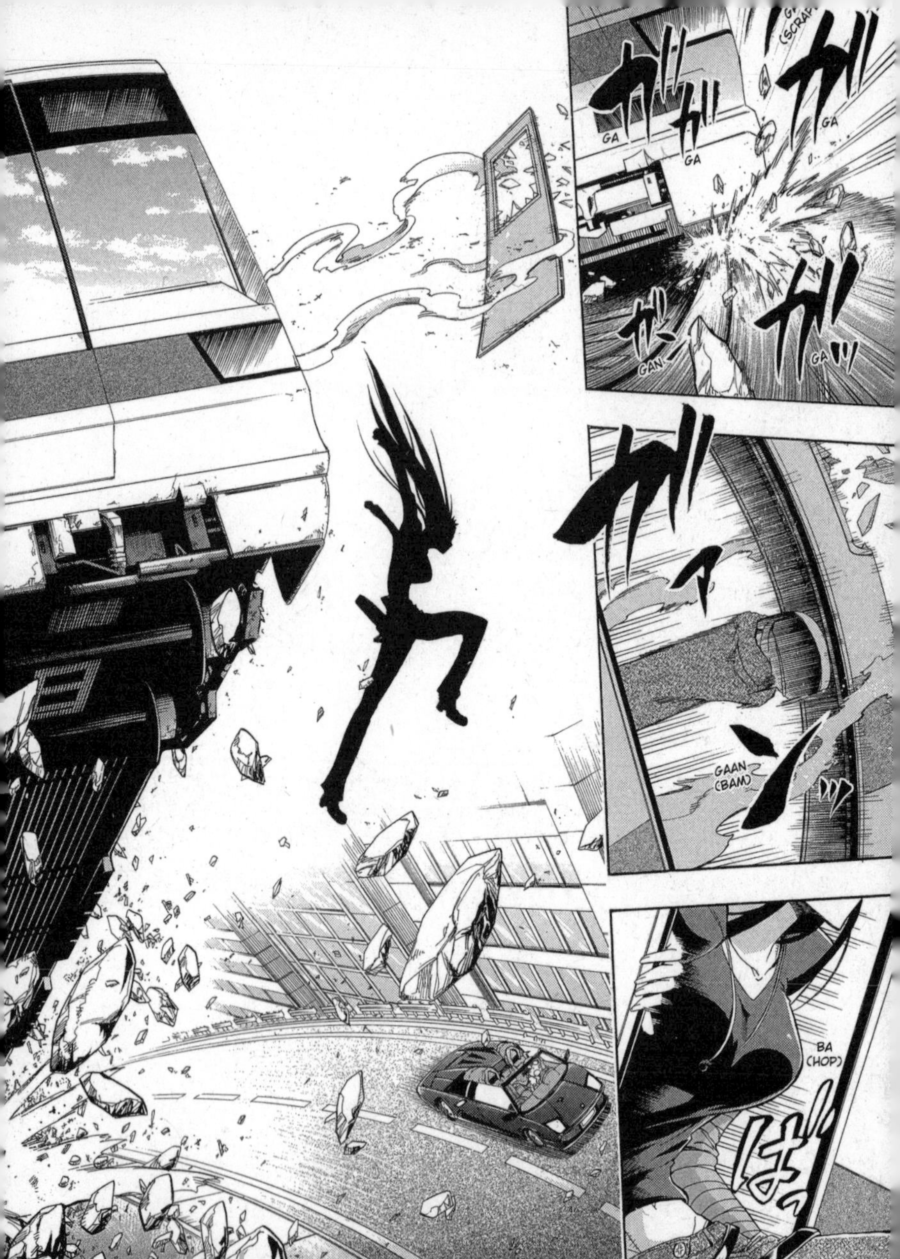

GA
GA
GA
GA
GAN
GAAN (BAM)
BA (HOP)

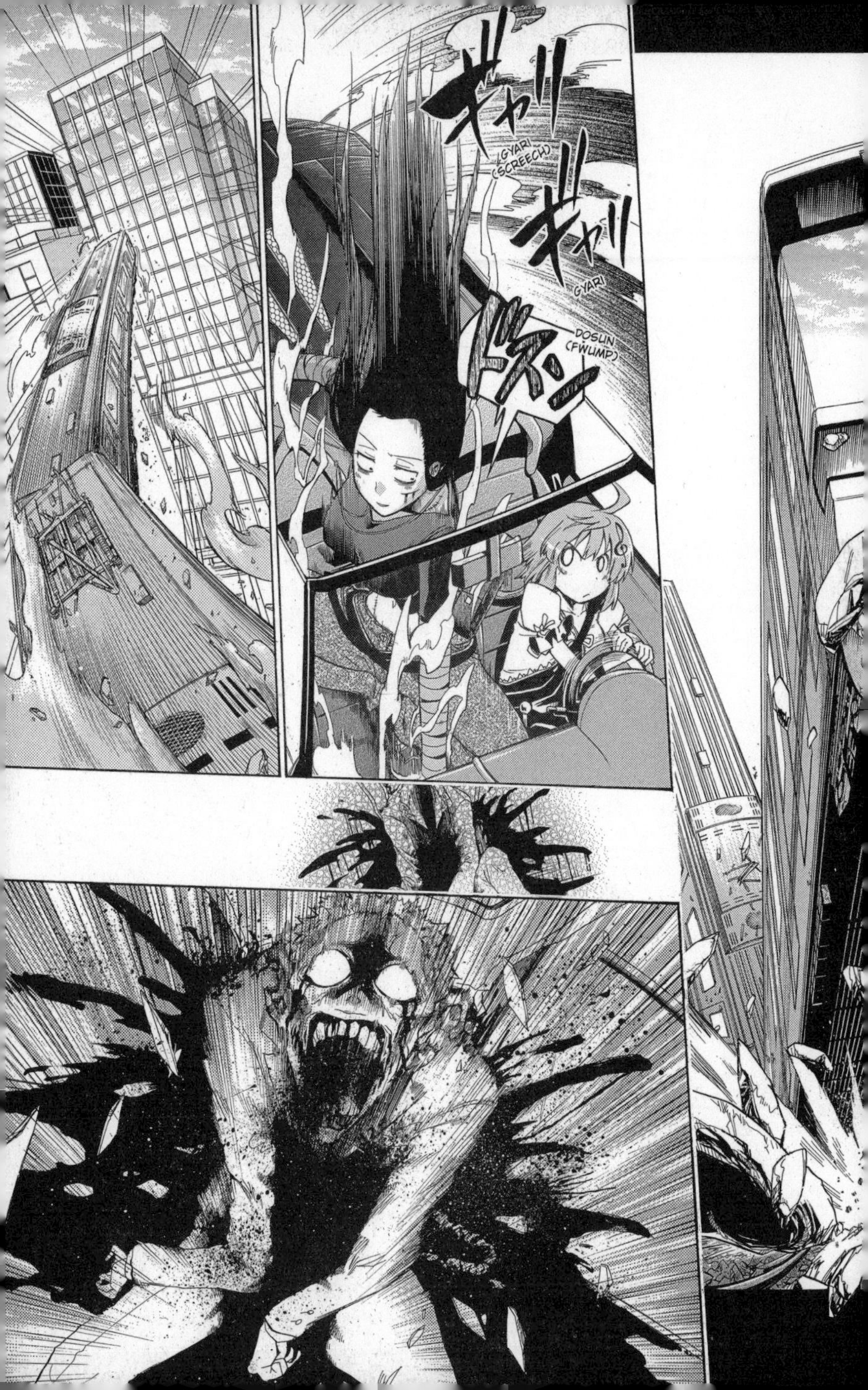
ギャリ
GYARI (SCREECH)
ギャリ
GYARI
ドスン
DOSUN (FWUMP)

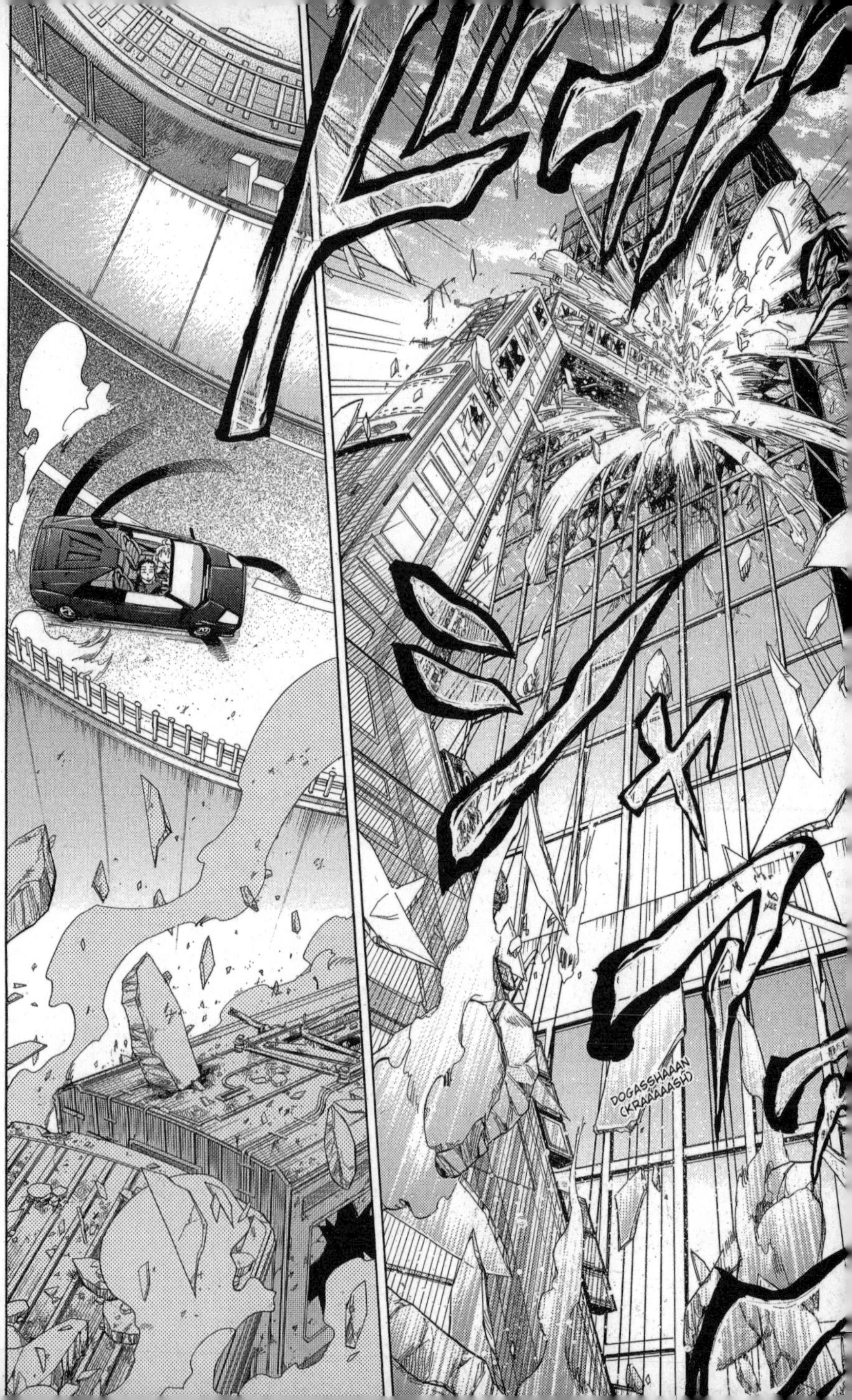
DOGASSHAAAN
(KRAAAAASH)

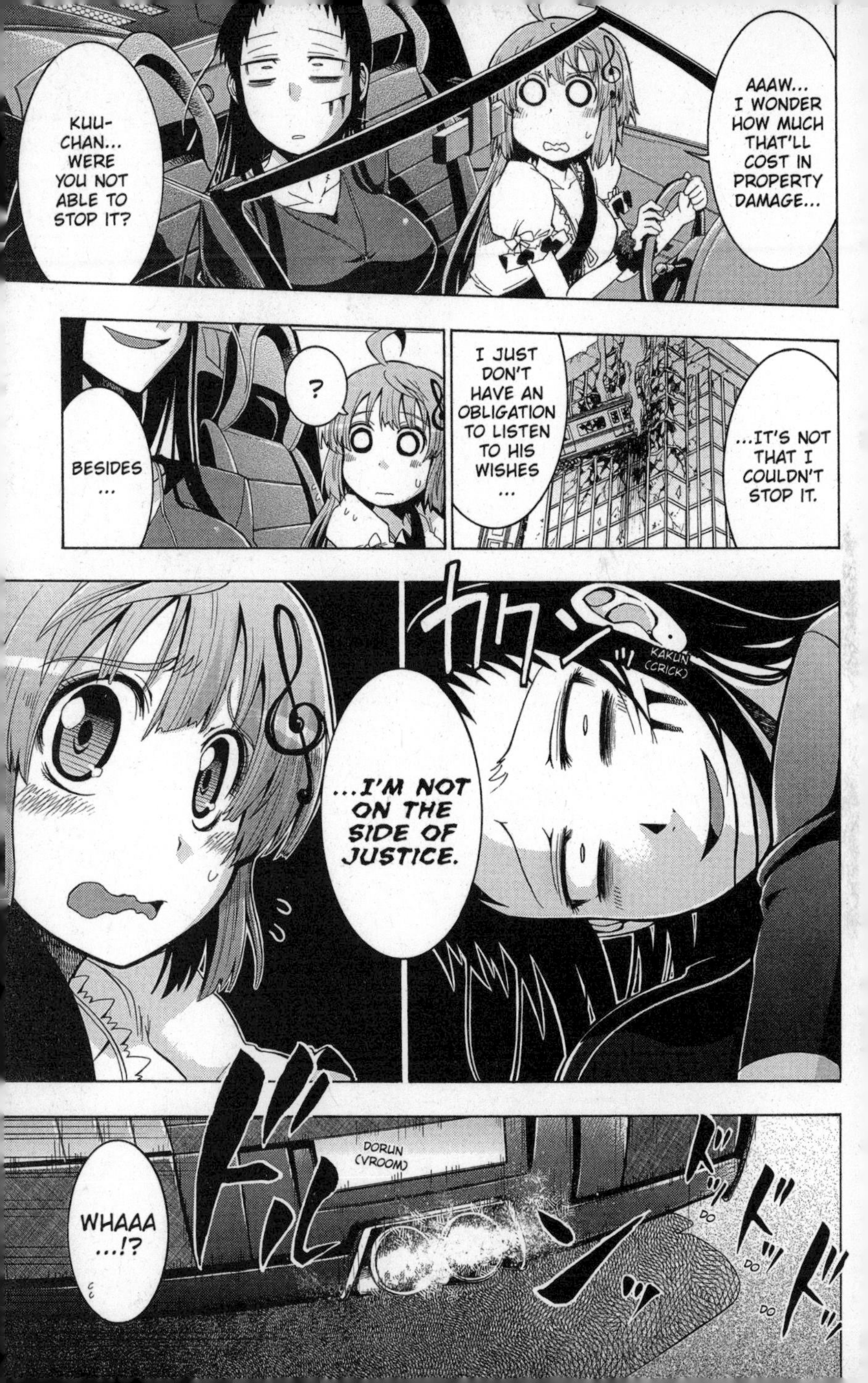

AAAW... I WONDER HOW MUCH THAT'LL COST IN PROPERTY DAMAGE...
KUU-CHAN... WERE YOU NOT ABLE TO STOP IT?
...IT'S NOT THAT I COULDN'T STOP IT.
I JUST DON'T HAVE AN OBLIGATION TO LISTEN TO HIS WISHES ...
?
BESIDES ...
KAKUN (CRICK)
...I'M NOT ON THE SIDE OF JUSTICE.
DO
DO
DO
DORUN (VROOM)
WHAAA ...!?

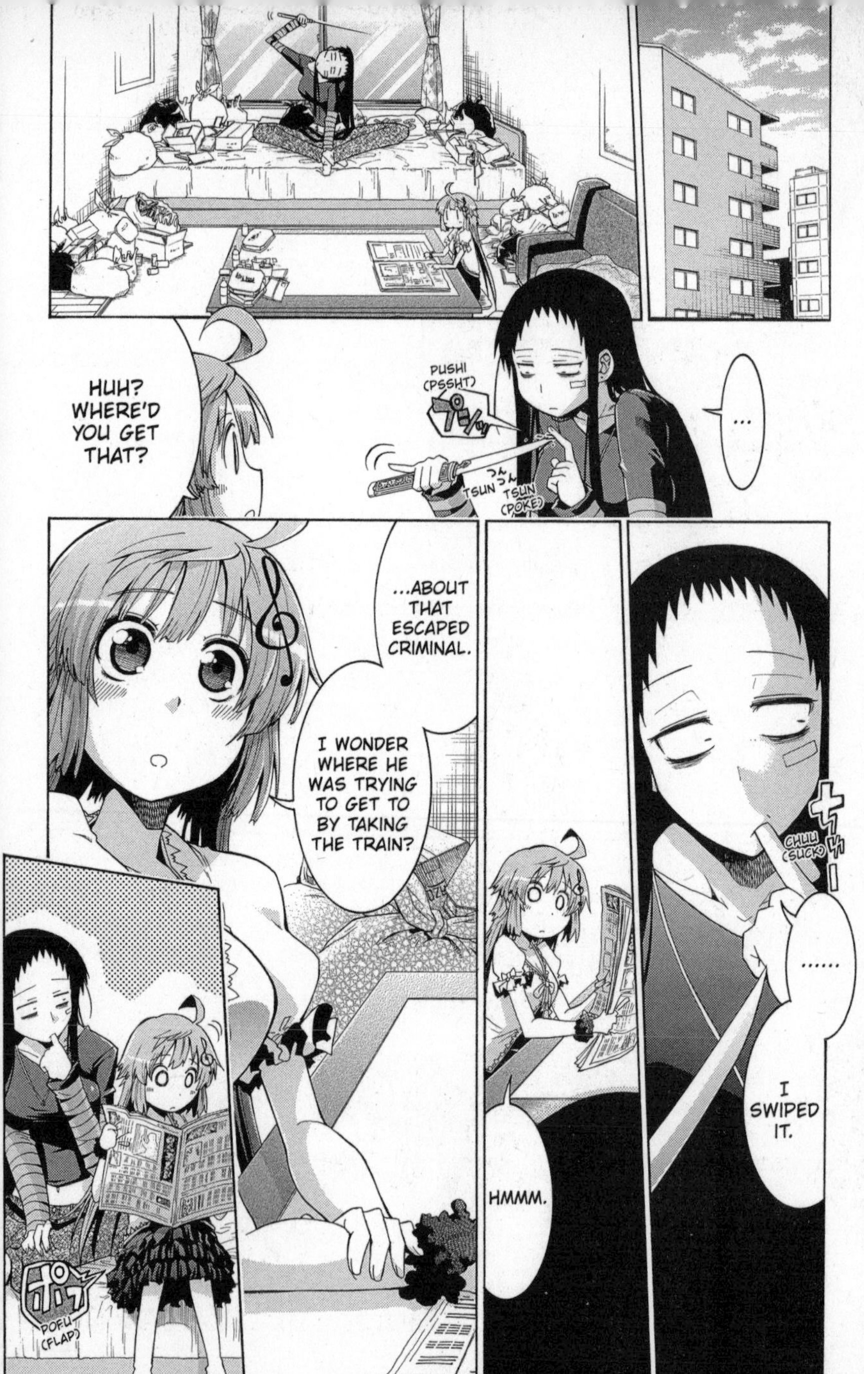
...
PUSHI (PSSHT)
TSUN TSUN (POKE)
HUH? WHERE'D YOU GET THAT?
CHUU (SUCK)
......
I SWIPED IT.
HMMM.
...ABOUT THAT ESCAPED CRIMINAL.
I WONDER WHERE HE WAS TRYING TO GET TO BY TAKING THE TRAIN?
POFU (FLAP)

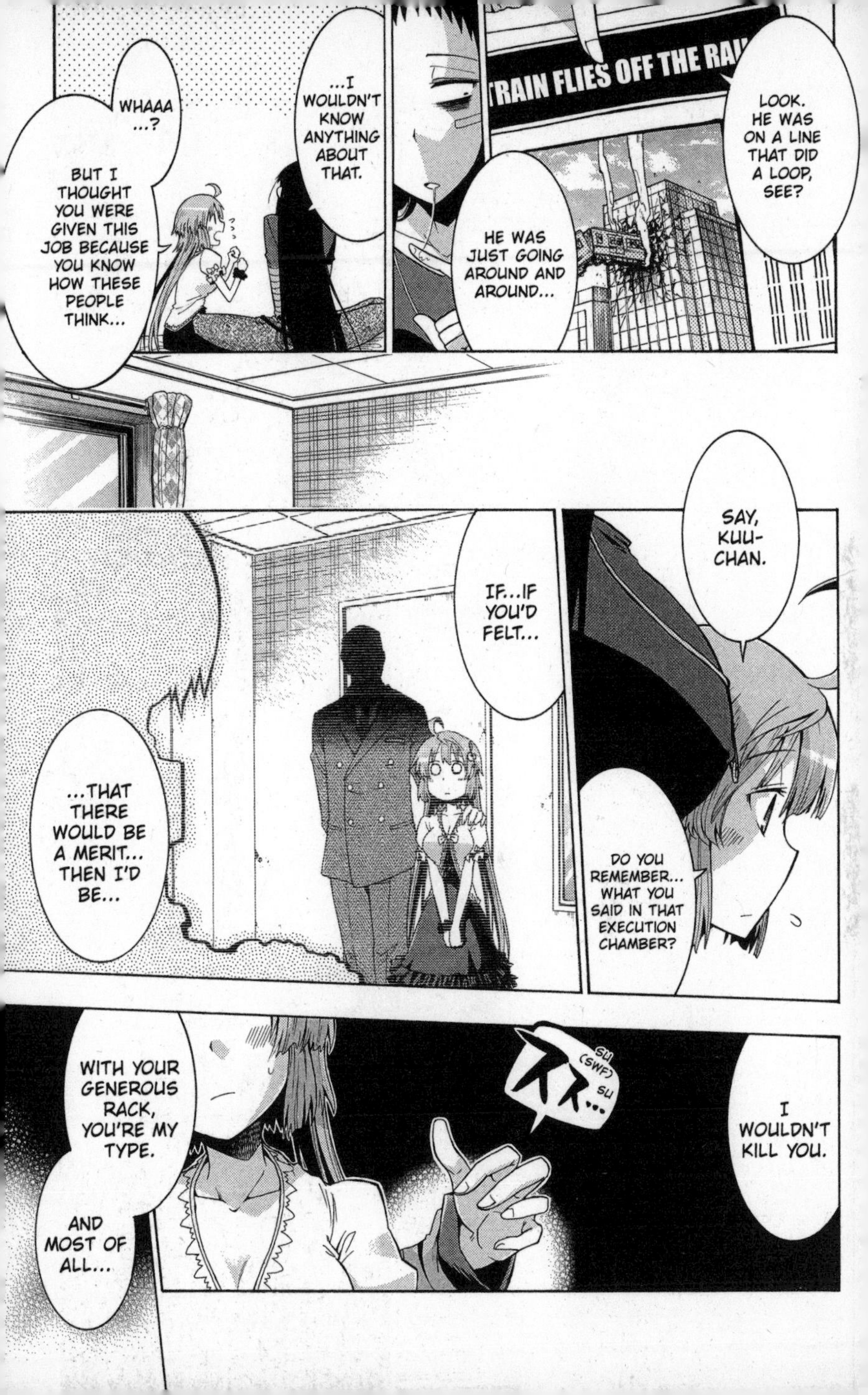
TRAIN FLIES OFF THE RAI
LOOK. HE WAS ON A LINE THAT DID A LOOP, SEE?
HE WAS JUST GOING AROUND AND AROUND...
...I WOULDN'T KNOW ANYTHING ABOUT THAT.
WHAAA...?
BUT I THOUGHT YOU WERE GIVEN THIS JOB BECAUSE YOU KNOW HOW THESE PEOPLE THINK...
SAY, KUU-CHAN.
DO YOU REMEMBER... WHAT YOU SAID IN THAT EXECUTION CHAMBER?
IF...IF YOU'D FELT...
...THAT THERE WOULD BE A MERIT... THEN I'D BE...
I WOULDN'T KILL YOU.
SU (SWF) SU
WITH YOUR GENEROUS RACK, YOU'RE MY TYPE.
AND MOST OF ALL...

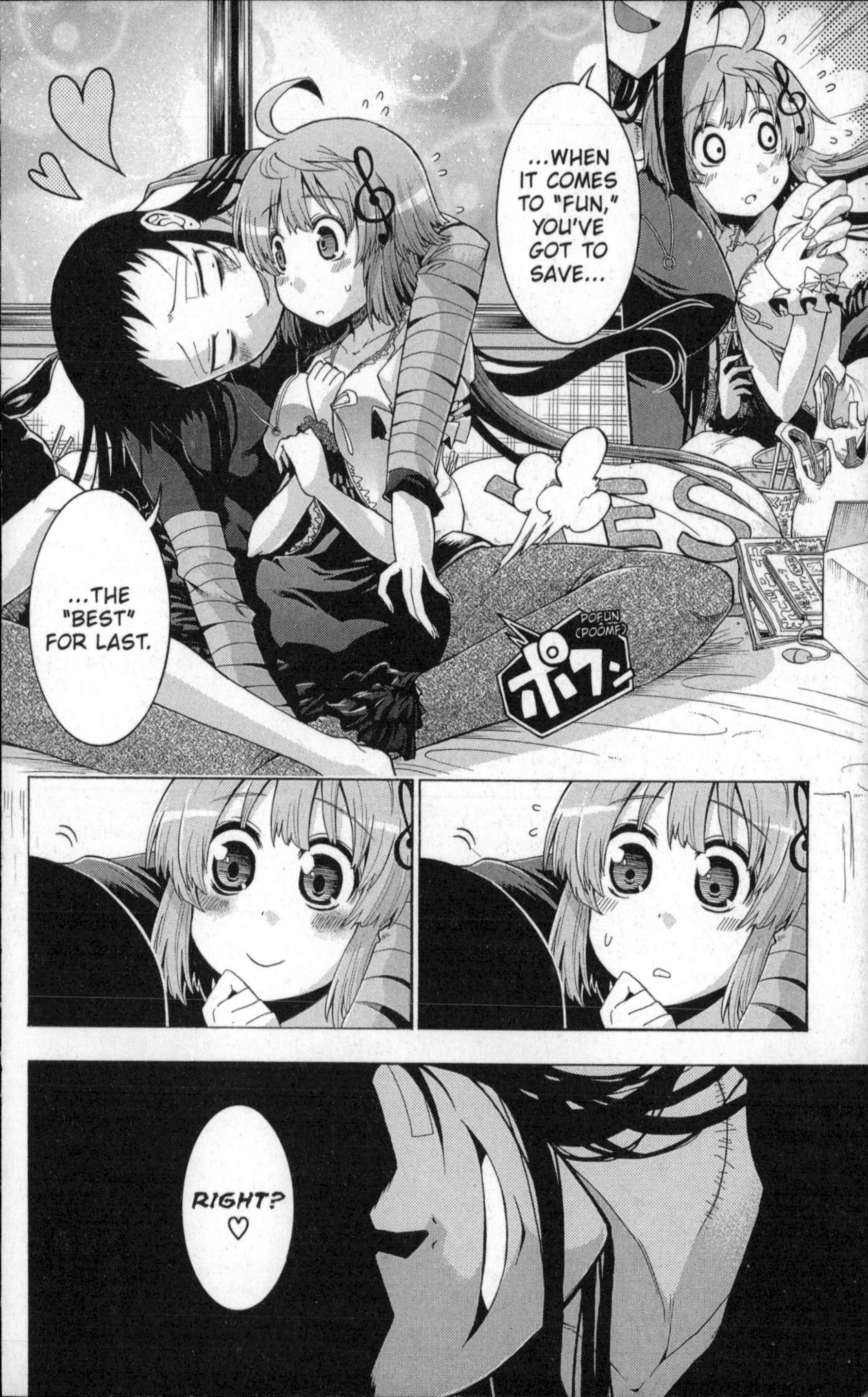
...WHEN IT COMES TO "FUN," YOU'VE GOT TO SAVE...
...THE "BEST" FOR LAST.
ポフン
POFUN (POOMF)
RIGHT? ♡

Translation Notes

Common Honorifics
no honorific: Indicates familiarity or closeness; if used without permission or reason, addressing someone in this manner would constitute an insult.
-san: The Japanese equivalent of Mr./Mrs./Miss. If a situation calls for politeness, this is the fail-safe honorific.
-sama: Conveys great respect; may also indicate that the social status of the speaker is lower than that of the addressee.
-kun: Used most often when referring to boys, this indicates affection or familiarity. Occasionally used by older men among their peers, but it may also be used by anyone referring to a person of lower standing.
-chan: An affectionate honorific indicating familiarity used mostly in reference to girls; also used in reference to cute persons or animals of either gender.
-senpai: A suffix used to address upperclassmen or more experienced coworkers.
-sensei: A respectful term for teachers, artists, or high-level professionals.

General
Murciélago is Spanish for "bat."

Page 11
The city of **Ruruie** is a reference to R'lyeh, a fictional lost city in H.P. Lovecraft's *The Call of Cthulhu*.

The **Nambu** pistol was a type of semiautomatic firearm produced in Japan during the first half of the twentieth century. The "New Nambu" is a fictional version based on the original.

Page 15
In the pro wrestling business, a heroic wrestler is called a **babyface**, or "face" for short.

Page 21
The drug **Cesare** is a reference to a character in the 1920s German silent horror film *The Cabinet of Dr. Caligari*. Cesare is hypnotized by Dr. Caligari into a dreamlike state, during which he murders people.

Page 69
The counterpart to the "babyface" in the pro wrestling business is the **heel**, or villainous wrestler.

Page 73
Enzuigiri is a wrestling move where the performer twists their body in the air and delivers a kick to the back of the opponent's head. Literally meaning "brainstem cutter" in Japanese, the move is the creation and signature finishing move of Antonio Inoki, one of Japan's most beloved and influential pro wrestlers.

Page 93
Hamburger steak: Known as *hamburg* in Japanese, this hamburger-like patty is made with ground beef, egg, breadcrumbs, and other ingredients. It is usually eaten with utensils rather than on a bun, and is closer to a meatloaf or Salisbury steak in terms of consistency.

Page 144
Nee-chan, literally "big sister" in Japanese, refers to a girl or woman who is older than the speaker but still relatively young.

Page 174-175
"Freude, schöner Gotterfunken...": The song the killer is singing is the German version of "Ode to Joy."

Page 188
"You are a 'bat' in limbo.": The Japanese word for bat is *koumori*, which sounds just like Kuroko's last name.

Page 205
"I'll say I have a Lamborghini!": One type of Lamborghini is the "Lamborghini Murciélago."

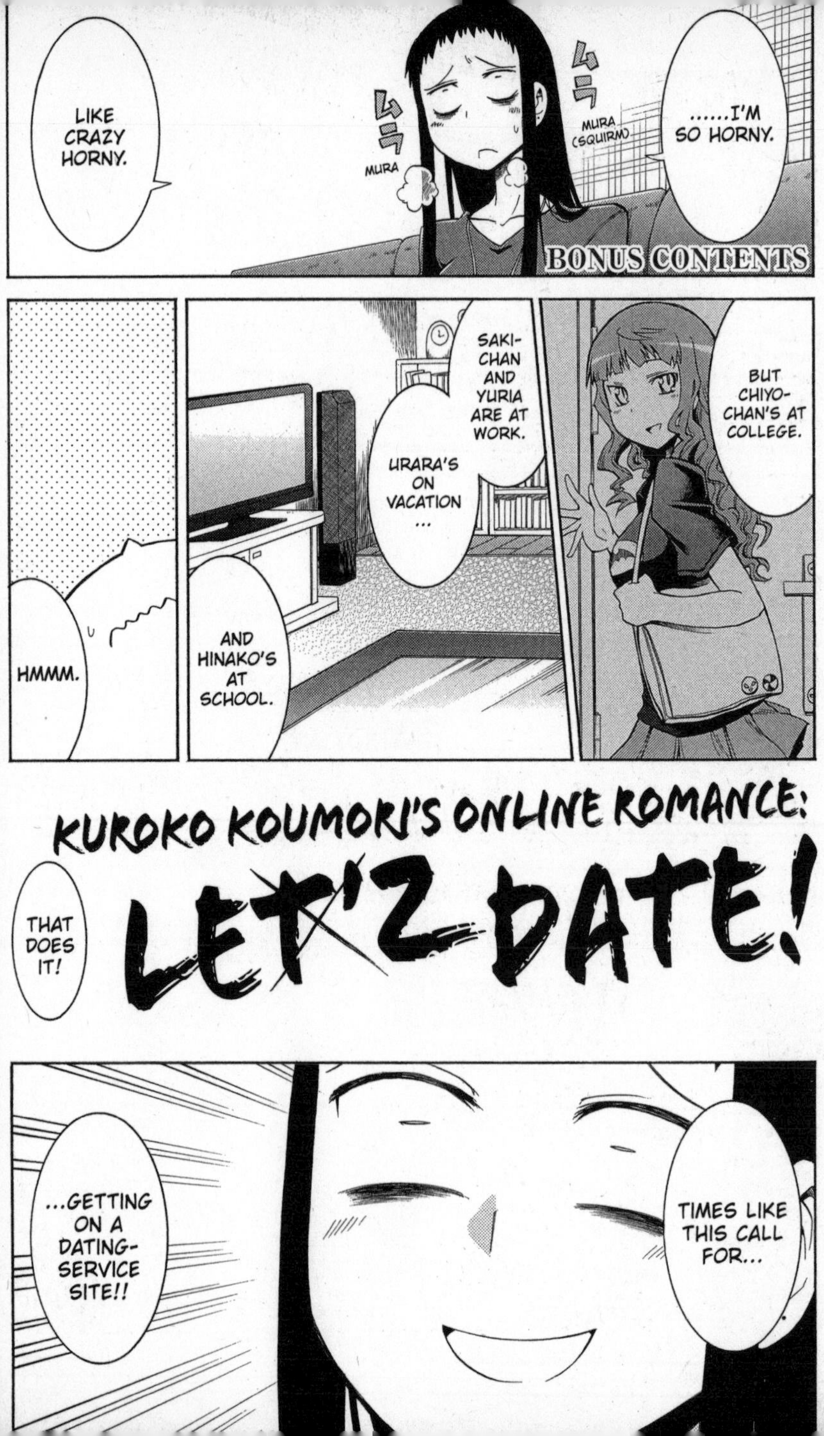

......I'M SO HORNY.
ムラ
MURA (SQUIRM)
ムラ
MURA
LIKE CRAZY HORNY.
BONUS CONTENTS
BUT CHIYO-CHAN'S AT COLLEGE.
SAKI-CHAN AND YURIA ARE AT WORK.
URARA'S ON VACATION ...
AND HINAKO'S AT SCHOOL.
HMMM.
KUROKO KOUMORI'S ONLINE ROMANCE:
LET'Z DATE!
THAT DOES IT!
TIMES LIKE THIS CALL FOR...
...GETTING ON A DATING-SERVICE SITE!!

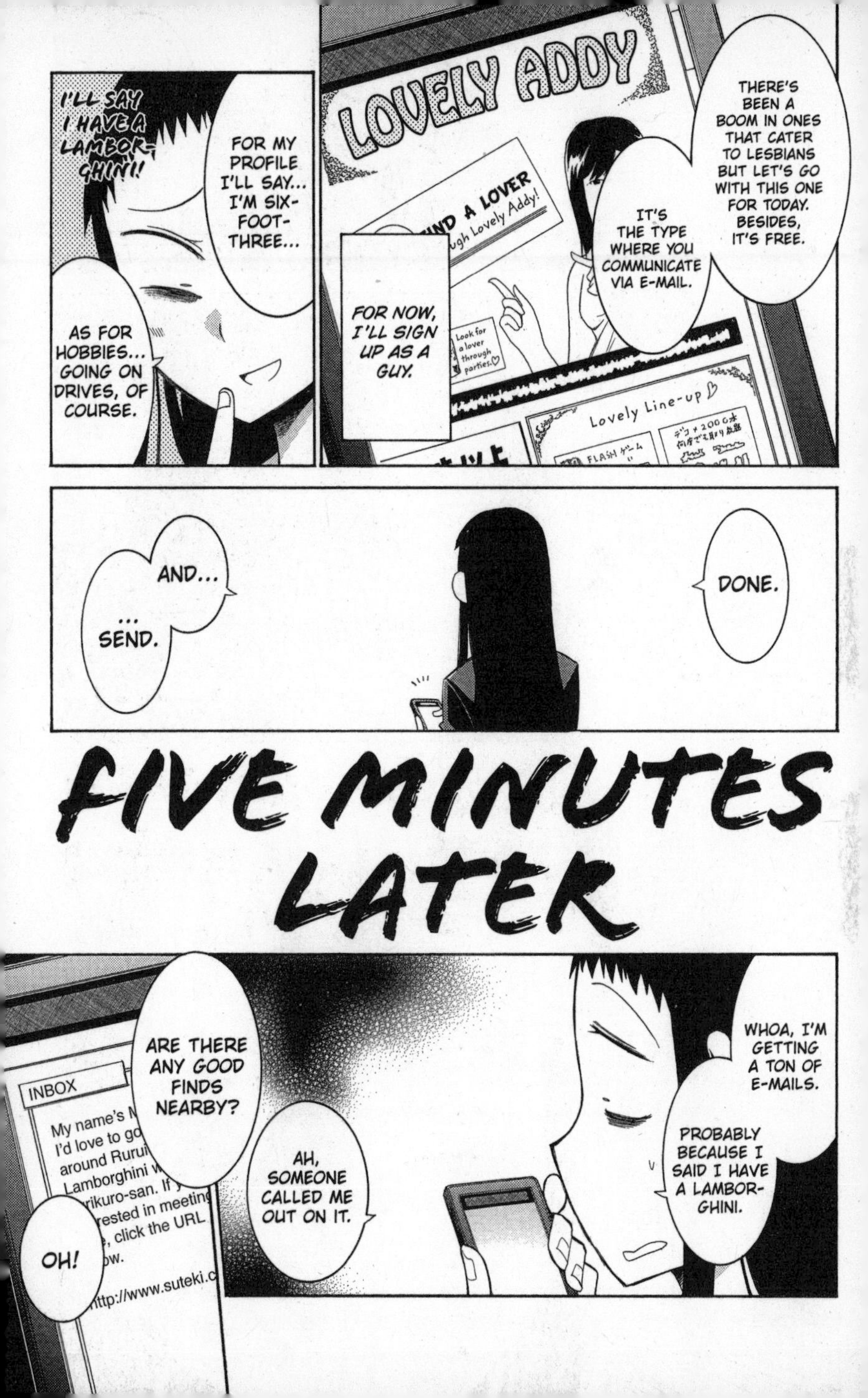
LOVELY ADDY
THERE'S BEEN A BOOM IN ONES THAT CATER TO LESBIANS BUT LET'S GO WITH THIS ONE FOR TODAY. BESIDES, IT'S FREE.
IT'S THE TYPE WHERE YOU COMMUNICATE VIA E-MAIL.
Look for a lover through parties.♡
Lovely Line-up♡
FOR NOW, I'LL SIGN UP AS A GUY.
FOR MY PROFILE I'LL SAY... I'M SIX-FOOT-THREE...
I'LL SAY I HAVE A LAMBORGHINI!
AS FOR HOBBIES... GOING ON DRIVES, OF COURSE.
DONE.
AND...
... SEND.
FIVE MINUTES LATER
WHOA, I'M GETTING A TON OF E-MAILS.
PROBABLY BECAUSE I SAID I HAVE A LAMBORGHINI.
ARE THERE ANY GOOD FINDS NEARBY?
AH, SOMEONE CALLED ME OUT ON IT.
INBOX
OH!

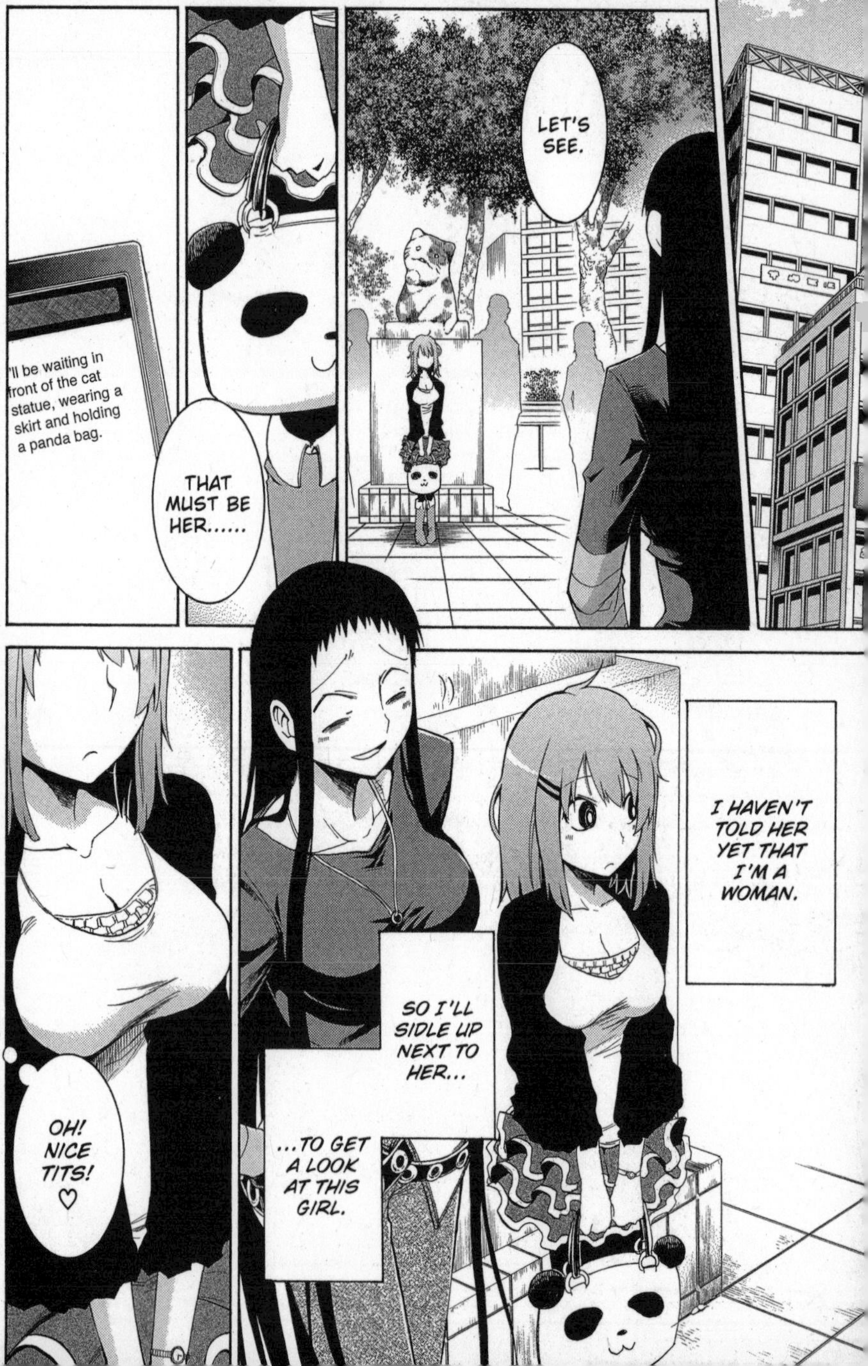

LET'S SEE.
THAT MUST BE HER......
'll be waiting in front of the cat statue, wearing a skirt and holding a panda bag.
I HAVEN'T TOLD HER YET THAT I'M A WOMAN.
SO I'LL SIDLE UP NEXT TO HER...
...TO GET A LOOK AT THIS GIRL.
OH! NICE TITS! ♡

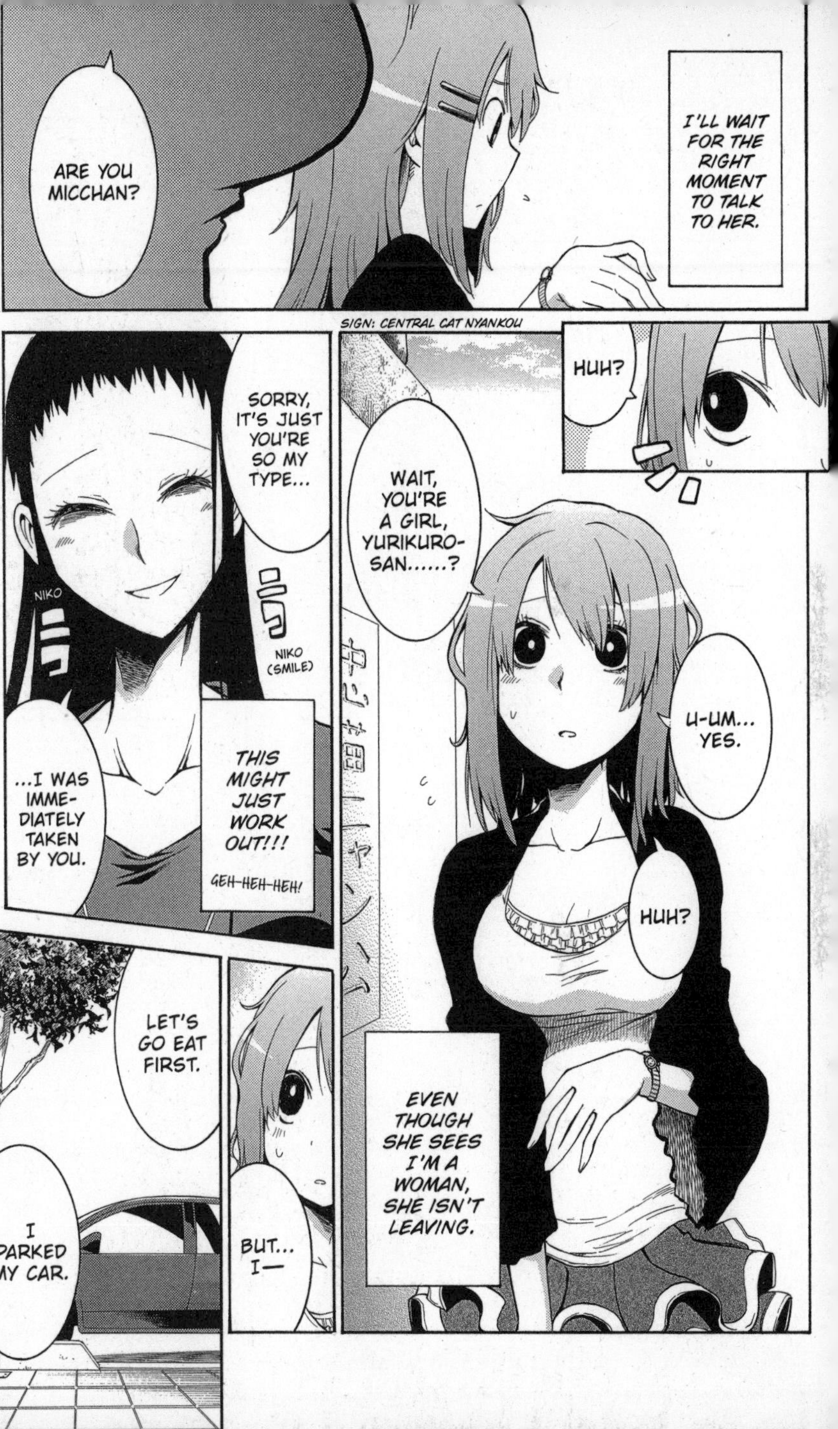
I'LL WAIT FOR THE RIGHT MOMENT TO TALK TO HER.
ARE YOU MICCHAN?
SIGN: CENTRAL CAT NYANKOU
HUH?
WAIT, YOU'RE A GIRL, YURIKURO-SAN......?
U-UM... YES.
HUH?
EVEN THOUGH SHE SEES I'M A WOMAN, SHE ISN'T LEAVING.
SORRY, IT'S JUST YOU'RE SO MY TYPE...
NIKO (SMILE)
NIKO
THIS MIGHT JUST WORK OUT!!!
GEH-HEH-HEH!
...I WAS IMMEDIATELY TAKEN BY YOU.
BUT... I—
LET'S GO EAT FIRST.
I PARKED MY CAR.

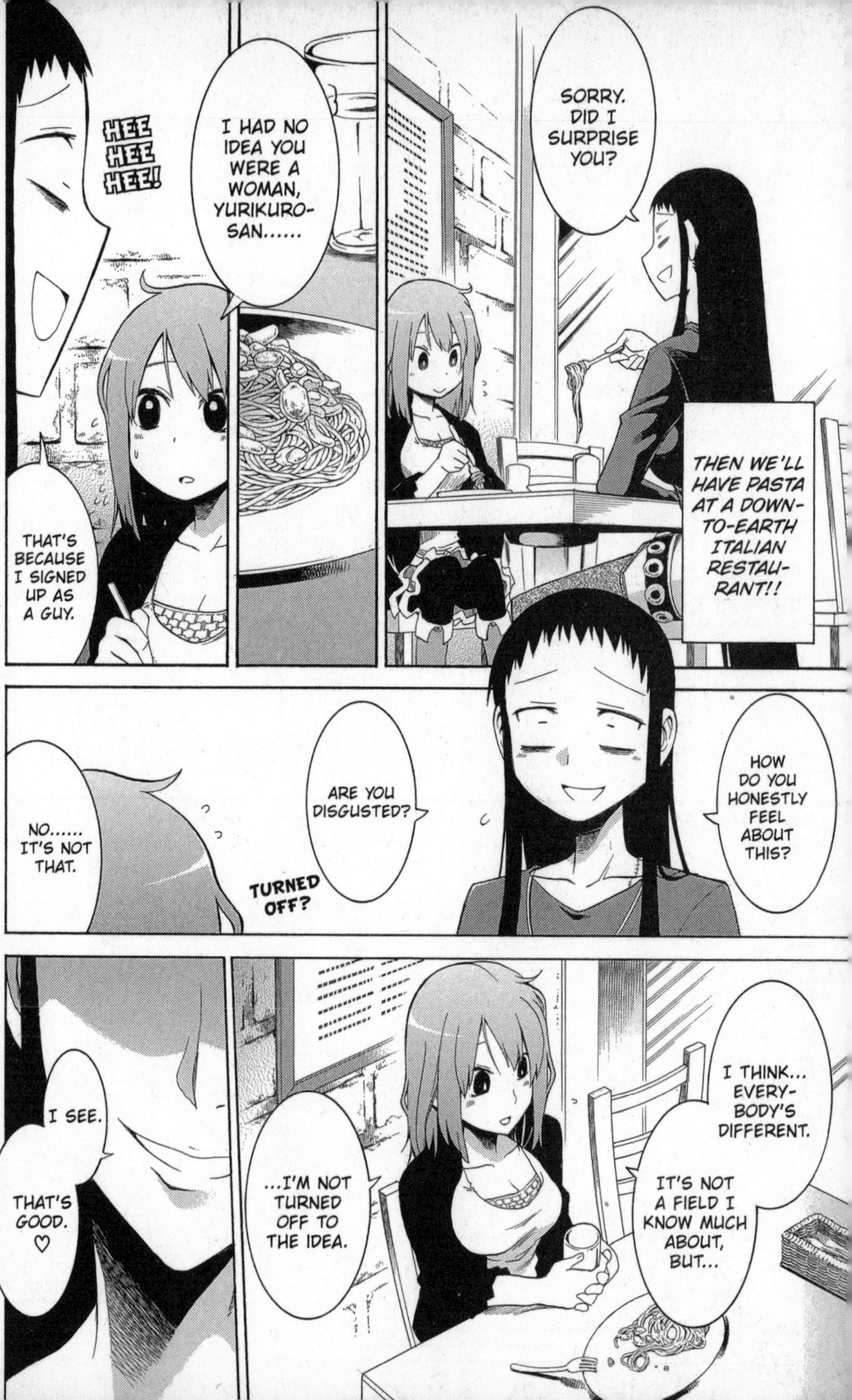
SORRY. DID I SURPRISE YOU?
THEN WE'LL HAVE PASTA AT A DOWN-TO-EARTH ITALIAN RESTAURANT!!
I HAD NO IDEA YOU WERE A WOMAN, YURIKURO-SAN......
HEE HEE HEE!
THAT'S BECAUSE I SIGNED UP AS A GUY.
HOW DO YOU HONESTLY FEEL ABOUT THIS?
ARE YOU DISGUSTED?
TURNED OFF?
NO...... IT'S NOT THAT.
I THINK... EVERYBODY'S DIFFERENT.
IT'S NOT A FIELD I KNOW MUCH ABOUT, BUT...
...I'M NOT TURNED OFF TO THE IDEA.
I SEE.
THAT'S GOOD. ♡

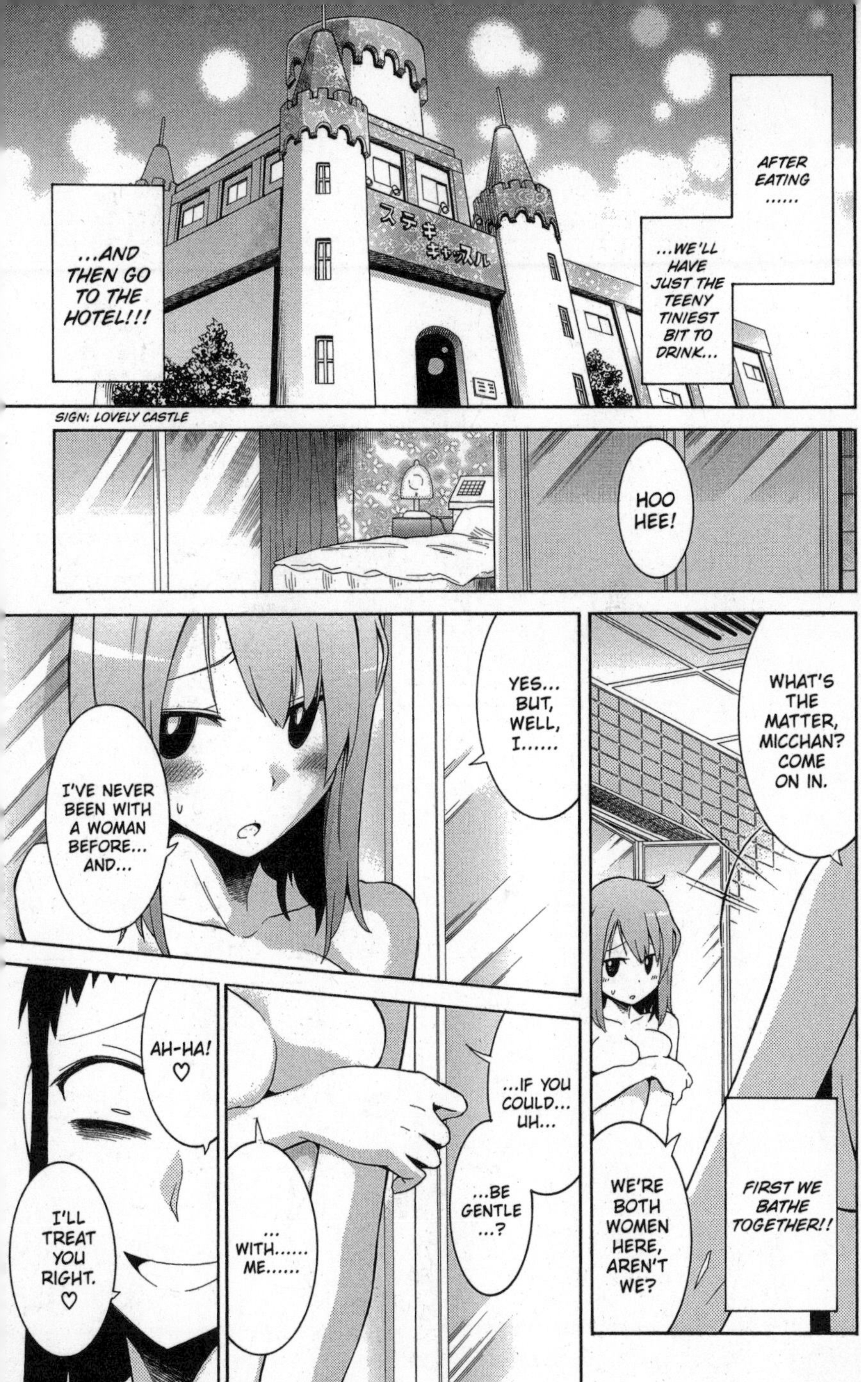
AFTER EATING ......
...WE'LL HAVE JUST THE TEENY TINIEST BIT TO DRINK...
ステキキャッスル
...AND THEN GO TO THE HOTEL!!!
SIGN: LOVELY CASTLE
HOO HEE!
WHAT'S THE MATTER, MICCHAN? COME ON IN.
FIRST WE BATHE TOGETHER!!
WE'RE BOTH WOMEN HERE, AREN'T WE?
YES... BUT, WELL, I......
I'VE NEVER BEEN WITH A WOMAN BEFORE... AND...
...IF YOU COULD... UH...
...BE GENTLE ...?
... WITH...... ME......
AH-HA! ♡
I'LL TREAT YOU RIGHT. ♡

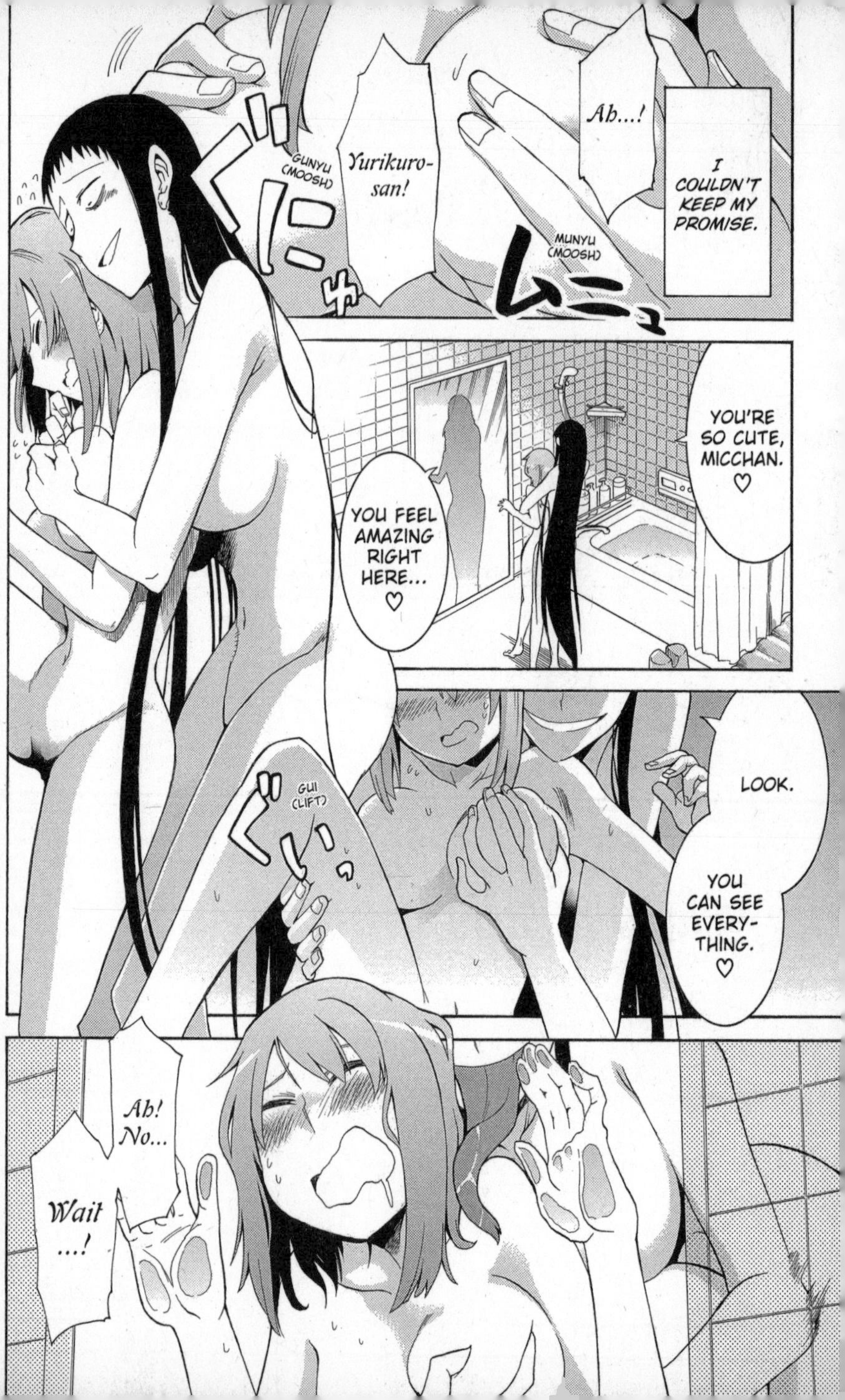
I COULDN'T KEEP MY PROMISE.
Ah...!
MUNYU (MOOSH)
YOU'RE SO CUTE, MICCHAN. ♡
YOU FEEL AMAZING RIGHT HERE... ♡
LOOK.
YOU CAN SEE EVERY-THING. ♡
GUI (LIFT)
Yurikuro-san!
GUNYU (MOOSH)
Ah! No...
Wait ...!

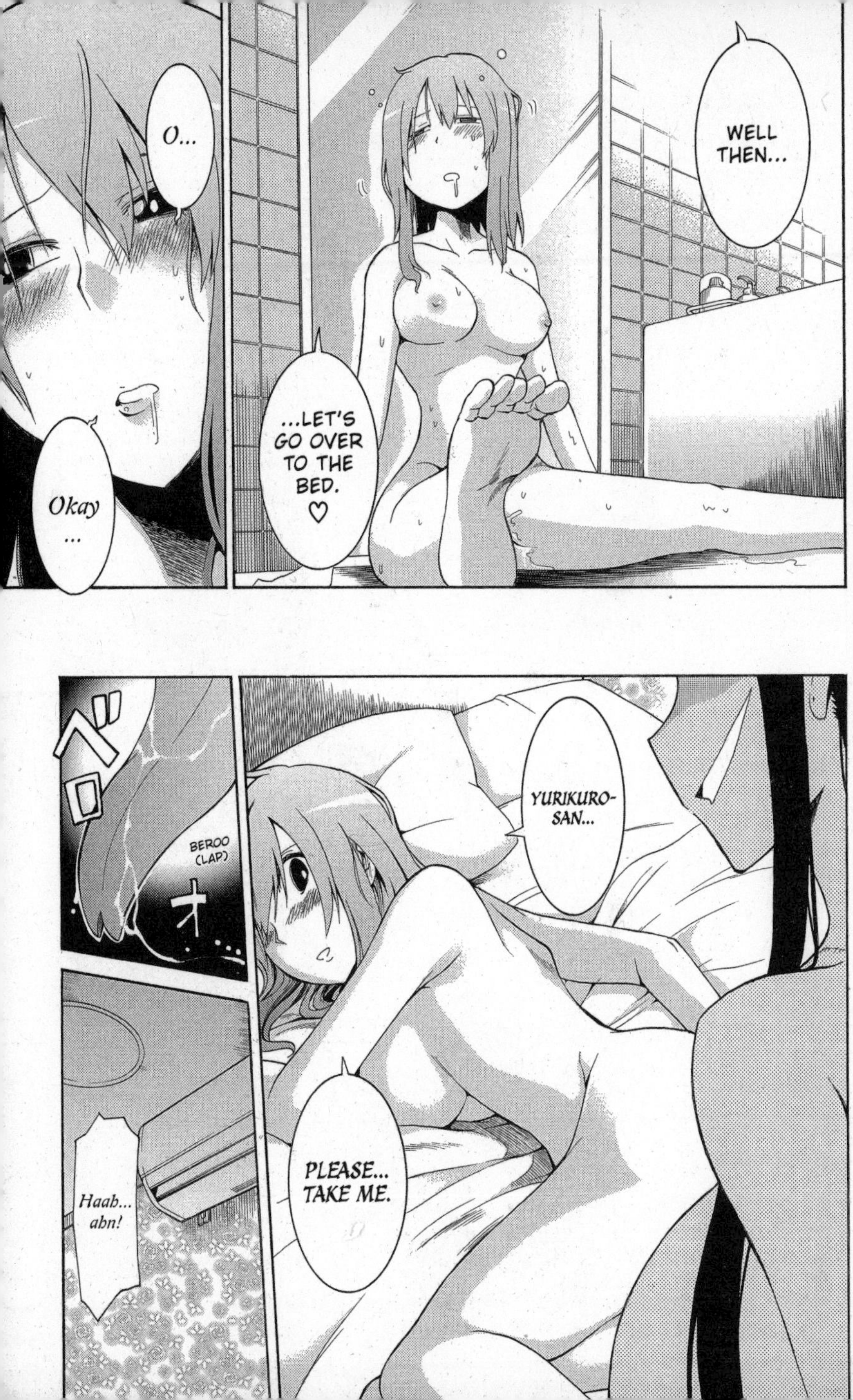
WELL THEN...
...LET'S GO OVER TO THE BED. ♡
O...
Okay ...
YURIKURO-SAN...
PLEASE... TAKE ME.
ベロオ...
BEROO (LAP)
Haah... ahn!

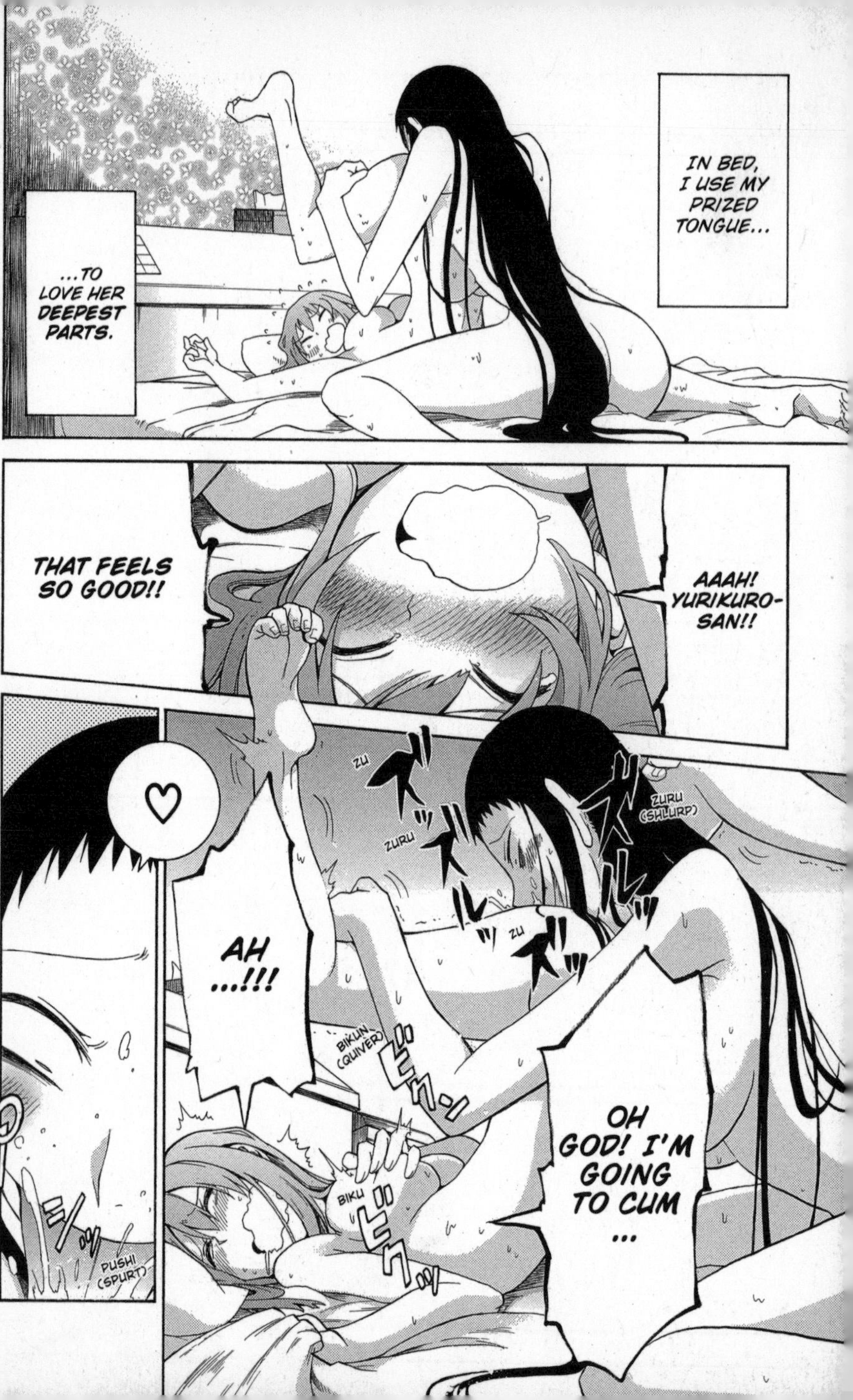
IN BED, I USE MY PRIZED TONGUE...
...TO LOVE HER DEEPEST PARTS.
AAAH! YURIKURO-SAN!!
THAT FEELS SO GOOD!!
ZURU (SHLURP)
ZU
ZURU
ZU
AH ...!!!
OH GOD! I'M GOING TO CUM ...
BIKUN (QUIVER)
BIKU
♥
PUSHI (SPURT)

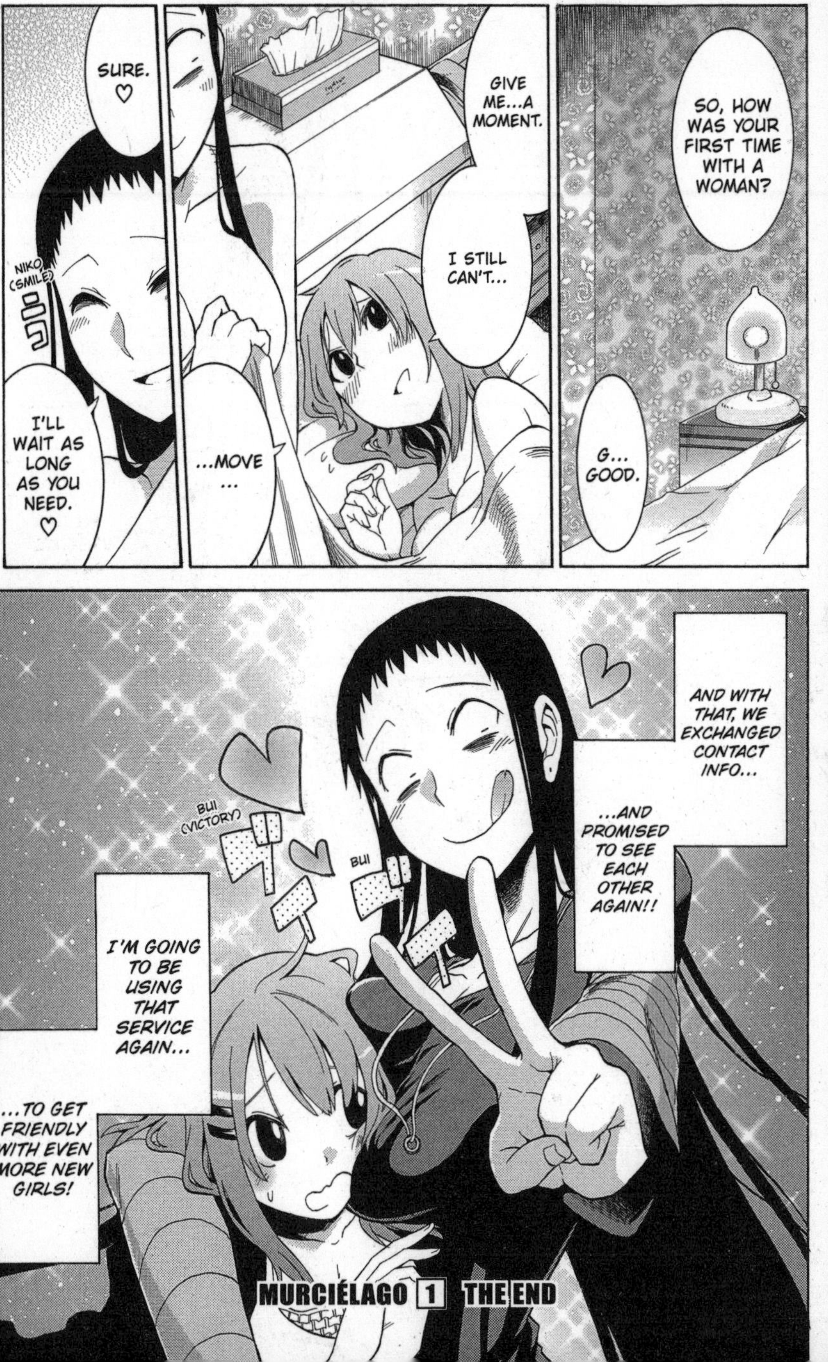
SO, HOW WAS YOUR FIRST TIME WITH A WOMAN?
G... GOOD.
GIVE ME...A MOMENT.
I STILL CAN'T...
...MOVE ...
SURE. ♡
NIKO (SMILE)
I'LL WAIT AS LONG AS YOU NEED. ♡
AND WITH THAT, WE EXCHANGED CONTACT INFO...
...AND PROMISED TO SEE EACH OTHER AGAIN!!
BUI
BUI (VICTORY)
I'M GOING TO BE USING THAT SERVICE AGAIN...
...TO GET FRIENDLY WITH EVEN MORE NEW GIRLS!
MURCIÉLAGO 1 THE END

MURCIÉLAGO

Yoshimurakana

Translation: Christine Dashiell ✦ Lettering: Alexis Eckerman

MURCIÉLAGO vol. 1
© 2014 Yoshimurakana / SQUARE ENIX CO., LTD.
First published in Japan in 2014 by SQUARE ENIX CO., LTD. CORPORATION.
English translation rights arranged with SQUARE ENIX CO., LTD. and Yen Press, LLC
through Tuttle-Mori Agency, Inc.

English translation © 2017 by SQUARE ENIX CO., LTD.

Yen Press
1290 Avenue of the Americas
New York, NY 10104

Visit us at yenpress.com
facebook.com/yenpress
twitter.com/yenpress
yenpress.tumblr.com
instagram.com/yenpress

Yen Press is an imprint of Yen Press, LLC.
The Yen Press name and logo are trademarks of Yen Press, LLC.

First Yen Press Edition: January 2017

Library of Congress Control Number: 2016958266

ISBN: 978-0-316-50460-7 (paperback)
978-0-316-51011-0 (ebook)

10 9 8 7 6 5 4 3 2 1

BVG

Printed in the United States of America

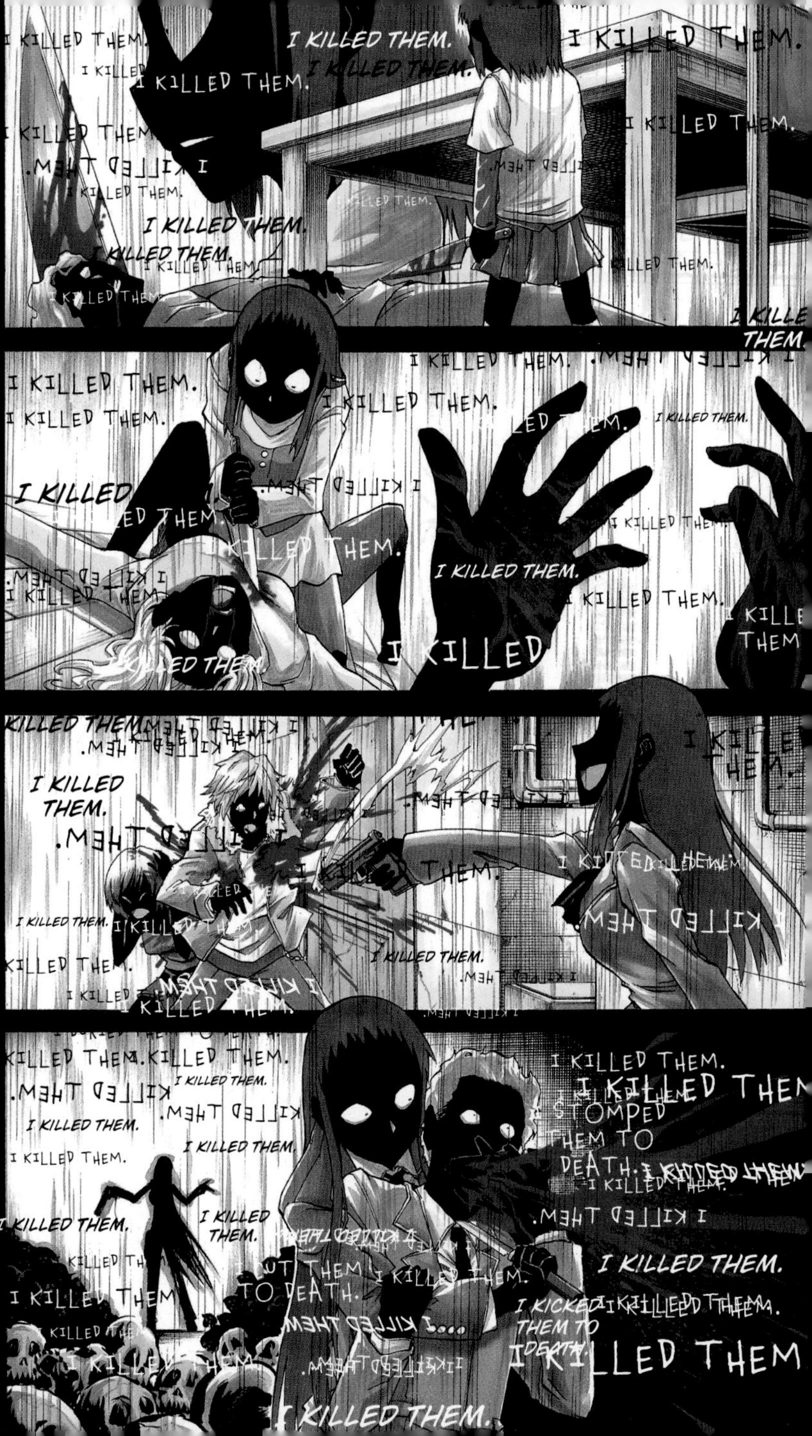
I KILLED THEM.
I KILLED THEM.
I KILLED THEM.
I KILLED THEM.
I KILLED THEM.
I KILLED THEM.
I KILLED THEM.
I KILLED THEM.
I KILLED THEM.
I KILLED THEM.
I KILLED THEM.
I KILLED THEM.
I KILLED THEM.
I KILLED THEM.
I KILLED THEM.
I KILLED THEM.
I KILLED THEM.
I KILLED
I KILLED THEM.
I KILLED THEM.
I KILLED THEM.
I KILLED THEM.
I KILLED THEM.
I KILLED THEM.
I KILLED THEM.
I KILLED THEM.
I KILLED THEM.
I KILLED THEM.
I KILLED THEM.
I KILLED THEM.
I KILLED THEM
I STOMPED THEM TO DEATH.
I KILLED THEM.
I KILLED THEM.
I KICKED THEM TO DEATH.
I KILLED THEM
I KILLED THEM.
I KILLED THEM.
I KILLED THEM.
I KILLED THEM.
I KILLED THEM.
I KILLED THEM.
I KILLED THEM.
I CUT THEM TO DEATH.
I KILLED THEM.
I KILLED THEM.

I KILLED THEM.